ACTIVE PSYCHOTHERAPY

The Editor

Harold Greenwald, who received his doctorate from Columbia University, is professor of clinical psychology and chairman of the program in humanistic clinical psychology of the United States International University in San Diego, California. He is a diplomate in clinical psychology of the American Board of Examiners in Professional Psychology of the American Psychological Association and a former president of the National Psychological Association. Before coming to San Diego, Dr. Greenwald taught at the University of Bergen in Norway, as well as at the Universities of Oslo and Copenhagen, the New School for Social Research, Pratt Institute, and Columbia University. In addition to his teaching, he also conducts a private practice in group and individual therapy and has recently been invited to lecture on his particular approach to psychotherapy, "direct decision therapy," in various parts of the United States, Europe, and the Near East. Dr. Greenwald is the author of *Decision Therapy, Great Cases in Psychoanalysis, The Elegant Prostitute* (formerly *The Call Girl*), *The Sex-Life Letters* (with Ruth Greenwald), and *Emotional Maturity in Love and Marriage* (with Lucy Freeman).

COMMENTARY

"Greenwald has given us in this volume a collection of excellent papers on the many faces of psychotherapy. His introduction suffices to establish the point about therapist intervention. If one is interested in a taste of many points of view regarding psychotherapy, rational-emotive psychotherapy, short-term therapy, treatment of psychopaths, behavior therapy, treatment of specific clinical problems such as impotence and frigidity, learning theory, implosive therapy, group psychotherapy and psychodrama, transactional analysis, and so on and on, this is a veritable treasure of a book."

Max Siegel
Contemporary Psychology

ACTIVE PSYCHOTHERAPY

HAROLD GREENWALD
EDITOR

𝒜

New York • Jason Aronson • London

CONTRIBUTORS

NATHAN W. ACKERMAN, M.D. Professor of Clinical Psychiatry, Columbia University

ALFRED ADLER, M.D. Founder of individual psychology

ERIC BERNE, M.D. Chairman of the San Francisco Social Psychiatry Seminars

SALAH EL-BATRAWI, Ph.D. Testing and Counseling Center of George Washington University

ALBERT ELLIS, Ph.D. Executive Director, Institute for Rational Living, Inc.; private practice, New York City

MILTON H. ERICKSON, M.D. Private practice, Phoenix, Arizona; Editor, *American Journal of Clinical Hypnosis*

SANDOR FERENCZI, M.D. Early psychoanalyst, initiator of "active" psychoanalysis

VIKTOR E. FRANKL, M.D. Professor of Neurology and Psychiatry, University of Vienna Medical School; President, Austrian Medical Society of Psychotherapy

SIGMUND FREUD, M.D. Founder of psychoanalysis

HAROLD GREENWALD, Ph.D. Private practice, New York City; President, National Psychological Association for Psychoanalysis; Faculty: Metropolitan Institute for Psychoanalytic Studies and Institute of Practicing Psychotherapists

JAY HALEY. Research associate, The Mental Health Research Institute of the Palo Alto Medical Research Foundation

ROBERT A. HOGAN, Ed.D. Associate professor, Illinois State University

ARON KRICH, Ed.D. Faculty: Marriage and Family Life Department, Teachers College, Columbia University; private practice, marriage counseling and psychotherapy

GOODHUE LIVINGSTON, Ph.D. Private practice, Seattle, Washington

PERRY LONDON, Ph.D. Director of Clinical Training, University of Southern California

J. L. MORENO, M.D. Psychiatrist; Founder of Psychodrama and Sociometry

MARIE COLEMAN NELSON. Editor, *Psychoanalytic Review*

HERBERT A. OTTO, Ph.D. Professor, School of Social Work, University of Utah

DONALD R. PETERSON, Ph.D. Professor, University of Illinois

E. LAKIN PHILLIPS, Ph.D. Testing and Counseling Center of George Washington University

K. PLATONOV, M.D. Central Clinical Psychoneurological Hospital of the Ministry of Railways, U.S.S.R.

HYMAN SPOTNITZ, M.D. Psychiatrist, private practice, New York; Faculty: Training Institute of the National Psychological Association for Psychoanalysis

CHARLES T. SULLIVAN. Social psychologist; associated with John Rosen at the Doylestown Foundation

THOMAS S. SZASZ, M.D. Professor of psychiatry, State University of New York, Upstate Medical Center in Syracuse

LEWIS R. WOLBERG, M.D. Dean, Post Graduate Center for Psychotherapy; Clinical Professor of Psychiatry, New York Medical College and Flower Fifth Avenue Hospital, New York City

JOSEPH WOLPE, M.D. Professor of Psychiatry, Temple University, Pennsylvania

INTRODUCTION

Breaking loose from the bonds of tradition, psychotherapy has recently undergone such a vast proliferation that it is almost impossible for even the most nimble of researchers in the field to keep up with the almost infinite variety of new approaches and new techniques. One unifying factor in all these new approaches, whether they be Fritz Perl's imaginative wedding of psychodrama and psychoanalysis as Gestalt Therapy, Berne's Transactional Analysis, Glasser's Reality Therapy, the Bio-Energetic variety of Reichian Therapy, or Primal Scream Therapy, is the increased activity of the therapist. The once-remote doctor sitting quietly behind the couch has become a rarity in a time when therapists have apparently begun to actively apply what they have learned in a more energetic and direct manner.

After a long period of relatively slow change and development, the practice of psychotherapy has now entered a phase of vigorous experimentation. The greatly increased public recognition of the merit of psychological approaches has brought about a dramatic upsurge of demand for mental health services on the part of broader segments of the population than ever before. The psychoanalyst's consulting room, frequented in Freud's day almost exclusively by neurotic nobility and *haute-bourgeoisie,* is entered today by artisans and stenographers by way of the clinical facilities that are proliferating under government and local sponsorship. Many kinds of people now seek aid, and they display a far greater variety of symptoms and life problems than are recorded in the earlier case-history literature.

The professional response to this new demand was minimal at first, but in recent years has markedly increased in creativity and imagination. While it is difficult to devise a precise rubric to cover all forms of such experimentation in psychotherapy, one major characteristic has been an increase in *activity*.

Obviously, activity cannot be defined quantitatively by measuring the number of therapist communications. The non-directive or client-centered therapist frequently speaks almost as much as his client, yet he is not considered active, since he attempts to limit his communication to the reflection of the client's feelings.

More frequently an attempt is made to distinguish between insight-oriented therapies and active therapies in terms of differing goals. Viewed in these terms, the insight therapies include all variations of psychoanalysis that focus on making the patient more conscious of the psychodynamic forces that motivate him. Active psychotherapy, on the other hand, is seen as being concerned with those techniques that focus directly on the removal of symptoms, such as anxiety or maladaptive overt behavior. This is perhaps a more viable distinction, except that therapies, like the difficulties they are designed to cope with, are not easy to categorize. For example, many of the variants of psychoanalytic techniques described in this volume entail the use of an active approach to promote insight, and many therapists work to promote insight and modify overt behavior. The need to establish a clear dichotomy between insight and behavior modification has often been challenged: many of the therapists who stress insight do so in the belief that increased insight, no matter how arrived at, will modify overt behavior and felt anxiety.

Some writers, such as Ellis, use the term *active* as a synonym for *directive*. If we define "directive" strictly, we will find hardly any therapy entirely devoid of directives. Even the most passive of psychoanalysts directs the patient through instructing him in the "fundamental rule"—namely, that he is to say whatever comes to his mind, no matter how embarrassing, foolish, or trivial. And both the psychoanalyst and the client-centered therapist usually set the hours, the length of the session, and the fee—in effect structuring much of the relationship.

The difference appears to be primarily a matter of degree and attitude. Psychotherapy can be seen as a continual experiment in which the therapist introduces a variety of stimuli and studies the responses. If the response is in the desired direction, then the stimulus may be repeated until optimum movement is achieved. At times the therapist must refrain from introducing any stimuli, in order to observe if the desired change can occur spontaneously.

The active therapist tends to utilize consciously devised interventions for a specific preconceived goal. As we said before, this goal may be increased insight, decreased anxiety, the modification of overt behavior, or all of these.

Some of the most dedicated active therapists do not insist that this method be prescribed for all: there are patients who seem to do best when activity is held to an absolute minimum. In such cases, activity is indicated either when the therapist feels that the patient cannot move ahead on his own or when activity would shorten treatment time significantly without sacrificing treatment goals.

The fact that this book is devoted to the active therapies does not mean that they are intended as substitutes for the more passive modes, such as classic psychoanalysis and the non-directive approach. In many circumstances they might well be the therapist's ideal choice: he will carefully assess the weaknesses and strengths of the patient and choose from his arsenal the technique that seems to him the most effective for dealing with that particular individual. Moreover, with any patient different approaches may be required at different times. For example, at the beginning of the relationship it is often useful, even for the usually very active therapist, to keep his own contributions to an absolute minimum—in fact, to limit his conversation to greeting and parting remarks. At other times the most intense activity may be indicated.

It would be too easy to suggest that the decision to act or not to act depends on the art rather than the science of psychotherapy. We need more careful research to pinpoint the precise conditions for which different techniques are indicated. Unfortunately, too often research has been aimed at proving the superiority of one technique over others. Also, too much research has been devoted solely to patient variables, important though they are. If therapy is thought of as an interactional relationship between patient and therapist, then the ideal research may well be designed to study which therapy can best be used by which therapist with which patient. In essence, it is the editor's hope that exposure to the wide variety of therapies included in this book will encourage readers to do their own experimenting, the aim of which would be to find out which technique a therapist, given his own assets and limitations, could most effectively employ for which conditions, given the patient's strengths and limitations.

Because of the fact that in recent years there have been so many new and active approaches, it has of course been impossible to be all-inclusive. Each reader, depending upon his interests, will be able to compile his own list of significant omissions. The mere existence of such omissions is in itself proof of the growth of the active therapies and the increase in activity to be shown in the more classical therapies. It is hoped, though, that the examples included will be illustrative of the new breath of active intervention which is sweeping through the whole field.

Harold Greenwald

CONTENTS

ACTIVE PSYCHOTHERAPY

SIGMUND FREUD

Lines of Advance
in Psychoanalytic Therapy

The following address was read by Freud before the Fifth International Psychoanalytical Congress, held at Budapest on September 28 and 29, 1918, shortly before the end of the First World War. It was written during the previous summer, while he was staying with Anton von Freund at his house in Steinbruch, a suburb of Budapest. The paper, in which the main stress is on the "active" methods chiefly associated later with the name of Ferenczi, was the last of Freud's purely technical works before the two which he published nearly twenty years later, toward the end of his life.

Since much of the opposition to active psychotherapy comes from orthodox Freudians, it is instructive to realize that Freud himself foresaw and even encouraged many of the future developments in activity. It is unfortunate to realize how many analysts prefer to be Freudians rather than Freud-like.

GENTLEMEN: AS YOU KNOW, we have never prided ourselves on the completeness and finality of our knowledge and capacity. We are just as ready now as we were earlier to admit the imperfections of our understanding, to learn new things and to alter our methods in any way that can improve them.

Now that we are met together once more after the long and difficult years of separation that we have lived through, I feel drawn

From *Standard Edition of the Complete Psychological Works of Sigmund Freud,* James Strachey, Ed. (London: The Hogarth Press, 1955), Vol. 17. The present translation, with a modified title, is based on the one published in 1924.

to review the position of our therapeutic procedure—to which, indeed, we owe our place in human society—and to take a survey of the new directions in which it may develop.

We have formulated our task as physicians thus: to bring to the patient's knowledge the unconscious, repressed impulses existing in him, and, for that purpose, to uncover the resistances that oppose this extension of his knowledge about himself. Does the uncovering of these resistances guarantee that they will also be overcome? Certainly not always; but our hope is to achieve this by exploiting the patient's transference to the person of the physician, so as to induce him to adopt our conviction of the inexpediency of the repressive process established in childhood and of the impossibility of conducting life on the pleasure principle. I have set out elsewhere[1] the dynamic conditions prevailing in the fresh conflict through which we lead the patient and which we substitute in him for his previous conflict—that of his illness. I have nothing at the moment to alter in that account.

The work by which we bring the repressed mental material into the patient's consciousness has been called by us psychoanalysis. Why "analysis"—which means breaking up or separating out, and suggests an analogy with the work carried out by chemists on substances which they find in nature and bring into their laboratories? Because in an important respect there really is an analogy between the two. The patient's symptoms and pathological manifestations, like all his mental activities, are of a highly composite kind; the elements of this compound are at bottom motives, instinctual impulses. But the patient knows nothing of these elementary motives, or not nearly enough. We teach him to understand the way in which these highly complicated mental formations are compounded; we trace the symptoms back to the instinctual impulses which motivate them; we point out to the patient these instinctual motives, which are present in his symptoms and of which he has hitherto been unaware—just as a chemist isolates the fundamental substance, the chemical "element," out of the salt in which it had been combined with other elements and in which it was unrecognizable. In the same way, as regards those of the patient's mental manifestations that were not considered pathological, we show him that he was only to a certain extent conscious of their motivation—that other instinctual impulses of which he had remained in ignorance had cooperated in producing them.

Again, we have thrown light on the sexual impulses in man

1. [Cf. Freud's technical paper, Recollecting, Repeating and Working Through (Standard Edition, Vol. 12), and Lecture 27 of his Introductory Lectures on Psychoanalysis, Sta. V. 17 (1916-17).]

by separating them into their component elements; and when we interpret a dream we proceed by ignoring the dream as a whole and starting associations from its single elements.

This well-founded comparison of medical psychoanalytic activity with a chemical procedure might suggest a new direction for our therapy. We have *analyzed* the patient—that is, separated his mental processes into their elementary constituents and demonstrated these instinctual elements in him singly and in isolation; what could be more natural than to expect that we should also help him to make a new and a better combination of them? You know that this demand has actually been put forward. We have been told that after an analysis of a sick mind a synthesis of it must follow. And, close upon this, concern has been expressed that the patient might be given too much analysis and too little synthesis; and there has then followed a move to put all the weight on this synthesis as the main factor in the psychotherapeutic effect, to see in it a kind of restoration of something that had been destroyed—destroyed, as it were, by vivisection.

But I cannot think, gentlemen, that any new task is set us by this psychosynthesis. If I allowed myself to be frank and uncivil I should say it was nothing but an empty phrase. I will limit myself to remarking that it is merely pushing a comparison so far that it ceases to have any meaning, or, if you prefer, that it is an unjustifiable exploitation of a name. A name, however, is only a label applied to distinguish a thing from other similar things—not a syllabus, a description of its content, or a definition. And the two objects compared need only coincide at a single point and may be entirely different from each other in everything else. What is psychical is something so unique and peculiar to itself that no one comparison can reflect its nature. The work of psychoanalysis suggests analogies with chemical analysis, but it does so just as much with the intervention of a surgeon or the manipulations of an orthopedist or the influence of an educator. The comparison with chemical analysis has its limitation: for in mental life we have to deal with trends that are under a compulsion toward unification and combination. Whenever we succeed in analysing a symptom into its elements, in freeing an instinctual impulse from one nexus, it does not remain in isolation, but immediately enters into a new one.[2]

In actual fact, indeed, the neurotic patient presents us with a

2. After all, something very similar occurs in chemical analysis. Simultaneously with the isolation of the various elements induced by the chemist, syntheses which are no part of his intention come about, owing to the liberation of the elective affinities of the substances concerned.

torn mind, divided by resistances. As we analyse it and remove the resistances, it grows together; the great unity which we call his ego fits into itself all the instinctual impulses which before had been split off and held apart from it.[3] The psychosynthesis is thus achieved during analytic treatment without our intervention, automatically and inevitably. We have created the conditions for it by breaking up the symptoms into their elements and by removing the resistances. It is not true that something in the patient has been divided into its components and is now quietly waiting for us to put it somehow together again.

Developments in our therapy, therefore, will no doubt proceed along other lines; first and foremost, along the one which Ferenczi, in his paper "Technical Difficulties in an Analysis of Hysteria" (1919),[4] has lately termed "activity" on the part of the analyst.

Let us at once agree upon what we mean by this activity. We have defined our therapeutic task as consisting of two things: making conscious the repressed material and uncovering the resistances. In that we are active enough, to be sure. But are we to leave it to the patient to deal alone with the resistances we have pointed out to him? Can we give him no other help in this besides the stimulus he gets from the transference? Does it not seem natural that we should help him in another way as well, by putting him into the mental situation most favorable to the solution of the conflict which is our aim? After all, what he can achieve depends, too, on a combination of external circumstances. Should we hesitate to alter this combination by intervening in a suitable manner? I think activity of such a kind on the part of the analyzing physician is unobjectionable and entirely justified.

You will observe that this opens up a new field of analytic technique, the working over of which will require close application and which will lead to quite definite rules of procedure. I shall not attempt today to introduce you to this new technique, which is still in the course of being evolved, but will content myself with enunciating a fundamental principle which will probably dominate our work in this field. It runs as follows: *Analytic treatment should be carried through, as far as is possible, under privation—in a state of abstinence.*[5]

3. [The synthetic function of the ego is discussed at greater length in Chapter III of Freud's *Inhibitions, Symptoms and Anxiety* (Standard Edition, Vol. 20).]

4. [According to a statement by Ferenczi in the same paper, and to another in a later one (see pp. 10ff. of this book—Ed. note, H. G.), the idea of this was based on an oral suggestion originally made to him by Freud himself.]

5. [Freud had already mentioned this principle in connection with "transference-love" (Observations in Transference Love, Standard Edition, Vol. 12).]

How far it is possible to show that I am right in this must be left to a more detailed discussion. By abstinence, however, is not to be understood doing without any and every satisfaction—that would of course not be practicable; nor do we mean what it popularly connotes, refraining from sexual intercourse; it means something else which has far more to do with the dynamics of falling ill and recovering.

You will remember that it was a *frustration* that made the patient ill, and that his symptoms serve him as substitutive satisfactions[6] It is possible to observe during treatment that every improvement in his condition reduces the rate at which he recovers and diminishes the instinctual force impelling him toward recovery. But this instinctual force is indispensable; reduction of it endangers our aim—the patient's restoration to health. What, then, is the conclusion that forces itself inevitably upon us? Cruel though it may sound, we must see to it that the patient's suffering, to a degree that is in some way or other effective, does not come to an end prematurely. If, owing to the symptoms having been taken apart and having lost their value, his suffering becomes mitigated, we must reinstate it elsewhere in the form of some appreciable privation; otherwise we run the danger of never achieving any improvements except quite insignificant and transitory ones.

As far as I can see, the danger threatens from two directions in especial. On the one hand, when the illness has been broken down by the analysis, the patient makes the most assiduous efforts to create for himself in place of his symptoms new substitutive satisfactions, which now lack the feature of suffering. He makes use of the enormous capacity for displacement possessed by the now partly liberated libido, in order to cathect with libido and promote to the position of substitutive satisfactions the most diverse kinds of activities, preferences, and habits, not excluding some that have been his already. He continually finds new distractions of this kind, into which the energy necessary to carrying on the treatment escapes, and he knows how to keep them secret for a time. It is the analyst's task to detect these divergent paths and to require him every time to abandon them, however harmless the activity which leads to satisfaction may be in itself. The half-recovered patient may also enter on less harmless paths—as when, for instance, if he is a man, he seeks prematurely to attach himself to a woman. It may be observed, incidentally, that unhappy marriage and physical infirmity are the two things that most often supersede a neurosis. They satisfy in particular the sense of guilt (need for punishment)

6. [See the opening pages of Freud's Types of Onset of Neurosis (Standard Edition, Vol. 12).]

which makes many patients cling so fast to their neuroses. By a foolish choice in marriage they punish themselves; they regard a long organic illness as a punishment by fate and thereafter often cease to keep up their neurosis.

In all such situations activity on the part of the physician must take the form of energetic opposition to premature substitutive satisfactions. It is easier for him, however, to prevent the *second* danger which jeopardizes the propelling force of the analysis, though it is not one to be underestimated. The patient looks for his substitutive satisfactions above all in the treatment itself, in his transference-relationship with the physician; and he may even strive to compensate himself by this means for all the other privations laid upon him. Some concessions must of course be made to him, greater or less, according to the nature of the case and the patient's individuality. But it is not good to let them become too great. Any analyst who, out of the fullness of his heart, perhaps, and his readiness to help, extends to the patient all that one human being may hope to receive from another, commits the same economic error as that of which our nonanalytic institutions for nervous patients are guilty. Their one aim is to make everything as pleasant as possible for the patient, so that he may feel well there and be glad to take refuge there again from the trials of life. In so doing they make no attempt to give him more strength for facing life and more capacity for carrying out his actual tasks in it. In analytic treatment all such spoiling must be avoided. As far as his relations with the physician are concerned, the patient must be left with unfulfilled wishes in abundance. It is expedient to deny him precisely those satisfactions which he desires most intensely and expresses most importunately.

I do not think I have exhausted the range of desirable activity on the part of the physician in saying that a condition of privation is to be kept up during the treatment. Activity in another direction during analytic treatment has already, as you will remember, been a point at issue between us and the Swiss school.[7] We refused most emphatically to turn a patient who puts himself into our hands in search of help into our private property, to decide his fate for him, to force our own ideals upon him, and with the pride of a creator to form him in our own image and see that it is good. I still adhere to this refusal, and I think that this is the proper place for the medical discretion which we have had to ignore in other connections. I have learned by experience, too, that such a far-

7. [Cf. the later part of Section III of Freud's *History of the Psychoanalytic Movement* (Standard Edition, Vol. 14).]

reaching activity toward patients is not in the least necessary for therapeutic purposes. For I have been able to help people with whom I had nothing in common—neither race, education, social position, nor outlook upon life in general—without affecting their individuality. At the time of the controversy I have just spoken of, I had the impression, to be sure, that the objections of our spokesmen—I think it was Ernest Jones who took the chief part[8]— were too harsh and uncompromising. We cannot avoid taking some patients for treatment who are so helpless and incapable of ordinary life that for them one has to combine analytic with educative influence; and even with the majority occasions now and then arise in which the physician is bound to take up the position of teacher and mentor. But it must always be done with great caution, and the patient should be educated to liberate and fulfill his own nature, not to resemble ourselves.

Our honored friend, J. J. Putnam, in the land of America which is now so hostile to us, must forgive us if we cannot accept his proposal either—namely, that psychoanalysis should place itself in the service of a particular philosophical outlook on the world and should urge this upon the patient for the purpose of ennobling his mind. In my opinion, this is after all only to use violence, even though it is overlaid with the most honorable motives.[9]

Lastly, another quite different kind of activity is necessitated by the gradually growing appreciation that the various forms of disease treated by us cannot all be dealt with by the same technique. It would be premature to discuss this in detail, but I can give two examples of the way in which a new kind of activity comes into question. Our technique grew up in the treatment of hysteria and is still directed principally to the cure of that affection. But the phobias have already made it necessary for us to go beyond our former limits. One can hardly master a phobia if one waits till the patient lets the analysis influence him to give it up. He will never in that case bring into the analysis the material indispensable for a convincing resolution of the phobia. One must proceed differently. Take the example of agoraphobia; there are two classes of it, one mild, the other severe. Patients belonging to the first class suffer from anxiety when they go into the street by themselves, but they

8. [This may be a reference to the paper read by Ernest Jones at the Fourth (Munich) International Psychoanalytical Congress held in 1913. Ernest Jones, *The Attitude of the Psychoanalytic Physician Toward Current Conflicts: Papers on Psychoanalysis,* 2nd Ed. (London, 1918), Chap. XVII.]

9. [Some further comments on Putnam's psychoanalytic views will be found in Freud's Preface to Putnam's *Addresses on Psychoanalysis* (Standard Edition, Vol. 18, p. 269).]

have not yet given up going out alone on that account; the others protect themselves from the anxiety by altogether ceasing to go about alone. With these last, one succeeds only when one can induce them by the influence of the analysis to behave like phobic patients of the first class—that is, to go into the street and to struggle with their anxiety while they make the attempt. One starts, therefore, by moderating the phobia so far; and it is only when that has been achieved at the physician's demand that the associations and memories come into the patient's mind which enable the phobia to be resolved.

In severe cases of obsessive acts a passive waiting attitude seems even less indicated. Indeed in general these cases incline to an "asymptotic" process of recovery, an interminable protraction of the treatment. Their analysis is always in danger of bringing to light a great deal and changing nothing. I think there is little doubt that here the correct technique can only be to wait until the treatment itself has become a compulsion, and then with this counter-compulsion forcibly to suppress the compulsion of the disease. You will understand, however, that these two instances I have given you are only samples of the new developments toward which our therapy is tending.[10]

And now in conclusion I will cast a glance at a situation which belongs to the future—one that will seem fantastic to many of you, but which I think, nevertheless, deserves that we should be prepared for it in our minds. You know that our therapeutic activities are not very far-reaching. There are only a handful of us, and even by working very hard each one can devote himself in a year to only a small number of patients. Compared to the vast amount of neurotic misery which there is in the world, and perhaps need not be, the quantity we can do away with is almost negligible. Besides this, the necessities of our existence limit our work to the well-to-do classes, who are accustomed to choose their own physicians and whose choice is diverted away from psychoanalysis by all kinds of prejudices. At present we can do nothing for the wider social strata, who suffer extremely seriously from neuroses.

Now let us assume that by some kind of organization we succeeded in increasing our numbers to an extent sufficient for treating a considerable mass of the population. On the other hand, it is possible to foresee that at some time or other the conscience of society will awake and remind it that the poor man should have

10. [Cf. the technical device described in the first section of the "Wolf Man" analysis (From the History of an Infantile Neurosis, Standard Edition, Vol. 17, pp. 3, 11).]

just as much right to assistance for his mind as he now has to the life-saving help offered by surgery; and that the neuroses threaten public health no less than tuberculosis, and can be left as little as the latter to the impotent care of individual members of the community. When this happens, institutions or out-patient clinics will be started, to which analytically-trained physicians will be appointed, so that men who would otherwise give way to drink, women who have nearly succumbed under their burden of privations, children for whom there is no choice but between running wild or neurosis, may be made capable, by analysis, of resistance and of efficient work. Such treatments will be free. It may be a long time before the state comes to see these duties as urgent. Present conditions may delay its arrival even longer. Probably these institutions will first be started by private charity. Some time or other, however, it must come to this.[11]

We shall then be faced by the task of adapting our technique to the new conditions. I have no doubt that the validity of our psychological assumptions will make its impression on the uneducated too, but we shall need to look for the simplest and most easily intelligible ways of expressing our theoretical doctrines. We shall probably discover that the poor are even less ready to part with their neuroses than the rich, because the hard life that awaits them if they recover offers them no attraction, and illness gives them one more claim to social help. Often, perhaps, we may only be able to achieve anything by combining mental assistance with some material support, in the manner of the Emperor Joseph.[12] It is very probable, too, that the large-scale application of our therapy will compel us to alloy the pure gold of analysis freely with the copper of direct suggestion; and hypnotic influence, too, might find a place in it again, as it has in the treatment of war neuroses.[13] But, whatever form this psychotherapy for the people may take, whatever the elements out of which it is compounded, its most effective and most important ingredients will assuredly remain those borrowed from strict and untendentious psychoanalysis.

11. [At the time at which this address was delivered Anton von Freund was planning the foundation of an Institute of the kind suggested here. See Freud's obituary of von Freund (Standard Edition, Vol. 18, p. 267).]

12. [The Emperor Joseph II of Austria (1741-1790), about whose unconventional methods of philanthropy many legends were current. He is referred to in the same connection in one of Freud's earlier technical papers (On Beginning the Treatment, Standard Edition, Vol. 12).]

13. [The treatment of war neuroses was a main topic at the Congress before which this address was given.]

SANDOR FERENCZI

The Further Development of an Active Therapy in Psychoanalysis[1]

In the history of psychoanalysis, Sandor Ferenczi's name is synonymous with active therapy. It was in reference to Ferenczi's innovations in technique that Freud wrote the preceding paper.

Many of the forms of active therapy practiced by psychoanalysts that are described in this book were originated by Ferenczi. In the following paper we see early indications of the rise of role-playing and psychodramatic techniques as well as the foundations for what later became the "interpersonal" approach in psychoanalysis.

In his biography of Freud,* Jones says of Ferenczi, "He had a warm and lovable personality and a generous nature. He was a highly gifted analyst with a remarkable flair for divining the manifestations of the unconscious."

I

THE FUNDAMENTALS of psychoanalytic technique have undergone little essential alteration since the introduction of Freud's "fundamental rule" (free association). That my proposals do not aim at this either, I would emphasize at the beginning; on the contrary, their intention was and is to enable the patient, by means

From Ferenczi, S., *Further Contributions to the Theory and Technique of Psycho-Analysis* (London: Hogarth Press, 1950).

1. *Zeitschrift*, 1921, Bd. VII, 233.

* Ernest Jones, *The Life and Work of Sigmund Freud*, Vol. III (New York: Basic Books, 1957).

of certain artifices, to comply more successfully with the rule of free association and thereby to assist or hasten the exploring of the unconscious material. Besides, these artifices are only required in certain exceptional cases; for most patients the treatment can be carried out without any special "activity" on the part of either doctor or patient, and even in those cases in which one has to proceed more actively the interference should be restricted as much as possible. As soon as the stagnation of the analysis, the only justification for and the only motive of the modification, is overcome, the expert will immediately resume the passively receptive attitude most favorable for the efficient cooperation of the doctor's unconscious.

Like almost every innovation, "activity" on closer inspection is found to be an old acquaintance. Not only has it played an important part already in the early history of psychoanalysis; it has in a certain sense never ceased to exist. We are dealing here, therefore, with the formulation of a conception and of a technical expression for something which, even if unexpressed, has always *de facto* been in use. Nevertheless I consider such a definition and terminological fixation as not unimportant from a scientific point of view; only by this means does one become conscious in the true sense of the word of one's own actions, and only by its becoming conscious is the methodical, critical, and selective practice of a method of procedure rendered possible.[2]

The period of the Breuer-Freud *cathartic* procedure represented a phase of marked activity on the part of the doctor as well as on that of the patient. The doctor made the greatest efforts to revive the memories relating to the symptoms and made use of every assistance that the procedures of waking or hypnotic suggestion put at his disposal. The patient, too, made every endeavor to follow the directions of his guide and had therefore to engage in marked psychic activities, had often indeed to exercise all his intellectual faculties.

Psychoanalysis, as we employ it today, is a procedure whose most prominent characteristic is *passivity*. We ask the patient to allow himself to be guided uncritically by his "ideas"; he has nothing to do but to impart these ideas without reserve—of course after overcoming the inner resistances that struggle against this. The doctor should not fix his attention rigidly on any particular intention (for instance, on the desire to cure or to understand) but should also

2. The significance of bestowing names in scientific matters deserves a psychological research of its own.

yield himself passively to the play of his fantasy with the patient's ideas. Of course, if he is to influence the patient's further ideas, he cannot continue this fantasying indefinitely; as I have explained elsewhere, as soon as he has been able to crystallize certain really valid opinions, he must direct his attention to them and on mature reflection must decide upon an *interpretation*. Communicating such an interpretation is, however, in itself an active interference with the patient's psychic activity; it turns the thoughts in a given direction and facilitates the appearance of ideas that otherwise would have been prevented by the resistance from becoming conscious. The patient must comport himself passively during this "midwifery of thought."

More recent knowledge of the decisive significance which the distribution of the libido has for the formation of neurotic symptoms helped Freud to another method of procedure.[3] He distinguishes two phases in the therapy; in the first all the libido is forced from the symptoms into the transference; in the second the struggle with the libido that has been transferred to the doctor is dealt with, and the attempt is made to free it from its new object. This setting free of the libido is rendered possible by the alteration of the ego under the influence of education by the doctor. Of course, by the forcing of the libido into the transference an active encouragement of this tendency on the doctor's part is not meant—the transference occurs spontaneously; the doctor needs only the skill not to disturb this process.

The education of the ego, on the other hand, is distinctly an active interference of which the doctor is capable because of the authority which has been heightened by the transference. Freud does not evade calling this kind of influence "suggestion," but indicates the essential characteristics that distinguish this from nonpsychoanalytic suggestion.[4]

This influencing of the patient is certainly an active thing, the

3. Freud, *Introductory Lectures on Psychoanalysis*, from the *Standard Edition of the Complete Psychological Works of Sigmund Freud*, James Strachey. Ed. (London: The Hogarth Press, 1955), Vol. 3, p. 534.

4. Earlier suggestion generally consisted in persuading the patient of a conscious untruth. ("There is nothing the matter with you"—which is certainly not true, as the patient is suffering from the neurosis.) Psychoanalytic suggestion employs the transference to make one's own conviction of the unconscious motives of the illness accessible to the patient. The psychoanalyst himself must have a care that the belief so accepted is no "blind belief" but the patient's own conviction, based on memory and actual experience ("repetition"). This also distinguishes psychoanalysis from the persuasion and explanation treatment of Dubois.

patient behaving passively toward this endeavor on the part of the doctor.

In what has been said so far, the passive and active conduct respectively referred exclusively to the patient's *psychic attitude*. Analysis demands no *activities* from the patient except punctual appearance at the hours of treatment; except for this no influence is exercised on the general mode of life: indeed it is expressly emphasized that the patient must deal with important decisions himself or they must be deferred till the power of making decisions is attained. The first exception to this rule occurred in the analysis of certain cases of *anxiety hysteria*; it happened that the patients, in spite of close compliance with the "fundamental rule" and in spite of a deep insight into their unconscious complexes, could not get beyond "dead points" in the analysis until they were compelled to venture out from the retreat of their phobia, and to expose themselves experimentally to the situation they had avoided because of its painfulness. As was to be expected, this brought with it an acute exacerbation of the anxiety, but, in exposing themselves to this effect, they at the same time overcame the resistance to hitherto repressed material that now became accessible to analysis in the form of ideas and reminiscences.[5]

I really meant that the description of "active technique" should be applied to this proceeding, which does not so much represent an active interference on the part of the doctor as on the part of the patient upon whom are imposed certain tasks besides the keeping of the fundamental rule. In the cases of phobia the task consisted in the carrying out of painful activities.

I soon had the opportunity to apportion to a patient tasks that consisted in her *renunciation* of certain hitherto unnoticed *pleasurable activities* (onanistic stimulation of the genitals, stereotypies, and ticlike twitchings or stimulation of other parts of the body), and in the control of the impulse to such activities. The result was that new memories became accessible and the progress of the analysis was visibly accelerated.

The inference from this and similar experiences has been drawn by Professor Freud in his Address to the Congress at Budapest.[6] He was even able to generalize the theory obtained from these observations, and to lay down the rule that, in general, the treatment must be carried out in a condition of *abstinence*; the same

5. A verbal statement of Freud's gave me the indication for this proceeding.
6. Turnings in the Ways of Psychoanalytic Therapy, *Collected Papers* (London: The Hogarth Press, 1953), Vol. 2, p. 392.

renunciation that led to the symptom formation must be preserved throughout the whole treatment as the motive for the desire to get well; it is even useful to deny just *that* satisfaction which the patient most intensely desires.

In what I have just said I believe I have mentioned everything essential that has so far been published about activity in psychoanalytic technique, and everything in the generally recognized methods that can be designated as "activity."

II

I should now like to give excerpts from some analyses calculated to substantiate what has been said, and to deepen to some extent our insight into the play of forces at work in "active technique." The case of a young Croatian woman, a musician, who suffered from a host of phobias and obsessional states, occurs to me at once. I shall mention only a few of her endless symptoms. She suffered torments of stage fright; if she was asked to play in front of others at the music school, she became scarlet in the face; finger exercises which, when she was alone, she readily performed automatically without any effort seemed to her prodigiously difficult; she made mistakes on every occasion and had the obsessive idea that she *must* disgrace herself, which she accordingly did pretty thoroughly in spite of her unusual talent. In the street she believed herself constantly observed because of her too voluminous breasts, and did not know how to hold or conduct herself in order to conceal this (imagined) bodily deformity. Now she would fold her arms across her chest, now compress the breasts tightly against the thorax; but, as is customary with obsessional patients, each precaution was followed by the doubt whether she were not by these very means attracting attention to herself. Her behavior in the street was now excessively shy, now provocative; she was unhappy if in spite of her marked beauty no attention was paid her but was no less disconcerted when actually spoken to by someone who misunderstood (or, rather, correctly interpreted) her behavior. She was afraid that she had an offensive breath and went constantly to the dentist and the laryngologist, who naturally could discover nothing the matter. She came after an analysis of many months' duration to me (as the colleague concerned had been obliged to break off the treatment) and was already well initiated into her unconscious complexes; on continuing her treatment, however, I had to endorse the observation of my colleague that the progress of the cure had no relation to the depth of her theoretic insight and to the memories already laid bare. Things went on with me in the same way for weeks. At one interview a street song occurred to her that her elder sister (who tyrannized over her in every way) was in the habit of singing. After hesitating for a long time she repeated the very ambiguous text of the song and was silent for a long time; I extracted from her that she had thought of the *melody* of the song. I did not delay in asking her to sing the song. It took nearly two hours, however, before she could bring herself to perform the song as she really intended it. She was so embarrassed that she broke off repeatedly in the middle of a verse, and to begin with she sang in a low uncertain voice until, encouraged by my persuasions, she began to sing louder, when her voice developed more and more and proved to be an unusually beautiful soprano. This did not overcome the resistance; after some difficulty she confessed that her sister was in the habit of accompanying the song with expressive and indeed quite unambiguous *gestures,* and she made some clumsy arm movements to illustrate her sister's behavior. Finally I asked her to get up and repeat the song *exactly* as she had seen her sister do it. After endless spiritless partial attempts she showed herself to be a perfect *chanteuse,* with all the coquetry of facial play and movement that she had seen in her sister. From now on she seemed to take pleasure in these productions and began to fritter away the hours of analysis with such things. When I noticed this, I told her we knew now that she enjoyed displaying her various talents and that behind her modesty lay hidden a considerable desire to please; it was no longer a matter of dancing but of getting on with the work. It was astonishing how favorably this little interlude affected the work. Presently memories of her early childhood, of which she had never spoken, occurred to her, memories of the time when the birth of a little brother had had a really unholy effect on her psychic development and had made of her an anxious, shy, and abnormally good child. She remembered the time when she was still "a little devil," the darling of all her family and friends, when she displayed all her talents before people and generally showed an unrestrained pleasure in muscular movement.

I followed up this active measure and constrained the patient to carry out activities of which she had the greatest fear. She conducted in front of me (while at the same time she imitated the sounds of an orchestra) a long phrase from a symphony; the analysis of this notion led to the discovery of the penis jealousy by which she had been tormented since the birth of her brother. She played to me the difficult piano piece that she had to play at the examination; it was shown soon afterward in the analysis that her fear of disgracing herself when playing the piano referred back to onanistic fantasies and onanistic disgrace (forbidden "finger exercises"). She did not dare to go to the swimming baths on account of her idea that her breasts were disproportionately large; only after she had overcome the resistance on my insisting was she able to convince herself during analysis of her latent desire to exhibit. Now that the approach of her most hidden tendencies was opened up, she acknowledged that during the analytic hour she occupied herself a great deal with her sphincter ani; sometimes she would play with the idea of passing flatus, sometimes contract the sphincter rhythmically, and so on.

As with every technical rule, the patient then tried to reduce activity to absurdity by exaggerating the tasks allotted her. I let her be for a time and then bade her give up these games, and after a not too prolonged labor we came upon the anal-erotic explanation of her anxiety that her mouth smelt offensively; soon after the reproduction of the associated infantile memories, while maintaining the prohibition against anal play, this showed marked improvement.

We owed the most marked impulse toward betterment to the patient's *unconscious onanism* which was rendered manifest by the help of "activity." Sitting at the piano she experienced, on every more vehement or passionate movement, a voluptuous sensation of the genital parts stimulated by the movement. She had to acknowledge these sensations to herself after she had been bidden to behave, as she saw many artists do, very passionately at the piano; but so soon as she began to take pleasure in this play she had on my advice to give it up. As a result we were then able to take cognizance of reminiscences and reconstructions of infantile genital play, the chief source perhaps of her exaggerated sense of shame.

It is time now to consider what exactly we were doing by these interferences, and to attempt a formulation of the play of psychic forces to which we owed the undeniable progress of the analysis. In this case our activity may be divided into two phases. In the first, the patient, who guarded herself from certain activities by a phobia, had to be commanded to carry out those activities, contrary to inclination; after the hitherto repressed tendencies had become pleasurable, she had in the second place to deny herself—that is, certain activities were *forbidden*. The commands had the result of rendering *fully conscious* inclinations hitherto repressed, or only manifested as unrecognizable rudiments, and ultimately rendering them *conscious as desires*, as ideas agreeable to herself. Then when the satisfaction of the now pleasurable activity was denied her, the psychic impulses, once roused, found the way to long-repressed material, to infantile reminiscences, or they had to be interpreted as repetitions of something infantile, and the peculiarities and conditions of the childish procedures had to be reconstructed by the analyst with the help of the other analytic material (dreams, fancies, etc.). It was easy for the patient to accept such reconstruction, as she could deny neither to herself nor to the doctor that she had recently actually *experienced* these activities and their accompanying affects. Thus the "active therapy," hitherto regarded as a single entity, breaks up into the systematic issuing and carrying out of *commands* and of *prohibitions,* Freud's "attitude of renunciation" being constantly maintained. I have already had occasion in a number of cases to make use of this measure, and not only (as in the case described) by the activation and control of sexual and erotic tendencies, but also of highly sublimated activities. Following certain hints, I constrained a patient who—apart from naïve attempts during adolescence—never wrote poetry to put her poetical notions on paper. In this way she managed to unfold not only an unusual degree of poetic talent but also the whole content of her—till then—latent longing for masculine productivity in general, which was connected with her predominantly clitoric eroticism and her sexual anesthesia for men.

In the period of interdiction, however, during which literary work was forbidden her, it became evident that in her case we were dealing rather with a misuse than a use of a talent. Her whole "masculinity complex" proved to be a secondary affair, the result of a genital trauma suffered in childhood that had turned her character—till then thoroughly feminine and yielding—in the direction of autoeroticism and homosexuality by rendering heterosexuality disagreeable to her. The discoveries made during analysis enabled the patient to estimate her real penchant correctly; she is aware now that she usually seizes her pen when she fears that she cannot function fully as a woman. This analytic experience has assisted not a little in the return of the normal feminine capacity for gratification.

When the patient is "active" from the beginning without being so commanded, when he masturbates, carries out obsessive and symptomatic acts and "transitory symptoms," then naturally the first, "the command period," falls out of itself, and the patient's task narrows itself to discontinuing such activities meantime for the purpose of furthering the analysis. (Of course, these little symptoms are often only rudiments of the latent tendencies, and the patient has first to be encouraged to develop them fully.) Among symptoms that have appeared and have been forbidden in the course of treatment I would mention the need of urination immediately before or after the analytic session, a feeling of sickness during the session, unseemly wriggling, plucking at and stroking the face, the hands, or other parts of the body, the playing with the sphincter already referred to, the pressing together of the thighs, and so on. For instance, I noticed with one patient that, as soon as the contents of the association began to be uncomfortable or painful for him, instead of continuing the work he manifested affects, screamed, wriggled, and generally behaved in an unseemly fashion. Of course, it was the resistance against the analytic material already disturbed that caused this; he wanted literally to "shake off" the painful thoughts.[7]

In seeming contradiction to the fundamental rule of analysis I had in a few cases to decide to encourage or discourage patients directly toward or against the production of *thoughts* and fantasies. I have in this way induced patients to carry out this plan who threatened to deceive me—for instance, to feign dreams. But where I became aware of the "misuse of the freedom of association"[8] by means of misleading, futile, and sidetracking ideas or fantasies, I did not hesitate to show the patient that by this he was only trying to escape the more difficult task, and to bid him resume the interrupted train of thought. These were just cases in which the patients wished to avoid what touched them closely but painfully, by means of the so-called talking past (Ganser)—one might rather say *thinking past*. This directing of the course of association, this hindering and furtherance of thought and fantasy, is certainly also an activity in the sense of the word employed here.

III

Little of general applicability can be said about the *indications* for activity; here, if anywhere, one must proceed on individual lines. The main thing about this technical auxiliary is, and remains, the utmost economy of its employment; it is only a makeshift, a pedagogic supplement, to the real analysis whose place it must never

7. The tics and so-called stereotypies require special consideration, which I have attempted in another paper. [*International Journal of Psychoaanlysis*, 2:19.]

8. See Ferenczi, On the Technique of Psychoanalysis, *Further Contributions to the Theory and Technique of Psychoanalysis* (London: The Hogarth Press, 1950), pp. 177-83.

pretend to take. On another occasion I have compared such measures to obstetric forceps that also should only be used in extreme need and whose unnecessary employment is rightly condemned by medical art. Beginners, or analysts of no great experience, do better generally to refrain from it as long as possible, not only because they may easily mislead the patient by it (or are misled by them), but also because they easily lose in this way their only opportunity of obtaining the criteria and proofs of the dynamics of the neuroses, which are only to be gathered from the behavior of the patient who is under no external control and subjected solely to the "fundamental rule."

I instance only a few of the many *contraindications*. Such technical artifices are bad at the beginning of an analysis. Habituation to the fundamental rule affords the patient quite sufficient occupation, and at the beginning, too, the doctor must conduct himself with all possible reserve and passivity in order not to disturb the patient's spontaneous attempts at transference. Later during the actual course of the treatment, according to the nature of the case, activity may more or less frequently be of use or even unavoidable. Of course, the analyst must know that such an experiment is a two-edged sword; he must also have certain indications of the *powers of endurance of the transference* before he determines on it. Activity always works, as we have seen, "against the grain"— that is, against the pleasure principle. If the transference is weak— that is, if the treatment has not yet become an obsession (Freud) for the patient, he easily makes use of the new and irksome task to free himself entirely from the doctor and to escape from the treatment. This is the explanation of the failure of "wild psychoanalysts" who usually proceed too actively and masterfully and thus frighten away their clients. The conditions are different toward the end of an analysis. The doctor now need feel no anxiety lest his patient should run away; usually he has rather to combat the patient's attempt to carry on the treatment indefinitely, that is, to cling to the treatment instead of to reality. The "end-game"[9] of the analysis is seldom successful without active interferences or tasks respectively that the patient must perform beyond the exact adherence to the fundamental rule. As such I would mention: the setting of a term to the conclusion of the treatment, the constraining to an already formed decision which has been postponed owing to resistance, the performance now and then of some particular sacrifice prescribed by the doctor, of a charitable or other alms. Sometimes after an at

9. [The author uses a term employed in chess.—TRANS.]

first compulsory and unwilling performance on the part of the patient, one is presented (as for example in Freud's case of "Infantile Neurosis")[10] with his final explanations and reminiscences as a parting gift, and not infrequently at the same time with an often small but symbolically significant present that is really donated by the patient in these cases and not "solved" as at other times during the analysis.

Indeed there is no kind of neurosis in which activity might not be employed. I have already said of obsessive acts and anxiety-hysteria phobias, that one seldom manages without this technique. It is rarely necessary in true conversion hysteria, but I remember a case that I once treated in a similar fashion many years ago, without knowing that I was employing an active therapy. I will report the case briefly.

A man of bucolic appearance visited my consulting room at the worker's polyclinic, complaining of attacks of loss of consciousness. I considered his attacks to be hysterical and took him to my house to examine him more closely. He told me a long-winded family history of trouble with his father, a well-doing farmer, who would have nothing to do with him on account of his unsuitable marriage, so that he "had to work as a canal cleaner, while—" At these words he became pale, swayed, and would have fallen, had I not caught him. He seemed to have lost consciousness and muttered incomprehensible stuff. I did not let myself be misled, however, shook him quite severely, repeated the sentence he had begun, and demanded forcibly that he should finish his sentence. He then said in a feeble voice that he had to work as a canal cleaner while his younger brother saw to the tillage; he would see him walking behind the plow with its span of six beautiful oxen and then going home after work was done and having his meals with his father, etc. He was going to faint a second time, too, when he spoke of the dissension between his wife and his mother; I forced him, however, to tell this to an end also. In a word, this man had the knack of hysterical fainting which he did whenever he wanted to escape from the unhappy reality into the beautiful world of fantasy, or from too painful trains of thought. The "actively" compelled, conscious thinking out of the hysterical fantasies to their completion affected the patient like a miraculous cure; he could not get over his astonishment that I could cure him thus "without medicine." Sokolnicka[11] recently reported a hysterical attack, in a child suffering from an obsessional neurosis, which was similarly influenced by

10. [Gesammelte Schriften, Bd. VIII. Collected Papers, Vol. 3.]
11. "Analyse einer infantilen Zwangsneurose," Zeitschrift, Bd. VI. S. 228.

activity. She also suggested the very valuable idea that one should try to get at the symptoms that are in the service of the secondary "gain of illness" by pedagogic means.

I take this opportunity to mention Simmel's analyses of traumatic war hysterias[12] in which the duration of treatment was appreciably shortened by active interference, and the experiences Hollós communicated to me orally in Budapest of the active treatment of catatonics. The *neuroses of children* and *mental illnesses* in general should offer a fruitful field for the employment of pedagogic and other activity, but it must not be forgotten that such activity can only be described as a psychoanalytic one when it is used, not as an end in itself, but as an aid to the exploration of the depths.

IV

I myself have repeatedly been in the position of repudiating unmotivated, and in my opinion superfluous, or, indeed, quite misleading proposals for the modification of psychoanalytic technique. If I now advance some new proposals myself, then I must either withdraw my previously declared conservative views, or must show that these proposals are reconcilable with my earlier utterances. I am also prepared that my opponents of those days will not let slip the opportunity to tax me with inconsistency. I recall my criticisms of the technical proposals of Bjerre, Jung, and Adler.

Bjerre suggested that one should not be content in analysis with the discovery of the pathogenic sources but should also undertake the patient's spiritual and ethical guidance. Jung wanted the psychotherapeutics to lead the patient's attention away from the past—and to direct it toward the actual duties of life; Adler said that one had to concern oneself not with the analysis of the libido, but of the "nervous character." My present proposals show some analogy with these modifications, but the differences are far too striking to escape objective judgment.

The instructions that I propose to give the patient—and only, as stated, in certain exceptional cases—are not in the least concerned with the practical or spiritual conduct of life in general; they relate only to certain particular dealings, they are not *a priori* directed to morality, but only against the pleasure principle; they hinder the erotic tendencies (the nonmoral) only in so far as it is

12. [Translated in Psychoanalysis and the War Neuroses, International Psychoanalytic Library, Vol. II.]

hoped they will thereby remove an obstacle to practicable analysis.

It may just as well happen, however, that one tolerates or even encourages, an erotic tendency that the patient has guarded against. An examination of character is never put in the foreground of our technique, for it does not play here the striking part it does for Adler; instead it is only touched on when certain abnormal traits comparable to the psychoses disturb the normal course of the analysis.

It might be objected that the "active technique" is a return to the banal suggestion or cathartic-abreaction therapy. The answer to that would be that we certainly do not employ suggestion in the old sense, as we only prescribe certain lines of behavior and do not foretell the result of the activity—do not, indeed, even know it ourselves. In requiring what is inhibited, and inhibiting what is un-inhibited, we hope for a fresh distribution of the patient's psychic, primarily of his libidinal, energy that will further the laying bare of repressed material. What, however, this material will be we tell the patient all the less as we gladly let it take us ourselves by surprise. Finally, we neither promise ourselves nor the patient an immediate "betterment." On the contrary, the provoking of an opposition by activity disturbs to no small degree the comfortable but torpid quiet of a stagnating analysis. A suggestion, however, that only promises something so unpleasant differs not a little from the hitherto health-assuring medical suggestions and can hardly be any longer designated by the same name. Not less marked are the differences between "activity" and the cathartic therapy. It was the task of catharsis to evoke reminiscences and to achieve the abreaction of inhibited affects by the awakening of memories. Active technique rouses certain activities in the patient—inhibitions, psy-chic discrepancies, or a discharge of affect—and expects *secondarily* the accessibility of the unconscious or of the memory material. In any event the activity roused in the patient is only a means to the end, while the discharge of affect in catharsis was regarded as an end in itself. Where then the task of catharsis ends, the real work of the "active" analyst only begins.

While, however, laying stress on the difference (to some extent the direct contradiction) between the methods and modifications just described, on the one hand, and active technique, on the other, I do not deny that the uncritical employment of my proposals may easily lead to a distortion of analysis after the fashion of Jung, Adler, or Bjerre. One reason the more to employ these technical helps with the greatest care and only after a complete mastery of correct psychoanalysis.

In conclusion I should like to mention some conceptions by means of which I attempted to explain to myself the theory of the efficacy of active technique. Activity, in the sense described, chiefly effects an increase of the resistance, since it stimulates the ego sensibility. This causes an exacerbation of the symptoms due to the increased severity of the inner conflict. Active interference, therefore, recalls the stimulating treatments that are employed in medicine for certain torpid or chronic processes; a mucous catarrh that has become chronic proves refractory to any teatment; the acute exacerbation, however, brought about by artificial stimulation not only leads to the discovery of latent sources of disease, but also rouses the resisting powers of the organism that may be indispensable for the process of cure.

Quite another kind of theoretical consideration throws light upon the efficacy of active technique from the standpoint of psychic economy. When the patient gives up pleasurable activities or masters painful ones, there arise in him new states of psychic tension, most often increases of tension that disturb the peace of remote or deeply repressed psychic domains hitherto spared by the analysis, so that the derivatives from this—in the form of ideas that can be interpreted—find their way into consciousness.

The necessary shortening of the duration of treatment for external reasons—the numbers to be dealt with in the army and the polyclinics, etc.—would suggest activity on a larger scale rather than the normal individual psychoanalysis. At any rate, I can here draw attention from my own experience to two dangers. The one is that the patient as a result of such interferences is cured *too quickly* and therefore not completely. For instance, I rapidly succeeded in encouraging an obsessional neurotic and phobic patient to seek out with enjoyment all the situations that formerly she had anxiously avoided; from a timid creature who had always to be accompanied by her mother she became an unusually gay, independent lady who let herself be surrounded by a whole host of admirers. But it never came to the second, the renunciatory, part of the active technique with her at all; I discharged her in the certain expectation that she would have to undergo the reverse of the active technique in a second analysis as soon as external difficulties had once more heightened the merely superficially resolved inner conflict to the pitch of symptom formation. The other danger is this: that as a result of stimulation of the resistances the treatment that was to have been shortened by the activity is much protracted, contrary to expectation.

Among the special indications for more active analysis I again mention cases of onanism, whose larval and often chameleonlike interchanging forms have consequently to be developed and inhibited, and this often occasions true onanistic activities for the first time. The unconcealed forms of onanism should be observed for a time till they have, so to say, developed themselves fully; one will probably never get hold of the unconscious (Oedipus) nucleus of the self-gratification fantasies without previous interdiction of the satisfaction itself.

In the treatment of impotence, too, the patient's attempts—mostly fruitless—are observed for a time without interference. In every case, however, these endeavors at self-cure must be forbidden at least for a period, and attempts at coitus disuaded, until as a result of analysis the real libido with its unambiguous characteristics becomes apparent; cases certainly do occur in which one can carry out the treatment to a conclusion without any such influencing of the sexual capacity. It also happens that for the purpose of deepening the analysis sexual intercourse must temporarily be forbidden even subsequent to the attainment of sexual capability. I have had to make a pretty extensive use of activity in the cases that might be called "character analyses." In a certain sense every analysis has to reckon with the patient's character when he is being gradually prepared to accept painful pieces of insight. There are cases, however, in which it is not so much neurotic symptoms but rather abnormal qualities of character that predominate. Qualities of character are distinguished from neurotic symptoms primarily in that with them, as in the psychoses, the "insight into the illness" is lacking; they are as it were private psychoses endured, nay acknowledged, by the narcistic ego—at any rate abnormalities of the ego whose modification is chiefly resisted by the ego itself. As we know from Freud, the patient's narcissism can limit the influence of analysis, especially as character is apt to form a wall of defense against the approach to infantile memories. If it is impossible, in Freud's phrase, to remove the patient into "the seething heat of the transference love" in which even the most reserved qualities of character melt, then a last attempt may be made by the opposite method, and traits of character that are often only suggested may be stimulated by setting the patient unpleasant tasks—that is, by activity—which will cause the former to be fully developed and reduced *ad absurdum*. That *this kind* of stimulation may easily lead to the breaking off of the analysis hardly needs to be mentioned, but if the dependence of the patient withstands this test, then the effort of technique may be rewarded by the progress of the analysis.

In the cases so far dealt with, the doctor's activity has consisted in his prescribing certain rules of conduct for the patients—that is, he gets them to assist actively in the treatment by their behavior. The question here principally concerned is whether the doctor is in the position to further the treatment *by his own behavior in relation to the patient.* By compelling the patient to activity we are really showing him the path to self-education, which will facilitate the enduring of the material still repressed. The question now arises whether we may also employ the other pedagogical means of assistance, of which praise and blame are to be considered the most important.

Freud said once that in children analytic aftereducation is not to be separated from the actual lessons of pedagogy. Neurotics, however, have all—especially during analysis—something childlike about them, and one has in fact sometimes to cool down a too impetuous transference by something of reserve, or to make some advances to the shy, and by these means to establish the "optimum temperature" of the relations between doctor and patient. The doctor must never, however, rouse expectations in the patient that he cannot or should not fulfill; he must answer for the sincerity of every statement till the end of the treatment. But within the limits of complete sincerity there is room for tactical measures as regards the patient. Once this "optimum" is reached, one will naturally not occupy oneself further with this relationship but, as soon as possible, turn to the consideration of the main task of the analysis, the exploring of the unconscious and of the infantile material.

The efficacy of activity becomes partly understandable perhaps from the "social" aspect of analytic therapy. How much more profoundly confession operates than self-acknowledgment, or being analysed than self-analysis, is a matter of general knowledge. The Hungarian sociologist Kolnai has just lately adequately acknowledged this effect. We aim, however, at a heightening of this effect when by our commands we constrain one or another patient not only to own deeply concealed impulses to himself, but to *enact them before the doctor,* and, by setting him the task of *consciously controlling* these impulses we have probably subjected the whole process to a revision that was dispatched at some other time in a purposeless fashion by means of *repression.* It is certainly no accident that just infantile *naughtinesses* are so often developed during analysis and must then be given up.

The fact that the expressions of emotion or motor actions forced from the patients evoke secondarily memories from the unconscious rests partly on the reciprocity of affect and idea emphasized by Freud in *The Analysis of Dreams.* The awakening of a memory can—as in catharsis—bring an emotional reaction with it, but an activity exacted from the patient, or an emotion set at freedom, can equally well expose the repressed ideas associated with such processes. Of course, the doctor must have some notion about *which* affects or actions need reproducing. It is also possible that certain early infantile unconscious pathogenic psychic contents, which never were conscious (or preconscious) but which date from the period of "uncoordinated gestures or magical behavior," cannot be simply remembered at all, but can only be reproduced by a reliving in the sense of Freud's repetition. In this, active technique only plays the part of *agent provocateur*; its commands and prohibitions assist in obtaining of repetitions that must then be interpreted or reconstructed respectively into memories. "It is a triumph for the therapy," says Freud, "when one succeeds in releasing by means of the memory what the patient would fain discharge in action." Active technique desires nothing more and nothing less than to lay bare the latent tendencies to repetition and by this means to assist the therapy to these triumphs a little oftener than hitherto.

ALFRED ADLER

The Drive for Superiority

Adler de-emphasized Freud's findings in sexual matters. A term which has passed into general usage as "inferiority complex" was coined by Adler and is the one thing most people think of in connection with his name. However, Adler actually contributed many other ideas and had great influence outside the field of psychoanalysis—in education, criminology, and medicine, for instance, as well as on the development of American psychoanalysis in particular. His emphasis on social factors probably influenced such American therapists as Erich Fromm, Carl Rogers, Karen Horney, and Harry Stack Sullivan.

Adler saw that the inevitable result of feelings of inferiority would be strivings for superiority. He later developed the theory that social interest rather than striving for superiority is the only true and natural compensation for feelings of inferiority.

In the cases described in the following article, Adler stresses some of the neurotic ways in which striving for superiority is sometimes carried out. The cases also illustrate Adler's emphasis on the life style—that is, the way in which the individual organizes his life to compensate for his feelings of inferiority. His therapy for these conditions was quite active, both in demonstrating the life style and in making suggestions for change. As Adler indicates, he is willing to tell his patient "how to mount a horse."

In this excerpt from Adler's writings there is also an early example of the use of negative suggestion, which we later see more fully developed in the work of Haley and of Frankl. The

From Chapter VI, *The Problems of Neurosis* (London: Cosmopolitan Book Co., 1939).

example is at the end of Adler's paper, where he advises an air
swallower, "If you want to go out, and feel in a conflict about it,
swallow some air quickly."

A CURIOUS CASE of depression which I once treated illustrates very
clearly how sadness may be used to heighten the feeling of superiority. This was the case of a man of fifty, who said he felt perfectly
healthy except when he was in a notably comfortable situation. It
was when he was at a concert or theater with his family, for instance,
that a fit of melancholy would descend upon him: and in such depression he always remembered an intimate friend who had died
when he was twenty-five. This friend had been his rival, not only
in business but as a suitor for the hand of his wife—an unsuccessful
rival, however, for by the time he contracted his fatal illness, my
patient already had the advantage over him both in love and in
business.

Success had been his lot, both before and after the friend's death;
he was the favorite of his parents, unsurpassed by brothers and
sisters, and prosperous in the world. His wife, however, was an
ambitious character who strove to solve every domestic problem by
a personal triumph or conquest, moral or otherwise: and between
two such persons, the struggle was naturally continuous and severe.
The wife sometimes gained the ascendancy very cleverly, not by
quarreling or domineering in any way, but by becoming very nervous in disadvantageous situations, and conquering him by her painful condition. She never expressed her excessive jealousies, but
sought to shackle him as required by her fits of anxiety. Thus, successful as he was in all but one relation of life, the man felt uncertain of having reached his goal of superiority, and his excessive
ambition was demanding compensation.

I know that many psychologists would seek for a "guilt complex"
to explain this depression. They would investigate the patient's
childhood to find out a very early desire to kill someone—probably
the father. This patient, however, had been the favorite of his
father, and there was not the least reason why he should ever have
desired his death, as he had always been able to manage him in his
own interest. Such a mistaken search for a "guilt complex" might
also lead a psychologist to think that the patient had secretly wished
to murder his friend and rival, and that after having triumphed
over him and having had the death-wish granted by fate, he remained still unsatisfied. If that were so, the guilt complex might
be developed by the striving of the patient to see himself in an
intenser light. He would want to express his good feeling and

liking for his former rival with the highest sincerity and honesty; and at the same time he would be shaken by the memory of his rival's fatal end and the thoughts which he had been unable wholly to dismiss before it happened. This would amount to the complicated state of self-accusation and repentance at the same time which we call a guilt complex, which is always a superiority-striving on the useless side of life. As I have already observed, it means: "I have reached the summit of error" or "My virtue is so lofty that this slight stain upon it is killing me."

However, in this case I found no indications of the kind, and the man's valuation of honesty as a virtue was not abnormally developed. His depressions were an attempt to show himself superior to his wife. To be depressed in very favorable situations called attention to his good fortune much more than if he had allowed himself to enjoy them. Everyone was surprised at his depression, and he constantly asked himself, "You happy being, *why* are you depressed when you have everything you want?" The unmanageable wife was the one sorrow in his comfortable life, and he compensated for this by *remembering his victory* in the most difficult phase of his history—when he outstripped his friend and won the woman from him. Loyalty forbade him to rejoice in the memory of his dead friend, but he could nevertheless feed upon this ancient triumph by being depressed in the box of the theatre. The more melancholy he was and the brighter the occasion, the more he was able to think of his past conquest and to elevate the consciousness of his estate. Deeper inquiries confirmed my conclusion. His friend had died from paralysis after syphilis, a disease which they had both contracted at the same time. My patient was cured, however; and now, surrounded by his healthy wife and six children, could not but recall, together with the triumph over his friend, his conquest of the disease.

Such, then, were his consolations. In his marriage this man did not feel superior; but at least his wife was the woman his friend had desired, and she had chosen him instead. By contemplating his friend's disaster in a discreet gloom he heightened the sense of victory. Consolation of this nature is on the useless side, however, and tends, as we see, toward disease.

A man of thirty-six came to me for advice about sexual impotence after having tried various treatments. He was a self-made man, in a good position, and physically healthy, but not very well educated, and he had a love relation with a well-educated girl. He was a second child between two girls and had lost both parents at the age of five. He remembered that his family had been very poor, but that he had been a spoiled child, very pretty and quiet, to whom the neighbors liked to give presents: and that he exploited their generosity, behaving like a beggar. One of his earliest remembrances was of walking the streets on Christmas Eve and looking into the shop windows at the Christmas trees destined *for others*. In the orphanage to which he was transferred at the age of five he was strictly treated, but his habitual docility and the striving nature he possessed as a second child enabled him to surpass others. His servility stood him in good stead, for he was promoted to be the principal servant of the institution. In this occupation he had sometimes to wait for a long time at an old and deserted railway station in the country; and at these times, when only the humming of the telegraph wires relieved the dead stillness of the night, he felt utterly isolated and alone in a friendless world. He preserved strong memories of this experience.

Often, in later life, he complained of buzzing in the ears, for which no aurist could find the cause. It proved, however, to be quite coherent with his style of life. When he felt isolated, which happened very often, the memory of the humming wires returned with all the liveliness of a hallucination. After this had been explained to him, and he had been a little more socially reconciled and encouraged to marry his sweetheart, the humming ceased.

It is quite usual for children who are brought up in an orphanage to make the strongest efforts to hide the fact, as though it were a disgrace. This man justified his concealment by asserting that many orphans do not succeed in later life. He regarded failure in life as the inexorable fate of orphans, which gave him his tense and striving attitude in business. For the same reason he halted before the problem of love and marriage, and his neurotic impotence was the immediate result of this profound hesitation.

This man's style of life, as we have seen, was to be a beggar. In business, however (as previously in the orphanage), begging had paved the way to domination. In business he enjoyed nothing more than a begging attitude on the part of his subordinates. He was only a beggar until he could be a conqueror, and he played the second role as heartily as the first. There is no need to drag in the idea of "ambivalent" characteristics, as some psychologists would do immediately. Rightly understood, the whole of this mental process —working from below to above, expressing an inferiority but compensating with a superiority—is not ambivalence but a dynamic unity. Only if it is not understood as a whole do we see it as two contradictory and warring entities. In his business we find the man with a "superiority complex," but if he were to lose his position and have to start again he would promptly go back to the expression of inferiority and make capital out of it. In his love problem he was, for the time being, upon the submissive line of action, begging for love, but trying to reach domination. His sweetheart liked him and wanted to marry him, so she responded to his hesitancy by taking up more and more of a begging attitude toward him! He was well on the way, in fact, toward getting the upper hand with her, and frequently did so in minor matters.

He had still not overcome his hesitant attitude, but after having had his style of life explained to him and having been encouraged, his state improved and his impotence disappeared. He then set up a second resistance, which was that every woman attracted him, and these polygamous desires were an escape from marriage. At this time he dreamed that he was lying upon a couch in my room and he became sexually excited and had a pollution.

There is no couch in my consulting room. My patients sit, stand, or move about as they please; but the couch in this dream was in the room of a doctor who had formerly treated him for a few months. This dream extracted a confession which he had never made before. He believed that both the other doctor and I belonged to a secret society, the object of which was to cure patients such as himself by providing sexual intercourse for them. For this reason he had been trying to find out which of my women patients would be chosen for him. The fact that he missed the couch in my room was like an accusation against me. I was not the right doctor. He had come to me *begging*, expecting me to settle his difficulties, take over his responsibilities, and to assist him to escape from marriage. My collusion in stopping his marriage was to go to the length of being his procurer, a fantasy to which his fright, his impotence, and his polygamous tendencies were all contributory. Failing that, he would solve his sexual problem by pollutions, as others might resort to masturbation or perversion.

He married, but it was difficult to prevent him from developing a tyrannical attitude toward his conciliatory wife.

Another case of the begging attitude was brought to me by a man fifty years old, the youngest of a very poor family. He had been indulged by his mother and the neighbors because of an apparent weakness, and early developed a very timid manner. He always tried to lean on his mother and to appeal to the sympathies of weak persons, especially in difficult times when he exhibited great depression and cried until help came. We have already seen the use which is made of crying by both children and adults. This man's earliest memory was that he had fallen down and hurt himself. The choice of this incident to treasure in the memory out of all possible recollections is explained only by his desire to impress himself with the danger of life. His technique of life was to perfect himself in the role of a beggar, to attract support, consolation, and favor by calling attention to his infirmities. Every incident was made into a matter for tears.

As a child the man had been very backward in learning to talk, and his mother, as always happens in such cases, had to attend all the more carefully to him to find out what he wanted. In this way he was able to feel like a little king. As Lessing said, "The real beggar is the only real king." He became a master of the begging art, expressing his inferiority in the power of his plight over others. "How can I make the poor weak child a king?" was the problem of life as he saw it, and he answered it by elaborating his own individual and essentially mendicant style.

This is one way of living, and so early an apprentice becomes a past master of its technique. He will not change it unless the cost becomes clearly too great, when he may be brought to see that his childish method is inadequate for present problems. Otherwise change is impossible for him, because he has all his life ascribed every success to the begging art and every failure to lack of proficiency in it. Such a goal as this is not calculable from the inheritance or the environmental stimuli, for the child's individual conception of the future is the dominant causal factor, and this patient's conception was such that whenever he wanted to attain superiority he had to make a mistake or get himself into a mess of some kind. All his feelings were appropriately ordered toward the goal of thus getting something for nothing.

After a few days' treatment this man was very much impressed by what I told him, and he sent me a pamphlet he had written some years before. It was entitled "An Association of Beggars."

Habitual criticism, anger, and envy are indications of a useless striving for superiority: they are motions toward the suppression of others, either in reality or fancy, so as to be supreme. Useful criticism of a constructive tendency is always in some comprehensible relation with social feeling, but where the motive is merely relative self-elevation by lowering or degrading others the tendency is neurotic. Neurotics often make use of the truth in order to undervalue others, and it is important, when checking a neurotic criticism, not to overlook the element of truth in the observation.

Anger is usually a sign that the person who is angry feels at a disadvantage—at least temporarily. Neurotics use it freely as a weapon to intimidate those who are responsible for them. Although occasional anger is an understandable attitude in certain critical relations, when it is habitual it is a sign of anxiety, of impatience, or of feelings of helplessness or suppression. Patients of this habit are often very clever in the selection of vulnerable points to attack in others and are also great strategists in preparing such situations that they put others slightly in the wrong before they begin a fight.

Envy is universally an expression of inferiority, though it may sometimes be a stimulus to useful action. In neurosis, however, envy of another's good does not go so far as practical emulation. It stops like a tram before the journey's end, leaving the patient irritable and depressed.

In a certain popular music-hall turn the "strong man" comes on and lifts an enormous weight with care and immense difficulty, and then, during the hearty applause of the audience, a child comes in and gives away the fraud by carrying the dummy weight off with one hand. There are plenty of neurotics who swindle us with such weights, and who are adepts in the art of appearing overburdened. They could really dance with the load under which they stagger like Atlas bearing the world on his shoulders. Yet it cannot be denied that neurotics feel their burden very keenly. They may be continually tired. They may sometimes perspire very freely, and their symptoms may suggest the possibility of tuberculosis. Every movement is very tiring, and they often suffer from palpitation of the heart. Usually depressed, they continually demand more zealous care from others, and yet find it continually insufficient.

I had a case of agoraphobia in a man of fifty-three, who found that he could not breathe properly when he was in company with others. He was living with his sister and had a son whose characteristics were very much like his own. When I investigated the cause of this man's unusual concentration of interest upon himself, I found that he had been orphaned at ten years of age and there were two elder brothers in the home. It was when they quarreled that he had had his first attack. This indicates the tendency to meet a difficult situation by breakdown. The man was the next-youngest of a family of eight and educated by his grandfather. A grandparent is almost invariably a spoiling foster parent. The patient's father and mother had been happily married; the father was superior and the mother rather cold, so the boy was attracted to his father.

A child's first good-fellowship in life is always with the mother if she is present, so that if it inclines more toward the father we may assume that the mother does not give the child sufficient attention: she is probably unkind, otherwise occupied, or more attentive to a younger child. In such circumstances the child turns to the father if possible, and in this case the resistance to the mother was very marked.

People are often unable correctly to remember their earliest situations, but experience enables us to reconstruct their circumstances from comparatively slight indications. This man said he could remember only three incidents from early childhood which had deeply impressed his memory. The first of these occurred at the age of three, when his brother died. He was with his grandfather on the day of the funeral, when his mother returned from the cemetery, sorrowful and sobbing, and when the grandfather kissed her, whispering some words of kindness and consolation, the boy saw that his mother smiled a little. He was very much upset by this, and for long afterward resented his mother's smile on the day that her child was buried. A second memory that he had preserved was of a friendly reproof from his uncle, who had asked him, "Why are you always so rough toward your mother?" A third remembrance from the same period of his life related to a quarrel between his parents, after which he turned to his father, saying, "You were brave, daddy, like a soldier!" He depended much upon his father, and was pampered by him, and he always admired his father more than his mother, although he realized that his mother's character was of a better type.

All these memories, which appeared to date from his third or fourth year, showed the fighting attitude toward the mother. The first and the third remembrances were clearly ruled by his goal, which was to criticize the mother and to justify him in turning toward the father. His reason for turning away from the mother is easy to guess: he had been too much spoiled by her to be able to put up with the younger brother's appearance upon the scene—that same younger brother who figures in an apparently innocent manner in the first recollection.

This patient had married at the age of twenty-four, and marriage had disappointed him, because of his wife's demands upon him. Marriage between two spoiled children is always unhappy, because both remain in the expectant attitude and neither begins to give. This man went through varied experiences and tried different occupations without success. His wife was not sympathetic, and complained that she would rather be the mistress of a rich man than the wife of a poor one, and the union ended in a divorce. Although the man was not really poor, he was very stingy toward his wife, and she divorced him by way of revenge.

After his divorce he turned misogynistic and developed homo-sexual tendencies; he had no actual relationships with men but felt a desire to embrace men. This homosexual trend was as usual a kind of cowardliness. He had been twice defeated and balked by women—first by his mother and afterward by his wife—and he was now trying to divert his sexuality toward men so as to evade women and further possibilities of humiliation. To confirm himself in such a tendency a man can easily falsify the past by recollecting and magnifying the importance of certain common experiences which are then taken by him as proofs of inborn homosexual tendencies. Thus, this patient remembered that he had been in love with a schoolmaster, and that in his youth a boy friend had seduced him into mutual masturbation.

The determining factor in this man's behavior was that he was a spoiled child who wanted everything for nothing. His agoraphobia resulted from the fear of meeting women on the one hand, and on the other hand it was also dangerous to meet men, because of pos-sible erotic inclination toward them. In this tension of feelings about going out of doors he developed stomach and respiratory troubles. Many nervous people begin to swallow air when they get into a state of tension, which causes flatulence, stomach trouble, anxiety, and palpitation, besides affecting the breathing. When I made him realize that this was his condition he asked the usual question: "What shall I do not to swallow air?" Sometimes I reply: "I can tell you how to mount a horse, but I can't tell you how *not* to mount a horse." Or sometimes I advise: "If you want to go out, and feel in a conflict about it, swallow some air quickly." This man, like some other patients, swallowed air even in sleep, but after my advice he began to control himself, and discontinued the habit. Air swallowing at night and vomiting upon waking occur in these patients who suffer from stomach trouble and anxiety when they are bothered by a difficulty which must be confronted upon the following day. The patient in question began to recuperate when he came to understand that, as a pampered child, he expected con-tinually to take without giving. He now realized that he had first stopped his normal sexual life, looking for something easier, and afterward adopted a fictitious homosexuality in which he also stopped short of danger, the whole process being an elaborate way of coming to a standstill. The last obstacle to be removed was his fear of mixing with strangers who did not care for him, such as the people in the streets. This fear is produced by the deeper motive of agoraphobia, which is to exclude all situations in which one is not the center of attention.

THOMAS S. SZASZ

Psychoanalytic Treatment as Education

While Szasz bases his therapy on the psychoanalytic model, he emphasizes certain special aspects. He sees psychoanalysis as primarily an educational activity and not a medical specialty. This leads him to describe the kind of educational effort in which therapist and patient collaborate. He specifically makes it clear that he does not advocate a nondirective technique or passivity but believes in active and meaningful participation in a particular kind of dialogue; a dialogue in which therapist and patient should be interested in the discrepancies which manifest themselves by complaints and symptoms and the patients' adaptation to them; by contradictions between statements made at various times; and by inconsistencies between words and acts. He sees the analyst's function as including the active challenging of the patient's explanations, asking questions, and suggesting alternative explanations. This is interestingly similar to Albert Ellis's technique in "Rational-Emotive Therapy," despite the fact that Ellis considers himself in active disagreement with psychoanalytic technique.

THE SEMANTICS OF PSYCHOANALYSIS and psychotherapy commit us to the view that the client is a "patient" and the expert helping him a "therapist." However, the opposite idea, that the client in search of this sort of help is *not* sick and that his helper is *not* a medical therapist, is nearly as old as psychoanalysis. Freud never

From *The Ethics of Psychoanalysis*, © 1965 by Thomas S. Szasz (New York: Basic Books, Inc., Publishers, 1965).

tired of resisting efforts to assimilate psychoanalysis to a medical psychiatry. His judgment about this was shared, not only by Adler and Jung among the psychoanalytic pioneers, but also by many outstanding psychotherapists who followed them (for example, Wilhelm Reich, Theodor Reik, Erich Fromm, and Rollo May).

Accordingly, the proposition that psychoanalysis is an educational, not a medical, enterprise is not new. In 1919, Freud asserted that the analyst's task was "to bring to the patient's knowledge the unconscious, repressed impulses existing in him";[1] in 1928, he repeated his "wish to protect analysis from the doctors" (and the priests);[2] and in 1938, at the end of his life, he wrote: "We [analysts] serve the patient . . . as a teacher and educator."[3]

If psychoanalysis is not a medical but an educational enterprise, so are other forms of psychotherapy (in which the therapist has no physical contact with the client and uses no drugs). Today, this view is warmly accepted in some quarters and heatedly rejected in others. Behind the scientific problem posed by this distinction lies the problem of institutional loyalties and power, which I shall not consider here. On the basis of evidence and reasoning presented in *The Myth of Mental Illness* and elsewhere,[4] I shall regard psychoanalytic treatment as a form of education.

The question may now be asked: If psychoanalysis is education, what are the similarities between it and other, more familiar, types of educational situations? I shall try to throw light on this question by offering a new view of education and especially of the teaching and learning that characterize various types of psychotherapy. This analysis will be based on the organizational complexity of the educational situation and on the type of influence that the teacher exerts on the student. It will reveal a pattern of increasingly higher levels of educational ("psychotherapeutic") experiences. This classification will differ from those we now use in psychiatry, for the latter are based either on the therapist's intentions (e.g., uncovering, reconstructive, supportive, etc., psychotherapies) or on the material scrutinized in the therapeutic situation (e.g., id, ego, character, etc., analyses).

1. Lines of Advance in Psychoanalytic Therapy (see pp. 1ff. of this book).
2. *Psychoanalysis and Faith: The Letters of Sigmund Freud and Oskar Pfister*, eds. Heinrich Meng and Ernest L. Freud, trans. Eric Mosbacher (New York: Basic Books, 1963). p. 126.
3. Sigmund Freud, *An Outline of Psychoanalysis* [1938] (New York: Norton, 1949), p. 77.
4. Thomas S. Szasz, "Human Nature and Psychotherapy," *Comprehensive Psychiatry, Vol. III* (1962), pp. 268-83, and "Psychoanalysis and Suggestion," Vol. IV (1963), pp. 271-80.

HIERARCHIES OF LEARNING

The simplest kind of educational situation is exemplified by giving and receiving advice. For example, if you are in a strange city, you may ask for directions and be given them; or you may ask the French word for "bird" and be told that it is *l'oiseau*.

The characteristics of this type of educational situation, which I call "protoeducation," are:

1. Learning is limited to a specific item. The traveler who receives directions learns nothing about reaching any other part of the city.

2. The student has no effective means of checking the validity of the instruction when he receives it. His choice is limited to accepting or rejecting the advice. If he accepts it, he can test the accuracy of the advice only by following the instructions. He will know that he has been misled only after making a mistake.

The method of teaching and learning increases in complexity when the instructor teaches and the student learns more than advice; and yet, from the information the student acquires, he can derive advice. This sort of education could be called "meta-advice." If you are traveling and want meta-advice, you ask for a map; if you are learning a language, you ask for a dictionary and a grammar book.

The characteristics of this type of educational situation, which I call simply "education," are:

1. Learning is not limited to a particular question or item; instead, if the student knows how to use meta-advice (e.g., how to use a map or a dictionary), he will be able to learn about many things, all belonging in the same logical class (e.g., how to go from any point on the map to any other).

2. The student is better able to gauge the validity of the information so acquired than he is in the situation of protoeducation. If, despite the correct use of a map, it does not yield correct information, he will distrust it the second time; and, if the error is repeated, he will be even more wary. In brief, the student's confidence in the validity of a map develops over a period of time, through repeated satisfactory use.

Most of the familiar teaching-learning situations fall into these two categories. Indeed, is there such a thing as "meta-education"? In our example of the student who receives advice and then a dictionary and a grammar, what would he receive or learn in the meta-educational situation? The answer must be: a catalogue or filing system of books and instruction in its use. Should the student want to speak another language or acquire other information, he would not have to ask for advice or wait to be given a dictionary. He would know what to do and how to do it. He would also understand that, to achieve his goal, he must use the method and tools properly. I shall presently show that learning about how one learns —that is, metaeducation—is an important aspect of psychoanalysis.

The characteristics of this type of educational situation—"metaeducation"—are:

1. Learning is not limited to a single class of items. Instead, the metateacher teaches the student how he has learned and what personal and social consequences result from this style of learning. The aim of metaeducation is to teach and learn about teaching and learning.

2. Since the purpose of metaeducation is not to impart factual information, the truth or falsity of the teacher's communications is not a significant consideration. The teacher's task is to help the student to acquire a metaeducational perspective toward himself. Accordingly, his effectiveness must be measured in terms of whether —or, better, to what extent—his student achieves this goal.

An important corollary of these three educational transactions remains to be noted. In each, the educator (therapist) communicates on two levels: explicitly, he conveys informational content; implicitly, he imparts a method of learning. In the case of protoeducation, the teacher provides advice and encourages the student to learn by asking for guidance; in education, he provides a body of knowledge and teaches the student to learn through a method of self-help; finally, in metaeducation, he provides a system for organizing knowledge and encourages the student to use a more autonomous and critical method of learning.

LEARNING, PSYCHOTHERAPY, AND PSYCHOANALYSIS

Let us now apply the concepts of protoeducation, education, and metaeducation to various types of psychotherapy.

There have always been people who say that all psychotherapy, including psychoanalysis, is suggestion. If by this they mean the giving and getting of advice (or protoeducation), their perspective on psychotherapy is limited. This view is so simple and patently false that it does not deserve serious consideration.

Many psychiatrists and psychologists have held that psychoanalytic treatment is a more sophisticated sort of education; the patient is not given advice, but is taught certain things about himself which he did not know (e.g., about his unconscious, his Oedipus complex, etc.). This was essentially Freud's view. So far as it goes, it is sound; but it does not go far enough.

My main objection to this view is that it holds—I think incorrectly—that the psychoanalyst is a teacher more or less like other teachers, differing only in the subject he teaches. According to classical analysis, he teaches the patient about his early family situation, the Oedipus complex, infantile sexuality, dreams, transference, and resistance. According to Sullivan, he teaches about the history and vicissitudes of interpersonal relations. Were the analyst to perform only these functions, his role would not differ greatly from that of other teachers.

Let us focus here on the differences, rather than on the similarities, between the psychoanalyst and other teachers. In general, teachers teach so-called subjects, such as history, geography, physics, and so forth, and skills, such as dancing, swimming, driving, and so forth. The analyst, of course, does both; he teaches content, as mentioned above, and he cannot help but teach certain skills as well. But this is not all. In my opinion, the analyst's distinctive contribution to the analytic process lies, not so much in what he teaches, but in raising the teaching-learning situation to a new and higher level of discrimination and discourse.

We are now ready to specify the educational processes which distinguish psychoanalysis from other forms of psychotherapy. To begin with, the psychoanalyst eschews giving advice. This is not to say, however, that the analysand makes no use of such learning; he usually does. The analyst's conduct and values may serve as models which the patient may choose to imitate; if he does, he learns from advice. To be sure, this sort of guidance is not presented through verbal direction or exhortation, but by example. Though the analyst must not give advice, he cannot forbid the patient to use his knowledge of the therapist as though it were advice. In analysis, the only proper device for minimizing this sort of learning is to interpret it and its basis to the patient.

Most forms of nonanalytic psychotherapy teach by advice. If the therapist deals with an acute situation and if the therapeutic contact is brief, this might be legitimate, just as it is reasonable to direct a traveler changing trains in a large city from one station to another. Should the stranger decide to stay for a while, however, and wish to become independent of seeking repeated advice, it would be best to give him a map and, if necessary, teach him to use it. Similarly, helping a patient learn by psychotherapeutic education (i.e., meta-advice) eliminates his need for re-peated advice. This is what makes education useful to the patient who wants to be emancipated from anaclitic relationships—and threatening to the therapist who wishes to foster such relationships.

Education, in this special sense, means meta-advice. Much of the teaching and learning in analysis belongs in this class. For ex-ample, through the analyst's decoding of the patient's symptoms and dreams, the patient learns about his unacknowledged ("un-conscious") concerns and inclinations; and, through the interpreta-tion of his transferences, the patient obtains an inventory of his major interpersonal strategies, their origins, and aims. In all these ways, the analytic teacher (therapist) gives more to his student (patient) than does the therapist who gives advice. And yet, in a sense, he also gives less, for he requires the student to work his own way from meta-advice to advice.

Psychoanalytic insight or understanding may be put to various uses; the choice rests with the patient. Once more, this is like giving a tourist a map of a strange city: the analytic traveler may, with a map, orient himself, but not find out where he *should* go.

A properly conducted analysis—presupposing an analysand in-terested in this sort of learning and an analyst competent in analyz-ing—is a dual learning experience; the patient learns both about himself and about self-analysis. Unfortunately, this fact has be-come obscured in modern psychoanalysis, largely because of the progressive discrediting of the idea of self-analysis. Although the analytic situation and the patient's analytic experience require two persons—an analyst and an analysand—this does not mean that self-analysis is impossible. For example, a person may analyze himself in relation to someone other than the analyst. However, I do not want to digress further on this subject.

Although characteristic of analysis, learning of this type (by education or meta-advice) is not limited to it. Certain professional pursuits, traditionally regarded as sublimations, can afford oppor-tunities for such education. Thus, sexual anxieties and doubts in adolescence may lead to hypochondriasis and the search for advice about imaginary ailments; they may also lead to the choice of medicine as a career. In the latter case, the student will learn, not only about specific sexual facts, but also about sex in a more abstract and complex manner, through anthropology, endocrinol-ogy, and psychology.

It now remains for us to clarify the metaeducational elements in psychoanalysis. In my view, the basic operation of psychoanaly-sis is the sharing of information between the participants. This is, of course, true of all types of psychotherapy. What distinguishes psychoanalysis is that it encompasses all three types of learning and places special emphasis on learning about learning (metaeducation). Other methods of psychotherapy encompass fewer categories or emphasize only one—usually advice (protoeducation). The principal method of psychoanalytic metaeducation is the analysis of the therapeutic situation and of extra-analytic situations in which the patient plays a significant part. Each of these "games" must be scrutinized to lay bare its structure; in other words, to ascertain who makes what rules for whom and why.

THE CONTENT OF PSYCHOANALYTIC TREATMENT

From a theoretical point of view, the form of psychoanalytic treatment is more important than its content. This is because the rules of the analytic game may be stated generally, whereas the moves that players make must be particularized. Despite this, the rules of this game have received much less attention in the psychoanalytic literature than has its content. Conversely, I have placed more emphasis on the strategic behavior of analyst and analysand, the negotiations between them, and the contract to which they commit themselves than on the patient's productions or the analyst's interpretations. Although I have relegated the cognitive content of the analytic relationship to second place, it deserves serious attention.

The History of Psychoanalytic Treatment

Like so much else in psychoanalysis, psychoanalytic treatment can be understood only from the historical point of view. As Freud's work developed, there were changes in his ideas and in those of other therapists about the content of analytic therapy. The result was much confusion and disagreement about what psychoanalysis "really" was or what deserved this name. Indeed, in the early days of psychoanalysis, much factionalism centered on the question of what the psychoanalyst should "teach" his patient.

During the period between the publication of *Studies on Hysteria* and *The Interpretation of Dreams*, Freud was laboring under the influence of hypnosis and the cathartic method. His principal therapeutic aim was to uncover the patient's "traumatic" memories and make them conscious, that is, to help the patient accept them. The rationale of this method lay in the assumption that the patient's neurosis was caused by unconscious traumatic memories whose effect could be dissipated by making them conscious. Furthermore, Freud assumed, on the basis of good evidence, that the traumatic memories were sexual in nature. Hence, during the initial period of psychoanalysis (before 1900), the client's traumatic sexual memories were the main subject of instruction.

This specific and limited topic, which the analyst taught and the analysand learned, grew rapidly in many directions. Freud soon discovered that what he thought were the patient's memories were actually his fantasies. This widened the scope of analytic therapy to include the patient's fantasies as well as his dreams.

Next came the realization that so-called neurotic illness was not a discrete phenomenon, caused by one or more traumatic events in the past, but an aspect of the patient's total personality. Thus, the analysand's entire childhood history, not just parts of it, became significant. At this point, the reconstruction of the childhood neurosis became the major topic of treatment. Nor was this enough. Soon Freud's attention was directed to the difficulties which the patient—or his so-called unconscious defenses—placed before the therapist who was trying to understand the analysand's infantile neurosis. With this in mind, Freud stated that the aim of analytic therapy was to overcome the patient's internal resistances to the treatment. From the initial discovery of the psychoanalytic method, some three decades elapsed before the analysis of transference became the central theme of the analytic situation.

This sketch of the development of Freud's thought reflects the changes in subject matter which the analyst, as teacher, expected the analysand, his student, to learn. How was the analyst to decide which of these topics was important? Which was the most important, if they were not all equally important?

The expanding scope of the subject which the analyst-teacher expected his analysand-student to master resulted in two major developments in psychoanalysis. One was a marked lengthening of the analytic treatment. (By now this inflation of the time investment demanded of the analysand has gone beyond all reasonable limits, but still the end is not in sight.) The other was a luxuriant growth of psychoanalytic factionalism, based largely on divergent views as to what constituted the most important topic for analytic instruction. The history of this factionalism, which is still raging, provides an inventory of the subjects which various analysts considered interesting, important, or indispensable for analysis. We need a perspective on this controversy to understand psychoanalysis as an educational enterprise.

Once the disagreements among Freud, Jung, and Adler were settled, the identity of psychoanalysis as a therapeutic method and profession seemed well established. However, the wide range of topics that could be included in the repertory of the analyst-instructor produced a new series of debates and secessions.

First, there was Sandor Ferenczi, with his idea of abandoning transference-analysis and, indeed, analysis of any kind, in favor of dwelling sympathetically on the patient's past disappointments and making heroic efforts to undo them. Then came Otto Rank, with his notion of the trauma of birth and its alleged implications for therapy; then Melanie Klein, with her views about the significance of preverbal memories and the early depressive and paranoid positions; then Harry Stack Sullivan, with his emphasis on the present rather than the past; then Sandor Rado, with his concept of neurosis as biological maladaption rather than as psychosocial creation; then Franz Alexander, with his new edition of the traumatic theory of neurosis, according to which the patient suffers from various parental attitudes which the analyst must repair with "corrective emotional experiences."

Another, more traditional, way of subdividing the scope of the analyst's subject is by dichotomizing it. We thus have unconscious and conscious materials; id and ego (and superego) materials and their derivatives; drives and defenses; instincts and social influences; and so forth. Some analysts claim that analyzing one member of these pairs is more important than analyzing another, or that one should be analyzed before the other. My point is that these emphases all serve to distinguish different types of psychoanalysis, each based on the subject which the therapist considers especially significant for effective therapy.

Whatever theoretical convictions the analyst may have, the analysand's unconscious fictions are of practical significance only insofar as he expresses or communicates them. The patient may do this through complaints, symptoms, dreams, allusions, transferences, nonverbal acts, and his whole life style. Much of the analyst's work consists of attempts to comprehend and decode the patient's disguised communications and of encouraging the patient, by means of the analytic contract, to address the analyst clearly and explicitly in his everyday language and to decode his own concealed messages.

My aim in presenting this brief historical survey of psychoanalytic treatment was not to condense into a few pithy phrases the vast bulk of psychoanalytic literature accumulated over the past seventy years. I intended merely to place in proper historical perspective the question "What does the psychoanalyst teach?" and the many answers to it that have been offered. The expansion of subject matter in analysis is not in itself a bad sign. Since 1900, the scope of such fields as physics and medicine has also broadened. However, there is a difference. In physics and medicine, our values are based on fact and established by practice; we know what is good and bad, what is progress and regress. But in psychiatry, psychotherapy, and, regrettably, even in psychoanalysis, we lack such standards. Thus, we must first establish well-defined criteria for judging psychotherapy. Until we do, we shall not be able to appraise various claims but will continue to denigrate our opponents by name-calling and to enhance our own position by proselytizing.

To summarize, during the first few decades of its existence, psychoanalysis consisted only of the analysis of reconstructions. Gradually, in the 1920s and more systematically in the 1930s, psychoanalytic treatment came to mean analysis of the transference neurosis. The educational scope of analysis was thus raised to a higher level and included, in addition to the patient's productions, the therapeutic relationship itself. Psychoanalysis need not and indeed cannot stop here. A further extension of its educational scope is inherent in its aims, principles, and spirit. Analytic scrutiny must be turned back on itself; "therapy" must thus include analysis of the analytic situation. Nothing less than this can achieve the classic aim of psychoanalysis—the complete emancipation of the patient from the forces that bind him to the person of the analyst.

The Psychoanalyst as Expert on the "Repressed"

Although the foregoing historical survey may have clarified somewhat the nature of the psychoanalytic dialogue, the question remains: What should be the content of the communications between analysand and analyst? There is no simple answer to this question. The best one can do is to analyze the problem it raises.

I wish to re-emphasize that the content of the therapeutic transaction must be defined largely by the patient. This is true especially at the beginning of the relationship. The client must be free to formulate his reasons for consulting the therapist and the ways in which he expects the therapist to help him. Even as treatment progresses, the therapist should avoid intruding his own interests or theories on the patient (so far as possible) and should let the patient chart his own course.

This does not mean that I advocate a nondirective technique. The autonomous therapist is not a dummy echoing what the patient says; nor is he a "passive" analyst responding chiefly with

"Hm . . . ," "Yes, I understand," "Yes, go on . . . ," or with silence. The analyst—as I understand his task—participates actively and meaningfully in a particular kind of dialogue. After the patient determines the topic, the analyst, though less active than the analysand, is by no means inactive. How does he contribute to the dialogue?

At this point we encounter another familiar aspect of the analyst's function as teacher. I refer to the analyst as a specialist in repressions or in "the unconscious." For example, the patient may be concerned about his relations with his mother and father. He describes his present situation with them and then begins to reminisce about his childhood and his parents' roles in it. By definition, this is the patient's conscious version of his relations with his parents; this is all that he can tell; it is all he knows.

The analyst's task is to listen; but to what? To inconsistencies between what the patient says and how he acts; to unacknowledged feelings and thoughts; to accounts of the patient's relations with persons other than his parents; and to his behavior toward the analyst—to the transference. In all these ways (and in others not mentioned), the analyst tries to transcend the conscious account of the situation presented by the patient and to construct another, less fictional, version of it. The therapist can accomplish this by observing, over long periods and in close detail, the actual games the patient plays, rather than accepting his account of them.

I am describing, of course, what is ordinarily referred to in psychoanalysis as "making the unconscious conscious," that is, replacing the patient's conscious (but "false") constructions of reality with his own unconscious (but "correct") versions of it. I agree with the basic idea of this formulation, but not with the impression that it is likely to create.

Traditional psychoanalytic ideas, framed in terms of id, ego, superego, unconscious, and so forth, create the impression that all the information necessary for a complete analysis is stored *in* the patient. The analyst's task is to "liberate" the information so that the analysand can communicate it to the analyst. Those who hold this view assume that, in addition to conscious conceptions of events, persons, and relationships, people also possess (stored somewhere?) another set or perhaps several other sets of conceptions of the "same" events, persons and relationships. Like the archaeologist uncovering one city buried under another, the analyst—the expert on "uncovering therapy"—exposes the patient's unconscious affects and memories that have been buried beneath his conscious "rationalizations."

Actually, the situation is different. Like everyone else, the patient lives by what he sincerely believes to be the truth (to simplify this presentation, I shall disregard the patient who lies). He lives according to a more or less fictional view of reality. But so do we all. In many areas of life, the patient who comes for analysis is likely to be no less honest, no less sincere, and no less realistic than most people and may very well be more so.

The point is that both patient and analyst will be or ought to be interested in those aspects of the patient's life which reveal *discrepancies*. These manifest themselves in many ways: by complaints and symptoms and the patient's adaptation to them; by contradictions between statements made at various times; by inconsistencies between words and acts; and so forth. It is at these points that the analyst must enter the dialogue; he challenges the patient's explanations; asks questions; suggests alternative hypotheses to explain the patient's conduct. If these interventions are appropriate and if the client is able to look at himself in a new light, then, by small steps, there will be some change in the patient's personality. He will view himself with new eyes (perhaps at first partly borrowed from the analyst); he will observe new sights; he will change and see himself and others differently. His new vision is what we have been calling his "unconscious." Like most words, it is a good term only if we understand it properly and use it carefully.

What do I mean when I say that the analyst is a specialist who teaches the patient about the "repressed," the "unconscious," the "unacknowledged," and the "inexplicit"? The term "the repressed" denotes an unusual class.[5] It differs from other kinds of subject matter, such as algebra, ancient history, or Latin. The student's personality does not alter these subjects, although the teacher's personality may cause some variations in them. Practically, however, these subjects consist largely of information *external* to the personality of both student and teacher.

But, in the class of events called "repressions," the content varies with the personality of the student. Not only does the specific subject vary from patient to patient, but also among patients from differing cultural circumstances and social settings. We must remember that repression is something each person does for himself. The subjects to be repressed are, however, determined largely for him by his family and culture. In Victorian Vienna, where Freud made his initial observations, infantile sexuality and, to an extent,

5. See Sigmund Freud, Repression [1915], Standard Edition, Vol. 14, pp. 141-58; The Unconscious [1915], *ibid.*, pp. 159-215.

even adult sexuality were repressed; a cultivated person was expected to have the appropriate fictions behind which to hide such indelicacies. But other sensitive subjects dealt with dishonestly elsewhere were not subjected to repression in the Vienna of those days, for example, financial chicanery in high government circles or social conflicts among religious or national minority groups.

Repression, then, is a particular form of obedience and hence a result of protoeducation. It is easy to see how the person taught this kind of obedience (the so-called hysteric) could easily be taught to obey the command of another authority (the advice of the suggestive therapist). In a sense, hypnosis is the "logical" therapy of hysteria.

These considerations help to explain why psychonalysis began as a socially "subversive" enterprise and why, if it is to remain true to its historical and intellectual mandate, must remain so. Its task was, and remains, to "demythologize" personal and social fictions. Freud, of course, sought to destroy the Victorian myths of family and sex rampant in his day. Today, in the United States, these are not the main areas shrouded in personal and social repressions; hence, the analyst's attention cannot be directed solely or often even mainly to these subjects.

HYMAN SPOTNITZ

The Toxoid Response

In this paper, Spotnitz presents a rationale for the therapist's utilization of his counterfeelings. He emphasizes the value to certain carefully selected patients of having the analyst communicate emotionally. However, Spotnitz carefully cautions against the indiscriminate use of such emotionality. Freud thought that the patient's transference was a hindrance until he learned to use it to further the therapy. Similarly, many therapists consider their own counterfeelings a hindrance. Spotnitz indicates how such counterfeelings can be put to therapeutic use.

A DEFENSIVE PREOCCUPATION with the unrecognized and inappropriate reactions of the analyst to his patient has characterized the literature on countertransference since Freud introduced the term in 1910 to encompass "what arises in the physician as a result of the patient's influence on his [the physician's] unconscious feelings."[6]* The "perfectly analyzed" practitioner having been conceded as nonexistent—a derivative of the Myth of the Hero, according to Glover[7]—deliverance of the human instrument from the insidious clutches of the "patient's influence" has been the major concern. In striking contrast to the reliance on transference as a conceptual tool, the "counter" phenomenon has been viewed, by and large, as a wholly unwelcome intruder bent on disrupting

From *Insulation and Immunization in Schizophrenia* (New York: Stuyvesant Polyclinic, 1963).

* Superior numbers refer to the list of references at the end of this article.

the analytic process. Vigilant attention to the analyst's subjective and unconscious reactions as a contribution to therapeutic failure has tended to obscure, or at least to retard, the recognition of those reactions which are realistically induced in him by the patient as a valuable component of psychoanalytic therapy.

These objective derivatives of the therapeutic encounter are certain to gain increasing acceptance in the future. Their potential value is now being explored as an aspect of various developments in the field. For example, the application of psychoanalytic therapy to a broadening spectrum of psychiatric conditions entails the investigation of new modes of functioning to meet the special requirements of those who are severely disturbed. Continuing efforts to expedite the therapeutic process and enhance its effectiveness for patients in all categories also expose the traditional attitudes and practices to searching inquiry. Some modifications are suggested by our growing understanding of the ingredients of a corrective emotional experience, and by the related new concept of the meeting of maturational needs. These considerations presage a more discriminating approach to countertransference.

The attitude most prevalent today, however, is that the development and expression of feelings for the patient are out of order. In most respects this attitude is unassailable, for reasons too familiar to detail here. It is in the interest of patients that the analyst remain free from emotional involvement with them. Such freedom also facilitates his professional functioning. Moreover, there can be no quarrel with the strictures against his exploiting the treatment relationship as an outlet for his own emotional gratification. But what if the patient has a maturational need to experience feelings from his partner in the relationship? His need challenges the attitude of emotional detachment. And observations of the therapeutic effectiveness of certain types of countertransference reactions strengthen the challenge.

A more flexible approach is encouraged, for example, by reports of cases being expedited by the direct communication of the analyst's negative feelings about a patient's resistant behavior. In the light of Breuer's abrupt termination of the case of Anna O. when he became aware of the strong reaction she was provoking in him[8,9] and of the still respectable policy of referring patients to other practitioners as a solution to countertransference problems, it is novel to read of treatment relationships that were preserved and even moved forward dramatically *after* the analyst had communicated his feelings.

Such an incident is disclosed by Alexander[2] when he reports having ended an apparent stalemate by venting his impatience, explaining the transference situation and admitting his dislike of the patient. Stekel[17] and others have also reported cases that took a good turn after the analyst had expressed his anger to the persons concerned. Tower[18] acted out extreme irritation with an abusive woman by "unconsciously and purposely" forgetting their appointment one day. After the incident, the analysis proceeded more productively.

In these cases the therapeutic effectiveness of the analyst's emotional confrontations was inadvertent. In each instance the analyst had reached the limits of his tolerance, but the frank admission of that fact had by no means been calculated to further the progress of the provocative patient. Another breach in the recommended attitude of emotional detachment is more fundamental. It involves the acceptance of countertransference as a dynamic tool in the therapeutic armamentarium.

Excluded from this formulation are subjective reactions based on the practitioner's unanalyzed or insufficiently analyzed adjustment patterns. Feelings developed for significant figures in his personal history and transferred to the patient are differentiated from those that are justified by objective observation of the latter. The influence and communication of such transferred feelings may continue to be regarded as highly undesirable, whereas feelings that are empathically induced in the analyst by the patient may be utilized in various ways to meet the patient's treatment needs.

Induced feelings may be employed solely as an aid in the fact-finding process—that is, to facilitate the understanding of the patient or an issue in the case. Saul[13] points out that these feelings are a "sensitive indicator of what is going on in the patient." But more active use may also be made of induced emotions. Rado[11] utilizes them to "provoke a relieving outburst" in a depressed patient whose retroflexed rage reaches an alarming degree. Winnicott[19] reports that his feelings are at times the "important things in the analysis of psychotic and antisocial patients." Carefully sorted out from subjective reactions, he holds the "truly objective countertransference," especially his hatred, in reserve until it becomes available for interpretation.

THEORETICAL CONSIDERATIONS

My own experience and findings with respect to induced feelings agree with the observations just outlined. Emotional states created in me by objective study of a patient's personality and behavior serve as a direct tap on his unconscious; these states also influence and eventually enter into my interpretations. However, my communications to the patient based upon induced feelings are as a rule planned, rather than adventitious, and are not limited to interpretation. I also communicate these feelings as an additional method of dealing with the resistances of the highly narcissistic patient.

In cases of schizophrenia, psychotic depression, and other severe disturbances, one encounters resistances, chiefly preverbal, that do not respond to objective interpretation. Their resolution is thwarted by toxic affects that have interfered with the patient's maturation and functioning. In my experience, these resistances yield to an emotional working-through process, in contradistinction to the customary working-through on an intellectual basis.

The troublesome affects are of two kinds. They are either those of the patient himself or the negative affects of the original object to which the patient's infantile ego was unduly sensitive. Exposure to these emotions creates either similar or antithetical states—induced neurosis or psychosis—in the analyst. If he is able to recognize and tolerate these emotional states indefinitely without acting on them, they can be utilized to neutralize the pathological effects of the patient's past experiences and immunize him against sensitivity to similar emotions stimulated by other people in the future.

It might be pointed out that successful analysis and interpretation of the defensive and repressive forces that hold toxic emotions in check may secure their discharge in language. Nevertheless, the kind of patient we are considering is highly vulnerable to recurrences of the pathological affects. The precise nature of the emotional upheavals to which he is inordinately sensitive depends on the pattern of his life experience; whatever that has been, the affects are approached as foreign bodies that have impeded maturational processes. To reduce his disposition to these upheavals in the future, he is given verbal injections of the emotions he has induced in the analyst, carefully "treated" to destroy their toxicity and to stimulate the formation of antibodies. In brief, *the induced emotions are employed as a toxoid.*

The science of immunology contributed to the elaboration of this concept, but it is compatible with the spirit and principles of resistance analysis and has been suggested in the literature. Ackerman, for one, writes about the need for injecting the "right emotions to neutralize the patient's wrong ones."[1] Rado refers to "emotional neutralization" as the therapeutic task and the "contagiousness of emotions" as a significant mechanism in the inter-action of patient and therapist.[12] Marie Coleman Nelson and Benjamin Nelson write about the "gradual dosing" of patients with specific responses to immunize them against pathological reactions.[10] Freud himself, in describing the permanent change wrought in the mental life through the successful handling of resistances, stated that the patient is "lifted to a higher level of development and remains proof against fresh possibilities of illness."[5]

The assumption prevails that Freud was fundamentally opposed to the exertion of emotional influence by the psychoanalyst. Indeed, references to it are absent from his statements on technique, and he developed a system of analyzing all of the induced feelings and of interpreting them in an unemotional manner. Nevertheless, one of his most illuminating statements on countertransference contradicts this belief.

In a letter written to Binswanger in 1913 (but not published until some forty years later) Freud refers to countertransference as one of the most difficult problems in psychoanalysis, one more easy to solve in theory than technically. The letter continues: "What is given to the patient should indeed never be a spontaneous affect, but always consciously allotted, and then more or less of it as the need may arise. Occasionally a great deal, but never from one's own unconscious. This I should regard as the formula. In other words, one must always recognize one's countertransference and rise above it; only then is one free oneself. To give someone too little because one loves him too much is being unjust to the patient and a technical error."[3]

The exclusion of any reference to the negative feelings induced by the analysand is characteristic of Freud. A letter he wrote in 1915 refers to a patient who "actually has been running away from me, since I was able to tell her the real secret of her illness (revengeful and murderous impulses against her husband.)" He then dismisses the woman in these words: "analytically unfit for anyone."[4] If Freud ever confronted this patient or any others with feelings of hatred, he appears not to have done so through the "consciously allotted" affects that he had already advocated for conveying feelings of love. This may help to explain his pessimistic views about the treatment of the narcissistic disorders.

Subsequent experience has borne out Freud's conviction that the resistances of narcissistic patients cannot be safely overcome by the customary analytic method; but we have also learned that they respond to other methods.[14] Like Hill, Winnicott, and others who have focused on the destructive impulses as the most troublesome in such cases, I have found that the narcissistic defense can be resolved when it is dealt with as a defense against feelings of hatred and self-hatred, and joined and reinforced until it is outgrown.[16]

Apart from Freud's failure to address himself to the induced feelings of hatred, his 1913 statement on countertransference is entirely compatible with the modern psychoanalytic approach to the deeply narcissistic person.

The utilization of the induced neurosis or psychosis as an ally in treatment represents a preliminary foray into the psychodynamics of the psychoanalyst, an area that requires more thorough exploration in the future. Nevertheless, it is my impression that many analysts who do not accept the giving of feelings as an essential aspect of the therapeutic process, do expose their patients to feelings that facilitate appropriate behavior and thus ease their adjustment to reality. Their need to experience feelings consonant with their maturational needs probably accounts in some measure for the time-consuming nature of the working-through process, even in cases of neurosis. Some patients manage to pick up toxoid emotions from other people at the same time that their progress in the analytic situation is slowed up by the intellectual nature of the established working-through process.

This process will be expedited, I believe, when both the phenomenon of emotional induction and psychological needs at each level of maturation are better understood. Effective utilization of the objective countertransference to meet these needs would then become an important aspect of all forms of analytic psychotherapy.

CLINICAL APPLICATION OF THE CONCEPT

Early in my psychiatric practice I treated a young woman suffering from paranoid psychosis and epilepsy, who was regarded as unsuitable for classical psychoanalysis. The case was handled on a research basis during the period when I was undergoing my personal analysis. In investigating her responsiveness to various techniques, I operated mainly on the assumption that, since I was intensely interested in curing her, verbalizations of the feelings induced in me by her personality and behavior would benefit her.

My unconscious could not have carried the burden that this approach entailed had I not been working on the subjective countertransference problems, one by one as I became aware of them, with my own training analyst. The identification and understanding of reactions associated with my own adjustment patterns helped me to recognize and work for the verbal discharge of the patient's latent emotions. These created reactions which I felt free to voice. The induced feelings also prompted me to make occasional comments on her functioning and appearance. I knew when she aroused anger in me and, in due time, let her know it.

An interpretation of her paranoid attitude was responded to as if it were a signal to dominate the treatment situation. Calm explanations of her problems branded me in her mind as a weakling bent on forestalling another outburst of rage. On the other hand, when I confronted her with the emotions induced by her psychotic tendencies, my interventions had a tremendous impact. She developed some respect for me and became amenable to therapeutic influence.

That was the first case in which I operated on the basis of the induced feelings. In verbalizing my reactions, I attempted to be sufficiently stimulating to produce movement in the case and yet not so stimulating as to force the patient off the couch. How to achieve the first and avoid the second effect I learned chiefly by trial and error.

It soon became clear that to act immediately on an impulse to respond to an unconscious resistance with an emotional communication was not consistently therapeutic. Spontaneous verbal expressions of my reactions rarely met with indifference, but they were harmful at times rather than helpful. A communication that stimulated an outpouring of anger in one situation could crush the patient into silence in another. But when my interventions were predicated on a study of what was going on between us—the emotional dynamics of the session and her discharge tendencies from moment to moment—she behaved in a more controlled way. The withholding and tempering of my communications until they became acceptable and meaningful to her ego permitted a therapeutic process to develop.

This process was conceptualized as one of immunizing a patient against toxic affects long before the pivotal role played by emotional induction in our relationship was recognized. Mutual contagion emerged as a basic factor: The analyst has to experience the patient's feelings in order to "return" them to him; the patient, through experiencing them from the analyst, is helped to discharge the feelings in language. The significance of this discharge became clearer after I had accumulated considerable evidence that nonverbal resistance patterns could be effectively dealt with when they were approached as primitive forms of communication rather than as manifestations of outright defiance of the rule of free association.

When the patient is helped to maintain these resistance patterns, they are eventually outgrown. These three formulations—emotional induction, immunization, and resistance reinforcement—are integrated in the clinical concepts I now employ.

The more ill the patient, the less capable he is of talking about himself in an emotionally significant way. Presumably, he is forced to use infantile modes of communication because of his previously unmet maturational needs; their nature is reflected in the type of resistance patterns to which they give rise and which the patient stubbornly maintains. But feelings that were intolerable to his infantile ego come into awareness when the analyst expresses the similar or complementary feelings induced in him by the patient. By "matching" the feelings in this way, the analyst apparently helps the patient to meet his maturational needs because he becomes capable of discharging the warded-off feelings in language. As he feels and verbalizes these toxic affects through his identification with the emotionally responsive analyst, the resistance pattern is outgrown and the patient commits himself more easily to spontaneous self-revelation through language.

Departures from a passive attitude are not indicated while a resistance pattern is being investigated earily in treatment. The standard approach is maintained as long as the patient functions cooperatively or remains self-absorbed. The timing of the emotional response is regulated by the patient's contact-functioning; that is, his direct attempts to elicit some personal information about the analyst or to involve the analyst in some emotional problem he, the patient, is unable to express in words. The induced feelings, tempered with understanding of their origin, may then be "returned" to the patient by the analyst through a response that reflects the pattern of the patient's resistance.

The confrontations are carefully timed and graduated to prevent uncontrollable reactions. The duration of the exposure and strength of the dosage are regulated by the intensity of the emotions generated. If the patient proves indifferent or is overstimulated, the emotional confrontation is discontinued. Otherwise, it goes on as long as it produces new understanding or ideas that the patient was unable to deal with previously.

Emotional responses figured prominently in the resolution of the resistances of the highly narcissistic young man I shall call Fred.[14,16] Directly or indirectly, during the early stages of his treatment, he would start to verbalize thoughts of getting off the couch to attack me and then quickly lapse into silence. My interventions at the time were designed to help him talk about his destructive impulses and to tame them somewhat through such release. Feelings of guilt about what he might say clammed him up. He also had strong fears that talking about his impulses would force him to act on them. He was convinced that his destructive urges proved that he was incurable.

I noticed that the repetitive quality of his threats aroused a great deal of resentment in me; even more, I was aroused by his insistence that his troublesome feelings and fantasied acts of primitive violence made him unique. He fought strenuously against accepting the notion that such impulses were natural and that an important aspect of one's rearing was to learn to control them.

It occurred to me that the way to solve this problem was to demonstrate to Fred that I had similar thoughts and feelings about him. My first attempts to convey this idea were ineffectual. "Don't try that stuff," he said when one of his threats was turned back at him. "You're repeating what I say but you don't really feel it." But I had the impression that he was unconsciously egging me on. I bided my time until the feelings induced by his outbursts of rage permitted me to respond with equal vehemence.

Fred appeared to be ready for such a response when he shouted in a moment of fury: "I'll bash your head in." "No you won't," I exploded back at him, "because I'll bash yours in before you can get off the couch." Though he felt no need to defend himself against attack, he responded to this expression of genuine feelings by exclaiming: "You really do hate me as much as I hate you, and you can be even more vicious!"

He garnered relief and security from my emotional responses. As his terror of speaking about his destructive urges gradually diminished, they lost their toxic quality. If someone he respected and relied on could accept and verbalize such urges, so could he. When he permitted himself to dwell voluntarily on long-outlawed feelings and thoughts of violence and found that he could do so without acting impulsively, the toxoid responses were discontinued.

As positive feelings for his own ego mounted, Fred matured sufficiently to accept, either spontaneously or with the aid of interpretation, many libidinal as well as aggressive impulses that had been ego-alien. By that time the induced feelings I had stored up for long periods during the first two years of the case were rarely employed as a therapeutic instrument. Interpretations tend to dissipate these feelings; but I made no effort to sustain them when the interpretations were acceptable to his ego.

Toxoid responses are often employed late in the treatment process to immunize a patient against the return of resistant attitudes.

Daniel, a business man in his forties, demonstrated the need for a "booster" during the last few months before I discharged him. He had pulled out of a severe depression and resumed his normal activities, but from time to time he slipped back into despondency. In one such interlude[15] he complained of bungling the impromptu talk he had given earlier in the day before a trade convention. After castigating himself for half an hour he paused, obviously appealing to me to lift his spirits.

Instead, I vigorously reproached him. I expressed surprise that a man of his experience had not prepared some remarks for the occasion. The feelings of irritation and annoyance that he induced were mobilized for the response; the expression of these feelings had been withheld during the many months when he was too sick to defend himself. At this point, however, my reflection of his self-attacking attitude stimulated a lively counterattack. This was my signal to proceed and step up the dosage.

To my criticism that he had muffed his opportunity and had been a rank failure, Daniel retaliated easily. He insisted that he had not acquitted himself so badly; it would have been in poor taste for him to "hog the occasion." Eventually his gloom vanished. With dramatic self-esteem, he ended the heated exchange with these words: "Enough, enough. What have I done to get your bowels in such an uproar? Why did you get involved in my business anyway? You're just my analyst."

After he had won the argument on rational grounds, he was rewarded with an interpretation. "All you ever want is to be attacked; you just beg for it. I gave it to you and now you feel better."

Daniel readily accepted the interpretation. In fact, all he needed at that time were a few more reminders of the connection between his once unconscious need to secure love by making "mother" sorry for him and the self-attacking tendency that had reasserted itself once again in that session. The final toxoid responses were administered in the case to invigorate him with sufficient understanding to recognize and protect himself in the future under circumstances that might encourage a revival of this tendency. A few more confrontations of this sort were helpful in dissolving the resistance.

IMPLICATIONS FOR THE ANALYST

To provide a gravely narcissistic person with "treated" doses of the toxic emotions he experienced in childhood and re-experiences in the transference facilitates the therapeutic task of releasing the intense emotions he has held in check. However, the very fact that the emotional quality of the transference reactions is thereby intensified introduces the possibility of a new source of error: contamination of the analytic situation by an incorrect confrontation.

An incorrect confrontation can be more damaging than an incorrect interpretation. Transference reactions are damped by the neutral attitude of the analyst who limits himself to the classical approach. The treatment edition of the patient's nuclear conflict is weaker, so that wrong interpretations are of relatively little significance. They do not create reactions in the patient that are likely to distort or change the toxic emotions of the transference neurosis.

Such distortion is a greater danger if the patient is exposed to feelings developed by the analyst in relation to other people. Hence, countertransference cannot be utilized with complete confidence unless it has been purged of its subjective elements. These "foreign" influences have to be "analyzed out" of the objective countertransference before they contaminate the transference reaction. The toxoid response is compounded in the pure culture of the feelings induced in the analyst by the patient as a real person.

The time may come when we will discover that certain types of contaminated responses are also helpful. However, my own experience leads me to believe that the only emotional confrontations that are consistently therapeutic for the deeply narcissistic patient are those based exclusively on the feelings he induces. Certainly, the induced feelings promote a transference climate; in a sense, they add an important new dimension to transference.

A situation about which a student analyst recently consulted me illustrates how the presence of subjective elements of countertransference can take one off on a tangent. The case she brought up for discussion was that of a young male schizophrenic who had been in treatment with her for about two years. In the negative transference he had already resolved his fears of becoming violent if he verbalized his destructive urges, but he was still in a state of conflict about remaining infantile or growing up. He repeatedly complained that his year-old marriage was going on the rocks because his wife was prodding him to get a better job.

During one session that his analyst discussed with me, the man said that when his wife brought up the subject, he would become aware of pains in his head. He felt like "sticking a knife through it."

"At that point," the analyst continued, "I wanted to say something that would make him feel that I was as hostile as his mother had been. I asked him: 'Why don't you go ahead and do it?' He replied: 'I think you are trying to destroy me.' If I had followed up by asking what difference that could make when he was set on destroying himself anyhow, he would have vigorously denied the self-destructive impulse and verbalized the feeling. But somehow I just couldn't give him that response. I said instead that I was just trying to get him to say whatever occurred to him. A little later he said that he was getting to feel hopeless about his treatment. I seem to have developed a resistance to responding as I should, and this is what is holding up the case. Since that session I've had a couple of dreams about it."

In the first dream, her patient repeated his statement: "I think you are trying to destroy me." Then he got off the couch and stood before her. "I was terrified that he would kill me," she went on. "That ended the dream, but the next night I had another one about him. In the midst of a session, a stranger walked in and my patient left the office with him. The stranger returned alone and tried to rape me. I cried for help but no one heard me. I woke up in a state of terror."

Associating to the first dream, the analyst connected it with a fear that the patient really believed that she wanted to harm him. His standing up in the dream probably signified that he intended to attack her sexually. The second dream indicated to her that she actually wanted to be raped, but by someone other than the patient. The stranger in the second dream represented the supervising analyst.

Eventually she recognized that her difficulty in responding to her patient in harmony with the induced feelings of anger was linked with her own sexual needs. Because of her husband's extended absence abroad, she labored under an unconscious wish to have someone "stand up" for her. This wish had checked her readiness to verbalize hostility. The analysis of her own sexual feelings and their influence on the case was necessary to resolve her counterresistance.

The ideal way to deal with countertransference problems that tend to develop when one works with profoundly narcissistic patients is to be in analysis oneself when one begins to treat them. As I have already indicated, this helped me to understand my resistances to treating narcissistic patients and also increased my tolerance for the feelings they induced. Even experienced practitioners who have no difficulty in treating neurotics may find it necessary to return to their training analyst or secure other aid in resolving personal problems that they become aware of when they start to work with more intractable patients. The therapist who is unable to analyze the severe neurosis or psychosis they induce courts the actual development of psychotic or psychosomatic reactions unless he secures immediate help.

For the well-trained analyst who approaches treatment as an intellectual undertaking and has inhibitions about expressing his emotional reactions, the approach I have described above will be repugnant. On the other hand, the practitioner who can permit himself to experience the induced feelings, convert them into toxoid responses, and communicate these as necessary in the course of resistance analysis works comfortably with narcissistic patients. As a matter of fact, such an analyst is more comfortable when he works in harmony with the induced emotions than when he tries to suppress them; to keep them out of his interventions entails the expenditure of considerable energy.

If the practitioner's personality is adapted to this approach, emotional induction operates in his interest as well as in the interest of his patients. A therapy based on the empathic understanding that develops in the analytic situation is beneficial for patient and therapist alike. For the recovery of the severely narcissistic person, this type of treatment experience is essential. Ultimately, we shall learn how best to create it.

REFERENCES

1. Ackerman, N. W., Transference and Countertransference, *Psychoanalysis and the Psychoanalytic Review*, 46, 3:17-28, 1959.
2. Alexander, F., *Psychoanalysis and Psychotherapy* (New York: Norton, 1956), pp. 90-92.
3. Binswanger, L., *Sigmund Freud: Reminiscences of a Friendship*, trans. N. Guterman (New York: Grune & Stratton, 1957), p. 50.
4. Binswanger, *op. cit.*, p. 62.
5. Freud, S., *A General Introduction to Psychoanalysis* (New York: Permabooks, 1953), p. 459 (28th lecture).
6. Freud, S., The Future Prospects of Psychoanalytic Therapy, *Collected Papers* (London: Hogarth Press, 1933), Vol. 2, p. 289.
7. Glover, E., *The Technique of Psychoanalysis* (New York: International Universities Press, 1955), p. 4.
8. Jones, E., *The Life and Work of Sigmund Freud* (New York: Basic Books, 1953), Vol. 1, pp. 224-25.
9. Karpe, R., The Rescue Complex in Anna O's Identity, *Psychoanalytic Quarterly*, 30:1-27, 1961.
10. Nelson, M. C., and Nelson, B., Paradigmatic Encounters in Life and Treatment, in M. C. Nelson, *Paradigmatic Approaches to Psychoanalysis: Four Papers* (New York: Psychology Department, Stuyvesant Polyclinic, 1962), p. 14; also *Psychoanalysis*, 5, 3:39, 1957.

62 | HYMAN SPOTNITZ

11. Rado, S., Psychodynamics of Depression from the Etiologic Point of View, in *Psychoanalysis of Behavior* (New York: Grune & Stratton, 1957), p. 240.
12. Rado, S., Recent Advances in Psychoanalytic Therapy, *ibid.*, pp. 265-66.
13. Saul, L. J., *Technic and Practice of Psychoanalysis* (Philadelphia: Lippincott, 1958), p. 140.
14. Spotnitz, H., and L. Nagelberg, A Preanalytic Technique for Resolving the Narcissistic Defense. *Psychiatry*, 23:193-97, 1960.
15. Spotnitz, H., *The Couch and the Circle* (New York: Knopf, 1961), pp. 145-47.
16. Spotnitz, H., The Narcissistic Defense in Schizophrenia, *Psychoanalysis and the Psychoanalytic Review*, 48, 4:24-42, 1961; published as a Monograph by the Psychology Department, Stuyvesant Polyclinic, New York.
17. Stekel, W., *Technique of Analytical Psychotherapy*, trans. E. and C. Paul (New York: Liveright, 1950), p. 180.
18. Tower, L. E., Countertransference, *Journal of the American Psychoanalytic Association*, 4:237-39, 1956.
19. Winnicott, D. W., Hate in the Countertransference, *Collected Papers* (New York: Basic Books, 1958), pp. 195-96.

MARIE COLEMAN NELSON

Effect of Paradigmatic Techniques on the Psychic Economy of Borderline Patients

In collaboration with sociologist Benjamin Nelson, Marie Coleman Nelson coined the term "paradigmatic psychotherapy." In this paper she provides us with verbatim material which clarifies her technique. Though her training is essentially Freudian, there are some interesting similarities between her work and that of Frankl and Haley as represented in this volume.

IN THE PSYCHOANALYTIC TREATMENT of pathological disturbances that are rooted in early infancy, the analyst is often aware of the need for more subtle intervention than is possible through classical interpretation,[1] and for methods capable of initiating profound shifts in the patients energy economy. In this paper I propose to explore certain effects of an approach to borderline patients which

From *Psychiatry*, Vol. XXV, No. 2, May 1962, pp. 119-34.

1. See *International Journal of Psychoanalysis*, 39, 1958: Ralph R. Greenson, Variations in Classical Psychoanalytic Technique: An Introduction, 200-201; Kurt R. Eissler, Remarks on Some Variations in Psychoanalytic Technique, 222-29; Rudolph M. Loewenstein, Variations in Classical Technique: Concluding Remarks, 240-42; Harold F. Searles, Positive Feelings in the Relationship Between the Schizophrenic and His Mother, 569-86. See also Leo Nagelberg, Hyman Spotnitz, and Yonata Feldman, The Attempt at Healthy Insulation in the Withdrawn Child, *Orthopsychiatry*, 23:238-52, 1953; Hyman Spotnitz, Leo Nagelberg, and Yonata Feldman, Ego Reinforcement in the Schizophrenic Child, *Orthopsychiatry*, 26:146-64, 1956; Milton Wexler, The Structural Problem in Schizophrenia: The Role of the Internal Object, in *Psychotherapy with Schizophrenics*, Vol. 26, Eugene B. Brody and Fredrick C. Redlich (New York: International University Press, 1952), pp. 176-215.

has been called *paradigmatic psychotherapy*, and to relate these observations to the findings of researchers in other areas of psychological science.

Knight conceptualizes the borderline case as one in which ". . . normal ego functions of secondary-process thinking, integration, realistic planning, adaptation to the environment, maintenance of object relationships, and defenses against primitive unconscious impulses are severely weakened. . . . Some ego functions have been severely impaired—especially, in most cases, integration, concept formation, judgment, realistic planning, and defending against eruption into conscious thinking of id impulses and their fantasy elaborations. Other ego functions, such as conventional (but superficial) adaptation to the environment and superficial maintenance of object relationships may exhibit varying degrees of intactness. And still others, such as memory, calculation, and certain habitual performances, may seem unimpaired. Also, the clinical picture may be dominated by hysterical, phobic, obsessive-compulsive or psychosomatic symptoms. . . ."[2]

Fairbairn calls particular attention to three general characteristics of the schizoid personality: an attitude of omnipotence, an attitude of isolation and detachment, and a preoccupation with inner reality. He speaks of the tendency of schizoids to "treat libidinal objects as means of satisfying their own requirements rather than as persons possessing inherent value . . . a tendency which springs from the persistence of an early oral orientation toward the breast as a partial object." He also emphasizes "an over-valuation of mental contents corresponding to the over-valuation of bodily contents implied in the early incorporative attitude of early childhood." Moreover, ". . . when a fixation in the early oral phase occurs, an incorporative attitude inevitably becomes woven into the structure of the ego . . . [hence] there is a general tendency on the part of individuals with a schizoid component to heap up their values in the inner world. . . . In the case of individuals whose object-relationships are predominantly in the outer world, giving has the effect of creating and enhancing values, and of promoting self-respect; but in the case of individuals whose object-relationships are predominantly in the inner world, giving has the effect of depreciating values and of lowering self-respect. When such individuals give,

2. Robert P. Knight, Borderline States, in *Psychoanalytic Psychiatry and Psychology: Clinical and Theoretical Papers, Austen Riggs Center*, Vol. 1, eds. Robert P. Knight and Cyrus R. Friedman (New York: International Universities Press, 1954), p. 102.

they tend to feel impoverished, because, when they give, they give at the expense of the inner world."[3]

The critical treatment problem posed by the borderline patient is thus twofold: How may he be enabled to withdraw an excess of investment of psychic energy from his own mental and bodily contents and reinvest this energy in objects and object-related activities, and how may this be accomplished without inducing in him further resistances resulting from feelings of violation and impoverishment?

Freud had already begun to recognize the importance of disturbing pathologically conditioned modes of psychic economy when in 1899 he remarked, "From time to time I visualize a second part of the method of treatment—provoking patients' feelings as well as their ideas. . . ."[4] Rank's emphasis on revival and working through of the birth trauma as the goal of treatment,[5] and Ferenczi's encouragement and prohibition of various forms of physical discharge during analysis[6] had a similar basis, however mechanistic their rationales may have been. Spitz, Kubie, Greenacre, Fries and Woolf, and Bak have shown pioneer concern with the developmental vicissitudes of early patterning, and Hartmann's intensive studies of the transformation of psychic energy have led to his concept of neutralized and deneutralized energy.[7] In general, the established clinical observation that maintenance of a certain degree of tension in the analytic patient is requisite for treatment implicitly acknowledges the somatic correlates of psychic change.

3. W. Ronald D. Fairbairn, *An Object-Relations Theory of the Personality* (New York: Basic Books, 1954), pp. 13, 15, 18.

4. Sigmund Freud, *The Origins of Psychoanalysis; Letters to Wilhelm Fliess, Drafts and Notes: 1887-1902* (New York: Basic Books, 1954).

5. Otto Rank, *The Trauma of Birth* (New York: Brunner, 1952).

6. Sandor Ferenczi, The Principle of Relaxation and Neocatharsis, *Final Contributions to the Problems and Methods of Psychoanalysis* (New York: Basic Books, 1955), pp. 108-250.

7. René A. Spitz, Infantile Depression and the General Adaptation Syndrome, in *Depression*, eds. Paul A. Hoch and Joseph Zubin (New York: Grune & Stratton, 1954); Lawrence S. Kubie, Instincts and Homeostasis, *Psychosomatic Medicine*, 10:15-30, 1948; Phyllis Greenacre, Toward an Understanding of the Physical Nucleus of Some Defence Reactions, *International Journal of Psychoanalysis*, 39:69-76, 1958; Margaret E. Fries and Paul J. Woolf, Some Hypotheses on the Role of the Congenital Activity Type in Personality Development, *The Psychoanalytic Study of the Child* (New York: International Universities Press, 1953) Vol. 8, pp. 48-64; Robert Bak, Regression of Ego-Orientation and Libido in Schizophrenia, *International Journal of Psychoanalysis*, 20:64-71, 1939; Heinz Hartmann, Contribution to the Metapsychology of Schizophrenia, *The Psychoanalytic Study of the Child* (New York: International Universities Press, 1953), Vol. 8, pp. 177-98.

To render comprehensible the body of my discussion, I shall summarize, as briefly as possible, the rationale and procedures of paradigmatic psychotherapy, which have been expounded more fully in earlier papers.[8]

1. The term *paradigm* means essentially "a setting forth by example." Hence *paradigmatic psychotherapy* means the systematic setting forth of examples by the analyst to enable the patient to understand the significant intrapsychic processes or interpersonal situations of his life, past and present. Presenting a paradigm to the patient is not anything so crude as deliberately acting as a model for the patient to imitate—although this tactic might be selectively introduced to provide a dynamic context in which a given patient could become aware of chronically imitative behavior.

The setting forth of paradigms for the patient may also be regarded as an *active* form of mirroring.

2. Paradigmatic techniques are employed in the analysis of resistances and defenses that are not amenable to the classical modes of interpretation. They are designed to educate the irrational ego and are unnecessary, by and large, with patients who respond therapeutically to standard interpretation—that is, with patients in whom the ego is predominantly rational.

3. Although for this writer, Freudian theory provides the essential framework of psychoanalysis, nothing inherent in the methods of paradigmatic psychotherapy precludes its use by analysts of different theoretical persuasions.

4. Paradigmatic psychotherapy assumes that borderline states are fundamentally problems of fixation and retardation rather than of regression, and that the treatment process is one of promoting remedial emotional growth and mental synthesis. Hence, all data presented by the patient—logical and pathological—are subject to scrutiny, just as all thoughts and feelings are—ideally—to be expressed as they occur.

5. To train the borderline ego to assume responsibility and learn to recognize self-destructive impulses, paradigmatic psychotherapy often utilizes the concept of "self-dosing."[9] From time to time the patient is invited to recommend procedures for the analyst to follow.

8. Marie L. Coleman, Externalization of the Toxic Introject: A Treatment Technique for Borderline Cases, *Psychoanalytic Review*, 43:235-42, 1956; Marie L. Coleman and Benjamin Nelson, Paradigmatic Psychotherapy in Borderline Treatment, *Psychoanalysis*, 5, 3:28-44, 1957. See also *Roles and Paradigms in Psychotherapy*, Marie Coleman Nelson, ed. (New York: Grune & Stratton, forthcoming).

9. Herbert S. Strean, The Use of the Patient as Consultant, *Psychoanalysis and Psychoanalytic Review*, 46, 2:36-44, 1959.

Recommendation or refusal to recommend becomes material for analysis. Where therapeutically indicated, the patient's recommendation may be carried out, provided it falls within the basic verbal framework of the analytic rule.

6. The method recognizes that borderline patients have not developed an integrated concept of self and that the ego is composed chiefly of partial introjects and multiple identifications. Hence, the paradigmatic psychotherapist views the patient as a group—an aggregate of selves—as well as an individual.[10] Thus the therapist may elect to impersonate in his communication with the patient any one of these selves, in order to enable the patient to ventilate fantasies, experiences, and feelings associated with the particular imago.[11] In response to the material presented by the patient, the analyst may decide to remain silent, to make a classical interpretation, or to make an observation (a) that is characteristic of the imago currently occupying the patient's conscious or unconscious attention, (b) that accords with some relevant self-image of the patient, or (c) that accords with the patient's temporary or prevailing transference image of the analyst.

Similarly, when a patient reports, without insight, some interpersonal experience that reveals a flagrant misperception of its reality components, the analyst may—in the same session—"duplicate" the essence of the reported experience in his interaction with the patient. Duplication creates a dynamic situation in which the patient may achieve insight into the original misperception.

The above approaches are predicated on the recognition that the borderline patient's overvaluation of mental contents, and close association of "giving" with self-revelation, cause him to perceive classical interpretation as intrusion and attack. When the analyst supports the patient's conscious or unconscious projections and resistances as described above, the patient tends to respond in the following order: (a) He observes the analyst's paradigm of these mechanisms—he see them *outside* of himself. (b) He ventilates thoughts, feelings, and fantasies evoked by the paradigms, thereby exercising and strengthening the healthy portion of the ego that repudiates the toxic introjects, the pathological projections, and the self-destructive resistances. (c) Through this strengthening, which

10. Gustav Bychowski, Struggle Against the Introjects, *International Journal of Psychoanalysis*, 39:182-87, 1958; Harold F. Searles, Integration and Differentiation in Schizophrenia, *British Journal of Medical Psychology*, 32:261-81, 1959. See also Coleman and Nelson, *op. cit.*; and Searles, Poistive Feelings in the Relationship Between the Schizophrenic and His Mother, *loc. cit.*

11. See Coleman and Nelson, *op. cit.*

may be regarded as the development of nonpathological resistances to pathological elements in the ego, the patient becomes willing to recognize the analyst's paradigms as representative of elements in his own psychic contents.

7. Until the patient is able to profit by classical interpretation, he is analyzed by any of the following approaches deemed appropriate, which are, of course, presented in highly schematic and condensed form.

Analysis of resistances:

(a) By active mirroring (either imitative or exaggerated joining of resistance).

(b) By duplicating reported interpersonal experience.

Analysis of introjects and imagos:

(a) By assuming role of self-image (patient's idealized, hated, or unconscious self).

(b) By assuming role of introject (patient's idealized, hated—toxic— or unconscious introject).

(c) By assuming role of "stranger" (alien, uncomprehending, distant).

Analysis of fantasies and transference:

(a) By entering into ongoing fantasy.

(b) By following patient's self-dosing recommendations.

(c) By adopting any of methods listed under resistances and introjects.

8. Analysts employing these methods systematically have found them to be self-dissolving. The ego strengthening that occurs through their use finally renders paradigmatic tactics superfluous, and the final phase of treatment is conducted as a classical analysis, with spontaneous understanding by the patient of what has gone before.

The following verbatim report of a treatment session demonstrates the use of some of the above procedures.

Robert Jones, A 32-year-old advertising executive, comes from an upper-income family and is the elder of two sons. Both parents are retired professionals. The mother worked before and after the patient's birth, and much of his care in infancy and childhood fell to nurses, maids, and progressive schools. Jones describes his father as overbearing, egocentric, and somewhat paranoiac; his mother as detached, intellectual, and coldly objective. As a small child, the patient was encouraged toward independent decision-making. He recalls only two occasions on which he received physical punishment.

As far back as he can remember, his mother (reputed to have undergone psychoanalysis before having children) employed psychological explanations to give him insight into his behavior and the situations that arose in the family. Jones has never ceased to feel bitter toward her for what he calls her "therapeutic domination" and lack of emotional concern with him. He is almost phobic about interpretations, perceives them as disguised attack, and had abandoned three therapists prior to entering treatment with me.

The patient has poor relations with colleagues and clients, is accident-prone, and has great difficulty in concentrating on his professional responsibilities even though he is intelligent and creative. He moves from one position to another frequently. He has had very few sexual experiences and rarely alludes to sex. Despite a deteriorated relationship with his parents, he is still deeply involved in their lives and cannot remain away from them for any length of time. He feels chronically exhausted and dissociated. Whatever behavior he "adopts" he senses as spurious; his utterances sound unreal and forced to his ears. Although Jones's facial expression is still juvenile, his physique is attractive. His movements are childlike and impetuous.

The session that follows is Jones's forty-sixth hour of treatment by the writer. The situation discussed during the first part of the hour is that Jones has missed three sessions—the first canceled with 24 hours' notice (not chargeable); the second canceled a few minutes before the hour (chargeable); the third missed without notification (chargeable). When canceling the first missed (Tuesday) hour, the patient requested that his Tuesday appointment be eliminated because he was unexpectedly and unavoidably required to attend conferences with a client regularly on that day. He asked for a lunchtime hour instead, which the therapist could not arrange.

It may also be mentioned that the extensive verbalization by both patient and therapist in this session is unusual rather than typical of paradigmatic techniques.

A TRANSCRIBED HOUR

[Long pause.]

P1: I suppose I should mention, for your edification, where I have been. [*Laughs nervously.*] Let's see, I—uh, let's put it this way. Even today it's been very difficult. I've been very busy. It's very difficult getting out of the office. This afternoon there was some pressing matter Hackett wanted me to take care of, and I made—I told him I was going out to see an account, and ran out. After all I had done all afternoon. I mean, we're busy. But I mean, I don't know, busy. I mean, this may affect—this would affect a twelve o'clock perhaps. In other words, I—I—here I'm in a situation where it's actually the—it was actually difficult for me, even though I've been *planning* just to leave now. And it was even—uh—they were all ready to throw a monkey wrench in. What can they do? Let's see, it was, yeah, the other evening—Oh, have you gotten any lunchtime hour?

T1: Have I gotten a lunchtime hour?

P2 [*exasperated*]: Yeah—you said you might get another lunch hour— you know, an hour for me to come during my lunchtime on a weekday, on a day other than Friday.

T2: Didn't you say it would be just as hard for you to do that?

P3: No—well, I turned down one of yours which was a Friday because I already have one on Friday. I mean, that was the idea. You said you have one lunch hour on Friday, but the hour I have on Friday was convenient, so that was silly. I mean—*Look*, I mean I *want* the hour, so— [*sighs*]. In other words, if it could be, uh, any other lunch hour.

T3: Well, if something opens up, I'll let you know.

P4: At this point you have nothing—

T4: No.

[*Intervening silence.*]

P5: I take it you have no hours over the week end—

[*15-second pause.*]

P6: Then what do I get charged for in this past month? I mean how does that work?

T6: Well, what do you figure?

P7 [*sarcastically*]: What *I* figure? I'd like to know what *you* figure, because what you figure is probably going to be closer to what I'll pay than what I figure. [*Pause*] Do you want me to figure? I mean, honestly?

T7: Why shouldn't you figure?

P8: Because obviously there are two viewpoints. I know from past experience two viewpoints are represented here, but— What do I figure? I mean, in fairness—I mean, I don't know the total number. Let's see now, I think two—I think I missed two. Am I correct? I don't even know, I haven't figured it out. But—oh—yes, that's right. This is only—I mean, I would figure that I would have to pay for the rest, which to me is quite in keeping with anyone's income, as it is a chunk out of mine. I mean, I'm not—that's all I can do.

T8: You mean you figure that you pay just for when you've been here, not for what you've contracted for—is that it?

P9 [*combatively*]: You want to make it into a—uh—I mean, I can be a bastard too.

T9 [*sharply*]: No, I'm not trying to make it into anything.

P10: Then don't put words into my mouth—"contracted." A contract has to be a written agreement to be important. I didn't contract with you.

T10: You contracted for certain hours during the week.

P11: So it's a verbal agreement. It's a verbal agreement. Since that tape recorder is on I suppose I shouldn't even go further.

T11: Why not?

P12: Because I might say something that could be held against me on tape. I mean, I'm not— [*gasps with exasperation*]. Right? In other words [*voice rises*] when you talk contract, you're talking as if there was actually—you're throwing into it your *interpretation* of what actually transpired, not what transpired. Right?

T12 [*factually*]: Look, Mr. Jones, there is only one contract that analysts make with patients, not just myself—

P13: Yeah.

T13: —it's a verbal contract, a verbal agreement—

P14: Yeah.

T14: —and there is an understanding, which is made clear—

P15: Yeah.

T15: —that the patient pays for whatever hours are agreed upon as his scheduled hours.

P16 [*angrily*]: How about your comment the time I phoned—I think it was primarily that you—that, uh—well, you said, "Well, it seems a shame that you have to have these hours," and—I mean you said something to the effect—something which I interpreted as, as meaning, "It is so clear that you can't make the hours you have contracted that maybe. . . ." and "You're telling me well in advance," would be implied also, therefore—uh —I mean, "This is not a violation of the contract not to. . . ." or "It's not a *change*" of the contract not to pay for the total—uh.

T16: You mean that you thought I meant something other than what I said?

P17: Oh, no. I thought you meant just what you said.

T17: Well, isn't it too bad that you should have hours that you contracted for, that you have to pay for, without having the benefit of them?

P18: That isn't what you said. I mean, if you want to— Maybe you can explain what you said, because when you said to me something that sounded quite understanding, this was already—I mean—after a couple were missed—and then the preceding Tuesday, which I told you well in advance. [*Adopts bawling-out tone to end of communication.*] *Part* of the contract was twenty-four hours in advance for avoidable things, anyway. And these are avoidable—uh, *unavoidable*. I mean, when you have a cancellation and you're told well in advance and this is all discussed—I mean, this isn't a—perhaps if I were a millionaire, as it is I have to pinch pennies to come here. Now when I have a job where I have to meet with the accounts, and I have to meet with them when they're in town, which sometimes happens to coincide with this hour—I mean, undoubtedly I'm anticipating an argument that will say, "The reason you're keeping this job is so you don't have to come here," but unfortunately— You know, I— it sounds like I'm back with Dr. R again. You've got to be dead before you can—before you get excused. And I guess you get billed—uh, your estate gets charged, probably!

T18 [*with cheerful resignation*]: Well, it looks like it's very difficult and very inconvenient for you to be analyzed—

P19: Is that what I'm saying?

T19 [*blandly*]: —and maybe that's true. Maybe you should do it some-time when you have more time, when you can spare the time for it.

P20: Maybe I should. Is that what you think? [*10-second pause*] Hmm? Is that what you think? [*Pause.*] That wasn't rhetorical.

T20: Why should I tell you what I think?

P21 [*sullenly*]: You don't *have to*. Keep it to yourself, I don't care. I'm asking you, but you don't have to tell me. [*With rising voice*] I don't know why it's impossible to recognize another side of it.

T21 [*wholeheartedly*]: I *do* recognize it. I recognize it so well that I suggest that maybe this is the only solution.

P22: Well, that was how it was mentioned the last time—I don't know why—I don't think you've made clear what—I don't understand. I am, in fact, perhaps anticipating, because you were very general. Now what is—what is the last time—when I spoke with you I said, "All right, from now on I just have trouble Fridays." Right? Last Friday I called you up.

T22: You asked me to hold one more—oh, you mean the last Friday you didn't come?

P23 [*angrily*]: No, I asked you to release Tuesday. Now *look*—

T23 [*interrupting sharply*]: Excuse me, I'm asking you a question.

P24: Yeah.

T24: Are you thinking about the last time we spoke?

P25: That's right. That's right. The last time I spoke to you on the phone. Last Friday.

T25: Yeah.

P26: I asked you to release Tuesday, right?

T26: Sure.

P27 [*in a cross-examining tone*]: O.K., so Tuesday is no longer con-tracted for by me. Last week it wasn't, right? I told you Friday. That comes before Tuesday. Therefore, I don't have Tuesday, right?

T27: That's correct.

P28: And I didn't have it last week. [*Mollified*] I mean—this—that's all I want. No, the others I understood. I mean, in the name of—well, from a—frankly, from what I consider the—uh, rather a fair point of view, I shouldn't—I shouldn't be paying for the ones I missed. I mean, like this month particularly.

T28: Why shouldn't you?

P29: In this particular month? Because—uh— [*haughtily*] there's what you call the human element. Now I know—

T29 [*indignantly*]: And yet *you* weren't even considerate enough to give me a phone call and tell me you weren't coming in!

P30: Uh—in which are we talking about?

T30: Well, for example—

P31: With Friday it's true.

T31: —on the eighteenth.

P32: The eighteenth.

T32: September eighteenth.

P33: Let's see. Now what—is—that—two weeks ago from today?

T33: That's right.

P34: Yeah. [*Thinking*] On the eighteenth—wait a minute—when did I start again after vacation?

T34: You started on September fifteenth.

P35: On the fifteenth—a Tuesday. Then so far I didn't—didn't—and Tuesday. But Tuesday I called you up on—so before, on Friday. Tuesday, yeah. [*Patient leaves couch, goes into foyer to his coat and brings back his appointment book, which he consults.*] I didn't call you on the eighteenth. I don't recall—oh yes, that's right. I didn't. It completely escaped me. I didn't remember. I mean the pressure of work—you may or may not believe it, but the pressure of work is really incredible. I mean—

T35: Well, I have no objection to your not calling me, if you want to do it that way, but—

P36: What do you mean, if I want to do it that way? Obviously, I— I wouldn't do it unless I forgot about it. This is not—

T36: Well, I mean if you want to forget about it, I have no objection.

P37: You know, you can read something into it, but there can be also very realistic—uh—reasons.

T37 [*cheerfully*]: I'm not reading anything into it.

P38: I normally have—

T38: You said you forgot about it. I agree with you. You forgot about it. What am I reading into it?

P39: Well, forgetting is a great variable, because—

T39: *You're* reading something into it I'm not making any interpretations about—

P40: Well, I think I'm fairly safe in making the one I'm making. I mean, it's a great—you say I can if I want to. You're implying that subconsciously I want to. If I—I mean, it's very difficult to dissociate subconscious from conscious or unconscious, *but*—uh—the point I'm making is that—uh, under the circumstances I—it was impossible to remember because there was much—there were *very serious* things that had to be done. I mean, these things I—you can't imagine it, but I mean, we—they—we get the—we get run through the mill daily. We have emergencies—actors stand by waiting to go to work—depending on the O.K.—families—and pressure from everyone you can think of—to do all kinds of crazy things. And so I mean, this just knocks you—the responsibility—it—it just succumbs you. People's jobs—and livelihood—depending on—

T40: So? All you're telling me is that you care less for yourself than you do for all these other people.

[*Both talk at once.*]

P41: You're talking about my petty little—

T41: Your own interests are subordinated—

P42: My petty—

T42: —to the interests of all these other people.

P43 [*dramatically*]: Yeah, but one thing is a neurosis and the other is actually—

T43: Your life is of less importance to you.

P44: Mine is just a little neurosis. I'm sorry, but I'm so selfish—I mean I can be, up to a point. Just this afternoon—

T44 [*interrupting*]: How is it you can't be selfish about this, but you can be selfish about your hour? I'm supposed to be as magnanimous as you are. But I'm not.

P45: You're supposed to—what do you mean by "magnanimous"?

T45: Well, *you're* willing to give up your hour' for all these other people, but *I'm* not willing to give up the fee for your hour, for all these other people. *You're* a much more generous person than I am.

P46: Well, obviously. And—and—in contrast to my trying, you have a lot more [*laughs nervously*], uh—from an economic point of view. So, uh—

T46: Well, what's the comparison? You sell your time and I sell mine.

P47: In other words—

T47: You sell your labor time and I sell my labor time.

P48 [*in a tone of resignation*]: I see. We—we're all a bunch of monads. I know. Uh— [*sigh*]. Look, I mean, you can, uh—I mean, I can recognize a good—a good line when I hear one, and [*permissively*] you go right on. This is—I don't know, uh, I mean it's great to—it's a great way to handle the—the—financial aspect by throwing things in about unconscious motivations.

T48: I'm not imputing *any* unconscious motivations. I say you're a very generous person. You're willing to give up your time and your analytic hour.

P49: You're being sarcastic.

T49: What's sarcastic about it, *I* give up three hours a week working in a clinic free, but I don't give up these hours working free.

P50: Well, maybe I should come to the clinic.

T50: Maybe you should. That's a very good idea.

P51: Yeah, I'd have to wait for years, I'm sure. You have long waiting lists, right?

T51: At this point? No.

P52: Could I apply there?

T52: Why not?

P53: I didn't ask why not. I asked, could I?

T53: Anybody can apply there.

P54: Could I be accepted?

T54: I don't know.

P55: For—for what reasons would I or wouldn't I?

T55: It would depend on the Chief of the Psychology Department.

P56: Why would he? I—I'm quite serious, because—I mean—this is quite a hardship on me in—

T56: Why should I tell you? Go down. Take a chance.

P57: I don't even know what the name of the clinic is. [*10-second pause*] I mean, you don't think it's a good idea that I go to the clinic where you're working—

T57 [*encouragingly*]: Where I'm working? Why? Why would I object?

P58: Then what's the name of the clinic?

T58: The X Clinic.

P59: Oh, it's on the East Side, right?

T59: It's on the West Side.

P60: I passed it. Oh, is that on Y Avenue? In between A and B Streets, or so?

T60: That's right.

P61: We have several accounts right nearby.

T61: It would be very convenient for you.

P62: It sure would. [*20-second pause*] Well, I don't know. Do you think, I mean—from your point of view, would it fit my needs? In other words, hours—as far as hours go, financially. I assume it would, uh—stuff like that.

T62: It depends on what hours are assigned. You'd have to talk about that to the person who schedules.

P63: Well, it isn't so much the specific hours. Well, there's Number 1: Would I get in? And Number 2: I mean, is it a good—is it a good clinic?

T63: Why don't you go there and find out?

P64: You don't find out by going there. [*Scornfully*] What, are they going to tell me it's a *bad* clinic?

T64: If there are all people like me working there, it must be a terrible clinic.

P65: How do I know they're all like you? You work three hours a week there. Maybe you do that to give them your name for their letterhead, or something. I don't know what the setup is.

T65: Well, can't you take a chance?

P66: Is it a question of a chance? Do you think I have so much time that I can take chances all over the place?

T66: Everybody else has to take a chance.

P67: I mean—that I just have time to go and explore? I mean, you must think I do nothing all day. I don't have time for lunch.

T67: Why not?

P68: Because I'm working, because it's very busy. I—I run out, and I run in again. And there is a brief space in between when I put my lunch in. But anyway, the point is that I don't have time for—I mean, I—I don't have time to look for another job. I took off some time. It's incredible how little you can spare. That's why I'm asking you these questions. Is it wrong to ask you these questions?

T68: It's *perfectly* all right.

P69: So why don't you tell me the answers?

T69: I don't know the answers.

P70: You have an *opinion,* you know *me.*

T70: Well, like everywhere else in the world, some people are good, some people aren't so good. You know, therapists are just like other people.

P71 [*explosively*]: Oh, Jeez! What are you? I—

T71 [*flatly*]: You're asking me, I'm telling you.

P72: Just like everywhere else.

T72: Just like anywhere else in the world.

P73: What are you, afraid to— This is being tape-recorded, you don't want to sound—

T73: What do you mean? What do you want me to say? Do you want me to say it's wonderful? It's wonderful. If you want me to say its terrible, it's terrible.

P74 [*interrupting*]: Don't you have an impression? Oh, you have absolutely no opinion, is that it? I mean, I lose confidence in you when you show this—when you're now presenting yourself as having no opinion. I mean, I don't know if you have an opinion or if you don't.

T74: You don't want my opinion.

P75: What do I want?

T75: I gave you an honest answer. You don't want an honest answer.

P76: What was your honest answer?

T76: I said, it's like everyplace else. Some people are good, some people are better, some people are poor. Just like anywhere else in the world.

P77: Ah. You can be so glib. I didn't know if you meant it.

T77: Why not?

P78: I said, because you can be so glib. But, uh— [*laughs*] in other words, *whom* do they take? Do they concentrate—are they like the Z Center? Do they concentrate on one type? Do they want a certain—you know. Are they doing *studies?* Or do they take people who can't possibly afford it? In which case it would probably exclude me. You know—can't afford private therapy.

T78: I don't know what their policy is about taking people—

P79: You really don't?

T79: —because I think their fees are scaled to income.

P80: You don't know what—

T80: They don't take *anybody* for less than a dollar an hour.

P81: You don't know *what* range they—

T81: And *above* that, the fees are scaled according to income.

P82: What's their tops? Do you have any idea?

T82: No, I don't.

[*15-second pause.*]

P83: All right. I'll drop in there. Can I go down there during the day? Or is it just open in the evenings?

T83: It is *only* open in the day.

P84: It's only open in the day, huh? Uh-*huh!* Do I mention—oh, I guess I mention everything, right? What I earn.

T84: It's all right with me. I have no objection.

P85: I mean—I—yeah. [*10-second pause*] Do they have a large staff?

T85: I don't know how large it is.

[*20-second pause.*]

P86: Can you suggest any other places?

T86: Why should I?

P87: Why shouldn't you? Because we're just discussing the situation. [*Voice rises.*] I mean, the only reason— All right. Yeah, [*Quietly, seriously*]

I don't know why you should, and frankly—I don't like—I mean, I don't want to switch again, really. I mean, this is—I just—I talk as if—I mean, the economic burden is quite great, but, uh—I was hoping to go to work on—I may have to do free-lance work week ends, as well. But uh—you don't—

[3-minute 25-second pause. What follows takes place in last 20 minutes of the hour.]

T87: Have you left for the X Clinic already?

P88 [laughs]: Yeah. I—uh, let's see now. I can't hear a word you're saying. No, uh—[stretches]. This is part of my exhaustion. I almost left for [laughs] sweet dreamland. Um, what am I supposed to say? [Humorously] I can't report this dream, I haven't had it yet. [5-minute 15-second pause] Gee, I'm really very tired.

T88 [quietly]: Well, that was a pretty exhausting exchange we had there. I don't blame you!

P89: Maybe all the work I did—and other things—like I go to the office two nights a week. [Hums gently; 20-second pause] Why don't you talk for a change? Don't you have anything to say?

T89: Why are you rubbing your feet together? Are you masturbating?

P90 [laughs]: Oh, all right. I thought you had something to say. Why not?

T90: You're not supposed to masturbate in here.

P91: Who said?

T91: I said.

P92: [alluding to therapist's standing request that he not remove his jacket during sessions]: With my jacket on, I could. I have my tie on, isn't that good enough? [20-second pause.] Well, give me something more interesting to do, like listening to you.

T92: I'm not here to entertain you.

P93: Then I'll have to masturbate when I dream.

[15-second pause.]

T93: Well, would you like me to read to you?

P94: You got something interesting?

T94: Well, I have a pamphlet here on office linoleum. Do you want to hear about office linoleum?

P95 [petulantly]: No.

T95: I have a new book here, the *Collected Papers of Frieda Fromm-Reichmann*—

[13-second pause.]

P96: Well, whatever you think is interesting.

T96: Well, you're the one who wants me to read, why shouldn't I read something that *you* think is interesting?

P97: *You're* not here to entertain me.

T97 [magnanimously]: I'll entertain you. I've got nothing to talk about, but I'll read to you, if you want.

P98: Have you *read* any of the Frieda Fromm-Reichmann?

T98: Yes, sure.

P99: Why don't you tell me what—what you thought of it. That would be more interesting.

T99: You want to know what *I* think, huh?

P100 [*laughs*]: Well, it— [*laughs*]. Well, it's more or less—not really. Tell me a funny story. I don't care. Or you could tell me—uh—about your vacation. I really, I'm not really interested. I mean, you know, not particularly. We've got to have *something* to fill up the hour.

T100: Why? Why can't you fill it up with resting?

P101: Well, I am. I might even drop off to sleep in the middle of—whatever you're doing.

T101: Why should I start? You can drop off right now. You've got— [*consults watch*] 10 minutes left. Get a little nap in.

P102: Oh, what an expensive nap! I mean, this month is—very expensive for— [*stretches*].

[*30-second pause.*]

T102: Well, you know what the Captain of the Guard said to Jesus.

P103: What did he say to Jesus?

T103: "If you can't carry the cross, get out of the parade."

P104: The Captain of the Guard said to Jesus— [*laughs nervously*]. The Captain of the Guard—is that a joke, or, uh—or what? Huh? Is that a joke?

T104: I don't know. You think it's funny?

P105: No.

T105: Then it isn't a joke.

P106: So what does it mean?

T106: It means what it says.

P107 [*stubbornly*]: I don't see Jesus, a Captain of the Guard, or a cross.

T107 [*playfully*]: You don't?

P108: No.

T108: Your mind's a blank?

P109: I didn't say that. I just said, I can't see Jesus, a Captain of the Guards, or a cross.

T109 [*with mock horror*]: You've gone blind!

P110: You think I am? I mean, if *you* see Jesus, maybe *you* should start talking and maybe I could—uh, help you out. Uh, is that supposed to mean that if I—is that—am I—is this analogous to me?

T110 [*flatly*]: This is supposed to be a joke. You asked me to tell you a joke, right?

P111: No I didn't. I thought you were going to read me—a joke. Um, is that supposed to be a joke? If you can't carry a cross—I'll laugh—if you really tell me it's a joke, I'll laugh.

T111: You don't have to laugh. Why should you laugh?

P112 [*satirically*]: Because I want to encourage you to tell me more jokes. Maybe you'll get to a good one eventually. Was that—was that supposed to mean something?

T112: What makes you look for hidden meanings in things?

P113: Hidden?

T113 [with mock disgust]: You're always looking for interpretations, hidden meanings. My God!

P114: Aw-w-w, look. Why don't you—tell me another joke? Do you know any other jokes?

T114 [indignantly]: Why should I tell you another joke? You really want interpretations. Even when I don't interpret to you, you take everything so—so seriously.

P115: Well, if you don't know any *funny* jokes, don't bother. But I thought maybe you'd know some funny ones. Aw, *[laughs]*, this is a fine expenditure of my dough! *[60-second pause.]* I mean, I'm being silent, which I see nothing wrong in, and the explanation is that, uh—there are— that, that—I mean, we are working at such a—I've been going, maybe, even more than the others. I mean, I'm just—at this point of the week I am just, frankly, just sort of used up. And, uh, so that's it. I mean, my effort has been expended so—so much. *[2-minute 35-second pause]* Oh, would it be possible to work with *you* at the X Clinic?

T115: No. I don't have any free time left.

P116: Might you, at some time?

T116: I couldn't anticipate when. *[2-minute pause.]* Well—

[Both rise.]

P117: I used up a lot of that extra tape, I'm afraid, on your tape recorder. You can cut out that last section *[laughs].*

T117: Why?

P118 [laughs]: The whole thing was absurd. *[With humorous condescension]* Tape must be worth a lot of money.

T118 and P119: Goodnight.

DISCUSSION[12]

The patient typically opened his sessions either by entering limply and flopping down in exhausted silence, punctuated occasionally by sighs and muffled allusions to his fatigue, or by sweeping in bulkily, as though itching for a fight. Because of his violently negative reaction to any remark approaching interpretation and his complaint that he had left his previous analysts because they were too silent or too full of interpretations that he already knew, it was necessary to provide a therapeutic experience without recourse to formal interpretative procedures. Somehow the patient

12. For valuable on-going discussion of the rationale of paradigmatic techniques, and for specific participation in the formulations of this section, I am indebted to colleagues of the Paradigmatic Behavior Studies Seminar: Benjamin Nelson, Arnold Bernstein, Arthur Blatt, Robert deNeergaard, Murray Sherman, and Herbert Strean, and a guest, John L. Herma. Also, many excellent suggestions made by the group after reading a first draft of this paper have been incorporated in this final version.

had to learn to communicate at the reality level, to recognize that his ascription of depth interpretation to all that happened in the hour was a resistance, and to come upon manifestations of the unconscious afresh, as, for example, in his slip of the tongue while bawling me out (*P18*): "*Part* of the contract was twenty-four hours in advance for avoidable things. . . . And these are avoidable—uh, *un*avoidable."

It became evident after I had observed Jones for a time that his two modes of presenting himself for treatment were attached to the following transference fantasies: When he was exhausted and silent, he perceived me as the mother, waiting to pounce on him with interpretations. When he behaved combatively, he saw me as the overtly aggressive father whom he must attack first in order to forestall being attacked (castrated).[13]

To relate to Jones in the traditional analytic manner, therefore, was to represent for him the mother whom he felt most justified in rejecting, as shown in his abandonment of the previous analysts. Moreover, since the mother had not displayed toward the patient the overtly accepting *or* prohibitive attitudes that a less sophisticated parent permits herself, it must be assumed that his Oedipal situation was ill defined and ill resolved; that conscious representation of the incest prohibition was structured almost solely in terms of fear of the father; and that the mother constituted far more an unknown quantity for the son than a specific love object forbidden by both parents in the usual symbolic and behavioral interaction of family life.

Accordingly, I elected to present Jones with a paradigm of the father—the parent who feels more real to him and with whom he will feel the least painful effects of deprivation. As the first portion of the treatment hour demonstrates (*T9* to *T29*), I entered into altercation with the patient; I got tough, spoke sharply, interrupted him, and laid down the law about paying for missed hours. When he suggested that paying for treatment was too much for him, I encouraged him to seek treatment at a clinic. From time to time he accused me of interpreting, which I vigorously denied, arguing— but not interpreting—that *he* was the one who was making in- terpretations (in *P18* to *T39*, assuming that I would make him pay

13. To the extent that the patient's concept of masculinity was patterned after the father, it is also evident that Jones was enacting the father's role toward me-as-himself; this observation, while valid, had no immediate thera- peutic utility. Other generalizations which the reader may deduce from the case material will not be explored unless they have relevance to the theme of this paper.

for a legitimately canceled hour, and in *P73*, *T73*, assuming that I was being evasive when I refused to designate the clinic as good or bad). In this highly charged atmosphere I deliberately avoided interpretation of the patient's use of the treatment situation to obtain sadomasochistic gratification, in favor of the more dynamically important nonverbalized message to him: "We can fight without murdering or leaving each other; I can stand your aggression without throwing you out or killing you off with cold interpretations; I am strong enough to be your father."

After Jones had tested my willingness to engage with him emotionally in the way he knew best, through combat, his anxiety was relieved. The emotional tone of the hour underwent a radical change (*P87*, *T87*, and following). He permitted himself to regress, to become a little boy who wants to be told a story or a joke. He wanted to be fed. I accepted his projection that I was now a mother; I stalled him a little to enable *him* to identify what was happening, if he so wished. When he did not attempt to interpret, I gratified his wish, but only partially, with a "sick" joke (*T102, 103*)—one that is funny, yet not funny, and one that he might refer to himself if he were so inclined, or reject as unrelated to himself. Like a dream, the joke was overdetermined. It could be perceived as a permissive statement: "If you are too tired to work today, take it easy," or "You are a Christlike fellow, a martyr, and if you can't take it, give up" (referring to his stated reason for missing an analytic hour—concern for the welfare of others), or "No matter what you do, you can't escape your sad, neurotic fate" (referring to the absurdity of Christ's being given the option of getting out of the parade). The joke fulfilled the patient's request for feeding—it came as milk. But its ambivalent content made it somewhat sour milk, a dubious fulfillment. Implicit in the joke was *the* interpretation of both the hour and the phase of treatment, since it related to the patient's characterological defense rather than to depth material. But it was a *virtual interpretation*, and as such demanded no overt acknowledgment by the patient unless he felt strong enough to attribute significance to it.

The ambivalent nature of the joke prevented it from serving as a simple gratification of the patient's wish (the self-dosing recommendation) and helped to sustain the degree of tension requisite for treatment. Jones received the joke as though it were sour milk; he was confused, suspicious, and curious. Again he tested me by trying to induce me to verbalize the interpretations which he had evidently perceived himself when he asked (*P110*), "Is this analogous to me?" Had I yielded, his deeper anxiety that I was out to kill him with interpretations would have been confirmed. Instead, I aligned myself with the less masochistic and more autonomous segment of his ego, the portion which did not relish painful interpretations or employ analytic thinking for ruminative, self-destructive purposes. I stated flatly, "This is supposed to be a joke." And when he continued to press me, I exclaimed in mock disgust (mirroring his resistance), "You're always looking for interpretations, hidden meanings. My God!"

The effect of the therapist's avoidance of the interpretive role is seen at the end of the hour, when the patient obliquely signified his intention not to run away. So that I would not be left with the impression that he wanted to leave me, Jones asked if I would be his therapist, were he to attend the clinic.[14]

Although the protocol of an analytic session that utilizes paradigmatic techniques only imperfectly conveys the dynamic nature of the encounter, it can best be likened to the end of a chess game in which the therapist relinquishes pieces of higher symbolic value in order to develop checkmating maneuvers elsewhere on the board with pieces that temporarily have greater *strategic* value.

For example, in the session with Jones the therapist yielded a traditional analytic tool, formal interpretation, to by-pass the chief obstacle to therapeutic contact—the patient's reality-reinforced hatred of interpretations. The necessity for evolving techniques that circumvent the resistances that certain patients mobilize when confronted by the logic of classical interpretation has been recognized by numerous writers.[15]

The utility of noninterpretive maneuvers, which nevertheless have the effect of interpretation, may be closely related to a perceptual mechanism that has been extensively explored by Poetzl, Fisher, Shevrin and Luborsky, and Klein.[16] In Poetzl's original ex-

14. This hour, and a subsequent one in which I signified my willingness to read to the patient whenever he felt too fatigued to conduct his share of the analytic work, had far-reaching consequences. His provocative introductory behavior largely ceased, he began to report his thoughts and feelings with seriousness and confidence, and he almost immediately developed a tolerance for some interpretation. He never followed up my offer to read to him.

15. See Eissler, Greenson, and Loewenstein, *op. cit.*

16. Otto Poetzl, Experimentally Provoked Dream Images in Their Relation to Indirect Vision, *Ztschr. of Neurology and Psychiatry*, 37:278-349, 1917; Charles Fisher, Dreams and Perception, *Journal of the American Psychoanalytical Association*, 2:389-445, 1954; Howard Shevrin and Lester Luborsky, The Measurement of Preconscious Perception in Dreams and Images:. An Investigation of the Poetzl Phenomenon, *Journal of Abnormal and Social Psychology*, 56:285-94, 1958; George S. Klein and others, Cognition Without Awareness: Subliminal Influences Upon Conscious Thought, *ibid.*, 57:255-66, 1958.

periments, images projected on a screen so briefly that they were seen only as a blur turned up in distorted but recognizable form in the subject's dreams. Holzman, commenting on the similarity between certain conclusions of these experimenters and Breuer's hypnoidal theory of neurosis, states:

"At the present time the most plausible explanation of these phenomena proposes that a stimulus perceived foveally, with optimum attention cathexis, is prevented, by the centering of attention on it, from undergoing transformations of a primary process character. Peripherally registered stimuli, on the other hand, are not bound by the hypercathexis of attention, and are therefore more plastic; they need not maintain an identity consistent with the laws of logic, demanded for stimuli in the center of attention."[17]

And Klein remarks, in discussing subliminal perception:

"Dreams, hypnosis, hypnagogic and mescaline states perhaps enable a relatively undifferentiated slice of incidentally registered experience to be re-experienced with an intensity which in the usual waking state of the laboratory can be accomplished only through passive, eideticlike imagery. As reality contact and reality requirements are minimized, so the prospects of incidentally registered material emerging in awareness in passive imagery may increase."[18]

If these observations are related to the analytic situation, it may be hypothesized that the nonverbalized interpretations implicit in the paradigmatic maneuver function similarly, as peripheral stimuli; that—like the blurred tachistoscopic image—the virtual interpretation registers at a more primary level than the overt interchange between analyst and patient. Because the nonverbalized interpretation in the paradigm demands no special, focused attention and because it emerges as an undifferentiated element of the ongoing, conscious encounter[19] it does not activate resistance as does logical confrontation. When, additionally the treatment of the borderline is regarded as a corrective emotional experience, it may further be deduced that the nonspecific, nonintellectual aspect of the paradigmatic encounter more closely approximates the hypnoidal learning situations of early childhood than do the more didactic aspects of formal interpretation.

17. Philip S. Holzman, A Note on Breuer's Hypnoidal Theory of Neurosis, *Bulletin of the Menninger Clinic*, 23:145, 1959.

18. Klein, *op. cit.*, p. 257.

19. For example, the therapist's frequent allusions in the hour—presented as countercharges rather than interpretations—to the patient's insistence on making interpretations (*T16, 35, 48, 74, 75, 106, 110, 113, 114*).

Recognition that the borderline ego is to a large degree irrational, and that it has erected multiple defenses to protect and conceal the primary fixations, necessitates the employment of various
subliminal procedures that touch more directly on the primary
process. The patient's eventual verbalization of insight that has
been gained at the preconscious and unconscious levels through
subliminal learning is similar to the evolution of the child's ego
that manifests itself in an increasing ability to structure random
impressions into formal concepts.

I should now like to consider the therapeutic management of
the borderline constellation that Fairbairn and others have observed. First, there is the overvaluation of bodily *contents,* and,
associated with it, the overvaluation of bodily *processes*—the gratification obtained from autistic thinking and autistic physical activities. A characterological attitude of contempt for the simple and
admiration of the complex is often derived from these. Finally,
there is a hypersensitivity to narcissistic injury; the internal life
is strongly defended.

I have been particularly impressed with the periodic compulsion of the borderline patient to generate intrapsychic fantasies
(sometimes, but not always, by inducing the environment to act
upon him) which are directly correlated with somatic tension, pain,
ecstasy—with libidinal or aggressive discharge.[20] However restricted
the physical mode or area through which he elects to somatize in
conjunction with the fantasies, the mechanism will eventually be
revealed through treatment.

At this point I wish to interject my interpretation of the very
real pain felt by the schizoid patient when the narcissistic constellation is subjected to analysis, for I believe it has some relevance
to the problem. (I should add that I am by no means certain that
this interpretation has not been advanced elsewhere.) The borderline patient's excessive preoccupation with himself, whether it be
ministrative or destructive, represents a relationship with the internalized mother; all of the self-inflicted psychic pain or pleasure,
of physical torment or ecstasy associated with the fantasies represents an attempt to achieve wholeness within himself through one-
ness with her, to correct the historic flaw in the mother-child
relationship that contributed to the illness. Hence *the therapeutic
intrusion upon the fantasy relationship with the internalized mother
produces the narcissistic pain and accounts for its intensity; it is as*

20. Patients with integrated patterns of repetitive physical discharge (exercise, the dance, perverse rituals, excessive masturbation or sexual activity, and
so forth) may be exempt, but only as long as the defense holds.

though the child were being torn from the mother's body. No other view, to my mind, suffices to explain either the seemingly disproportionate suffering experienced by these patients as they give up their critical narcissistic investments, or the affect of resentment when the healthier portion of the ego cooperates in withdrawing cathexis from autistic modes of gratification.

At the outset of the analytic hour with Jones, I argued with the patient, as I have indicated, in order to fulfill the paradigm of his father, thus mirroring and supporting the transference projection and preventing a situation from developing in which he would experience me as the detached mother. But I also argued with him for another reason: to create a more challenging and less predictable treatment situation. Highly sophisticated in matters psychoanalytic, Jones knew that analysts are "supposed" to remain emotionally uninvolved. In doing the unexpected, I precipitated a temporary withdrawal of the psychic energy usually invested in his autistic processes (namely, manifest exhaustion) and a redirection of this energy outward, in the form of active curiosity about *our* relationship and *my* role in the situation.

From the standpoint of energy economy the question arises: Why was Jones *willing* to disturb his usual state of psychic equiliprium? Why did he not withdraw from the encounter? *Because the therapeutic tactic allowed one form of narcissistic gratification to be substituted for another;* at no point was the patient narcissistically impoverished by the exchange. Any capitulation by a therapist is viewed, at some level, as a victory by the patient. Although he did not allude to it, Jones undoubtedly interpreted my abandonment of the "proper" analytic role, emotional uninvolvement, as an *involuntary* capitulation to him. The gratification derived from this fantasied triumph over me permitted the detachment of psychic energy away from deep preoccupation with the maternal introject and its outward release as impetus for the personal encounter. This also explains his subsequent willingness to present *himself* in a less defended role—as a little boy wanting pleasure from an external mother figure. Exploiting the allegory of the chess game, I sacrificed a "status" piece to engage the patient more dynamically elsewhere. To the possible objection that Jones was able to communicate effectively only on the basis of two unrealistic fantasies (that is, that I was like his belligerent father and that he had caused me to abandon the proper analytic role), I would reply that in time the patient comes to realize that whatever stance the therapist takes is an elected one, and that later in treatment, as classical analysis becomes feasible, he will openly allude to "those times when you acted like my father," or "when you let me think you weren't a real analyst," and so forth.

The analyst's voluntary manipulation of his and the patient's status roles in borderline treatment deserves closer examination. Eissler, in exploring the particular phenomenon in which the patient perceives the meaning of his own verbalization not when he utters it, but only when the analyst repeats it after him, suggests that ". . . the bulk of psychic energy, in such states, is engaged in countercathexis against the preconscious or unconscious systems. This particular hypercathexis of the defensive apparatus, resulting in a state of relative security, may, I assume, have permitted the entrance of a genuinely dangerous derivative. When, in this state, the person is confronted with the same content but coming, this time, from the outside against which the psychic apparatus is more or less unprotected, then the ego is taken by surprise and has no time to build up adequate defences."[21]

Confirmation of this explanation is found in the use of paradigms; the patient who avoids spontaneous insight and resists classical interpretation recognizes resistances, projections, and fantasies when they are in some fashion reprojected by the analyst.[22] Sherman has called attention to the similarity of this mechanism to the effects of surprise discussed by Reik.[23]

Amplifying the above observation, Eissler adds that, in instances where simple repetition of the patient's words results in insight, "the interpretive core is reduced to zero and the vehicle function is performed not by the repeated statement itself, but exclusively by distribution factors of psychic energy in the subject."[24]

While it is true that the semantic interpretive core is reduced to zero, another element is present in the situation which Eissler does not mention. The very repetition of the patient's words invests them with a significance that is not accorded words of his which are *not* repeated. But it is not merely the implication of special interest (investment of cathexis) by the analyst in the patient's words that precipitates the patient's understanding of what

21. Eissler, *op. cit.,* p. 225.
22. This does not hold true for the type of paranoid patient who channelizes the bulk of the paranoid projections into the transference. Here, the analyst's mirroring of the internalized hated object through paradigms may dangerously magnify the delusional projections. It can be successful where paranoid fantasies are diffusely projected on the persons in the patient's environment—including but not exclusively focused on the analyst.
23. Murray Sherman, Clues to the Third Ear, *Psychoanalysis and Psychoanalytic Review*, 46, 3:43-50, 1959; Theodor Reik, *Surprise and the Psychoanalyst* (London: Kegan Paul, 1936).
24. Eissler, *op. cit.,* p. 225.

he has himself said; it is the patient's involuntary emotional response to the analyst's repetition—the feeling that the analyst is interested and the idea that he has no ready interpretation—which impels the patient to step in the breach. A part of nature, the human psyche abhors a vacuum. The analyst's supposed failure to understand mobilizes the patient's aggressive and competitive energy, and the interpretation rides into his consciousness on the crest of this wave.

One of the most powerful obstacles to treatment of the borderline patient is his opposition to the inevitable reduction of an elaborate compensatory system to the primitive desires that underlie his illness. I have yet to see an intellectual who delights in juggling abstruse concepts derive pleasure from the revival of his yearning need to suck at the mother's breast. Hence, the sooner the narcissistic cathexis of internal processes becomes attached to the analytic process, the less impoverished the patient feels and the more he is able to tolerate unflattering truths about himself as they emerge. I have found it generally therapeutic, for example, to permit certain patients to conduct their own self-analyses (indulge their autism, if you will) for as long as they wish, *provided* there is concomitant evidence of improved functioning and object relationships outside the analysis. Periodically, however, it is desirable for the analyst to make neutral mention of this tendency so that the patient may know that it does not continue unobserved. If exclusion of the analyst from the treatment process does not wound the analyst's own narcissism to such a degree that he feels compelled to intrude upon the patient's solitary journey of discovery (the historic prerogative of the Hero!) the latter will eventually face his encounter with the analyst. He will question what his exclusion of the analyst means, thus signifying a readiness for joint exploration of the autistic pattern.

In handling the narcissistic constellation, the degree of participation required of the analyst depends to a large extent upon his sensitivity to establishing the tempo best suited to the progress of the patient. It is my impression that, just as the borderline patient tends to veer to extremes, so must the treatment atmosphere and the analyst's involvement veer, if dynamically matched rapport is to be achieved.[25] The paradigmatic hour frequently shows this quality of affective extremes, as in the quoted hour with Jones, which exerted such a beneficial influence on the further course of treatment.

25. Henry L. Lennard and Arnold Bernstein, *The Anatomy of Psychotherapy* (New York: Columbia University Press, 1960).

"Persistently stereotyped communication from the patient," says Searles, "tends to bring from the therapist communications which, over a long period of time, become almost equally stereotyped." He emphasizes the importance of self-differentiation by the therapist in affecting primary fantasies of symbiotic relatedness:

"What the therapist does which assists the patient's differentiation often consists in his having the courage and honesty to *differ with* either the patient's repressed feelings or, often most valuably, with the social role into which the patient's sick behavior tends to fix (transfix might be a more apt word) the therapist. This may consist in his candid disagreement with some of the patient's strongly felt and long-voiced views, or in his flatly declining to try to feel "sympathy"—such as one would be conventionally expected to feel— in response to behaviour which seems, at first glance, to express the most pitiable suffering but which the therapist is convinced primarily expresses sadism on the patient's part. . . ."[26]

As I mentioned earlier, the borderline patient tends to create psychic crises, and the analyst's imposition of a monochromatic feeling tone on treatment creates too sharp a dichotomy between the patient's narcissistic defenses—his pattern of autistic internal gratification—and the overt analytic situation; the analyst appears to the patient too alien, too "normal," and too far removed from the patient's crisis psychology. The analytic process proves boring compared to his more exciting inner world of fantasy.

The myth that the borderline patient requires a constant atmosphere of calm neutrality derives in turn from a magical allegiance to the myth that calm induces calm. In the same connection, the analyst frequently attempts, through rational discourse, to dispel internal difficulties of the patient which cannot heed the call to reason. As early as 1932, Luria demonstrated experimentally that acute affect in human subjects "destroys the normal associative activity, throwing the subject back on the primitive psychological structures."[27] Failure of the associative process, senseless extrasignalizing responses, perseveration, tendency of the motor set toward immediate realization—all are characteristic of states of acute affect, the chronic underlying condition of the deeply disturbed patient. The analyst, however, on perceiving these chaotic symptoms, tends to refer the patient's state of disorganization to his own behavior and the analytic setting, whereas the latter only provides the *arena* in which the symptoms (hopefully) manifest themselves. Thus the

26. Searles, Integration and Differentiation in Schizophrenia, *loc. cit.*, p. 275.
27. Alexander R. Luria, *The Nature of Human Conflicts*, trans. W. H. Gantt (New York: Liveright, 1932), p. 53.

analyst is frequently led into fruitless attempts to alleviate the patient's mental confusion by intellectual interpretation and explanation of content—that is, he attempts to give help from above, so to speak, even though the confused mental state, as an inevitable expression of the patient's affect disorder, will only abate through transformations occurring from below, in the energy economy.

Generally speaking, the writer has found that the atmosphere most conducive to the treatment of the borderline patient, for the various reasons discussed above, is one in which the patient remains slightly mystified concerning the motivations underlying the analyst's *overdetermined* interventions, somewhat intrigued by the analytic process, and rather competitive with the analyst. To put it baldly, until classical analysis becomes feasible the patient should be obliged to run a bit to catch up with the analyst. I do not mean by this that the analyst should be one jump ahead of the patient with interpretations; far from it—he should often in a sense be one jump behind, for he can keep the patient in pursuit with silence and apparent stupidity as well as with words and a show of brilliance. But in a mildly competitive atmosphere in which the patient is also allowed to win—that is, sometimes find the analyst wrong or stupid—the psychic energy of the narcissistic constellation is drained off in the form of aggression and enlisted in the service of the ego for analytic exploration.

CHARLES T. SULLIVAN

Recent Developments in "Direct Psychoanalysis"

Direct psychoanalysis is largely the creation of John Rosen. Unfortunately his writing on the subject has been fragmentary, and in addition copyright problems made it unfeasible to include any of his papers. However, a collaborator of his at the Doylestown Foundation, social psychologist Charles T. Sullivan, has written an excellent summary of Rosen's work.

John Rosen's first publications appeared at a crucial time, when the emphasis in psychiatric circles was tending to the physical treatment of psychoses by such methods as insulin shock, and electroconvulsive therapy. He helped turn attention to the psychological treatment of schizophrenia, which has since been greatly expanded. He also anticipated the present trend to the use of ancillary personnel in the therapy of psychoses.

Rosen bases his technique on an essentially Freudian formulation of the patient's dynamics. However, in his technique he departs widely from Freud. Many of his interventions are so far removed from classical psychoanalytic methods that they seem more a new departure than a "modification" as Sullivan terms them.

The departure seems to be chiefly in the direction of increased activity and a kind of role-playing which is akin to Marie Coleman Nelson's paradigmatic technique (pp. 63ff.). Also, Rosen, unlike the classical psychoanalyst, does not hesitate to employ direct physical contact with the patient.[28]*

From *The Psychoanalytic Review*, Vol. 51, No. 3, Fall 1964.

* Superior numbers refer to the list of references at the end of this article.

Fortunately, Rosen has not hesitated to submit his technique to the most careful objective scrutiny to establish its validity as well as to chart its methodology.[1, 21]

INTRODUCTION

"DIRECT PSYCHOANALYSIS" is a method of understanding and treating psychotics. It is essentially Freudian, as the name implies, although it includes some substantial modifications of Freud's theories and techniques.

Until recently, direct psychoanalysis was not widely known. Its originator, John N. Rosen, had published only a brief account of it in *Direct Analysis: Selected Papers* (1953).[25] Other writers, when referring to Rosen's work, did not have the advantage of first-hand observation or discussion. Consequently, they tended to base their remarks either on Rosen's own fragmentary account, or else on rumors and "impressions" of what he did.[2, 13]

To remedy this situation, Rosen invited a group of psychoanalysts and psychiatrists to study his work at length. The resulting publications by Brody,[3] Scheflen,[34] English,[9] and others,[5] indicate that direct psychoanalysis has been developed and refined considerably since Rosen first described it. Rosen has also completed his own report of the recent developments in direct psychoanalysis.[26] This includes a comprehensive description of the procedures used in treatment, and a detailed statement of the Freudian theory on which the treatment is based.

The historical background of these reports can be sketched briefly. In his first paper, Rosen described direct psychoanalysis as "a method of resolving acute catatonic excitement."[28] Later, he suggested that it could also be used with psychotic individuals diagnosed as hebephrenic or paranoid. He maintained that psychotic symptoms could be viewed as the manifest content of an interminable nightmare, that these manifestations were intelligible in terms of Freud's dream-psychology, and that interpretations to the psychotic could bring about a rapid resolution of the psychosis.

Rosen also reported the results of having treated 37 psychotics during his psychiatric residency at Brooklyn State Hospital and at the New York Psychiatric Institute and Hospital. According to his report, all 37 cases were recovered from psychosis, and all of them were non-psychotic when the report was first published, in 1947.[32] Rosen's follow-up statement,[25] in 1952, said that 31 of these individuals were non-psychotic at that time, while the remaining 6 had relapsed into psychosis (pp. 95-96).

The controversy aroused by Rosen's statements was bitter.[19, 23] In some quarters it has not yet subsided entirely;[24] in others, it has given way to a high estimation of the man and his accomplishments.[17, 18, 21] Perhaps its most unfortunate aspect for psychiatry has been the *ad hominem* level of the discussion.[16, 39] Until recently, no critic has published an evaluation of direct psychoanalysis on its own merits, apart from the merits of Rosen as its best-known practitioner.[22, 37]

Rosen himself seems to have ignored this controversy and to have persisted in developing and demonstrating the use of direct psychoanalysis as a method of psychiatry. In 1953 he published a collection of papers on the subject.[25] In 1956 he went to Temple University Medical Center to participate in a long-term research project with the Department of Psychiatry.

This project, known as the Institute for Direct Analysis, has been supported by grants from the Rockefeller Brothers Fund, the Doris Duke Foundation, the Webster Benevolent Foundation, and other sponsors. Its purposes have been to observe and define the procedures used by Rosen in direct psychoanalysis and to determine if these procedures can be taught. In order to minimize debate as to whether the patients treated by Rosen were actually psychotic upon arrival and actually recovered upon discharge, there has been a separate Selection and Evaluation Committee consisting of Doctors Kenneth E. Appel, Robert S. Bookhammer, and Irving Lorge* (pp. 5-9).[34]

In this research, direct psychoanalysis has been subjected to the scrutiny of many observers. The principal ones have been Dr. O. Spurgeon English, chairman of Temple's Department of Psychiatry, and Doctors Bacon, Brody, Devereux, Hampe, Harrower, McKinnon, Scheflen, and Settlage. Some observers, such as Dr. English and his associates, have spent innumerable hours in this study; others have limited themselves to weekly meetings for demonstration and discussion; still others have been present only a few times. Observers have included psychiatrists, psychoanalysts, clinical psychologists, sociologists, members of the clergy and students in all of these professions.

From their publications and Rosen's recent statements the reader can obtain a clear, intelligible picture of direct psychoanalysis as it now stands.

---

* Now deceased.

The first part of this paper will summarize the theory of direct psychoanalysis; the second part will discuss its procedures of treatment.

THEORY OF DIRECT PSYCHOANALYSIS

Definition of "Psychosis"

Essentially, direct psychoanalysis is Freudian. Psychosis is viewed as a psychogenic disorder, differing mainly in degree from what is considered neurotic and what is considered normal. According to Rosen, psychosis itself is also a matter of degree. He uses the term "psychosis" to include a number of manic-depressive, paranoid, hebephrenic, and catatonic states which other psychiatrists distinguish as separate kinds of psychogenic reactions, or as symptoms of separate kinds of disease entities.[26]

Phases of Psychosis

In *Direct Psychoanalytic Psychiatry*,[26] Rosen differentiates eight phases of psychosis, in a spectrum of severity from "least psychotic" to "most psychotic." He maintains that a psychotic individual can be observed to move from one of these phases to another, in either an upward or a downward direction. Certain "sticky cases" may remain in one phase for months or years, while other individuals may move from phase to phase fairly rapidly. As a psychotic recovers, he is said to move upward on this spectrum or scale (pp. 53-57).

Phases of Regression

Following Freud's idea[10] that psychosis is a regression to the pregenital stages of psychosexual development (pp. 428-29), Rosen says that his eight phases of psychosis can be viewed as levels of regression, from "late anal" (least psychotic) to "early oral" (most psychotic). As a Freudian, Rosen emphasizes that these levels of regression, or phases of psychosis, are not supposed to be clear-cut (p. 30).[11] Any psychotic individual in any of the phases might manifest oral, anal, or even genital characteristics. In other words, his behavior may not always be typical of the phase in which he seems to be located.[26]

The Purpose of Regression

According to direct psychoanalytic theory,[26] the psychotic has re-turned to his pregenital experience through regression, in order to "seek the mother he knew" (pp. 10-24). Each of the phases of psychosis is viewed as a re-experiencing of some aspect of the original infant-mother relationship. Originally, the individual suffered from the vicissitudes of "mother," i.e., his early maternal environment. The superego he acquired from this early maternal environment during the first year or two of life has never been integrated comfortably with his ego. It has been harsh, "toxic," impossible to satisfy, "indigestible." As an internalized representation of "mother" it is indispensable; and yet, representing a malevolent kind of "mother," it is deadly.[29]

When the ego ultimately gives up its struggle with this harsh superego and seeks relief in regression, Rosen describes it as moving out of the frying-pan into the fire.[29] The original relationship with the early maternal environment, no longer amnestic, is more painful than its counterpart, the ego-superego conflict, has been. The ego, however, cannot easily reverse its decision and terminate the regression (i.e., psychosis) at will. It can only try out the various modes of action which Rosen has attempted to distinguish in his eight phases of psychosis.[29]

The Early Maternal Environment

An early paper of Rosen's stated that a psychotic "is always one who is reared by a woman who suffers from a perversion of the maternal instinct."[30] This assertion, based upon the manifest and latent content of psychosis, is not supported by observation of mothers and infants. It has since been qualified. Rosen now speaks of the "early maternal environment," rather than of the actual mother only, as the source of psychosis in the child. He seems to have recognized that his understanding and treatment of psychotics does not require any condemnation of mothers and mothering. Direct psychoanalysis can address the psychotic as if the mother's "maternal instinct" had been "perverted." The reality of such an instinct and the possibility of its perversion are peripheral questions when the psychotic's current dilemma is central.[29]

The Superego as "Mother"

Psychodynamically, then, psychosis is understood in terms of regressive ego-superego conflict at the oral and anal levels. Here the theory of direct psychoanalysis has departed from Freud's theory of the origins and nature of the superego. Freud[11] described the super-ego as the "heir to the Oedipus complex," coming into existence during the child's fifth or sixth year, and serving as a psychical embodiment of parental and other "moral" influence (p. 121). Rosen[26] describes the superego as the psychical embodiment of the early maternal environment, coming into existence soon after birth, and acquiring its important characteristics during the child's first and second years[38] (p. 20).

According to Rosen,[26] the "normal" child gradually acquires a reasonable and comfortable superego through a process of imi-tation-incorporation-identification. The "deviant" child who will be neurotic if not psychotic in later life starts off by acquiring an unreasonable and uncomfortable superego. The "mother" he imi-tates, tries to incorporate, and tries to identify with is "indispensable but deadly." When he becomes psychotic such an individual may refer to this paradoxical "mother"/superego with such metaphors as "poisoned milk" or "a tree growing in his stomach and ripping him with its roots." Or he may refer to it with slips of the tongue, such as "murder-in-law." Or he may refer to it nonverbally by refusing to eat, or vomiting his meals, or overturning the breakfast table, or assaulting the person who prepares or serves his meals (pp. 101-103).

"Mother" in the Manifest Content of Psychosis

Rosen has gradually come to understand more and more of the psychotic's manifest content in terms of this essential ego-superego or infant-"mother" relationship. He has moved from the more ob-vious clues, such as the paranoid fear of being poisoned, to less obvious ones, such as the depressed psychotic's mournful appearance, which he views as a reaction to the loss of a loved object, i.e., "mother," the superego, the "breast." A large part of *Direct Psycho-analytic Psychiatry* is devoted to the understanding of specific ex-amples of psychotic behavior, such as "rapid talk" or "silly mood" or "submissive reaction," in terms of the general theoretical orienta-tion of direct psychoanalysis. In every instance, for some sixty items of behavior, the manifest content is related to the latent content of the individual's present phase of psychosis.

"Mother" in the Latent Content of Psychosis

For each of the eight phases of psychosis which he discerns, Rosen[26] has constructed a kind of Freudian motif to characterize its latent content: what the psychotic is unconsciously feeling and thinking. Each "motif" reflects some variation of the basic proposition that the psychotic is re-experiencing his oral and anal relationship with his early maternal environment. To enumerate these motifs descriptively, in order from the least psychotic phase to the most psychotic phase of psychosis:

1. "I am dreaming that I am mourning because I have lost the penis, feces, and breast."
Cf. manic-depressive reaction, depressed type.

2. "I am dreaming that I am very much alive because I am making-believe that I am united with the penis, feces, and breast."
Cf. manic-depressive reaction, manic type.

3. "I am dreaming that I am being harmed, or threatened with harm; therefore my problem is external, not internal."
Cf. schizophrenic reaction, paranoid type.

4. "I am dreaming that I know what to do because I have figured out my special importance in the world."
Cf. schizophrenic reaction, paranoid type.

5. I am dreaming that I am a silly baby, laughing and playing with my fingers and toes because I am trying to make-believe that I am the whole world."
Cf. schizophrenic reaction, hebephrenic type.

6. "I am dreaming that I am almost frightened stiff because mother refuses to love me unless I die."
Cf. schizophrenic reaction, catatonic type.

7. "I am dreaming that I am terrified of mother and screaming for her because she is both indispensable and deadly."
Cf. schizophrenic reaction, catatonic type.

8. "I am dreaming that I am frightened stiff because I must be dead to please mother."
Cf. schizophrenic reaction, catatonic type.

The first part of each motif attempts to characterize the outward appearance and behavior of the individual in that phase of psychosis, and to emphasize its dream-like quality. Rosen often speaks of psychosis as being an "interminable nightmare." The second part of each motif attempts to characterize the reasoning of the unconscious portion of the ego, in relation to the superego (pp. 54; 99).

Talking to the Psychotic

Rosen uses this series of motifs, in treatment and in teaching, as guides to what phase of psychosis an individual has reached.

When he addresses a psychotic, Rosen customarily use the kind of language in which the motifs are expressed. For instance, to a "depressed" psychotic, he might say: "You are sad because your mother [i.e., superego] has deserted you [i.e., ego]." He rarely uses psychiatric language—such as "hebephrenic"—or psychoanalytic language—such as "superego"—when talking to a psychotic. Even with a neurotic or with a neo-neurotic, (i.e., a recovered psychotic), Rosen seems to prefer the simpler, more direct language of the motifs.[29]

Being a "Foster Parent" to the Psychotic

Direct psychoanalysis of the psychotic, based on its understanding of psychosis, puts the psychiatrist in the role of foster parent.[35] He must act like a "good mother" to compensate for the malevolence of the original "bad mother" (i.e., superego). According to Rosen, the psychiatrist takes upon himself the responsibility of accepting the neo-infantile psychotic as one would accept a real infant, and of bringing up this neo-infant all over again. Earlier,[25] Rosen seemed to be saying that the psychiatrist must actually love the psychotic in order to accomplish this up-bringing (pp. 8-9). More recently,[29] Rosen has said that the psychiatrist need only *act like* a loving foster parent; often the psychotic will react to the statement "I love you" as a nonpsychotic might react to the real thing.

This point was only clarified by intensive interrogation of Rosen at the Institute for Direct Analysis, in seminars conducted by Dr. English.[9, 33] An equally important point was clarified earlier, during seminars conducted by Dr. Brody:[3] being a good foster parent does not preclude stern discipline when the situation calls for it, and does not preclude firm control of the treatment situation at all times (p. 60). Rosen has recently[26] revised his formulation of the governing principle of direct psychoanalysis to include these additional aspects of the psychiatrist's role (pp. 60-63).

Resolution of the Psychosis

The foster-parent approach,[26] to be described more fully later in this paper, includes the establishment of a separate treatment unit and staff as a foster home for each psychotic individual (pp. 64-81). According to Rosen, it also includes treatment beyond the resolution of the psychosis, into the postpsychotic phase which Rosen calls the "neo-neurosis." He maintains that the psychotic was neurotic before becoming psychotic, and that he returns to a modified form of this neurosis when the psychosis is resolved.[29]

Significance of the Neo-neurosis

It appears that Rosen's continuing concern with the neo-neurosis and its treatment has been ignored in published criticisms of direct psychoanalysis. Early critics, such as Fromm-Reichmann,[14] Eissler,[8] and Bychowski,[4] appear to have taken Rosen to task for allegedly neglecting the follow-up treatment of recovered psychotics. Observers who actually studied Rosen's procedures first-hand at the Institute for Direct Analysis imply that the treatment ends when the individual is allowed to go home from the treatment unit.[6, 34] And yet Rosen has been raising questions as to the merits of conventional psychoanalysis versus a modified form of analysis for the individual who has reached the neo-neurotic level of recovery, in publications as early as in his second paper (1947).[32] Once again, the more spectacular aspects of direct psychoanalysis appear to have taken attention away from aspects which are less spectacular but equally consequential.[14]

DIRECT PSYCHOANALYTIC TREATMENT

Setting for Treatment

Direct psychoanalysis of the psychotic is based upon the foster-parent concept described above. As mentioned, the setting for treatment is a separate unit for each psychotic: a small house or apartment staffed by three or four assistants who live on the premises like members of a foster family (pp. 16-18).[34] These assistants are carefully chosen for their responsibility and their responsiveness to the psychotic. Some are actually former psychotics themselves; others are students or graduates in medicine, psychology, and related fields. According to Rosen, a combination of former psychotics and intelligent students is ideal for the staffing of a treatment unit. The first group has its unique unconscious understanding of psychosis, while the second can provide supplementary conscious understanding.[26, 27]

Functions of the Assistants

The assistants are charged with caring for and protecting the psychotic at all times. This includes attention not only to his physical well-being, but also to the psychical needs expressed in his verbal or nonverbal manifest content. Prior to a treatment session the assistants make note of items which may be useful to the direct psychoanalyst. Following the session they attempt to keep the psychotic thinking about what transpired during the course of it.

Observers at Treatment Session

The treatment session is a face-to-face encounter between the psychiatrist and a psychotic. The assistants are usually required to be present in the background and there may also be an audience of students and other observers (e.g., during the research sessions at the Institute for Direct Analysis).[1]

Rosen maintains that the interaction of psychiatrist and psychotic is not materially affected by the presence of an audience even when it exceeds fifty or a hundred persons. He says that the psychotic's awareness is usually focused on an hallucinatory "internal environment"; occasionally it is focused on the psychiatrist; almost never on others who may be present.[29]

The Treatment Session

Manifestly, the treatment session is a conversation between psychiatrist and psychotic.[15] In certain phases of psychosis the psychotic is more likely to take the lead, e.g., in Rosen's Phase 2 (cf. manic-depressive reaction, manic type). The psychotic's lead is usually some fragment of his dreamlike manifest content. The psychiatrist's response might be a question, an interpretation, a simple yes or no, a gesture, or a demonstration of some emotional reaction such as anger or affection.

In certain other phases, e.g., Rosen's Phase 6 (cf. almost mute catatonic type), the psychiatrist is more likely to take the lead. Often he delivers a brief monologue which explains or interprets some aspect of the psychotic's manifest or latent content. The psychotic's response to this may be admission, denial, silence, an outburst of rage, assaultive behavior, or any of the innumerable other items of manifest content.

Rosen's *Direct Psychoanalytic Psychiatry* gives many examples of the exchanges which occur with individuals in various phases of psychosis.

Techniques of Direct Psychoanalysis

Scheflen[34] (pp. 70-105) and English[9] have published lists of "techniques" they observed in use by Rosen during direct psychoanalysis.

Such codification can be misleading, for while it seems a necessary step in the definition of direct psychoanalysis for research purposes, it does not accurately represent the spontaneity and the immediate, rapid give-and-take of the typical session.[36]

Rosen states[26] that he does not consciously use a series of techniques in treatment any more than a parent consciously uses techniques with a child. Instead, Rosen says, he does whatever seems therapeutically appropriate in response to the behavior of the psychotic. This always includes gestures, bodily movements, facial expressions and other actions which it would be ludicrous to classify as techniques (pp. 103-206).

A different way to formulate Rosen's mode of treatment would be to reduce the various items of the psychotic's manifest content to their lowest common denominators: the motifs which Rosen has constructed to describe eight phases of psychosis, and the basic understanding of "mother" which underlies these motifs. Often Rosen seems to be leading his dialogue with the psychotic back to the subject of "mother" and "mothering." This subject has two aspects: the "bad mother" (superego) and the "good mother" (direct psychoanalyst). During a long series of treatment sessions with a given psychotic Rosen appears to refer more frequently to "mothering" than to any other topic.[29]

Reference to the Phases of Psychosis

Another important feature of the treatment as it is practiced and described by Rosen is the psychiatrist's orientation in terms of phases of psychosis. Rosen's *Direct Psychoanalytic Psychiatry*, when it discusses treatment, is constantly referring to these phases and their motifs.

Critical publications on direct psychoanalysis have given scant attention to this feature of treatment.[1, 7] They seem to refer to "the psychotic" or "the schizophrenic" without differentiation.[20, 34] This is in contrast to the specificity of Rosen's descriptions of treatment.

Psychotic Transference

It appears that in the typical treatment session the direct psychoanalyst tries to weaken the influence of the "bad mother" (superego) and to introduce his own influence as the "good mother." Eventually, through the processes described as imitation-incorporation-identification, the psychiatrist may be "taken in" by the psychotic, to become a benevolent, reasonable component of the superego.

The basis of this "taking in" is the psychotic's transference, as defined by Rosen. Freud,[10] we recall, maintained (p. 455) that there is no transference in psychosis (i.e., the narcissistic neuroses). Rosen maintains that transference is an essential feature of psychosis. He defines transference to mean the tendency to seek and find "the mother you knew" in persons or objects which are palpably not that mother.

For Rosen, then, the therapeutic problem is not the absence of transference but the overabundance of it. The psychiatrist must find ways of focusing this psychotic transference upon himself instead of letting it diffuse in all directions.[31]

This seems to be Rosen's explanation for his frequent and controversial references to himself as "mother," "father," "God," "the boss," and other figures, when he is addressing a psychotic. Rosen makes such claims to the psychotic in order to get the psychotic's attention and interest. The psychiatrist pretends to have the maternal omnipotence and omniscience which the psychotic has been attributing, in transference, to voices, to bystanders, to inanimate objects, and to diverse other real or imaginary parts of the environment.[29]

Focusing the transference is evidently a gradual and subtle process. At times, the direct psychoanalyst is attacking the malevolent "mother" (superego); at other times, he takes the part of a "good mother." He describes his interest in the psychotic's physical well-being, in his physical comfort, and in his recovery from the nightmare of psychosis (pp. 39-40).[25]

Transference Interpretations

One of the few techniques specifically named and described by Rosen is the transference interpretation. Usually, this is a brief statement made to the psychotic at some critical point of the treatment session.

For example, a psychotic in Rosen's Phase 7 (cf. acute catatonic excitement) cries out—not necessarily to the psychiatrist—"Please don't cut my balls off, Pa." The transference interpretation of this manifest content might be: "I'm your father, and I have no intention of punishing you. I give you permission to have those thoughts about Mother."[25]

Or a psychotic in Rosen's Phase 1 (cf. depressed) says: "God will punish me for what I've done." The transference interpretation might be: "I am the one who does the punishing around here. If I decide that you have done no wrong, then there will be no punishment."

In each instance it appears that the direct psychoanalyst is claiming for himself the power to decide right or wrong and the power to punish or forgive. He denies the existence of any authority or powers greater than those he claims for himself.[29]

Direct Interpretations

The direct interpretation appears to be a more general version of the transference interpretation. It does not refer explicitly to the psychiatrist as an omnipotent, omniscient or parental figure. Evidently it is used when the psychotic's manifest content does not provide an appropriate cue for a transference interpretation.

For example, the psychotic in Rosen's Phase 3 (cf. paranoid) complains that his wicked bankers are preventing him from recovering a million dollars he has deposited in the bank. There is no factual basis to this complaint. After it has been elaborated and repeated several times the direct interpretation might be: "If you had a million dollars, then do you think your mother would love you?"[26]

Purposes of Interpretations

The purpose of the transference interpretation, as suggested already, is to focus the psychotic's transference upon the direct psychoanalyst and to intensify it so that the direct psychoanalyst will be "taken in" by the psychotic. Incidentally, this kind of interpretation also helps to make conscious for the psychotic an idea or feeling which has been unconscious.

This incidental purpose of the transference interpretations seems to be the primary purpose of direct interpretations. They help to make the latent content of psychosis more manifest to the psychotic. Rosen maintains[26] that it is extremely important for the psychiatrist to keep showing the psychotic that he understands him. The psychiatrist tries to encourage insight by impressing specific points of understanding upon the psychotic (p. 76).

The Psychotic's Reaction to Interpretations

Depending upon the phase of psychosis in which he seems to be located an individual's reaction to a particular transference interpretation or direct interpretation may be immediate or delayed, conspicuous or imperceptible. Optimally there is an immediate, obvious response; the psychotic may utter an impassioned denial, or he may burst into tears, or he may try to run away from the psychiatrist. At other times the psychotic may manifest no reaction to what has been said.[26]

The question of harmful or premature interpretations has been raised by critics of direct psychoanalysis[12] and more recently by Rosen himself.[26] He says that a psychotic, in any phase of psychosis, is always ready for a correct interpretation. And he maintains that an incorrect interpretation will do no harm; it will simply be ignored. He finds no evidence to support the claim that ill-advised interpretations to a psychotic will undo the good already done by the psychiatrist. The more explosive a psychotic's reaction, says Rosen, the better. This indicates that the psychotic has been paying attention to the psychiatrist and that the psychiatrist has for the moment made contact wth him; he has penetrated the internal environment of the psychosis (pp. 237-39).

The psychotic's long-term reaction to the direct psychoanalyst, in successful treatment, is supposed to be eventual incorporation of him as a benevolent component of the superego. This is followed by identification with him as a useful model for mature behavior.

The Course of Treatment

Resolution of psychosis by direct psychoanalysis may be achieved rapidly in a matter of weeks, or more slowly in a year or more, or it may not be achieved. Rosen's early report on 37 cases suggests an average treatment period of about four months.[32]

When he arrived at Temple University in 1956 Rosen seemed to feel that a psychotic could be recovered in even less than four months, granted "optimum conditions." This meant that the individual would begin treatment as soon as possible after becoming psychotic for the first time, with no exposure to institutional handling and institutional methods of treatment. Although no official report of treatment results has been published by the Institute for Direct Analysis, Rosen himself is of the opinion that his idea about optimum conditions has been proved sound.[29]

It is important to note that treatment does not terminate with the resolution of the psychosis. Therefore, figures referring strictly to the resolution of psychosis tend to be misleading. Follow-up treatment in direct psychoanalysis may go on for a year or longer.[29]

Follow-up Treatment

As explained above, the theory of direct psychoanalysis maintains that the individual whose psychosis is resolved moves into a neo-neurotic phase before he reaches an acceptably "normal" level of maturation.

Resolution of psychosis, according to Rosen, means identification with the psychiatrist following incorporation of him as a new, benevolent superego-component. Progress toward this goal is estimated from what the individual says and does and how he says and does it.

The neo-neurosis is regarded as the counterpart of a prepsychotic neurosis which may or may not have been conspicuous. As in any neurosis, the essential problem—from a Freudian point of view—is the Oedipus complex. Rosen[26] has his own definition of this complex (pp. 2-23). He maintains that the individual must develop a satisfactory relationship with Father, and that this can only be accomplished if he has identified successfully with Mother. The boy must learn to identify with Father; the girl must learn to imitate certain aspects of Mother's attitude toward Father. In neither case, according to Rosen, does the child actually wish to engage in sexual intercourse with the parent of the opposite sex.

Direct psychoanalytic theory holds that the individual whose psychosis has been resolved has successfully identified with "mother" (i.e., the psychiatrist taking the maternal role). The next step is to achieve a satisfactory relationship with "father"; as before, the psychiatrist takes the appropriate parental role.

Treatment sessions for the neo-neurotic are ordinarily held in private, although in the Temple research project they were sometimes conducted as demonstrations before professional audiences.

Sessions may be scheduled regularly on a weekly or biweekly basis, or they may be scheduled more flexibly, according to need. Outwardly they resemble the treatment sessions with psychotics; there is a face-to-face encounter between psychiatrist and neoneurotic, with conversation its most conspicuous feature.

The verbal content of these sessions with the neo-neurotic may include occasional direct interpretations but never a transference interpretation, since the transference is presumed to have subsided with the resolution of psychosis. Rosen is never more or less than "Dr. Rosen" to the individual. His tone and his attitude are cordial, positive, and paternal. What he says is usually a comment on what the individual has reported to him; it may be approval, disapproval, advice, warning, or merely friendly pleasantry. The subject matter usually embraces the individual's current circumstances, activities, and problems. Occasional references to psychotic or prepsychotic experience may be made by the psychiatrist to illustrate some point he is making about the present.[29]

Resolution of the neo-neurosis, like resolution of the psychosis, seems to be a gradual and subtle process, with only approximate behavioral criteria serving as guides for estimates of progress.

Long-Term Results of the Treatment

Rosen has not published a formal report of the results of his treatment since his addendum (1952) to the early paper on 37 cases. Other practitioners of direct psychoanalysis, perhaps to avoid controversy, have not made their results known. In recent years the only published estimate is the one by English[9] of Rosen's first twelve cases in the research project at Temple, "all but two of whom have recovered from the psychosis sufficiently to return to the community." One individual had committed suicide during a trial visit home and another was recovered from psychosis after more than two years of treatment.

It may be that Rosen, like other psychiatrists, is trying to stay out of the "batting average" competitions, such as the one which flourished in this country during the nineteenth century. In any event, the Selection and Evaluation Committee affiliated with Temple's Institute for Direct Analysis will sooner or later make its determination known. [They did so in November 1966.]

SUMMARY

This paper has attempted to present a clear, intelligible picture of the direct psychoanalytic approach to the psychotic. It has emphasized the recent developments in this approach, as described by John N. Rosen, the originator of direct psychoanalysis, and by observers of his work at Temple University Medical Center.

The first part dealt with the theory of direct psychoanalysis, as formulated by Rosen in his *Direct Psychoanalytic Psychiatry*. The theory maintains that psychosis consists of eight overlapping phases, which can be correlated with Freud's concept of regression and with the diagnostic classifications of descriptive psychiatry. It maintains further that the psychotic has regressed to the pregenital stages, in order to "seek the mother he knew" in his early maternal environment, who was indispensable but deadly to him.

The second part dealt with direct psychoanalytic treatment,

which has been described by Rosen and by Brody, Scheflen, and English. The treatment is based upon a "foster parent" concept, which holds that the psychiatrist must bring up the regressed, neo-infantile psychotic, first to a "neo-neurotic" level and later to maturity. The psychotic's extensive and continuous transference provides a means of access for the psychiatrist, who offers himself for "imitation-incorporation-identification" by· the psychotic. Eventually, the psychotic's "malevolent" superego is modified by the addition of "benevolent" components derived from the personality of the psychiatrist.

REFERENCES

1. Bacon, C. L., The Rosen Treatment of the Psychosis from the Viewpoint of Identity. In O. S. English et al., Direct Analysis and Schizophrenia (New York: Grune & Stratton, 1961), pp. 59-68.
2. Balint, M., Changing Therapeutical Aims and Techniques in Psycho-Analysis, International Journal of Psycho-Analysis, 31:117-24,1950.
3. Brody, M., Observations on "Direct Analysis" (New York: Vantage Press, 1959).
4. Bychowski, G., Review of J. N. Rosen, Direct Analysis: Selected Papers, Psychoanalytic Quarterly, 23:114-16, 1954.
5. Devereux, G., The Nature of the Bizarre, Journal of the Hillside Hospital, 8:266-67, 1959.
6. Devereux, G., A Psychoanalytic Scrutiny of Certain Techniques of Direct Analysis, Psychoanalysis and the Psychoanalytic Review, 46:45-49, 1959.
7. Devereux, G., Schizophrenia versus Neurosis and the Use of "Premature" Deep Interpretations as Confrontations in Classical Analysis and in Direct Analysis, Psychiatric Quarterly, 34:710-21, 1960.
8. Eissler, K. R., Remarks on the Psychoanalysis of Schizophrenia. In E. B. Brody and F. C. Redlich, eds., Psychotherapy with Schizophrenics (New York: International Universities Press, 1952), pp. 134, 143.
9. English, O. S., Clinical Observations on Direct Analysis. Comprehensive Psychiatry, 1:156-61, 1960.
10. Freud, S., A General Introduction to Psychoanalysis (New York: Washington Square Press, 1960).
11. Freud, S., An Outline of Psychoanalysis (New York: Norton, 1949).
12. Fromm-Reichmann, F., Principles of Intensive Psychotherapy (Chicago: University of Chicago Press, 1950), pp. 95-96.
13. Fromm-Reichmann, F., Psychoanalysis and Psychiatry (Chicago: University of Chicago Press, 1959).
14. Fromm-Reichmann, F., Some Aspects of Psychoanalytic Psychotherapy with Schizophrenics. In E. B. Brody and F. C. Redlich, eds., op. cit., p. 100.
15. Hampe, W. W., Some Observations on John Rosen Treating Psychotic People. In O. S. English et al., op. cit., pp. 44-45.
16. Horwitz, W. A., Polatin, P., Kolb, L. C., and Hoch, P. H., A Study of Cases of Schizophrenia Treated by "Direct Analysis," American Journal of Psychiatry, 114:780-83, 1958.
17. Kubie, L. S., Preface to A. E. Scheflen, A Psychotherapy of Schizophrenia: Direct Analysis (Springfield: Charles C Thomas, 1961).

18. Lewin, B. D., Review of A. E. Scheflen, *A Psychotherapy of Schizophrenia: Direct Analysis, Journal of Nervous and Mental Disease*, 134:578-81, 1962.
19. Lipton, S. D., Some Comparisons of Psychotherapeutic Methods in Schizophrenia, *Psychiatric Quarterly*, 23:705-11, 1949.
20. Mann, J., Review of J. N. Rosen, *Direct Analysis: Selected Papers, American Journal of Orthopsychiatry*, 24:434-35, 1954.
21. McKinnon, K. M., A Clinical Evaluation of the Method of Direct Analysis in the Treatment of Psychosis, *Journal of Clinical Psychology*, 15:80-96, 1959.
22. Pathman, J. H., Juggernaut Therapy: Review of M. Brody, *Observations on "Direct Analysis," Contemporary Psychology*, 5:344-1960.
23. Redlich, F. C., The Concept of Schizophrenia and Its Implications for Therapy, in E. B. Brody and F. C. Redlich, eds., *op. cit.*
24. Rogers, C. R., A Theory of Psychotherapy with Schizophrenics and a Proposal for Its Empirical Investigation, in J. G. Dawson *et al.*, eds., *Psychotherapy with Schizophrenics* (Baton Rouge: Louisiana State University Press, 1961).
25. Rosen, J. N., *Direct Analysis: Selected Papers* (New York: Grune & Stratton, 1953).
26. Rosen, J. N., *Direct Psychoanalytic Psychiatry* (New York: Grune & Stratton, 1962).
27. Rosen, J. N., Management of the Patient, in C. Whitaker, ed., *Psychotherapy of Chronic Schizophrenic Patients* (Boston: Little, Brown, 1958), pp. 184-96.
28. Rosen, J. N., A Method of Resolving Acute Catatonic Excitement, *Psychiatric Quarterly*, 20:183-89, 1946.
29. Rosen, J. N., Unpublished lectures and personal communications.
30. Rosen, J. N., The Perverse Mother, in *Direct Analysis: Selected Papers, op. cit.*, pp. 97-105.
31. Rosen, J. N., Transference, *International Journal of Psychotherapy, Psychosomatics, and Special Education*, 2:300-14, 1954.
32. Rosen, J. N., The Treatment of Schizophrenic Psychosis by Direct Analytic Therapy, *Psychiatric Quarterly*, 21:117-31, 1947.
33. Scheflen, A. E., Fostering Introjection as a Psychotherapeutic Technique in Schizophrenia, in J. G. Dawson *et al.*, eds., *op. cit.*, pp. 79-97.
34. Scheflen, A. E., *A Psychotherapy of Schizophrenia: Direct Analysis* (Springfield, Ill.: Charles C Thomas, 1961).
35. Searles, H. F., Dependency Processes in the Psychotherapy of Schizophrenia, *Journal of the American Psychoanalytic Association*, 3:126-48, 1955.
36. Settlage, C. F., On the Psychodynamics of Direct Analysis, in O. S. English *et al.*, *op. cit.*, pp. 77-98.
37. Stone, L., Two Avenues of Approach to the Schizophrenic Patient, *Journal of the American Psychoanalytic Association*, 3:19-66, 1955.
38. Wexler, M., The Structural Problem in Schizophrenia: The Role of the Internal Object, in E. B. Brody and F. C. Redlich, eds., *op. cit.*, pp. 179-200.
39. Wexler, M., A Temple for Rosen? Review of A. E. Scheflen, *A Psychotherapy of Schizophrenia: Direct Analysis*, and O. S. English *et al.*, *Direct Analysis and Schizophrenia*, in *Contemporary Psychology*, 7:171-72, 1962.

GOODHUE LIVINGSTON

The Role of Activity in the Treatment of Schizoid or Schizophrenic Patients

Livingston defines activity in a precise but rather special way as the therapist treating the patients' needs as real. Using that definition, he sees Freud as being opposed to "activity" despite what Freud had to say in the paper included in this volume.

Livingston's search for the underlying principle uniting the work of Rosen, Fromm-Reichmann, Sechehaye, Federn, and others is a valuable contribution to the understanding of an important dynamic in psychotherapy.

Livingston's chapter is a fitting sequel to the discussion of John Rosen's Direct Analysis (pp. 90ff.). Direct Analysis is seen as one of the techniques for establishing contact with the psychotic patient.

Livingston also demonstrates, from the literature, the benefits of gratification. Like all those interested in active therapy, he accurately shows Ferenczi's seminal contribution (pp. 10ff.).

IN THE CONTEXT of this paper, "activity" refers to those moments in therapy when the therapist treats some needs of the patient as real (*i.e.*, not transference) and either frustrates or gratifies them. For example, a patient asks you for a cigarette and you either hand him one or tell him that you do not wish him to smoke. Or a patient comes in wearing a new dress and asks if it is becoming. You admire the dress. A patient cries and is ashamed. You tell the patient

From *Psychotherapy*, Vol. 1, No. 4, Fall 1964. This paper was delivered at the Fourth Annual Mental Health Research Meeting held at the University of Washington on October 18, 1963, under the title *Activity Therapy Revisited*.

that situations sometimes demand tears. A patient ashamedly explains that he cannot refrain from masturbating. You say that in your experience almost everyone, including those who condemn it, has done it. You gratify or frustrate a need accepted by you and by the patient as real.

I

The feelings which led me to write this paper developed during my treatment of schizoid or schizophrenic patients. Such patients always cause something of a strain. Their great sensitivity, their tendency to misunderstand or reinterpret what is said to them, can cause them to lose contact with reality on short notice and can get them into serious trouble. In a scene in the movie *David and Lisa*, David turns his attention away from the schizophrenic Lisa and tells her, in effect, that he is busy. Unlike a neurotic who might be angry or try to clarify the situation with a question, Lisa loses contact with reality, wanders confusedly around town, and ends up stealing a copy of *Holiday* magazine, which to her symbolizes "travel to a warm climate." Frustrated by the storekeeper, who takes the magazine from her, she continues her flight until she ends up on the steps of a museum which contains the statue of a mother, onto whose lap she wants to crawl.

I feel this movie illustrates well how schizoid or schizophrenic persons react to frustration, real or assumed. They cannot express their feelings in words, or take up their troubles with the person who frustrates them. They lose contact with reality and act symbolically. One of my patients explained to me that words can be used to deceive; it is more meaningful to pantomime. Paul Federn[4]* recounts how a schizophrenic patient of his committed suicide as a result of his being late to her hour (p. 146). A neurotic would have complained, not acted. A patient of mine, in the early days of her therapy, would become confused if I kept silent. So, for a while, I found myself telling her my constructions of what she was feeling and had felt as a child, not so much because I was too sure of the interpretations, but because the sound of my voice was a symbolic gratification that reassured her.

Although at times I have gratified patients, congratulated them, joked with them, I have also frustrated them or at least taken a firm stand on acting out or psychotic behavior. (My stand was essentially that I was against it.) For instance, in one case I forbade

* Superior numbers refer to the list of references at the end of this article.

a patient to mail any letters until I had seen them and discussed their contents with him. In the case of a suicidal patient, I explained that suicidal ideas were not to be put into practice, that they were most likely connected with misunderstandings between her and me, and that the place to discuss such feelings was in my office.

If I conceptualized what I was doing, I kept in mind that while my main role was to understand the patient, from day to day I acted like the guardian of a mixed-up child—sometimes encouraging, sometimes prohibiting, occasionally interpreting. I kept certain general principles in the back of my mind, but felt free to do what seemed natural to me. If the patient was in obvious torture, I did what I could to relieve the pain. If the patient acted unwisely, I told him so and urged him to consider his motives. I was extremely active and manipulative on occasion.

I worried about my own motives, sometimes wondering if explaining to a patient how to balance her checkbook was really part of therapy. (I concluded that in that particular instance it was.) I also went to the library and began to study how others had dealt with the problem of when to be active and how.

II

As I began reading intensively, concentrating especially on the work of Rosen, Sechehaye, Fromm-Reichmann, and three journal articles by Boyer, Karon, and Haley, I had a "first impression" similar to that of David Rosenthal[13] who recently reviewed a collection of writings on schizophrenia:

"It is as though one had asked a group of distinguished painters or sculptors to represent their perception of a common entity, in this case, schizophrenia . . . and each had done so in his own unique way, retrospectively developing a rationale of the phenomenon represented to maintain perceptual and conceptual consistency" (p. 377).

How are we to reconcile such techniques as (1) John Rosen[11] forcing, with the aid of attendants, a psychotic to kneel before him and acknowledge that he, Rosen, was God and not the patient; (2) Sechehaye[14, 15] and Rosen himself (on other occasions) tenderly feeding the patient; (3) Bryce Boyer[3] using a standard psychoanalytic couch, free associations and all, with a number of schizophrenic patients; (4) Paul Federn[4] advising against free associations or the standard psychoanalytic technique; (5) Frieda Fromm-Reichmann[6, 7] warning against "encouragement of hostile expression in the schizophrenic"; (6) Karon[10] writing, "The patient is especially encouraged to hate, on the assumption that if you cannot hate, you cannot allow any feeling" (p. 27).

Actually, my second impression was more hopeful. In a very interesting article Jay Haley[8] suggests that the prize characteristic of the schizophrenic is his inability to relate. As Haley sees it, one can relate to others in two classic ways. One can enter into authoritarian relationships, telling others what to do or being told by them. Or one can relate in an equalitarian relationship as a co-worker. Fundamentally, the schizophrenic fears to relate and refuses to play ball. He will neither do as he is told, or direct what someone else does, nor share responsibility with a co-worker. Haley very ingeniously points out that the seeming discrepancies among the various therapists cover up an essential area of agreement: *They all use forcing techniques which demand that the patient relate.* As soon as a relationship is achieved, by whatever means, half the battle is won.

There exists a "fifth column" within the psychosis. Making a deal with the sane ego is the first objective, after which one can work together with the patient to observe and analyze the shambles. The first and never-to-be-forgotten rule for the therapist is never to betray this inner ally. Mistakes of all kinds will be forgiven, but not letting down the "friend within the psychosis."

Let me now give examples of how three very dissimilar therapists, Rosen, Boyer, and Sechehaye, treat this initial problem of contact. Boyer starts his therapy by imposing strict rules relative to procedure, hours, and payment which are addressed to the sensible ego. He explains how he works and how feelings should be handled. He speaks of how the material in analysis is confidential, and talks to the reasonable aspect of the ego. He implies that the patient may satisfy his needs but that he will be taught socially acceptable ways of so doing. He "assumes" that the patient is sane.

Rosen[12] postulates "a part of the psyche which remains in touch with the external reality at all times" (p. 58). As he sees it, psychotics who wish to be the next Pope must buy tickets to Rome, not Las Vegas. They walk through doors, not walls. Assuming such reasonableness, therapy becomes possible.

Sechehaye's method of dealing with sick patients[16] is probably closer to Rosen's than to Boyer's and employs such stratagems as speaking to the patient "in the third person," which permits, in some cases, almost immediate direct contact with the person within the psychosis. She describes how she addressed a schizophrenic boy who complained that "they had given him somebody else's clothes" and would destroy any clothes he wore (p. 46). Sechehaye approached him with the words, "The director sent me to see if I could help Jacques who has had such great sorrow." The previously mute patient answered: "He is pleading, he is pleading, he is earnestly pleading that they take off these clothes which were not made for Jacques and are too heavy to carry and they will give him clothes made to fit him, just for him."

III

Further rules as to when one should be active, and in what way, are derived from one's ideas about the origin and structure of the psychotic personality. In the literature on the schizoid or schizophrenic personality and its treatment, there is agreement on the personality structure found in these people and the circumstances under which it develops. Sechehaye, Rosen, and Boyer, representing quite different schools of thought (at least on the surface), all agree on the following four points:

1. The schizoid or schizophrenic personality is a psychogenic disorder which originates in early infancy as the result of the infant's belief that its mother does not wish it to live or to have pleasure. This belief may or may not have a foundation in fact. (Melanie Klein argues that it may not, being a by-product of the relative intensity of the infant's drives.) Be that as it may, the psychic reality of the patient contains this belief, and it has a profound effect on future mental structure.

2. Consequently, the adult comes equipped with a superego which literally makes the act of living a guilt-laden experience. The patient's problem is expressed by this dilemma: to live or enjoy pleasure means losing mother's love. The only way to be loved is to be dead.

3. Because the life instincts are in opposition to the superego, but fairly helpless, it is not hard to understand the anger of these schizoid people, their unrealistic, autistic way of gaining some fun, and their feelings of worthlessness and persecution.

4. The classic symptoms, including the thinking disorders, once thought of by Bleuler[2] as "primary symptoms," are seen as secondary effects of the root problem. Sechehaye demonstrates clearly that they disappear whenever contact with the therapist is successfully established.

The fact that there exists a fairly well agreed-upon picture of the schizophrenic personality is grounds for optimism, because on the basis of this picture one can classify three kinds of active intervention.

1. *Intervening to encourage the patient to satisfy his basic needs.* This rule is quite simple. The therapist essentially backs the patient in his lawful aspirations to be human, achieve love, grow, and live in the world of reality.

2. *Intervening to protect the patient from the onslaught of his destructive superego.* Sechehaye chacterizes the goal of psychotherapy as finding out the legitimate needs of the patient and gratifying them without arousing guilt. Siding with the patient's life instincts is psychically dangerous. It exposes both the patient and the therapist to retaliation from the superego. For this reason, the therapist should establish himself as soon as possible as a powerful but friendly person. Both Rosen and Sechehaye feed their patients themselves on occasion, thus taking the responsibility on their own shoulders for such behavior.

I find that whenever I encourage this kind of patient to do something constructive I can expect some kind of self-destructive impulse originating in the superego to appear soon after. One girl, having tidied herself up and fixed her hair (as the result of some prodding on my part), reported strong suicidal feelings that evening which were in retaliation for her daring. She dreamt that she was cutting off her hands. Intervention of this type is risky unless one is fairly sure of the balance of the forces one is dealing with. For this reason, with some patients, it can only be done under hospital conditions, where the patient can be protected from self-harm. To go back to the military analogy, a therapist who has established contact with a sane ego, and who furthermore is encouraging it in its aspirations, must continuously protect this isolated sector of the patient's personality. The "sane" ego has to feel that victory is ultimately possible and that strong forces are working with him. He needs continuous "air support."

3. *Intervening with activity designed to protect the therapist, the patient, or anyone else from acts of violence.* Because of the ego weakness of the schizoid personality, activity of some sort is indicated to control either self- or other-directed hostile impulses. The patient is caught between the superego and the id and needs protection in the form of controls to prevent harm. Sechehaye[16] describes a disturbed man who kept his eyes closed "so that he would not see the wicked things that he wanted to do" (p. 167). This patient later spoke of his relief at being placed under restraint and protected. He described how he "exaggerated his symptoms" to be sure he was not released too soon and left unprotected. To safeguard the thera-

pist, the patient, or anyone else is a primary duty. Rosen[11] writes: "Having concentrated the patient's attention on the malevolent behavior of his real mother while he is still hazy as to who is who, the therapist often finds the full fury of this free energy turned against himself" (p. 16). He goes on to state that the aggression must be kept under control with words or, if necessary, a restraint sheet. Not to do so is a failure to respond to a basic need of the patient— to be kept from doing real harm. In less disturbed patients, strictures against making permanent "life changes," getting pregnant, or becoming promiscuous, serve this function.

Summing up: direct intervention can be used: (1) to allow the patient to enjoy legitimate gratifications; (2) to protect the patient from superego retaliation; (3) to control and defend the patient from id or superego impulses which may harm him. The whole procedure may be summed up as "being a good parent."

I found myself in tune with Rosen's governing principle of direct analysis.[12] "The relationship should include," he writes, "not only benign administration but also discipline, education, companionship, dedication, self-sacrifice, and finally, that aspect of the mother-baby relationship that is least known to us, an 'X factor,' which distinguishes the normal from the perverse mother" (p. 61).

One very important stricture: It is important that the therapist, though acting spontaneously, should not be using the situation to gratify either his erotic or sadistic impulses. There has to be someone around with a strong ego.

IV

To gain perspective on these therapies, let us examine activity therapy in its historic context. Activity, on the part of the therapist, was construed as the gratification or frustration of needs by the therapist. In effect, he is rewarding the patient or punishing the patient.

Such activity was condemned rather strongly by Freud, especially in dealing with adult patients. In his paper on transference love, Freud[5] laid down a fundamental rule with regard to erotic needs which the patient directs toward the analyst. The analyst should neither gratify the need nor censor the patient. He should use these "transference needs" to understand the patient and help her gain insight.

Ferenczi's and Rank's names are usually associated with beginnings of "activity" therapy. Toward the end of his life, Ferenczi postulated that the patient had in childhood suffered deprivations which could only be corrected by new experiences. Freud, as was to be expected, was shocked by Ferenczi's departure from classical principles and attempted to reconvert Ferenczi to the orthodox position. The controversy was acrimonious; Sir Ernest Jones[9] gives the impression that Ferenczi had lost his mind. There exist other views on the subject, and Jones, unfortunately, died before Ferenczi's defenders had a chance to marshal their ammunition.

The real question is what happens when the therapist treats a patient's need in some other way than by strict neutrality. Rosen, for instance, sees his role as that of a psychotrophist, or mind-nourisher.

In 1946 Alexander and French,[1] acknowledging their debt to Ferenczi, put forth the notion of a "corrective emotional experience" which they felt was more important than insight and was the backbone of what makes therapy work. Accordingly, they attempted to match patients and therapists with the idea of satisfying needs which in childhood had never been satisfied. Therapy, they said, is a place where you get something you never got before and as a result of this experience you can get on to the next stage. Such gratifications are not to be understood as "spoiling." The corrective experience may involve disapproval or censure. On occasion, Rosen and Sechehaye call spades spades and speak strongly against certain kinds of behavior, especially the self-destructive behavior, but by so doing provide the patient with an experience of caring which he has not experienced before.

V

I would like to discuss the restoration of the "sense of reality." There is a connection, explicitly spelled out by Sechehaye,[14] between the satisfaction of a need and the patient's sense of reality. The famous example is the one where Mme. Sechehaye gives her patient an apple. Following this experience, Renée, the patient, reports:

"When we were outside I realized that my perception of things had completely changed. I saw reality, marvellous reality, for the first time. The people whom we encountered were no longer automatons, phantoms revolving around, gesturing without meaning; they were men and women with their own individual characteristics, their own individuality" (p. 79).

Using the phenomenon systematically, Sechehaye sets about

rectifying the unsatisfied needs of the patient. Such a course of action might be blessed by Ferenczi, but it poses a serious problem. As Bleuler[2] points out:

"According to current information, we should be led to believe that such therapy soon arouses demands unrealizable by the therapist, thence to deviant ideas of love and persecution, terminating in a more determined escape from the real world" (p. 176).

In attempting to answer Bleuler, Sechehaye[15] distinguishes between "essential" and "compensatory" desires. She describes the case of a six-year-old girl named Paulette who craved chocolate to an unnatural degree, consuming a whole box at a time without relief from her cravings. Her analyst gave her chocolate unrestrictedly with no effect. Sechehaye, when she took the case, gave her a daily bottle of orange juice and no more. Paulette's needs abated and after a while she lost her interest in the bottle. Why? Sechehaye is not sure but guesses that the chocolate was satisfying a compensatory need; it was not an object of "magic symbol participation," i.e., an essential need. Another difference was that in the case of the chocolate, the former analyst merely placed the box in front of the child and let her struggle with her conflicting desires for up to an hour. Sechehaye personally took the responsibility on her own shoulders and fed the child herself; just as in the case of Renée, the previously mentioned psychotic, she personally gave her the magic apples which restored to her the sense of reality.

Another example concerns a borderline psychotic who was infantilized by an inexperienced nurse who "did everything for her." The patient became more and more demanding, depressed, and suicidal. What had happened was that the nurse had been gratifying the woman's latent homosexual needs together with strong impulses of self-punishment.

VI

In this discussion I have emphasized the use of active methods mostly with reference to psychotics. However, psychotic elements are an exaggeration of trends which are in everyone. Every patient we treat has "psychotic" elements which may have to be dealt with quite actively.

Freud, in his insistence on keeping any kind of activity out of his therapy, may have made a mistake which has kept psychotherapists barking up the wrong tree for some time. His thinking may have been influenced by ideas current in child-rearing practices of the early twentieth century. Although Freud put his finger on the effect of the rigid child-rearing practices of the time, his therapy is closer to the idea of schedules than to demand feeding. Along with the pedagogues of his day, he feared that the effect of any indulgence, especially warmth on the part of the therapist, could be disastrous and certainly reduce the chance of insight. At least, he writes in this vein. He may not always have practiced what he preached. In spite of recognizing the continuity of all mental processes, seeing the child within the man, the neurotic within the healthy, the psychotic within the neurotic, he drastically isolated therapeutic techniques. Activity therapy or suggestion was appropriate for children, psychotics, psychopaths, not neurotics. Presently it seems that the difference between these clinical types is exaggerated, and activity, i.e., transference gratification, may be a needed tool in almost all cases, neurotic and psychotic.

Sometimes something as minor as using the patient's first name, or teasing him, or showing emotion oneself is all that is needed. At other times it is a very complex procedure.

REFERENCES

1. Alexander, F., and French, T. E., *Psychoanalytic Therapy* (New York: Ronald Press, 1946).
2. Bleuler, E., *Dementia Praecox*, J. Zinkin, trans. (New York: International Universities Press, 1952).
3. Boyer, B. Provisional Evaluation of Psychoanalysis with Few Parameters Employed in the Treatment of Schizophrenia, *International Journal of Psychoanalysis*, 42, 1961.
4. Federn, P., *Ego Psychology and the Psychoses* (New York: Basic Books, 1952).
5. Freud, S., Further Recommendations in the Technique of Psychoanalysis, *Collected Papers* (London: Hogarth Press, 1949), Vol. 2, pp. 377-92.
6. Fromm-Reichmann, Frieda, in *Psychoanalysis and Psychotherapy*, D. Bullard, ed. (Chicago: University of Chicago Press, 1959).
7. Fromm-Reichmann, Frieda, Notes on the Development of Schizophrenics in Psychoanalytic Therapy, in *Specialized Techniques in Psychotherapy*, G. Bychowski and L. Despert, eds. (New York: Basic Books, 1960).
8. Haley, J., Control in Psychotherapy with Schizophrenics, *Archives of General Psychiatry*, 5:340-53, 1961.
9. Jones, E., *The Life and Work of Sigmund Freud* (New York: Basic Books, 1957), Vol. 3.
10. Karon, B., The Resolution of Acute Schizophrenic Reactions: A Contribution in the Development of Nonclassical Psychotherapeutic Techniques, *Psychotherapy*, 1:27-43, 1963.
11. Rosen, J., *Direct Analysis* (New York: Grune & Stratton, 1953).
12. Rosen, J., *Direct Psychoanalytic Psychiatry* (New York: Grune & Stratton, 1962).

13. Rosenthal, David, A Review of Arthur Burton, ed., *Psychotherapy of the Psychoses*, in *Psychiatry*, November 1961, pp. 377-80.
14. Sechehaye, Marguerite, *Autobiography of a Schizophrenic Girl*, Rubin-Rabson, trans. (New York: Grune & Stratton, 1951).
15. Sechehaye, Marguerite, *Symbolic Realization*, Worsten, trans. (New York: International Universities Press, 1951).
16. Sechehaye, Marguerite, *A New Psychotherapy in Schizophrenia*, Rubin-Rabson, trans. (New York: Grune & Stratton, 1956).

ERIC BERNE

Transactional Analysis

While obviously still strongly influenced by the psychoanalytic model, Berne's system has the virtue of greater simplicity and comprehensibility. His chief emphasis, like Haley's, is on what goes on between therapist and patient, or, in group therapy, what goes on among group members. "Transactional analysis" is an ingenious method of combining intrapsychic with inter-psychic analysis. Thus structural analysis is basically focused on intrapsychic phenomena as it expresses itself in transactions among group members. Game analysis and script analysis also focus on both elements. The characteristic game one plays is similar in many respects to Adler's "life style" or Wilhelm Reich's "character analysis." However, the game is discovered by observations of the interaction going on within the group. It is also interesting to note the resemblances and the differences between Moreno's psychodrama and Berne's conceptualization of script analysis. Both see group therapy as a dramatic presenta-tion: Moreno makes the drama deliberate and directs the group players into a dramatic recreation of life problems; Berne on the other hand focuses on the drama inherent in the interaction among group members.

In one important sense Berne has returned to Freud. He has restored simple clear language to psychotherapy. Freud used the simple German words meaning the "it," the "I," and the "over-I," which were unfortunately translated into id, ego, and superego. Berne in his structural analysis also uses simple words: "child,"

From the *American Journal of Psychotherapy*, Vol. XII, No. 4, October 1958.

"adult," and "parent" (although these do not have the same meaning as Freud's terms). The trend to simplicity and clarity is a refreshing corrective to the complex jargon that so often appears in the work of less talented theorists who mistake pedantic obscurantism for profundity.

THERE IS NEED for a new approach to psychodynamic group therapy specifically designed for the situation it has to meet. The usual practice is to bring into the group methods borrowed from individual therapy, hoping, as occasionally happens, to elicit a specific therapeutic response. I should like to present a different system, one which has been well tested and is more adapted to its purpose, and with which group therapists can stand on their own ground rather than attempting a thinly spread imitation of the sister discipline.

Generally speaking, individual analytic therapy is characterized by the production of and search for material, with interpersonal transactions holding a special place, typically in the field of "transference resistance" or "transference reactions." In a group, the systematic search for material is hampered because from the beginning the multitude of transactions takes the center of the stage. Therefore it seems appropriate to concentrate deliberately and specifically on analyzing such transactions. Structural analysis, and its later development into transactional analysis, in my experience offers the most productive framework for this undertaking. Experiments with both approaches demonstrate certain advantages of structural and transactional analysis over attempts at psychoanalysis in the group. Among these are increased patient interest, as shown by attendance records; increased degree of therapeutic success, as shown by reduction of gross failures; increased stability of results, as shown by long-term adjustment; and wider applicability in difficult patients such as psychopaths, the mentally retarded, prepsychotics, and postpsychotics. In addition, the intellegibility, precision, and goals of the therapeutic technique are more readily appreciated by both the patient and the properly prepared therapist.

This approach is based on the separation and investigation of exteropsychic, neopsychic, and archaeopsychic ego states. Structural analysis refers to the intrapsychic relationships of these three types of ego states: their mutual isolation, conflict, contamination, invasion, predominance, or cooperation within the personality. Transactional analysis refers to the diagnosis of which particular ego state is active in each individual during a given transaction or series of transactions, and of the understandings or misunderstanding which arise due to the perception or misperception of this factor by the individuals involved.

I have discussed in a previous publication[1] the nature of ego states in general, and of their classification according to whether they are exteropsychic—that is, borrowed from external sources; neopsychic—oriented in accordance with current reality; or archaeopsychic—relics fixated in childhood. These distinctions are easily understood by patients when they are demonstrated by clinical material, and when the three types are subsumed under the more personal terms Parent, Adult, and Child, respectively.

As this is a condensation in a very small space of a whole psychotherapeutic system, I can only offer a few illustrative situations, choosing them for their relative clarity and dramatic quality in the hope that they will draw attention to some of the basic principles of structural and transactional analysis.

STRUCTURAL ANALYSIS

The first concerns a patient named Matthew, whose manner, posture, gestures, tone of voice, purpose, and field of interest varied in a fashion which at first seemed erratic. Careful and sustained observation, however, revealed that these variables were organized into a limited number of coherent patterns. When he was discussing his wife, he spoke in loud, deep, dogmatic tones, leaning back in his chair with a stern gaze and counting off the accusations against her on his upraised fingers. At other times he talked with another patient about carpentry problems in a matter-of-fact tone, leaning forward in a companionable way. On still other occasions, he taunted the other group members with a scornful smile about their apparent loyalty to the therapist, his head slightly bowed and his back ostentatiously turned to the leader. The other patients soon became aware of these shifts in his ego state, correctly diagnosed them as Parent, Adult, and Child, respectively, and began to look for appropriate clues concerning Matthew's actual parents and his childhood experiences. Soon everyone in the group, including the patient, was able to accept the simple diagram shown in Figure 1 as a workable representation of Matthew's personality structure.

In the course of Matthew's therapy, he asked the physician to examine his father, who was on the verge of a paranoid psychosis. The therapist was astonished, in spite of his anticipations, to see

1. Eric Berne, Ego States in Psychotherapy, *American Journal of Psychotherapy*, 11:293-309, 1957.

how exactly Matthew's Parent reproduced the father's fixated paranoid ego state. During his interview, Matthew's father spoke in loud,
deep, dogmatic tones, leaning back in his chair with a stern gaze,
and counting off on his upraised fingers his accusations against the
people around him.

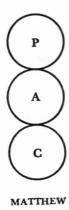

MATTHEW

FIGURE 1. *Structural Analysis*

It should be emphasized that Parent, Adult, and Child are not
synonymous with superego, ego, and id. The latter are "psychic
agencies,"[2] while the former are complete ego states, each in itself
including influences from superego, ego, and id. For example, when
Matthew reproduced the Parental ego state, he not only behaved
like a stern father but also distorted reality the way his father did,
and vented his sadistic impulses. And as cathexis was transferred
from the Parental ego state into that of the scornful Child, the
planning of his attacks and the accompanying guilt feelings had a
childlike quality.

In therapy, the first task was to clarify in Matthew's mind what
was Parent, what was Adult, and what was Child in his feelings
and behavior. The next phase was directed toward maintaining
control through the Adult. The third phase was to analyze the current conflicts between the three ego states. Each of these phases
brought its own kind of improvement, while the ultimate aim in
this prepsychotic case was to enable all three ego states to cooperate
in an integrated fashion as a result of structural analysis.

2. Sigmund Freud. *An Outline of Psychoanalysis* (New York: Norton. 1949).

There were two contraindications in this case. The first was the universal indication against telling the Child to grow up. One does not tell a two-year-old child to grow up. In fact, from the beginning it is necessary in every case to emphasize that we are not trying to get rid of the Child. The Child is not to be regarded as *childish* in the derogatory sense, but *childlike*, with many socially valuable attributes which must be freed so that they can make their contribution to the total personality when the confusion in this archaic area has been straightened out. The child in the individual is potentially capable of contributing to his personality exactly what a happy actual child is capable of contributing to family life. The second contraindication, which is specific to this type of case, was against investigating the history and mechanism of his identification with his father, which was a special aspect of his Parental ego state.

Simple Transactional Analysis

A patient named Camelia, following a previous train of thought, said that she had told her husband she wasn't going to have intercourse with him any more and that he could go and find himself some other woman. Another patient named Rosita asked curiously, "Why did you do that?" Whereupon Camelia, much to Rosita's discomfort, burst into tears and replied, "I try so hard, and then you criticize me."

This transaction may be analyzed according to the diagram drawn as Figure 2. This figure was drawn and analyzed for the

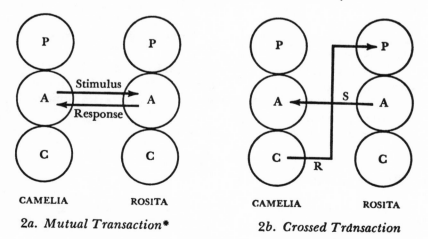

2a. *Mutual Transaction**   2b. *Crossed Transaction*

FIGURE 2.

* This terminology has now been changed to Complementary Transaction.

group as follows: The personalities of the two women are represented structurally as comprising Parent, Adult, and Child. The original transactional stimulus is Camelia's statement about what she had told her husband. She related this in her Adult ego state, with which the group was familiar. It was received in turn by an Adult Rosita, who in her response exhibited a mature, reasonable interest in the story. As shown in Figure 2(a), the transactional stimulus was Adult to Adult, and so was the *transactional response*. If things had continued at this level, the conversation might have proceeded smoothly.

Rosita's question ("Why did you do that?") now constituted a new transactional stimulus, and was intended as one adult speaking to another. Camelia's weeping response, however, was not that of one adult to another, but that of a child to a critical parent. Camelia's misperception of Rosita's ego state, and the shift in her own ego state, resulted in a crossed transaction and broke up the conversation, which now had to take another turn. This is represented in Figure 2 (b).

This particular type of crossed transaction, in which the stimulus is Adult to Adult, and the response is Child to Parent, is probably the most frequent cause of misunderstandings in marriage and work situations, as well as in social life. Clinically, it is typified by the classical transference reaction, which is a special case of the crossed transaction. In fact, this particular species of crossed transaction may be said to be the chief problem of psychoanalytic technique.

In Matthew's case, when he was talking about his wife, the crossing was reversed. If one of the other members, as an Adult, asked him a question, expecting an Adult response, Matthew instead usually answered like a supercilious Parent talking to a backward Child, as represented in Figure 3.

Therapeutically, this simple type of transactional analysis helped Camelia to become more objective about her Child. As the Adult gained control, and the Child's responses at home were suppressed for later discussions in the group, her marital and social life improved even before any of the Child's confusion was resolved.

THE ANALYSIS OF GAMES

Short sets of on-going transactions may be called *operations*. These constitute tactical maneuvers, in which it is the other members of the group who are maneuvered. Thus the conversation between Camelia and Rosita, taken as a whole, is an operation and has to be analyzed again at a deeper level, when it soon appears that the need of Camelia's Child to feel criticized was one of the motives for telling this particular story to the group.

A series of operations constitutes a "game." A game may be defined as a recurring series of transactions, often repetitive, superficially rational, with a concealed motivation; or, more colloquially, as a series of operations with a "gimmick."

Hyacinth recounted her disappointment and resentment because a friend of hers had given a birthday party which she herself had planned to give. Camelia asked, "Why don't you give another party later?" To which Hyacinth responded, "Yes, but then it wouldn't be a birthday party." The other members of the group then began to give wise suggestions, each beginning with "Why don't you . . ." and to each of these Hyacinth gave a response which began "Yes, but . . ."

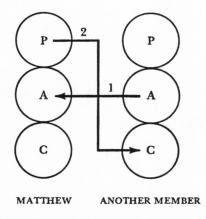

MATTHEW   ANOTHER MEMBER

FIGURE 3. *Crossed Transaction. Type II*

Hyacinth had told her story for the purpose of setting in motion the commonest of all the games which can be observed in groups: the game of "Why don't you . . . Yes, but . . ." This is a game which can be played by any number. One player, who is "it," presents a problem. The others start to present solutions, to each of which the one who is "it" objects. A good player can stand off the rest of the group for a long period, until they all give up, whereupon "it" wins. Hyacinth, for example, successfully objected to more than a dozen solutions before the therapist broke up the game. The gimmick in "Why don't you . . . Yes, but . . ." is that it is played not for its ostensible purpose (a quest for information or solutions), but for the sake of the fencing; and as a group phenomenon it corresponds to Bion's basic assumption "F."[3]

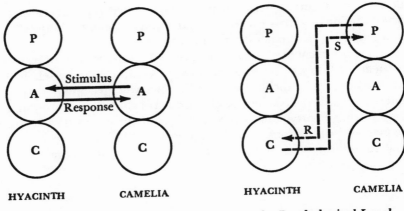

a. Social Level   b. Psychological Level

FIGURE 4.   A Game

Other common games are "How am I doing?" "Uproar," "Alcoholic," "P.T.A." "Ain't it awful?" and "Schlemiel." In "Schlemiel," the one who is "it" breaks things, spills things, and makes messes of various kinds, and each time says, "I'm sorry!" This leaves the inexperienced player in a helpless position. The skillful opponent, however, says, "You can break things and spill things all you like; but please don't say 'I'm sorry'!" This response usually causes the Schlemiel to collapse or explode, since it knocks out his gimmick, and the opponent wins. I imagine that at this point many of you are thinking of Stephen Potter, but I think the games I have in mind are more serious, and some of them, like "Alcoholic," with all its complex rules published by various rescue organizations, are played for keeps. "Alcoholic" is complicated because the official form requires at least four players: a persecutor, a rescuer, a dummy, and the one who is "it."[*]

The transactional analysis of Hyacinth's game of "Why don't you . . . Yes, but . . ." is represented in Figure 4. This figure was

3. W. R. Bion, Group Dynamics: A Re-View, *International Journal of Psychoanalysis*, 33:235-47, 1952.

* To this has now been added a fifth player: the connection or supplier.—E.B.

drawn and analyzed for the group. In the guise of an Adult seeking information, Hyacinth "cons" the other members into responding like sage parents advising a helpless child. The object of Hyacinth's Child is to confound these parents one after the other. The game can proceed because at the superficial (social) level both stimulus and response are Adult to Adult, and at a deeper psychological level they are also complementary, Parent to Child stimulus ("Why don't you. . . ?") eliciting Child to Parent response ("Yes, but . . ."). The second level is unconscious on both sides.

The therapeutic effect of this analysis was to make Hyacinth aware of her defensive need to confound and to make the others aware of how easily they could be conned into taking a Parental role unawares. When a new patient tried to start a game of "Why don't you . . . Yes but . . ." in this group, they all played along with her in order not to make her too anxious, but after a few weeks they gently demonstrated to her what was happening. In other words, they now had the option of playing or not playing this game, as they saw fit, where formerly they had no choice but to be drawn in.

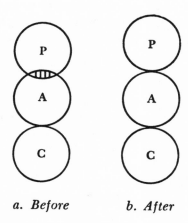

a. Before   b. After

FIGURE 5.   *Therapeutic Effect*

This option was the net therapeutic gain, which they were able to apply profitably in their more intimate relationships. In structural terms, this improvement is represented in Figure 5. Figure 5(a) shows the original contamination of the Adult by the Parent, and Figure 5(b) shows the decontaminated Adult who can now rationally control his behavior in this particular situation.

THE ANALYSIS OF SCRIPTS

A script is an attempt to repeat in derivative form not a transference reaction or a transference situation, but a transference drama, often split up into acts, exactly like the theatrical scripts which are intuitive artistic derivatives of these primal dramas of childhood. Operationally, a script is a complex set of transactions, by nature recurrent, but not necessarily recurring, since a complete performance may require a whole lifetime. A common tragic script is that based on the rescue fantasy of a woman who marries one alcoholic after another. The disruption of such a script leads to despair. Since the magical cure of the alcoholic husband which the script calls for is not forthcoming, a divorce results and the woman tries again. A practical and constructive script, on the other hand, may lead to great happiness if the others in the cast are well chosen and play their parts satisfactorily. A game usually represents a segment of a script.

The ultimate goal of transactional analysis is the analysis of scripts, since the script determines the destiny and identity of the individual. Space, however, does not permit a discussion here of the techniques, aims, and therapeutic effects of script analysis.

SELF-ANALYSIS

Structural and transactional analysis lend themselves to self-examination more readily than orthodox psychoanalysis does, since they effectively bypass many of the difficulties inherent in self-psychoanalysis. The therapist who has some knowledge of his own personality structure has a distinct advantage in dealing with his countertransference problems: that is, the activity of his own Child or Parent with its own favorite games, its own script, and its own motives for becoming a group therapist. If he has a clear insight, without self-delusion, as to what is exteropsychic, what is neopsychic, and what is archaeopsychic in himself, then he can choose his responses so as to bring the maximum therapeutic benefits to his patients.

I have condensed into this brief article material which would easily fill a book, and which is best made clear by six months or a year of clinical supervision. In its present form, however, it may stimulate some people to more careful observation of ego states in their patients, and to some serious and sustained experiments in structural interpretation.

SUMMARY

1. A new approach to group therapy is outlined, based on the distinction between exteropsychic, neopsychic, and archaeopsychic ego states. The study of the relationships within the individual of these three types of ego states, colloquially called Parent, Adult, and Child, respectively, is termed structural analysis and has been discussed in a previous publication.[4]

2. Once each individual in the group has some understanding of his own personality in these terms, the group can proceed to simple transactional analysis, in which the ego state of the individual who gives the transactional stimulus is compared with the ego state of the one who gives the transactional response.

3. In the next phase, short series of transactions, called operations, are studied in the group. More complex series may constitute a "game," in which some element of double-dealing or insincerity is present. In the final phase, it is demonstrated that all transactions are influenced by complex attempts on the part of each member to manipulate the group in accordance with certain basic fantasies derived from early experiences. This unconscious* plan, which is a strong determinant of the individual's destiny, is called a script.

4. Clinical examples are given, and the therapeutic gain expected from each phase of structural and transactional analysis is indicated.

4. See footnote 1, p. 121.

* It is now known that the script plan is not unconscious, but preconscious, or even fully conscious.—E.B.

J. L. MORENO

Reflections on My Method of
Group Psychotherapy and Psychodrama

In this paper, J. L. Moreno explains his concept of group therapy, while at the same time indicating those experiences of his own life which influenced the growth of his ideas. While Moreno is chiefly noted for his development of psychodrama, sociometry, and sociodrama, he has also exerted an indirect influence on the work of such therapies as those exemplified in this volume by Spotnitz, Nelson, and Greenwald. This influence can perhaps be thought of as deliberate assumption of role by the therapist, in order to supply what Franz Alexander called "the corrective emotional experience."

"GROUP PSYCHOTHERAPY" is a term that has established itself over the past twenty years, not only in medicine but also in psychology and sociology. In addition, it has become an indispensable aid in the pedagogic sphere, in industrial psychology, and in the armed forces. The basic concept of group psychotherapy still remains that which I originally expounded in 1932 at the annual meeting of the American Psychiatric Association:*

The method of group psychotherapy aims at grouping all those taking part in the manner most likely to produce favorable thera-

From *Ciba Symposium*, Vol. II, No. 4, 1963.

* I coined the terms "group therapy" and "group psychotherapy" at that meeting. See "Application of the Group Method to Classification" published by the National Committee on Prisons and Prison Labor, 1932, pp. 60, 74, and *The First Book on Group Psychotherapy*, Beacon House, 1957.

peutic results. Where necessary, regrouping is undertaken in order to bring the group constellation into line with the spontaneous motives and inclinations of the individuals concerned.

The underlying principle is that each individual—not just the physician himself—may act as a therapeutic agent for every other individual, and each group as a therapeutic agent for another group.

In 1932, I added the following postulate: Group psychotherapy treats not only the isolated individual, who is the main object of interest by reason of his inability to adapt himself and fit into his environment, but also the entire group and the sum of individuals who are in contact with him. In the last resort, a genuine therapeutic method must envisage nothing less than mankind as a whole.

The first aim of group psychotherapy is to promote the integration of the individual with respect to the uncontrolled forces surrounding him; this is attained through so-called sociometric analysis, whereby the individual ego explores his immediate environment. The second aim is the integration of the group. This method of approach from both sides, i.e., from the individual on the one hand and the group on the other, requires their reciprocal integration, which is realized by "spontaneous and free interaction" not only between the patients themselves but also between patients and the physician.

The methods I have evolved are closely bound up with my personal development, and this makes it necessary for me to refer here briefly to the more salient landmarks in my life story. I was born in Bucharest on May 19, 1892. Five years later, my parents moved to Vienna. The sources of psychodrama are to be found in my childhood games and youthful experiences. One Sunday afternoon, while my parents were out, it so happened that I and some of the neighbors' children decided to play at "God" in the enormous cellar of the house in which I lived. The first thing was to build our Heaven. To this end, we collected every available chair and piled them up on an enormous oak table until they reached to the ceiling. I now mounted my heavenly throne—mine "the kingdom, the power, and the glory"—while my angels "flew" round me singing. Suddenly one of the children called out: "Why don't you fly too?" Whereupon I stretched out my arms—and one second later lay on the floor with a broken arm. So ended my first psychodrama, in which I had filled the dual roles of producer and chief actor. This taught me that, in order to play a part, the requisite inward preparedness must first be conjured up by means of a special "warming-up" process; that even the "highest" of God's creatures require the help of others; and that other children besides myself like to play at being God from time to time. These factors—the "warming up" process, the help of others ("auxiliary egos"), and the psychodrama protagonists—we shall encounter again later when discussing psychodrama. Today, I am still convinced that the vertical structure of my psychodrama theater betrays the influence of these childhood experiences. The first level is that of the conception, the beginning of the action of psychodrama, the second that of its growth, the third that of its fulfillment, while the balcony—as a type of fourth dimension—is the realm of gods and heroes.

As a medical student possessed of an extremely fertile poetic imagination, I used to spend much of my free time in the parks of Vienna. One day, it came to pass that I began telling stories to a small group of children playing nearby. To my amazement, other children soon left their games and joined the band of listeners. Next came nurses with babies in prams, then mothers and fathers, finally park attendants, and even a few policemen! From this day onward, telling stories in the park became one of my favorite occupations. I would usually sit down under one of the old trees and—as if lured on by a magic flute—the children would flock toward me, sit down in a circle, and listen with rapt attention. What made so deep an impression on these children was not so much the subject matter as the plot, the action—the manner in which the unreal, the "fairy tale," became reality, actual experience.

It was during those years before the First World War, when, still a student, I assisted Professor Otto Pötzl at the Vienna Psychiatric Clinic, that I met Sigmund Freud. He had just finished a lecture on the analysis of a telepathic dream, and the students were leaving the lecture hall. Freud noticed me and questioned me on my work and my plans for the future. I answered, "You see patients in the unnatural surroundings of your consulting-room. I meet them in the streets, in their homes, in their natural environment. You analyse their dreams. I shall give them courage for new dreams."

In 1917, I obtained my medical degree at the University of Vienna and, from then until 1924, was in practice in Bad Vöslau. From 1915 to 1917, I had been in charge of a refugee camp at Mittendorf, near Vienna. I soon realized that the unhappy plight of displaced persons was made progressively worse by the immense psychological tensions to which they were subjected—tensions which often became unbearable, both for the community as a whole and for its members individually. It was then that I first hit upon my idea of exploring the psychological and sociometric structures and topography of groups of persons, without which any solution to this tension and any subsequent reorientation of the community seemed to me unthinkable. I set down my ideas in a letter addressed to the Austrian Government, but found no sympathy in that quarter.

It was at this time that I tried to develop my poetic bent, which bore a marked religious-existentialist stamp. In fact, this constitutes the philosophical basis of my entire therapeutic method—a fact unfortunately too often overlooked: "A meeting of two: eye to eye, face to face. And when you are near I will tear your eyes out and place them instead of mine, and you will tear my eyes out and will place them instead of yours, then I will look at you with your eyes and you will look at me with mine" (1914). About the same time, a number of my works were published in German (some of them anonymously) by the Anzengruber-Verlag in Vienna and by Kiepenheuer in Berlin: *Invitation to an Encounter; The Godhead as Author; The Godhead as Speaker; The Godhead as Comedian; The Words of the Father; The Speech on the Moment; The Speech on the Encounter; The Speech before the Judge; The King's Novel;* and *The Theater of Spontaneity.* I was also editor of the literary magazine, *Daimon,* which published contributions by Franz Werfel, Franz Kafka, Martin Buber, Arthur Schnitzler, Jakob Wassermann, Max Scheler, Francis Jammes, and others—many of these being original articles. Meanwhile, in the Maysedergasse, not far from the Vienna Opera House, the "Theater of Spontaneity" founded by me was transformed into a therapeutic theater. Had I been interested only in material and intellectual well-being, I would have had every reason to continue my activities as author and psysician in Europe.

Instead, in 1925, I emigrated to the United States. Only New York, the melting pot of the nations, the vast metropolis with all its ethnic and psychological problems and its freedom from all preconceived notions, offered me the opportunity to pursue sociometric group research in the grand style. I not only used my findings in my own psychiatric practice, but also made them the basis of my group-psychotherapeutic methods, more particularly psychodrama, in reform institutes, prisons, and schools. I invented a number of tests: the Acquaintance Test, the Role Test, and the Sociometric Test. They have received universal recognition and acceptance. My school of sociometry soon aroused interest and won recognition among American sociologists. In 1937 and 1938 I taught at Columbia University, and for some years now I have been professor at New York University. In the early forties, classes and seminars in sociometry were set up at various American universities, where they are now taught by former pupils of mine, who have contributed much to their development. During the Second World

War, my Sociometric Test was used by both the British and American armies, in an effort to promote the best possible interpersonal relations among the troops.

This Sociometric Test (the term is derived from *metrum* and *socius*, i.e., measurement of a person's relationship to his fellow men) is based on the following principles: The individuals of the group are asked to select (or exclude) other individuals on the basis of a clearly defined yardstick, such as, say: "With which of your comrades would you prefer to go into battle?"—or: "With which members of the group would you most like to work together in one room?"—or: "Which members of the group would you like to have as co-patients?" The results are reproduced graphically in the form of a "sociogram": the individuals are indicated by circles (females) or triangles (males), and the interpersonal relationships by connecting lines of various types, e.g., sympathy by a continuous line, antipathy by an interrupted one, etc. The sociogram gives a reliable picture of the degree of cohesion of a particular group and of the psychological currents within it. It also shows the sympathetic and anti-

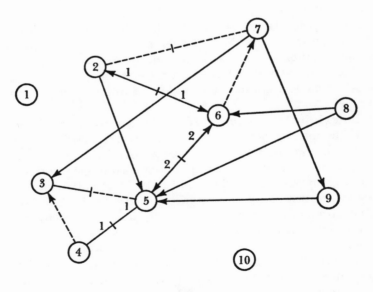

A Typical Sociogram

pathetic currents flowing toward a particular individual. Some individuals emerge as favorites in one or another respect, while other structures (e.g., pairs, triangles, chains) show which individuals exhibit an affinity for one another.

The emergence of certain definite structures is not a haphazard phenomenon but is determined by the degree of maturity of a particular group. From this we deduced the so-called sociogenetic law, which states that higher forms of group organization always proceed from simpler forms. In its ontogenesis, the group organization is to a large extent a mirror of the structural modifications which succeeding prehistoric communities of the species have undergone in the course of their development. An individual may enjoy a high sociometric status while exhibiting sociogenetically a lower stage of development. This explains why in school sociograms, for instance, a certain pupil often remains isolated because his social and emotional development is more advanced than that of the other members of the group. The most popular individuals in a sociogram are frequently those belonging to the same sociogenetic grade. Even where the test is repeated and the possible choices extended, the sociometric structures—so far from changing on the lines of a mathematically calculable probability—in fact constantly yield similar results.

From this recognition I developed the "sociodynamic law," which lays down that sociometrically isolated individuals, i.e., those who appear isolated, unnoticed, or little noticed in the sociogram, tend to remain isolated and little noticed in the formal social structures also; moreover, the greater the number of social contacts, the more marked this isolation tends to be. Conversely, individuals who appear markedly "favored" in the sociogram tend to remain favored, the more so in proportion to the number of their social contacts. This sociodynamic principle affects the group in exactly the same way, riding roughshod over all economic and cultural barriers and setting up new standards of "rich" and "poor"—namely, "emotionally rich" and "emotionally poor." These sociometric differences, which evidently exist in our society, are of immense importance for psychotherapeutic situations. It has, for instance, been recognized that an individual's chances of success and satisfaction in the psychological, social, and economic spheres depend on his sociometric status. It has also been observed that sociometrically isolated individuals tend to be less successful when applying for jobs and seem to be more prone to industrial accidents than the "favored" ones and those who find it easier to work together with others.

My sociometric researches led to the discovery of two further laws—namely, the law of "social gravitation" and the law of the "interpersonal and emotional network." In the medical domain, the introduction of "perceptual sociometry" has proved particularly valuable. In this, the individual draws a sociogram of the individuals living with him in a group situation, i.e., their relationships both with one another and toward himself. This sociogram is then compared with another sociogram based on objective selection, i.e., the selection of others. Disorders of social perception, as revealed by this comparison, are particularly characteristic of psychotic individuals, e.g., paranoid subjects and schizophrenics.

The analysis of the sociograms forms the basis on which the plan of treatment is then drawn up. The first problem is to establish whether a particular individual or the entire group, requires treatment; also what changes in the group structures are desirable in order to promote normalization of these structures, harmonization of the entire group, and hence also the restoration of the individual to emotional health. This is obtained by means of group psychotherapy and psychodrama.

Psychodrama begins with a talk between patient and physician. As soon as the patient begins to describe a concrete situation in which he finds himself face to face with his fellow men, the physician leads him onto the stage. Here, the free association is transformed into free action. With neither practice nor preparation, the patient now plays the part of himself in the particular situation.

The patient's fellow men—father, mother, wife, friend, or foe—are not present in the flesh, but are played by so-called *auxiliary egos*, i.e., members of the audience; in this way, they acquire a type of semireality which proves effective but is less awe-inspiring than the "real thing." At the crisis of the action, the physician, who is closely following the course of the psychodrama, orders the actors *to reverse roles:* the persecuted plays the role of the persecutor, the weakling the role of the strong man, the son the role of the father, etc. The individual thus gains direct experience of the behavior of his "opponent" or "adversary." As a result, he often gains a genuine insight into his fellow men which is something far more than a mere process of intellectual compulsion. The psychodrama method also helps the others to understand the often confused personality of the protagonist. When using the so-called *double method,* an auxiliary *ego* sits or stands behind the protagonist and imitates his bearing and each of his movements. As soon as the patient, in the course of the action of the psychodrama, falls into an inner conflict, the auxiliary *ego* speaks the thoughts, feelings, and impulses which are not really apprehended by him, thus encouraging him, exposing him, warning him. In this way, psychodrama brings about a type of *catharsis* of experience.

On an earlier occasion I once expressed this idea in the following terms: "The audience is the entire community. All are invited and assemble in front of the house. Yet this mad passion, this unfolding of life in make-believe, does not become a path of suffering, but only confirms the fact that each true second occasion means liberation from the first. 'Liberation' is a flattering description, for complete repetition renders the object of repetition ridiculous. One acquires the view of the creator in relation to one's own life, the feeling of true freedom, the freedom of one's nature. Through the second occasion, the first occasion makes us laugh. On the second occasion, too, everything is repeated (in appearance) on the stage—speaking, eating, drinking, begetting, sleeping, waking, writing, quarreling, fighting, winning, losing, dying. But the selfsame pain is no longer sensed as pain by audience and actors, the same desire is no longer desire, the same thought is no longer thought—all are painless, unconscious, thoughtless, deathless. Each figure from reality is extinguished through itself in make-believe, and reality and make-believe dissolve in laughter."

As soon as the drama is over, the make-believe world of the stage is extinguished for the patient. Sobering down, and with a feeling of having been robbed, he now faces the group, whom he scarcely noticed during the action of the play. The forces at work must now change for the third time—while he strove to portray his problems, he spurred his audience on to identify themselves with him. He now enters into direct contact with the spectators, the members of the group, while the latter come into direct contact with one another. It is here that the group therapy begins. One after the other, the members of the group now express their feelings, adding to these by revealing personal experiences of a similar kind. In this way, the patients now undergo a new type of *catharsis*—a "group *catharsis*." One of their group made them a gift of love, and now they return his love. The members of the group share their problems with him, just as he shared his with them. Each bears the other's burden, and gradually the *catharsis* purges all those present. However, this process of resolution is not devoid of conflict. Sharp criticism, even hostility—especially toward the physician—is by no means rare. The entire group is in a state of ferment, and the physician needs all his skill and resources to find a solution to the conflicts involved.

In the treatment of psychotic subjects in particular, psychodrama has achieved astounding results with this type of "love *catharsis*"— a *catharsis* born of encounter with fellow sufferers. The method is based on the principle that the physician and his assistants place themselves on the same level of spontaneity as the patient and so, as it were, move in his world. Whether or not one chooses to describe the spontaneity of the patient as his "unconscious" is of no importance whatever for the treatment prescribed. What is important, by contrast, is that the patient shall in fact embrace the spheres and objects of those persons who fill his psychotic world, no matter how confused or fragmentary his experience of them may be. It is not enough for the psychodrama leader, like the psychoanalyst, merely to observe the patient and translate his symbolic behavior into scientifically comprehensible terms. Instead, together with his auxiliary *egos*, he enters the psychotic world of his patient, partly as co-actor, partly as observer. He speaks with his patient in the psychotic language of signs and gestures, words and actions, just as the patient produces them. Such psychiatric practice naturally harbors certain dangers.

The following case history provides a good idea of the treatment of a schizoid patient by the psychodrama method.

Johnny,* a pale, 15-year-old youth, came to us in the summer of 1952 from the juvenile section of the Bellevue Nerve Clinic in New York. He looked older than his age and had strikingly intelligent features, putting one somewhat in mind of Napoleon. His mutism was apparent from the start—when one greeted him, the most one could hope for was a scornful glance. What little we knew of his childhood we learned from his father—and from the newspaper headlines: "Teenager Sees Himself as Adviser to President of the United States"—"Fifteen-Year-Old Youth Marches Fully Armed into White House"—"Police Arrest Young 'Freedom Hero' "—"Boyish Prank or Dementia?" These headlines referred to one of Johnny's trips to Washington (the second), which he undertook dressed in military uniform and fully armed. His plan was to give the American President advice on how to solve the East-West conflict. The police arrested him, had him psychiatrically examined, and brought him back by plane to New York, where he was placed in the Bellevue Clinic. Once there, he refused to have anything to do with either doctors or nursing staff.

Notwithstanding his negative attitude, we took him up on the stage of our theater one evening. To begin with, the auxiliary *egos* and I had to battle with his obstinacy and generally uncooperative behavior. Before long, however, Johnny responded in spite of himself to the "warming up process" and began giving us an *impromptu* description of his first trip to Washington. No awkward questions were asked of him, nor were any of his actions condemned out of hand. Johnny now went through the motions of buying his ticket, taking the bus to Washington, chatting with other passengers on the way, and finally approaching the White House. At this point we intervened, preventing him from entering the White House and forcing him, in-

* A forerunner of Lee Harvey Oswald, Johnny tried to attack President Harry Truman in 1952.

stead of firing the imagination of the President with his grand idea, to spend the night in a home for juvenile delinquents and to return the following day to New York, his task unaccomplished. Once the play was over, Johnny, waking out of the dreamworld of his reminiscences, suddenly found himself once more among the creatures he so despised—conceited doctors, stupid nurses, clueless fellow patients. What can they understand of my historic mission, he may well have thought to himself, and his first reaction was probably one of horror at the idea of his spontaneous communicativeness. At that moment, however, a warm wave of sympathy from the audience made itself felt: it was clear that "they" admired his courage, readily understood his disappointment and disillusionment, and were interested in the motives which had prompted his undertaking. Yet nobody, not even Johnny, was as yet aware of the miraculous transformation which had turned a hitherto mutistic patient into a man ready to converse with fellow men who had so far remained inaccessible for him. In a word, suspicion and mistrust had now given way to feelings of warmth, sympathy, and mutual confidence.

The following week, Johnny no longer occupied the forefront of interest in our group. At the same time, those who took the trouble to keep him unobtrusively under observation could see that—while he still remained very silent and something of an outsider—he was yet no longer a "foreign body" within the group. When we took Johnny up on to the stage a second time, he doubtless imagined that we should now go through his second journey to Washington—the one which had put an end to his long-cherished project of bringing freedom to the world. In fact, what interested us on this second occasion was his family background. Sure enough, in the course of this second play, we learned that his father, a modest street peddler from Armenia, supported his family financially but was completely engrossed in his business. In this he was helped now and again by Johnny's stepmother, a very primitive Armenian woman who looked after the home, and whose favorite was obviously not Johnny but his small stepbrother. Johnny was unhappy and ill at ease not only in his home surroundings but also at school, where the other boys were well below his intellectual level. As a result, he grew up into an outsider *par excellence*. His free time he devoted entirely to reading American history, and he was particularly fascinated by contemporary political and military events. Johnny now went up on to the stage, a newspaper under his arm, just as if he were returning home. An auxiliary *ego*, representing his stepmother, at once asked him why he was so late. Johnny's irritable retort immediately revealed the tension existing between him and his stepmother, and the audience must at once have wondered how this psychodrama was going to proceed. At this point, roles were reversed, and the next thing we witnessed was the spectacle of the poor defenseless auxiliary *ego*, who had taken over Johnny's part, being assailed by a torrent of abuse from Johnny, playing his own stepmother. The bone of contention was Johnny's allegedly one-sided interest in politics. His stepmother, who had lived for a time in Russia, sympathized with communism; Johnny by contrast, saw his supreme ideal in the American revolution, and—after the model of the minutemen of the American War of Independence—believed it was his mission to intervene in person in the cause of liberty. During the group discussions which follow the drama, Johnny expressed amazement that, with the reversal of role, he had had no difficulty in adopting the views of his stepmother and had even been able to argue her case with regard to the East-West conflict. Was it not possible, he queried, that all problems might ultimately find solution through mutual understanding? Thoughts such as these may well have helped to loosen up Johnny's hitherto unbending frame of mind.

A few days later, in a further psychodrama, Johnny had another violent quarrel with his stepmother. When "she" (realistically portrayed by the auxiliary *ego*), in response to the "compulsion of spontaneous action," sent him off the stage with a box on the ears, turning him symbolically out of the parental home, everybody burst out laughing, Johnny included. The Gordian knot had been cut. From this moment, Johnny became a cheerful, relaxed member of the group. By contrast, the group members were oppressed by all that they had learned, how Johnny had been turned out of house and home and had spent several nights in a New York cinema showing a non-stop program until one day he finally slipped into his father's store and stole money from the till, in order to buy his G.I. uniform and the revolver he so badly needed for his trip to Washington "in the cause of freedom."

It was not only Johnny who responded to this psychodrama with a more flexible attitude. We had with us a male opera singer, completely egocentric and a drug addict to boot, who from time to time acted as an auxiliary *ego*. Quite spontaneously, he told me how happy he was at the success so far achieved, and even made suggestions for Johnny's further treatment. In his case, too, the "love *catharsis*" had begun to take effect. With his aid, we now set about staging Johnny's plans for the future. For a youth like Johnny who had set his sights so high and failed so lamentably, it was vitally important to realize that not only his own world of fantasy but real life, too, could be an interesting experience, an exciting challenge. On the stage, Johnny finally came to realize that it was impossible for him to try and improve the world in the way he envisaged without arousing fear and enmity on all sides. Instead, he would do better to try and get himself a suitable and interesting job. Again and again, we put him through the motions of applying at labor exchanges, pilot training schools, and similar offices, to help him learn how to deal with his fellow men, more particularly his superiors.

Many weeks later, Johnny finally joined a training school for commercial pilots. Behind the everyday routine lay the lure of the wide,

wide world, and this appealed to his sense of adventure. The minute-men and their ideal of freedom seemed to have lost their appeal. We kept an eye on Johnny for a good year more. Throughout this time, nothing psychiatrically abnormal was observed. The "action therapy" of psychodrama had thus succeeded in steering the energies of this schizoid youth back along normal lines. Yet the success of this therapy was only made possible by the process of "love *catharsis*" which evolved round the patient within the group of co-sufferers, co-actors, co-patients.

It is a popular misconception that psychodrama demands an elaborate, "theatrical" *mise en scène*. In fact, it is a purely *ad hoc* performance, carried out wherever the patient happens to be. It is, as it were, a healing process based on reality, on human nature. According to the theory of psychodrama, the earliest stage of psychic development is not penetrated by the usual significant symbols of organized, grammatically-formed speech—it is the silent parts of the *psyche* which plays such a vital part in the development of neuroses and psychoses. When introducing psychodrama work, then, it is important to establish wherever possible some physical contact with the patient, i.e., some tactile, motor communication, whether through touch, caress, embrace, or through participation in silent motions such as eating, walking, etc. Physical contact, physical therapy, and physical training thus form an essential element of the psychodrama situation. For this reason, I have expended great care on devising a system to enable the physician and the auxiliary *egos* to find their way into the patient's own world and populate it with figures familiar to him. The great advantage of such figures is that they are neither pure illusion nor pure reality, but half invented, half actual. The auxiliary *egos* are in fact real persons, but enter the *psyche* of the disintegrated patient rather like some good fairy with a magic spell. Like good or evil spirits, they startle the patient, rouse him, surprise him, console him, as the case may be. He finds himself caught in a world half real, half unreal, as if in a trap. He sees himself act, he hears himself speak, but his thoughts and actions, his feelings and perceptions, derive not from himself but, strange though it may seem, from some other person, from the reflected therapeutic images of his mind.

When we come to deal, not with an individual patient, but with tensions affecting an entire group, e.g., a school class, a team of workers, a military unit, etc., the conflict is approached not by psychodrama but by so-called sociodrama. The effect of a group *catharsis* is often to transform the sociogram of the relevant community into a much more favorable one. Sometimes, sociodrama will reveal that the tension can be solved only by a process of regrouping, e.g., by moving pupils to other desks, laborers to other sites, etc. One word here about part-playing: acting gives the frustrated individual the chance of at least playing on the stage the part he has always longed to play, but never succeeded in playing, in real life. As a result, he often discovers new tasks which he can discharge satisfactorily in real life. Many a human life has been enriched by this means, many a choice of job made easier.

Between 1940 and 1950, my psychotherapeutic methods were gradually adopted in psychiatry, sociology, pedagogy, and other fields in the English-speaking world. The ensuing ten years witnessed their adoption on a world-wide scale—a development largely brought about by the numerous journeys I undertook, always accompanied and assisted by the untiring efforts of my wife Zerka. First we visited Italy, then Paris, where the French section of the New York Academy of Psychodrama and Group Psychotherapy was set up under the name of *Groupe français d'études de sociométrie*. In 1954, my main work, *Who Shall Survive?*, appeared first in a German translation (*Die Grundlagen der Soziometrie*) and soon after in a French version (*Fondements de sociométrie*). The German edition, together with the lectures I held during the Lindau Psychotherapy Week the same year, aroused widespread interest in the German-speaking countries of Europe. In subsequent years I visited Munich, Vienna, and Zurich. In 1957, I undertook an extensive lecture tour which took me through Hamburg, Bremen, Hanover, Göttingen, Marburg, Frankfort-am-Main, Heidelberg, Stuttgart, Freiburg, and finally Zurich, where I had the honor of opening the second International Congress of Group Psychotherapy. In 1962 I was elected President of the International Council of Group Psychotherapy, and in July 1963 I opened the Third International Congress in Milan, under the auspices of the President of the Italian Republic, Antonio Segni. Several persons taking part in this congress bore testimony to the world-wide interest shown in this new form of therapy. In the summer of 1957, I accepted an invitation to visit the Scandinavian countries. During all this time, my methods also found adoption in several countries of South America, in Israel, India, and Japan. In addition to these extensive travels, I continued working in the United States, teaching, conducting group psychotherapy and psychodrama, practicing psychiatry, and writing.

In the summer of 1958 I held lectures with demonstrations at the University of Barcelona, after which I conducted a forensic psychodrama in Tel Aviv and a polyglot sociodrama in a government hospital in Haifa. From Israel, I went on to Greece and Turkey. In the same year, I was for the first time invited beyond the Iron

Curtain, a series of lectures in Yugoslavia being followed by an invitation to the Czechoslovak Psychiatric Congress in Lazne Jesenik (Graefenberg). There was evident appreciation of the potential importance of the sociometric group method for the psychological well-being of workers in the East European countries, where free choice of a job or the site of a job is virtually unknown.

In the autumn of 1959, I was invited to meet Russian Psychiatrists in Leningrad and Moscow. Great was my surprise on finding one of my books there in a Russian translation! In the course of my lectures and demonstrations at the Institute of Psychology in Moscow (Prof. A. A. Smirnov) and at the Bechterev and Pavlov Institute in Leningrad, I gained the impression that sociometry has a part to play in bringing about better understanding between East and West and helping to bridge over ideological conflicts. As a result, the theme I chose for my speech to UNESCO in Paris on October 2, 1959, was "The Scientific Encounter between East and West."

To date, my books have appeared in twenty different languages, and my sociometric methods have won many friends all over the world. Some ascribe this gratifying development to the fact that these methods are not divorced from everyday life and are, above all, ultimately based on the power of human sympathy and love.

HERBERT A. OTTO

Toward a Holistic Treatment Program

Otto has made an effort to synthesize into his technique some of the most recent therapeutic methods, including the work of such psychoanalysts as Franz Alexander and Lawrence Kubie, together with the existential analysts Rollo May and Ludwig Binswanger, as well as some of the behavioral therapists who base themselves on Pavlov and Skinner. The emphasis on restructuring the life space can be regarded as an effort to modify or change the stimulus in order to obtain a new response.

A HOLISTIC TREATMENT program is concerned not only with obtaining optimal gains in the therapeutic sessions through utilization of a discrete set of concepts, *but is equally concerned with utilizing the patient's life span outside the office as a means of achieving therapeutic gains.* This includes helping the patient to become actively involved in making planned use of his living environment, his interpersonal environment, and his vocational setting in order to achieve growth.

Among the pioneers of holistic theory and the holistic approach must be numbered General J. C. Smuts, who originated the term; Karen Horney, Kurt Lewin, and Kurt Goldstein. More recently, Abraham Maslow,[1]* Ludwin von Bertalanffy,[2] and Andreas Angyal[3] have been prominent proponents of this viewpoint.

This article is a revised excerpt from a paper entitled "The Personal and Family Strength Research Projects—Some Implications for the Therapist," *Mental Hygiene*, Vol. 48, No. 3, July, 1964, pp. 439-50.

* Superior numbers refer to the list of references at the end of this article.

The basic framework and methods of a holistic treatment program gradually emerged as a consequence of findings from the Human Potentialities Research Project at the University of Utah. A brief résumé of the background and aims of that program is therefore presented. The Human Potentialities Research Project has been concerned with the development of both theory and methods in relation to the hypothesis that the so-called healthy or normal person is functioning at approximately 10 per cent of his potential. This hypothesis is by no means new; it can be found in the writings of William James at the turn of the century, and about fifteen years ago was "rediscovered" by investigators. A number of leading contemporary behavioral scientists, Fromm,[4] Kubie,[5] Maslow,[6] Mead,[7] Murphy,[8] Rogers,[9] to name but a few, subscribe to this hypothesis. This viewpoint is also shared by a growing number of influential scientists in the U.S.S.R.[10]

To date sixteen articles describing the work of the Human Potentialities Research Project have been published or accepted for publication by professional and scientific journals, as well as one book[11] in 1966, with two more[12, 13] scheduled to appear in 1967. Methods and approaches developed in the course of the research have been used in treatment programs with selected patient populations by psychiatrists, psychologists, and social workers.

BACKGROUND AND BASIC CONCEPTS

If the therapist accepts the hypothesis that the so-called average, healthy human being is operating at 10 to 15 per cent of his potential, he may then choose to undertake, as the paramount goal in life, the actualization of his own potential. An adequate assimilation or internalization of this viewpoint will have been accomplished only when the major and conscious life focus of the individual is directed toward translating his potential into action. This means that every possible conscious (and unconscious) effort is channeled in this direction and that the basic life pattern is one of consistently seeking experiences and deep interpersonal relations with the conscious aim of searching out and actualizing potentialities. Implicit is a total commitment which relegates goals, drives, values, and aspirations of the individual to a subsidiary or supportive role to this major aim. Realistically speaking, this is a very difficult task, made almost insuperable by our contemporary culture, which is overwhelmingly pathology-centered and which surrounds the individual with pathological vectors.[14]

Halbert L. Dunn's concept of high-level wellness similarly

focuses on "actualizing" the human potential. Kaufmann, in a recent article, points out the following:

"A *high-level* wellness for the individual, as defined by H. Dunn, is an integrated method of functioning which is oriented toward maximizing the potential of which the individual is capable, within the environment where he is functioning.

"It therefore involves: (*a*) direction in progress forward and *upward toward a higher potential of functioning,* (*b*) an open-ended and ever-expanding tomorrow *with its challenge to live at a fuller potential,* and (*c*) the integration of the whole being of the total individual—his body, mind, and spirit in the functioning process."[15] (Italics added.)

The basic viewpoint delineated in the previous paragraphs has a number of implications for the therapist. If a therapist subscribes to the point of view that man's primary goal should be the actualizing of his potential, then this becomes the major operational bond between therapist and patient. Consequently, the goal of therapy is not to help the patient work through his emotional pathology or to facilitate his social adaptation, but to assist him to discover and make maximum use of his potentialities—the range of his strengths, capacities and capabilities. At the same time, "working with" and "working through" pathology, the uncovering of unconscious motivation and the delimiting of intrapsychic conflict, are necessary and essential concomitants of the basic focus on individual strengths and potentialities. The seeking out and unfolding of an individual's possibilities cannot be separated from the process of achieving personal authenticity—an important dimension of existential freedom.

Within such a framework therapist and patient are engaged in a most challenging and demanding venture. Not only is it the therapist's task or function to encourage and to assist the patient in utilizing his potential, but the patient has a similar task, function, and responsibility. (We already recognize that not only does the therapist give to the patient, but the patient also deeply gives to the therapist.) The identification, utilization, and development of individual strengths and potentialities constitutes the basic and underlying premise in the interpersonal exchange. With this fundamental attitude or viewpoint in common, both therapist and patient bend every effort to create an atmosphere in which mutual confrontation, emotional honesty, and a sharing of basic goals and concerns (including the meaning of existence) become tools in an interaction process aimed at the development of potentialities by two individuals who have come together for this task.

A consistent finding from experimental groups focusing on the actualization of potentialities in "healthy" populations has been that the more aspects of a person's environment that can be involved in the process of actualizing potential, the greater the gains. Use of any and all aspects of the group member's physical and interpersonal environment in a "total environment push" has been one of the contributions of this research.

The importance of including the largest possible number of environmental vectors in the treatment process is placed in stark relief by findings from Sensory Deprivation Research. It is a highly significant finding of sensory-deprivation experiments that within a relatively short period of time (often three to four hours) a large proportion of individuals adjudged to be healthy and normal on the basis of psychological and psychiatric evaluations begin to have hallucinations, followed in many instances by a comparatively rapid personality disorganization or breakdown. Indications are that the personality disorganization is directly linked to the absence of most sensory inputs. After a comprehensive survey of the published literature on sensory deprivation, Berelson and Steiner concluded: "A certain amount of differentiated input seems necessary for normal orientation and even for mental balance in the human being."[16] This supports the position that environmental stimuli, inputs, or forces play a much more dominant role in relation to personality functioning than has heretofore been suspected and leads to the conclusion that personality, to a large extent, is a function of the field in which it operates.

It would follow that the deeply meaningful relationships with parents and others, which are of basic importance in relation to personality formation, must be understood as significant forces or components of the larger field which sustains the personality. The cradling force of the total environmental field, with its multiplicity of impinging stimuli and sensory inputs, is needed to sustain personality as a function. Proponents of the point of view that personality is, in essence, an organizing principle must now take into account the fact that the organizing principle is, to a much larger degree than previously assumed, dependent for its functioning on the environmental field or on the sensory inputs which are the object of its organizing task. As a result, the subject-object relationship has become considerably less distinct and emerges as a dualism of dubious value.

Until recently, the point of view has prevailed that personality as an organizing principle is the dominant factor in relation to the environment—personality was essentially seen as an independent variable. Or, to put it differently, personality was perceived as a separate entity from the environment and studied (and treated) in separation. The conclusion now appears inevitable that personality is, much more than previously suspected, a function of the total environment (social, interpersonal, physical) or field. This conclusion marks the emergence of a holistic concept of treatment. To effect maximal therapeutic gains and actualization of the patient's potentialities, the totality of the patient, including all possible facets of his life space, must be utilized in treatment.

If the therapist is committed to a holistic treatment approach, the environment of the patient becomes a major and integral component in the total treatment program. It is largely the responsibility of the therapist to involve the patient actively in utilizing his environment as a means to achieve treatment goals. This is the very essence of action therapy—the therapist through his outreach extends the range and scope of therapeutic possibilities, at the same time enabling the patient to become more totally and actively involved in attaining healthier and more nearly optimum functioning.

The development of a holistic treatment program involves the following basic propositions:

1. An adequate understanding of the personality includes an understanding *in depth* of the field in which it functions.

2. The exploration in depth of the individual's field or life space focuses on the identification of health vectors within the field as well as vectors which contribute to malfunction and pathology.

3. Health vectors in the patient's environment, including his physical and interpersonal environment, are consciously and purposefully used by patient and therapist in the development of a total treatment program.

4. The patient is encouraged to invest of himself in the conscious transformation of aspects of his environment consonant with the goals and aims of treatment, *with the emphasis on active participation in the treatment process during the period between office visits.*

5. The patient is helped to undertake an assessment of his *life style* with the view of discovering how unconscious and symbolic components incorporated into the life style prevent both the actualization of potential and the emergence of personal authenticity. The patient's world view and value structure is explored vis-à-vis his total functioning, so that his sharpened awareness of the meaning of existence will irradiate the nature of his being and becoming.

6. Identification of deeply established habit patterns is undertaken to determine how these habit structures impede functioning. (For example, recreational patterns are often quite rigid, sterile,

and devoid of meaning.) The patient is encouraged to undertake a conscious restructuring of habit systems to provide for more positive and enriching experiences.

7. An assessment of the pleasure economy of the patient is undertaken. The question is asked, "Are there sufficient experiences of genuine, deep and spontaneous joy in the patient's life; and how can these be provided?" (Again, recreational habit systems often yield very attenuated or minimal joy and pleasure.) Genuine joy and pleasure (positive inputs) are placed in the service of growth and the actualization of potentialities—the achievement of therapeutic gains.

8. The soma is actively and fully involved in the treatment process by encouraging the patient to participate in specific physical regimes tailored to his needs and the development of his potentialities. (This is based on the recognition that identity and soma are for all practical purposes inseparable.) Such regimes may include physical-exercise programs, swimming, the use of steam baths, sauna, massage, hydrotherapy, "free form" or expressive dance, etc.

9. The therapist's office environment can be successfully transformed, based on the needs of the patient, at specific points in therapy. This can be achieved through the selective use of art, including abstract, impressionistic, or representational paintings, reproductions of illustrations, sculpture as well as posters. The use of abstract art for the purposes of free association and as a projective device has received some attention. Relatively neglected is the planned use of art works throughout the treatment program, based on an understanding of the patient's personality and his needs. Aesthetic objects can also be used as a part of treatment. If, for example, lilies of the valley have a deep meaning to a patient and represent the possibility of an aesthetic or "trigger" experience, use of this flower at a specific point in treatment can be of considerable value. The practice of symbolic offerings (chewing gum, candy, etc.) by the therapist at certain times in therapy is fairly widespread. However, the selective use of diet as a treatment adjunct is relatively uncommon. Much more can be done here, as well as in relation to providing an environment of odors at specific points in treatment.

10. Key segments of the interpersonal-relationship web of the patient can be successfully utilized as a part of the total treatment program. Not only are joint sessions with the immediate family of value and should be routinely undertaken, but interviews with close friends and associates should also be routinely conducted and can significantly transform the patient's interpersonal environment.

Specific methods have also been devised so that the patient can utilize aspects of his interpersonal network as a part of treatment.

A holistic treatment program is concerned with the treatment of the whole man—his psyche, soma, and environment simultaneously. By working with as many facets of man's being as feasible, patient and therapist together begin to recognize the interrelatedness of these wholes and how they can contribute to bring wholeness to man.

METHODS

A number of methods and techniques have been developed as a part of the Human Potentialities Research Project which have direct application to individual and group therapy.[17, 18, 19] These methods focus on the improvement of the self-image and self-concept and are essentially ego-supportive. It must be stressed that these methods should be used only after there has been a considerable working through of pathology and when, in the therapist's judgment, the patient is ready to profit optimally from an ego-supportive type of experience. This is usually at some time beyond the midpoint in treatment.

Most of the following methods and techniques have application both to individual and group therapy. One, the Multiple Strength Perception Method, has application only to group therapy.

The Supportive Environment Approach

The use of "supportive environment" is by no means new. Murphy and Cattell,[20] discussing Sullivan's relation to field theory, mention ". . . Sullivan's conception of the rebuilding of the patient's world as a first step in interpersonal theory."

Existential analyst Ludwig Binswanger points out that man is not a detached ego but a *being-in-the-world*. He emphasizes the dynamic process character of this *being* which is necessarily in relation to the world. Binswanger and the other existential analysts see the world with which every man is polarized as threefold: the *Umwelt*, consisting of our biological and physical foundations; the *Mitwelt* of man's social and interpersonal relations; and the *Eigenwelt* of one's inner life and self-consciousness, i.e., the basis on which one orients to reality. Binswanger stresses that all three realms of relation must be taken into account if there is to be adequate therapy or treatment, and that it is an error to emphasize one realm to the exclusion of the other two.[21]

Alexander, referring to a number of therapeutic studies of the Chicago Institute for Psychoanalysis, summarizes a series of technical recommendations resulting from these studies:

". . . The essence of them is that, from the beginning, the therapist must be aware of the danger inherent in the regressive tendencies of the patients. To counteract this danger, the analyst must consistently give the patient as much independence as possible. Interpretations alone cannot accomplish this. The dependent tendencies can often be counteracted by reducing the contact with the patient to that minimum which is necessary to preserve the continuity of the treatment. Properly timed reduction of the frequency of the interviews, shorter and longer interruptions, are indispensable in every case. *Encouraging the patient to new life-experiences outside the treatment suitable to increase self-confidence and encourage hope are also potent devices in weaning the patient from dependence on the therapist.*"[22] (Italics added.)

Comparatively little use seems to be made by the majority of therapists of the many environmental vectors which could be employed as supportive measures and therapeutic adjuncts. Ignoring the principle that the supportive environment can become an important adjunct in the therapeutic and treatment process constitutes one of the vast wastelands of therapy.

As a part of the Human Potentialities Research Project experimental groups have made extensive use of the Supportive Environment Approach. A description of this method as used in laboratory groups is presented, since a direct transposition of both practice and principles to individual and group therapy can be undertaken by the interested practitioner.

Members of the experimental groups are acquainted with the principle of "total environmental push" during the first or second session. They are told that the task of actualizing potential is a difficult one and that the more aspects of their environment they can enlist to aid in this process the better. The range of environmental aids is briefly presented in lecture form and discussed. The choice and initiative as to the use of environmental push is then left entirely a matter of individual decision by group participants. The following facets of "total environmental push" are presented:

1. Analysis and restructuring of living space. The living space of the participant can be analyzed by him from a number of perspectives. For example, what sort of feelings do the furniture arrangement, color combinations, and interior decoration give to the group member? Can living space be analyzed in terms of the needs of the group member or the family? Can furniture or interior

decoration be changed in such a way as to give a greater feeling of freedom, lightness, airiness, space—or, conversely, hominess or snugness? The rationale here is that the home environment can serve to maintain and reinforce the participant's focus on personal growth and the aims and purposes of the group experience, which thereby is extended into the life space of the patient. Often a group member was able to "restructure" only one room, such as a bedroom. However, participants reported that every time the room was used, "It reminds me of the group and what I am working on."

2. Analysis and use of significant symbols. It is suggested that group members may be interested in identifying *significant symbols* in their home and examining the effect of these symbols on themselves. What keepsakes, paintings, or photographs are there to which the participant has emotional linkages? What is the meaning of these symbolic objects and how do they make the participant feel? From this viewpoint, does the photograph of father, mother, or aunt really belong on the mantelpiece? What does the symbol have to do with strengths and potentialities in the participant? On the other hand, can paintings, sculpture, keepsakes, or other symbolic or aesthetic objects be used in a supportive way to focus attention on the task of developing strengths and actualizing potentialities?

3. Use of diet and food. It is pointed out that a diet tailored to the individual needs of the group member can be used. Such a diet may be a reducing diet or one designed to assist in the gaining of weight. It may also be a so-called high-energy diet. The use of food in relation to energy, fatigue, and physical strength and the symbolic use of food are discussed. If necessary, an analysis is undertaken of how specific participants use food—is there monotony in meal patterns? Are meals too rushed and eaten in unaesthetic surroundings? What is the effect of this on the self-image and self-concept? It is pointed out that through diet and other uses of food group members can have a very satisfying experience three times daily, which at the same time reinforces and helps them to focus on the objective and goals of personal growth.

4. Use of personal restyling. It is suggested that group participants may be interested in examining the use of facial make-up, clothing styles, and color combinations, as well as hairdo, as means of contributing to a more positive self-image and to maintain the strength focus. Use of a highly trained beautician with a special interest in people is recommended. Similarly, men are asked to examine their use of wearing apparel, haircut, and style of eyeglasses. If indicated, the following questions are raised: What are

you presenting to the world through the personal symbolism of your make-up, clothing styles, etc.? What message does it give to others (group members)? *Is this the message you want to convey—the image you want to project?* Are you taking the best advantage of the physical assets you have through creative use of clothing styles (tailoring), color combinations, etc.?

5. Interpersonal relations as a source of support. It is pointed out that "we grew into what we are through interpersonal relations and we grow into what we can be through interpersonal relations." The statement is made that the complex web of interpersonal relations in which we find ourselves can be subjected to an analysis by asking ourselves: "Which relationships are experienced as especially supportive or strengthening?" Since certain interpersonal relationships are experienced as strengthening, then other relationships may be experienced as unhealthy and tending to weaken, or as restimulating pathological areas in the group member. The question is then raised: "Can interpersonal relationships be deliberately sustained with the idea of seeking primarily those associations which are experienced as strengthening and which will help you in your efforts to actualize your potential?"

6. Physical exercise as a supportive measure. It is pointed out that the development of strengths and potentialities must include physical as well as emotional and attitudinal aspects. The interrelatedness of psyche and soma is stressed. Participants are urged to examine their current use of physical exercise and their health status. A physical examination is suggested when indicated. The question is raised whether a regime of physical exercises is of importance in the development of personality strengths and resources. In this connection, the relationship of physical exercise to emotional states is discussed ("Exercise makes you feel good") and the effect of physical exercise on the self-image is briefly explored.

It is the writer's conclusion that if a regime of physical exercises which has symbolic and emotional significance to the individual is linked with the group experience, considerably accelerated progress in utilizing strengths and actualizing potentialities can be achieved. For example, preceding or following group sessions, participants should be able to swim in a heated pool, have an opportunity for massage and steam baths, and be able to exercise or dance in a gymnasium or studio-type facility. Currently, therapeutic programs are characterized by their failure to utilize physical regimes which can have definite ego-supportive values, as well as a profound effect on the patient's self-image.

Over the past two decades there has been a slowly growing recognition (especially on the part of practitioners of psychiatry and psychology) that aspects of the patient's environment should be included in treatment programs. In some measure the development of this viewpoint has been aided by the burgeoning growth of mental health clinics, which are often heavily staffed with social workers. Although the profession of social work has traditionally been identified with the concept of "environmental manipulation," not only has the word "manipulation" acquired negative connotations, but the whole concept of working with the environment has consistently been interpreted and used in a very narrow and superficial fashion. The same critique applies to the theoretical constructs associated with the term "environmental therapy," which also need extensive elaboration and development in depth. It is high time for the helping professions to re-evaluate and re-examine both the concept and role of environment as related to the treatment program. Perhaps the introduction of a different nomenclature can hasten this process and lead to more adequate utilization of the environment in a unified treatment program. The term "environmental reconstruction" is suggested to encompass the six areas previously discussed.

Action Programs

This method is useful in both individual and group therapy. It is based on the assumption that the interim period between appointments can be utilized plannedly and systematically in an effort to help the counselee achieve growth. Action programs are defined as *any activity, program, or interpersonal experience which the participant engages in outside of the office setting in order to facilitate the development of strengths or the utilization of his potential.* Selection of the type of action program to be undertaken is left very largely to the initiative of the patient. We begin where he is and encourage him to prescribe for himself. Again, this method is best used after the approximate midpoint of treatment has been passed. Action programs initially are of a very simple nature (improvements in grooming, buying a new dress, etc.) and gradually become more complex (building new friendships). Action programs are usually carried to conclusion in from three to seven days. On completion of an action program, patients discuss with the therapist what undertaking the program has done for them. If the action program has not been completed, resistances are examined.

If the method is to be used in group therapy, we have found it of value to point out that "this is not only a talking group, but an action group." It is stressed that increased utilization of strengths and problem-solving abilities does not take place solely as a result of one group meeting a week, regardless of the depth of personal exchange or experience. Group members are urged immediately to become involved in action programs, and are asked to use their best judgment in selecting that action program "which would do most for them."

Successes or failures with action programs are then reported back to the group by the individual members, and evaluation of these programs is constantly undertaken to determine to what extent the individual is helped to develop strengths and encouraged to use potentialities. When resistance or difficulties in sustaining action programs are encountered, group members are urged to ask the assistance of the total group. The group then brings its sensitivity and perceptivity to bear in an effort to help the individual reach an increased understanding of what is keeping him from utilizing a specific action program. By use of action programs, the therapeutic process is extended into the process of living as the patient invests himself in purposive action outside the office setting as a means of achieving therapeutic gains.

Strength-Role Assignment

A precursor of strength-role assignment is Kelly's Fixed Role Therapy.[23] There are, however, some significant differences in these methods. In fixed role therapy, the client is asked to act out a fictitious person over a period of time on the basis of a "fixed role sketch" furnished by the clinician. Assigned strength roles primarily used in a group setting encourages the participant to select and define his own role using the group or clinician as a resource.

This method also utilizes the life space outside the office setting. It requires the presence of some ego strength, motivation, and self-investment on the part of the patient. When, in the therapist's judgment, use of the method is indicated, the method is briefly explained to the patient. The choice of whether he would like to use the method is then left to him. If he agrees to try, he is handed a set of "strength roles" (these are best typed on 4-by-5-inch cards) and asked to select the particular strength role which he would enjoy carrying out. Following is a list of possible strength roles (which can be expanded by the therapist):

1. You are a very friendly and outgoing person. You like to share your ideas and thoughts with others and to take the initiative.

2. You are a person who thinks things through before taking action. You very rarely act impulsively and maintain an even temper.

3. You are a person with a good sense of humor, who likes to tell jokes and entertain people.

4. You are a creative (artistic) person, and you express your creativity through painting, drawing, writing, or you think up new and novel ways of doing things. You can, for example, lend touches of beauty to the home for the times the family has together.

5. You are a very honest person who never holds back the truth as you see it. You are completely honest with people.

6. You are a person who has definite latent leadership qualities. You seek opportunities to exercise these qualities. At meetings and other events you let your voice be heard and your influence felt.

7. You are a person with considerable "stick-to-it-iveness" or perseverance. You use this quality to tackle specific things that you have put off doing; you stick with it and persist in your efforts until there has been some change.

Strength roles can and should be made up and tailored to the specific needs of the person who chooses to participate in a strength-role assignment. After the patient has selected a strength role, it is next clarified that the selected strength role should be *lived* (or acted out) in the period between therapeutic sessions. (From four to seven days is the usual time period allotted for the planned living out of strength roles.) As a next step, it is suggested that patient and therapist define and "spell out" some of the concrete behaviors and actions which are involved in carrying out the strength role. (The initiative should here, as much as possible, rest with the patient.) It is best if the patient is encouraged to take notes at this point and to write out specific behaviors and actions.

During the session following completion of the strength-role assignment, the experience with the assigned strength role is discussed in detail as to its effect on the patient and those close to him. Growth or change which has taken place is identified and the feelings of the patient around the strength role are discussed. Resistances to the carrying out of the role are explored.

When used in a group, the method is first described in detail by the therapist and its voluntary aspects noted. Cards with one strength role typed on each are passed around at this time. Those wishing to participate in the method can then be asked to write their names on a slip of paper, which is folded and put into a receptacle. Selection is by a random drawing. Before beginning the process, the therapist should again carefully stress that the purpose of strength-role assignment is *not* to correct a person's shortcomings, weaknesses, or problems by asking this person to do something he may not wish to do. The purpose of the method is for everyone to help the person whose name has been drawn to work out a strength role which he will enjoy carrying out and which will strengthen him. To begin the process of strength-role assignment, the person whose name has been drawn should turn to the group and ask members the key question in words similar to the following, "What is the role which you think would strengthen me most?" It is only after the key question has been asked that all the other members should contribute their ideas as to what role would most strengthen the person selected.

Assignment of the strength role is on the basis of group discussion and consensus. Following the assignment specific behaviors associated with the strength role are spelled out by the group. Notes are taken by a volunteer who writes down these specific behaviors suggested by the group for the person selected. These notes are subsequently handed to him. Approximately a week later the person selected then shares with the group his experience with strength-role assignment.

The strength role which is assigned should be "tailored" to the specifications of the person, with his wishes a fundamental consideration in the role assignment. He should want to enter into the strength role assigned to him of his own accord and should be able to enjoy the role. Coercion, or forcing the strength role on a person through group pressure, should very rarely be attempted, and only under special circumstances, as, for example, when a person "wants to be persuaded" by the group into accepting a role.

Strength-role assignment often has a marked carry-over effect extending beyond the period of assignment and into the life of the individual. We have noted that in many instances family and associates will recognize changes in behavior and make comments such as "You are so much more outgoing" and "You are much more thoughtful and nicer." Such comments and observations tend to reinforce the behavior and contribute to growth and positive change. Especially toward the end of therapy, strength-role assignment can be a rewarding experience for the patient.

Use of "These Are Your Strengths" Forms

This method also is best used when the patient has passed the approximate midpoint in treatment. It is designed to provide the patient with a series of positive, ego-supportive experiences. A secondary aim is to mobilize and enlist aspects of the patient's interpersonal-relationship environment in his efforts to regain healthier and more optimal functioning. The very simplicity of this method is deceptive, as oftentimes complex forces are set in motion through its use. The method is first described in detail and the choice of whether or not to use it is left to the patient.

The method is briefly as follows: Mimeographed forms are used which are headed: "These Are What I See as Your Personality Strengths and Resources." The remainder of the page is blank, except that the right-hand part of the form contains, for use by the patient, the word "Name: _____" and under that the word "Date: _____." The explanation is given that it is the purpose of the method to provide a series of interpersonal experiences of a positive nature designed to give the participant an understanding of how people close to him perceive his strengths and personality assets. It is noted that "Oftentimes those close to us have a different perspective or clearer idea of our resources than we do, because we are too close to ourselves and not accustomed to thinking in terms of our strengths." It is pointed out that "These Are Your Strengths" forms can be given to family members or relatives, close friends and associates, or superiors in the vocational setting. Participants usually explain to those to whom they are handing the form that filling it out will be helpful to them and that this is part of a self-improvement program in which they are engaged.

Participants are urged to take as many forms as they wish and to use them with persons who know them well. It is further pointed out that they may wish to have an informal discussion with the person after he has filled in the form. Objectives of this informal discussion would be to seek clarification or amplification in relation to certain listed strengths, to ask for examples which have led the person filling out the form to the conclusion that the participant has a particular personality resource, and so forth.

It has been found that use of this method often brings about specific modifications in the interpersonal environment of participants. Sometimes complex and subtle changes are set in motion which are not noticed by those concerned until time has passed. Persons close to the participant will in many instances acquire a different perspective of the participant's worth and regard him with increased esteem. This can bring about attitudinal change and change in the manner of relating to the participant which is sometimes dramatic: "Since my boss filled out the form, he treats me like a different person"; "Two of my friends said they feel so much closer to me since they wrote out my strengths and talked to me about it." The patient's experience with "These Are Your Strengths" forms is discussed with the therapist and used in therapy as indicated. We have found that in many instances use of the forms not only fosters the patient's self-confidence but furnishes him with valuable insights.

The Multiple Strength Perception Method

This group method is often called "strength bombardment" by participants. Again, it is best to use this method beyond the mid-point of the group's approximate life span and after significant progress has been made in working out the individual problems of most group members. As a preliminary step to the use of the method, the group needs to develop its own frame of reference as to what is meant by "personality strengths." An alternative is for the therapist to present a broad frame of reference of personality resources, for which the Otto Inventory of Personal Resources has been found to be of special value. (This inventory is available in three forms from the Human Potentialities Research Project, the University of Utah. "Form A" is designed for adolescents aged four-teen to eighteen, "Form B" is for persons having a college-level educational background, and "Form D" is designed for persons having an educational background of one year of high school or more.) This is a self-scoring inventory including 18 strength areas, which describes in detail 198 strength items. The instrument is designed to give the user an overview and indication of his personality assets; it also contains a "strength profile."

We have found it best to employ the following procedure in the use of the M.S.P. method:

1. The method is first described in detail and the Key Questions are put on the blackboard.

2. The group then has the choice whether to use the method or not.

3. If the group wishes to use the method, volunteers are asked to write their names on a piece of paper, to fold it, and drop it into a receptacle. A name is then drawn at random, and the person selected becomes the "target person."

4. The target person now begins the process by verbally sharing with participants what he considers to be his strengths. After he has completed listing his strengths, the target person must then ask the group this Key Question, using the following or similar words: "What other strengths or potentialities do you see me as having, and

what factors or problems do you see as keeping me from using these strengths?"

5. Following this, all group members share with the target person what they perceive as being his strengths. This is done in an informal manner with all group members contributing their perceptions of the strengths of the individual who has volunteered to be the target person. Problems or obstacles which keep the person from using his strengths or actualizing his potential are also discussed, although the focus is predominantly on the identification of personality assets and resources.

6. When the group interaction begins to slow down, the therapist asks, "Are there any other strengths we see in John [or Mary] if he [or she] were to use all of these strengths or potentials? What do we see him [or her] doing five years from now?" The group now shares its dream or fantasy about the target person.

It is one of our findings that the shared-group fantasy often shows a surprising correspondence with the deepest wish-dreams of the individual. The fantasies of the group coincide in most instances with 60 per cent or more of the deepest dreams and wishes the target person has about himself. This is a profoundly ego-supportive and ego-building experience for the target person. As a closure for the method, some therapists prefer to ask the target person one of the following questions: "What dream do you have for yourself?" or "How did you feel when the 'bombardment' was going on?"

The use of the M.S.P. method over a period of four years resulted in a number of conclusions and findings:

1. Within a compartively short period of time group members are able to develop a significantly increased sensitivity or perceptivity of strengths, resources, or potentialities in group members or other persons. It became evident with the first experimental groups that group participants used a wide range of nonverbal clues in the process of searching out strengths. Remarks such as "I noticed that your voice changed when you said this during our last meeting" and "There was a sparkle in your eye when you talked about this three sessions ago" were frequent.

2. Use of the M.S.P. method appears to be related to positive changes in the behavior and functioning of participants. In peer group and family relationships, for example, participants tended to be increasingly aware of the strengths and potentialities of friends, associates, and family members.

3. Use of the M.S.P. method seems to have contributed to the

strengthening or enhancing of the self-image of participants. Group members reported feeling "more capable," "more competent," "more ready to try out new ideas or activities." They also pointed out that prior to this experience they did not have a clear idea of the range of their strengths and potentialities, whereas they had a fairly good grasp of their weaknesses and problems. They stated that use of the method had contributed to a clearer understanding of the "topography of their strengths," leading to a more realistic self-appraisal. This was evident from recurrent statements similar to the following: "This has given me a much more balanced picture of myself"; "I am much clearer about my personality assets and liabilities—this helps me select goals I can achieve and stick to, because I know I have the resources to carry through."

It is hoped that the foregoing methods will add to the armamentarium of the therapist interested in the use of action therapies and the practitioner concerned about the development of a holistic treatment concept. It is the combination of these approaches which offers a great challenge and a greater promise.

REFERENCES

1. Maslow, A. H., *Motivation and Personality* (New York: Harper & Row, 1954), pp. 20ff.
2. Bertalanffy, L. von, *Problems of Life* (New York: John Wiley and Sons, 1952).
3. Angyal, A., *Neuroses and Treatment, A Holistic Theory* (New York: John Wiley and Sons, 1965).
4. Fromm, E., *Man for Himeslf* (New York: Holt, Rinehart & Winston, 1947).
5. Kubie, L. S., *Neurotic Distortion of the Creative Process*, Porter Lectures, Series 22 (Lawrence, Kans.: University of Kansas Press, 1958).
6. Maslow, A. H., *Toward a Psychology of Being* (Princeton, N.J.: Van Nostrand, 1962).
7. Mead, M., Culture and Personality Development: Human Capacities, in *Man, Science, Learning and Education*, The Semi-Centennial Lectures at Rice University (Chicago: University of Chicago Press, 1963), pp. 241-54.
8. Murphy, G., *Human Potentialities* (New York: Basic Books, 1961).
9. Rogers, C. R., *On Becoming a Person* (Boston: Houghton Mifflin, 1961).
10. Pedagogical Quests, *U.S.S.R., Soviet Life Today*, 42-45, November, 1964.
11. Otto, H. A., ed., *Explorations in Human Potentialities* (Springfield, Ill.: Charles C Thomas, 1966).
12. Otto, H. A., *A Guide to the Release of Your Potential* (New York: Charles Scribner's Sons, 1967).
13. Otto, H. A., and J. Mann, eds., *Ways of Growth* (New York: Grossman, 1968).
14. Kubie, L. S., Social Forces and the Neurotic Process, in Alexander H. Leighton and others, *Explorations in Social Psychiatry* (New York: Basic Books, 1957).

15. Kaufmann, M., High-Level Wellness, a Pertinent Concept for the Health Professions, *Mental Hygiene,* 47:57-58, 1963.
16. Berelson, B., and Steiner, G. A., *Human Behavior—Inventory of Scientific Findings* (New York: Harcourt, Brace & World, 1964), p. 59.
17. Otto, H. A., The Personal and Family Resource Development Programs—A Preliminary Report, *International Journal of Social Psychiatry,* 8, 3:185-95, Summer 1962.
18. Otto, H. A., The Personal and Family Strength Research Projects—Some Implications for the Therapist, *Mental Hygiene,* 48, 3:439-50, July 1964.
19. Otto, H. A., Personal and Family Strength Research and Spontaneity Training, *Group Psychotherapy Journal,* 17, 2-3:439-50, June-September 1964.
20. Murphy, G., and Cattell, C., Sullivan and Field Theory, in *The Contribution of Harry Stack Sullivan* (New York: Hermitage House, 1952).
21. Binswanger, L., quoted in Rollo May, The Existential Approach, in Silvano Arieti, ed., *American Handbook of Psychiatry* (New York: Basic Books, 1959), Vol. II, pp. 1355-56.
22. Alexander, F., Development of the Fundamental Concepts of Psychoanalysis, in *Dynamic Psychiatry* (Chicago: University of Chicago Press, 1952).
23. Kelly, George A., *The Psychology of Personal Constructs* (New York: Norton, 1955), pp. 360-451.

ARON KRICH

Active Strategies in Marriage Counseling

In addition to describing a series of active interventions in the practice of marriage counseling, Krich also places this relatively recent discipline within the framework of psychotherapy in general. While he limits himself to describing the counseling of couples, there are interesting similarities between some of Krich's work and that of Haley in dealing with the total family interaction.

IN INDIVIDUAL COUNSELING or therapy, a single person brings himself, however reluctantly, for scrutiny. And though he may be, at first, fixated on "personal constructs" and more ready to communicate about externals than about his internal conflicts, anxieties, and confusions, he cannot—except by massive resistance—escape the fact that his difficulties, at least, are his own. The marriage counselor, by contrast, is presented with a crisis in living where immediacy not only belies the long twofold prehistory of the suffering partners but also hides a deteriorated intimate relationship behind institutional grievances. It is as though the old vaudeville "egg": *Marriage is a great institution; but who wants to be married to an institution?* has come to his office to hatch.

Therapeutic technique must, therefore, be determined not only with relevance to the cultural framework of the couple but also to the maturational level of each spouse. Motivational level, in turn, tends to correspond with stages in personality development. If significant emotional learning is to take place, the therapist's first order of business must be to raise the existing level of motivation for change in each spouse discretely as well as in the marital dyad. The counselor—not the counselees—begins with the awareness that when two people marry there ensues an interaction which can either be productive or destructive for themselves, their children, and the society around them. We, not they, are convinced that wherever unconscious goals exert a preponderant influence, the very qualities that drew the couple together become sources of tension. We, not they, feel it is by now redundant to elaborate on the part played by the family in the making of personality and on the unbelievable cost in human unhappiness when early life experience produces maladjustment, conflict, and fear.

This transfer of conviction must, in the ordinary setting of fairly short-term marriage counseling, be accomplished by encounters between the "professionally trained person" and "the other" which are usually limited to a single hour in the week. The traditional techniques of marriage counseling are an amalgam of approaches defined chiefly by client-centeredness. An eclectic "field," its theories and practices have derived—often on a folkloristic basis— from an empirical admixture of the original training of its founding fathers and mothers: social casework, dynamic psychiatry, clinical psychology, obstetrics and gynecology, and education. (A decade ago membership in the American Association of Marriage Counselors consisted of 19 per cent physicians—of whom 5 per cent were psychiatrists—16 per cent educators, 20 per cent social workers, 14 per cent clinical psychologists, 12 per cent sociologists, 15 per cent ministers, 4 per cent lawyers. These figures have shifted a little by the addition of a growing number of individuals coming out of accredited graduate training programs in marriage counseling per se.) The traditional posture of the individual counselor, overriding or complementing his basic discipline, has been one of warmth and acceptance with the aim of getting the client to "put out feelings."

The theoretical framework behind this approach has been posed by Emily H. Mudd[1] in the following hypothesis: "If an individual can experience during the counseling process, new understanding of himself and his marriage partner and more satisfying ways of using himself in his daily relationships in marriage and with his family, he should be able to apply these acquired abilities to other problem situations as these arise in his daily living." Given the differential that the focus of the counselor's approach is the relation-

1. Emily H. Mudd, Marriage Counseling: A Philosophy and Method, in E. H. Mudd and A. Krich, *Man and Wife* (New York: Norton, 1957).

ship between the two people in the marriage rather than, as in intensive individual psychotherapy, the reorganization of the personality structure of the individual, the acquisition of these new life abilities could well be said to be a goal common to both therapies.

By its nature, however, marriage counseling tends to put the counselor in the perceptual foreground. His clients are familiar with the image of the psychoanalytic patient stretched out on the couch with the bearded analyst taking notes behind him. They are also familiar with the image of the judge or arbitrator. They may even have the wish for, if not the familiarity with, the image of the wise man of yore. And all therapists have experienced the temptation to grant this primary wish of our clients for someone to take charge of their lives. This kind of pressure, it seems to me, is particularly great on the marriage counselor.

At first encounter, the couple who arrive at the door of the marriage counselor cannot be other than dependent—they have come to *him* for something, however denied or exaggerated. How directive should he be? As little, I would say, as the two parties can tolerate when the prior dependencies of the clients *and the counselor* are pushed aside.

On the whole, our clients are suffering from the fact that throughout their lives they have been constantly "told what to do." Often infantilized, or at best with indeterminate identities characteristic of adolescence, their autonomy of personality has been vitiated in spiritless acquiescence or petulant, rebellious disappointment around stereotypical responses, rather than preserved in authentic personal responses which are more appropriate to situations of intimacy. Often there resides in the individual a stubbornly held resistance to being "told what to do." But rooted as it is in a preadult developmental stage, this resistance, at its best, tends to be a skewed or confused last-ditch attempt to defend the precious autonomy of the personality. More often it takes the form of a neuroticized and encapsulated refusal "to listen." It is in these instances that active strategies are most effectively deployed. Indeed, they become the "treatment of choice."

Obviously the whole world has been "telling" the troublesome, idiosyncratic individual that he is "wrong." If he had within himself sufficient dynamic leeway to contemplate alternatives he would have "listened" long before. The counselor must, then, promptly differentiate himself from all the "others" in the client's historical and present existence. "No man is an island" is not an operative metaphor for the deviant or isolated human being. He is on an island and the water around him is rising. We must join him on that island and either help him back to the mainland or crowd his island with our presence until he experiences our invasion with enough paradigmatic "annoyance" to leave it solely to us. We therapists, it is assumed, can get back to the mainland on our own.

How active should the counselor be? As much as the sophistication of his techniques permit, to get the clients to take charge of their own lives right then and there. By way of illustration, I might point out that I find myself lately more and more—in the course of the first session, when normally the couple are together and intent on delineating the hopelessness of their situation—throwing up my hands in *real*, mock seriousness and saying things like: "Do you expect *me* to straighten this out? King Solomon died three thousand years ago!" Or, when a couple are belaboring each other with hostility: "Aren't you afraid to be sitting next to each other? Maybe one of you should be sitting across the room!" Or, if ten years of marital interaction are hurled at me in ten minutes: "How long did you say you've been married? Ten years? But I have only known you ten minutes! It'll take me at least a year before I can answer *that* question. Do you think you can stick it out with each other until I find out who is right and who is wrong?" Sometimes I tell the couple that they have come to the wrong place; that they really need the address of the nearest police precinct or the name of a good lawyer.

These are active techniques intended to turn the client's attention from complaint to communication. A few sessions later, these clients are likely to come in, grin at my silence, and announce with some pleasure: "Okay, I know what you want. You want me to take charge of my own session." A less compliant response might be: "I don't know what I'm paying you for. I do all the talking and you tell me you're making me an expert on myself!" Either way they have learned something of how people can grow and change through their own initiative and "become able to survive and even live creatively within the same framework that existed when they first sought help, or find the courage, initiative, and faith to effect difference in their surroundings by their own efforts."[2]

It is quite likely that such movement could be effected by less active techniques. Most people, if accepted as they are, without condemnation, will respond to naturalness and the relief of being permitted to be themselves. The amount of activity, it seems to me, is usually determined by an assessment of characters and defenses

2. Mudd, *op. cit.*

and the counselor's flexibility and freedom to bring these strategies into play. An attitude of receptivity to the client must, however, remain constant. What is the nature of this receptivity? Carl Rogers tells us it means that "whatever the client's feelings—fear, despair, insecurity, anger; whatever his mode of expression—silence, gestures, tears or words; whatever he finds himself being in this moment, he senses that he is psychologically *received,* just as he is."[3] But Rogers is careful to point out it is the "client's experience of this condition which makes it optimal, not merely the fact of its existence in the therapist."

Old hands know that such receptivity is never of itself a magical property of the therapist. And, as Rogers is careful to point out, even if its exists in the therapist he must get the client to experience it. Here, I believe, is the nexus which binds the activity of the therapist to the needs of his client. Someone with a gift for metaphor has called this dimension of therapeutic discipline "the will power of desirelessness." If love is not enough, neither is mere listening—though old hands know, too, that listening can be hard work. Rogers emphasizes, as well, that the other person needs to be understood. Experience in supervision of trainees in marriage counseling frequently brings forward occasions on which the tape recorder plays back an obscure or intriguing communication of a client. What does the client mean? The trainee does not know. I have learned by now that trainees need supervisory "permission" to ask the client what he means. The mystique of listening has somehow given the act of asking a straightforward, direct question such as "What do you mean?" the stigma of invasion of privacy. Sessions following supervisory encouragement to ask questions which lead to communication are usually highlighted by recorded exchanges of relief and pleasure at the breakdown of a basic communication barrier. This applies to the idiosyncratic or paleological communication of the more deeply disturbed patient, which may still remain somewhat obscure after the inquiry, as well as to the normally anxious communications of one person to another who is still something of a stranger.

Receptivity is not a technique but a basic attitude, a quality of the therapist as a person, which makes possible a variety of strategies, active and passive. Is not deliberate silence one of the most active—and provocative—of therapeutic events? Restraint from doing and saying may also be highly conscious strategic activities.

3. Carl R. Rogers, A Process Conception of Psychotherapy, *American Psychologist,* April 1958.

Out of theoretical commitments quite different from Rogers', Karl Menninger warns against the *furor sanandi* in his excellent book *Theory of Psychoanalytic Technique*. But he also derides "those constitutionally passive individuals who seem to operate on the theory that healing rays emanate from them so that patients should get well by virtue of merely being exposed to those benign influences."[4]

The task of the therapist to free himself of the frenzy to cure may, at first glance, seem to contradict the orientation of more active approaches to the patient. On the contrary, many active strategies take their form from an apparent refusal to cure. Let us consider the following actual exchange with a depressed housewife. This mother of two small children was finding her life at home increasingly disturbing, but felt too guilty about her negative feelings toward her maternal role to acknowledge openly that she wished to hire a housekeeper and return to the business world. Weeping, she announced that it was getting to be too much for her and that she had better go into a hospital. The therapist agreed with her. It was, indeed, too much for her to handle! Had she given some thought to which hospital she would go into? The patient acknowledged that she would not want to go into a public facility. She had in mind some pleasant type of rest home, but this was beyond her means. Mulling this thought over—with the therapist actively participating in trying to solve the dilemma by naming various institutions and speculating on the costs—the patient arrived at the conclusion that she would have to go to work to save up enough money to go into the hospital of her choice. Weeping turned into a wan smile. The patient had taken the first step to the actual solution of her life situation, which occurred shortly after. With guilt reduced she decided to take a part-time job. At the same time, of course, she had externalized her own profound fears of helpless collapse.

Menninger quite rightly memorialized Freud's restraint from "saying and doing"; but the patients of the formative years of psychoanalysis are not the patients of contemporary clinical practice. Would interpretation have as effectively led to self-confrontation as did "joining" this patient's own expression of hopelessness? After all, the whole world had been telling her to cheer up! Only her therapist was "on her side" in telling her she had the right to collapse. This strategic respect for the autonomy of the person

4. Karl Menninger, *Theory of Psychoanalytic Technique* (New York: Basic Books, 1958).

in emotional difficulty has had a long and somewhat convoluted history. Paradoxically, the tradition of patient acceptance begins with a reduction in the therapist's activity early in the formative period of psychoanalysis; but today much of the impetus toward a redefinition of the therapist's participation is in reaction to the model of the classically neutral, orthodox psychoanalyst.

This is not the occasion to pursue the development of psychoanalytic technique from cathartic abreaction to the "working through" of transference and resistance to the nuances of contemporary ego psychology. We know that as early as 1892, Freud had become bored with the monotony of repeating suggestions.[5] In that year he wrote to Charcot: "Neither the doctor nor the patient can tolerate indefinitely the contradiction between the decisive denial of the disorder in suggestion and the necessary recognition of it away from suggestion." In later years, Freud revealed his uneasiness in observing one of his French masters in hypnotism —probably Bernheim—raging at a hysteric: "You are countersuggesting! You are countersuggesting!" At any rate, by 1896 the term "psychoanalysis" was first employed in a published paper and Freud was putting his trust in the talking-listening interaction, which he found by following what he himself called "an obscure intuition."[6]

The point I want to stress is that from the time Freud transferred the operative center of therapeutic process from the authority of the doctor to the autonomy of the patient, it has become increasingly clear that authentic movement in personality change comes with the patient's ability to "take charge" of himself. Pressure to innovate and elaborate treatment procedures which push the activity of the patient beyond the parameter of free association, and the activity of the therapist beyond the parameter of interpretation, increased in our own era with the broadening of the milieu of psychotherapy from the consulting room into the playroom of the settlement house, the crowded office of the social agency, the examining table of the gynecologist. Group therapy with adolescents, dynamic intervention in family process, translation of sexual and reproductive dysfunction into terms of marital interaction introduce *in situ* therapies which complement the shift in preoccupation from the id to the ego.

Symbolically, we might say, this shift is represented by the movement of the patient population from the horizontal to the

5. Ernest Jones, *The Life and Work of Sigmund Freud* (New York: Basic Books, 1953), Vol. 1.
6. *Ibid.*

"sitting up" position. Whether we see ourselves in terms of the Sullivanian participant observer, the Rogerian empathic reflector, the existential being, or even the "blank screen" of classical psychoanalysis, the common denominator on the professional side of the person-serving process is a disciplined and acutely observed receptivity. This "set" in the therapist is the very antithesis of passivity. Nor does it imply a poverty of technique such as has been caricatured in the story of the "nondirective counselor" muttering, "Uh, huh," as the client goes sailing out of the window! Every word, every gesture, of the counselor is, after all, an intervention in the life of the counselee. The task is to get him to listen to us as actively as we listen to him.

Nor does "face to face" activity imply a limitation of material to daily realities. I have found, for example, that a kind of actively encouraged "role play" of a fantasied love object is quite effective in dealing with disappointment in a marital partner. If the client is not too intractable, it soon becomes apparent to him or her that disappointed romantic yearnings, being attached to a fantasy, are being used to reject the available, flesh-and-blood spouse.

Usually, the client is able to see that this is unfair competition, particularly if the counselor can show that he or she is being projected into the fantasy without blemish. Ordinarily, these clients will not "associate" in such directions. They usually require a device such as "pushing a button" to open the door of secret expectations and wishes. The mental relationship with the fantasied love object is also "counseled." The question "How is your love life going?" will be understood by the client to refer to the fantasy love life. The "relationship" with the fantasy partner is examined in every detail, including its sexual delights, until these become so "real" that the client becomes intrigued with the possibility of trying out some of the new experiences on the flesh-and-blood spouse. This approach, incidentally, originates from experiences in counseling the relationship where there actually is "a third party." On occasion, I have seen "the other woman" or "the other man" in the office, sometimes for a number of sessions. Where the extramarital relationship is viable it sometimes leads to a less disruptive termination of the old marriage and movement into the new one. Where the "third party" counseling reveals conspicuous acting-out, it usually leads to what Alfred Adler is said to have called "spitting in the patient's soup."

But counseling is not primarily the management of an external situation. Nor is it a process of indoctrination. As I have said earlier, the marriage counselor does have great demands placed upon him at the outset. The immediate life situation may be so pressing that the counselor must give it practical common-sense attention, while at the same time initiating the process of self-exploration and self-growth. His role, for the moment, may be that of a parent—a good one, we hope—with a child in trouble. But essential therapy occurs when we bring into movement the same processes of personality development, with a sequence of experiences and solutions, to which the growing child is exposed, but which, in our clients, have become static, blocked by repetition of inadequate solutions and incapacitating conflicts. There can be no violation of therapeutic canon in vigorously offering our clients a "second chance."

Thus, a client at a crucial stage in our relationship kept protesting: "I don't like what you're doing to me. You're making me selfish and self-centered. You're trying to make me into a bastard!" This man, a rotund, "jolly" philanthropist, was suffering from a particularly embarrassing manifestation of retarded ejaculation which covered marital resentments hidden by an idealized, democratic family life. His father had died during the patient's puberty; his mother committed suicide shortly after; his only brother was killed in an accident; his first wife had died in pregnancy. He resisted stubbornly—in his own jolly way—all acceptance of his anger. Gradually, as he became able to tolerate negative feelings, it became apparent that among other reasons for his inability to culminate the sex act intravaginally there was his anger at adding another child to his already large family.

Here the importance of working with the spouse as well is dramatically borne out. I was seeing the frustrated and bewildered wife intermittently. On this occasion, I asked her whether she was using her diaphragm even in those unterminated acts of intercourse which still took place. Learning that she was not—her response was "What's the use? He won't finish anyway!"—I urged her to make a special point of letting her husband know she was inserting the diaphragm. On the next occasion of intercourse, normal coitus took place. In reporting the event, the husband acknowledged his realization of the amount of hidden anger at increased family responsibilities, resentments against his wife, and a variety of long-buried pseudo-compliant patterns. Later he announced, "All my life I've felt like I was being pushed around by something outside myself—willingly—but never really feeling I was being myself." He had insight, too, which he expressed by saying that I had "not done anything" to him except to challenge him to take charge of his real feelings.

I can think of no better metaphor to describe this process of returning the personality to its existential core than that used by Freud himself, back in 1904,[7] in describing his "novel therapy for the neuroses" before the College of Physicians in Vienna. Freud assured the skeptical professors that his method, which "like sculpture, does not seek to add or to introduce anything new but to take away something, to bring out something" was not easy. He reminded his listeners that Hamlet's uncle had appointed two "psychotherapists"—the courtiers Rosencrantz and Guildenstern—to direct the "madman" back to compliance. But their efforts were so clumsy that Hamlet had to protest: "S'blood, do you think I am easier to be played on than a pipe? Call me what instrument you will, though you can fret me you cannot play upon me."

There is today increasing recognition of the therapist's role as "double agent."[8] Not only does he act as mediator between the public and private spheres of life; he must also become more flexibly involved in strategic operations at the balance point between the "therapeutic alliance" and the "therapeutic barrier." Rosencrantz and Guildenstern could not "play" Hamlet because they were not working for him. Paradoxically, it is often in the area of convincing the patient that the therapist is really working for him that active proof is required. It is as though the "double agent" must prove dramatically that he has come over from "the other side" before he can be trusted as an ally.

Consider the following clinical situation. A patient elaborates an airtight rationale of maternal and spousal deprivation to justify an extramarital affair. Astute and psychoanalytically sophisticated, his own "interpretations" reinforce the acting-out. There is nothing for it—he must "gratify his frozen impulses." The therapist not only agrees but offers practical advice to further the affair. (The highly ritualized "love affair," bearing all the hallmarks of pre-arranged "deprivation," had already proceeded to considerable involvement beyond the sphere of the therapist's influence. Assuming "disapproval" by the therapist, the patient had been bringing in to his sessions carefully selected "after the event" material.) The patient is puzzled and suspicious, but gradually begins to discuss his movement in the affair more openly and, in addition, begins to make the therapist privy to his anxieties within the hitherto paradisiacal relationship. Finally he openly confronts the therapist

7. Sigmund Freud, On Psychotherapy, *Collected Papers* (London: The Hogarth Press, 1950), Vol. 1.

8. Benjamin Nelson, The Psychoanalyst as Mediator and Double Agent, *Psychoanalytic Review*, Fall 1965.

with his bewilderment at the therapist's active interest in making the affair work. "You can't believe that I'm working for you," the therapist says. "Why should I want you to spend the rest of your life being cheated out of what's coming to you?" Long after the patient has "returned" to his wife and is reassuring the therapist that she is trying hard not to deprive him, the therapist continues to maintain his readiness to join the war against deprivation.

These gambits of the therapist's double agency are manifold. Sometimes they set up a byplay between a particular characterological manifestation and the vicissitudes of resistance to change. The dialectic of quantity into quality is evoked. An obsessional list maker is greeted at the door with "Do you have your list for me today? Why is it so short this week? I don't see thus and thus listed. Where is thus and thus this week?" A passive-aggressive woman is greeted with "Well, how many people did we kill this week?" Or a central theme of transference may be chosen for mimetic improvisation—therapist as bad mother, therapist as boss, therapist as grumpy husband.

The effectiveness of these strategies is, as always, most readily seen in the moment of their happening. Occasionally one has the opportunity to study variables of technique in more or less controlled circumstances. In a training situation where patients change counselors at the end of each academic year, the same patient may be studied in a continuity of audited tape recordings and verbatim transcripts. A woman exposed to traditional supportive-reflective counseling for two years with two different counselors was making little headway with her third counselor, against a constellation of dependencies, infantilized attitudes, and depressive hopelessness. A carefully supervised program of "joining" her in her hopelessness was initiated. Week after week, the counselor met the client's protestations of futility with agreement instead of challenge. The chiaroscuro of the client's own picture was blackened, always in her own terms, until there was nothing left to be seen even of the pseudomorphous pretenses of adjustment fostered by the prior counseling.

Although considerable supervisory time had been spent in communicating the feel of this strategy to the trainee, as the work went along, less and less attention had to be paid to the rationale of joining the client's hopelessness. Freed of the burden of concealing his own belief that the client's situation was indeed almost insurmountably hopeless, the counselor began to be inventive in collaborating with her in a minimum program of change within the framework of her now openly acknowledged inadequacies. By the end of the counseling term, the client was working, had made an effective separation from a schizophrenic husband, and, most surprising in view of her former resistance to the immensity of the idea, had accepted a referral and became engaged in intensive psychotherapy.

Just as trainees can be guided to employ active strategies in their work with clients, spouses can be taught to break long-standing impasses in marital interaction by consciously applying new ways of dealing with old situations. The wife of a severely obsessional chemist was regularly driven to tears by his inspection of her dish-washing. Her protests that she had applied almost laboratory methods in washing the dishes were to no avail. The repeated outcome of these inspections was screaming and tears. With some explanation of the futility of trying to "change" this particular piece of symptomatology in her husband, the wife was guided in a campaign of "joining" her husband's phobia. Instead of trying to convince him of the sterility of her dishes, she now offered them for inspection herself. "These dishes don't look clean enough to me. What do you think?" was her new approach. Seeing puzzlement and hesitancy on her husband's face, she would hasten to offer to wash them again. "You've taught me to appreciate a really clean dish." Not too long afterward, the husband was in the position of urging his formerly "sloppy" wife to forget about the dishes.

A timid "victim" complained that her depressed husband was falling asleep on the couch immediately after dinner. To her tears and complaints of neglect, the husband replied that he was merely exhausted from the difficulties of a trying job. The wife was guided into urging her "exhausted" husband into going right up to bed to get a good night's rest. Her approach now was along these lines: "I know how trying the job is. Please go right up to bed. I know it's only eight o'clock; but you need your rest." In time the husband could only offer counterprotests that it was too early to go to bed, that he really was not that tired, and so forth, until he was retiring at a normal hour. For the timid wife there was great gain in self-esteem. For one of the rare times in her life she was able to undo her own victimization.

These instructed approaches between spouses are particularly effective in the area of sexual adjustment. A husband of somewhat uncertain masculinity who interpreted the rather normal, easy-going responses of his wife as "frigidity" was soon speaking of her as "a ruthless tigress" after she "joined" his unspoken fantasies of sex at unconventional times in unconventional places. A wife who hid other, non-sexual resentments behind constant excuses of being "too tired" was soon making overtures to her husband after he joined her in acknowledging that her youth was on the wane. In every instance the conscious application of a "strategy" by the instructed spouse tended not only to break a particular stalemate in the relationship but eventually to add to the quality of the relationship by externalizing the underlying neurotic or unexpressed "childish" demand as well as by increasing the feeling of competence in one or both spouses to deal more actively with the destiny of their own interaction.

The gains in existential contact and operative freedom for the therapist in an approach which actively comes to grips with the client's difficulties as actualities, rather than symbolic derivatives of past experience, must not be minimized. The impulse toward activity is often blocked by the bugaboo of "manipulation." But, as I have tried to show, the patient's autonomy is best protected by deepening receptivity. As to the charge of manipulation, this too must be received frontally. I recall, in this connection, an exchange between the editor of this volume and a venerable pioneer in the field of child care. Having listened to Dr. Greenwald tell something of the active strategies he employs, the pioneer—uninhibited by decades of devoted service—voiced the big question which so many others in the audience obviously hesitated to ask: "But isn't that manipulation?" I remember her delighted smile when Dr. Greenwald cheerfully answered, "Yes!" While therapists would do well to keep in mind that the word *theraps* means nothing more than servant and that we and our techniques are the servants of our clients, it is also true that the wise servant knows his master best.

NATHAN W. ACKERMAN

The Family Approach to Marital Disorders

Ackerman is very much identified with the beginnings of the relatively new field of family therapy. His paper is a fascinating summary of marital disorder as well as a description of the therapist's function in dealing with such disorder. In describing how the clinician should use himself in marital therapy, Ackerman suggests that the therapist "must be open, flexible, forthright, at times even blunt." Anyone who has had the opportunity to observe Ackerman in action, either in person or on any of the films in which he has participated, cannot fail to observe how well he follows his own prescription.

IT IS COMMON KNOWLEDGE today that the social institution of marriage is not working as we would like it to. To be sure, the institution of marriage is here to stay, but it is not the same any more. It is rickety, its joints creak. It threatens to crack wide open. If marriage is ordained in heaven, it is surely falling apart on earth. Three generations survey the record with dismay. The older married folks look with silent reproach on the younger ones. The younger married folks look at themselves with shocked perplexity and wonder how on earth they got this way. The children look at their parents, not with reverent respect, but with bitter accusation. They indict their parents. "You are wrecking our family. What are you doing to yourselves and to us? You are failing miserably. Why?"

In the present-day community, anxiety concerning the instability of marriage and the family is widespread. The sources of worry are "sidewise" marriage, the teen-age marriage, infidelity, desertion, divorce, multiple marriages, the loosening of sex standards, the war between the sexes, "momism," the weakness of fathers, the reduction of parental authority, broken homes, emotionally injured children, the anarchy of youth, and the trend toward delinquency. With all this comes a growing disillusionment in the tradition and sentiment of marriage and family.

If today the marriage bond is unstable, it is because the entire constellation of the contemporary family itself is unstable. Since our way of life at all levels—family, community, and culture—is in a state of flux, the style of marriage must also echo the profound current of change and instability.

Healing forces do emerge, but the healing itself is often warped. It is something akin to what surgeons call "the pathological healing" of a wound. For a multiplicity of reasons, we are challenged to take a new look at this old problem and, if possible, to discover a fresh approach to the marital disorders of our time.

For me, a psychiatric clinician, the marital problem poses a tantalizing challenge, something like a complicated jigsaw puzzle. We find one part that fits; instantly we hope and expect that the others will quickly fall into place and uncover the hidden design; but it is not so easy.

Marriage is more than sex; it is a whole way of life. It is a joining in the work, joys, and sadnesses of life. Disorders of the marital relationship cannot be understood in a social vacuum. The fit or lack of fit of the partners can be properly appraised only within the framework of the family viewed as an integrated behavior system with dominant values and a definable organizational pattern. The marital adaptation needs to be seen within that larger network of relationships that reflects the identity connections of each partner with his respective family of origin and with the larger community. Relevant beyond sexual union are the basic functions of family, which have to do with security, child rearing, social training, and the development of the marriage partners both as a joined couple and as individuals.

To illustrate: A 24-year-old worker, married six months, was considering divorce. In the initial psychiatric interview, try as I might, I could not find the slightest hint as to her motive. Why divorce? Finally in desperation, I asked, "Is it your sex life? What in the world is wrong?" "Oh, no," she said, "my husband is an expert lover. Believe me, sexual intercourse is just great. The only trouble is that there is no verbal intercourse at all." Diagnosis: physical relations good; emotional interchange, none. The complaint of "silent treatment" in married life is a frequent one these days.

Interviewing another couple, a kewpie doll of a wife and a big burly police captain of a husband, I had a different experience. This couple had been married ten years and had three children. The wife threatened divorce. She was cute, childlike, but she blew fire out of her mouth. She let loose a barrage of bitter accusations. For the better part of an hour her husband sat mute; he couldn't get a word in edgewise. What was her complaint? Her husband had cheated her out of her rights as a woman. When they married she was naive and innocent. For ten years her husband had not given her the remotest hint that a woman is supposed to enjoy sex. Only now, at the New School for Social Research, did she learn for the first time that a woman may have an orgasm. Through her gnashing jaws, she spit out a furious ultimatum. It was her husband's duty to see to it that she had an orgasm or else!

An interesting phenomenon is that of marital couples who swap partners for a week end. Some of these marriages deteriorate rapidly. In a few cases, however, there is a paradoxical response. The adventure of infidelity seems to exert a remarkable healing effect on the marriage. It is a disturbing invasion of the life of both partners, but strangely enough if they get through this crisis each of them may then emerge a stronger person. They experience a piece of mutual learning; the companionship grows closer, the love life richer. They both grow as people. In one such case, the wife reacted to the shocking discovery of her husband's romance with an attractive Negro actress with the prompt dissolution of her sexual frigidity. This delighted her husband and impelled him then to characterize his Negro inamorata as the best psychotherapist he and his wife could have had.

This is but a small example of the attitude of the sex-seekers of our time. One way or another they engage in a frantic search for a new sexual kick that they expect will be the magic cure-all.

In another case, a wife reacted with a pathological jealousy. She was "bugged" on her husband's imagined sexual antics with other playmates; she plagued him incessantly. She was depressed, agitated, unable to sleep, nor did she let her husband sleep. She knew that her husband had erotic interest in women wrestlers and weight lifters. When her husband asked her to lift him or hold him in her lap she refused; it might break her back. She entered the role of detective in order "to get the goods" on her husband. She discovered in his desk a batch of pictures of female weight lifters in scanty attire. Finding a stain on her husband's underclothing, she sent a piece of it to a chemical laboratory. The report came back: "Positive; many spermatozoa were found together with large numbers of squamous epithelial cells. The finding of many squamous epithelial cells is indicative of the presence of vaginal secretion along with the spermatozoa." This clinched the wife's case. She crucified her husband with this "proof." She demanded that he confess the truth. What new sexual tricks had he learned from "these other broads"?

Both partners had been previously married, so that in this household there were three sets of children: the wife's children by her former marriage, the husband's children by his former marriage, and a new baby. From the word "go" the partners got off on the wrong foot and failed completely to build a true marital union. The courtship phase was intense. Both parties moved fast to dissolve their previous marriages to make way for this one. But they were hardly married before the husband began to withdraw interest. When his wife became pregnant, he stopped making sexual advances altogether. Sensing the sexual rejection, the wife began to build up her delusions of jealousy.

In this case, husband and wife came from very different cultural and religious backgrounds, but they had in common the special experience of a philandering, unfaithful father. They reacted, however, in different ways. The husband sided with his father. He felt convinced that his father had in fact been killed by his mother. Through her persistent nagging and accusations of infidelity she had caused his final heart collapse. The wife, on the other hand, entered an empathic alliance with her mother in an attempt to protect the wounded pride of the females of the family against what she felt was her father's cold, ruthless, indiscriminate indulgence in sexual escapades.

In therapy the wife related four dreams in succession. In each of these she depicted a threesome involved in a horrible tangle, reflecting the profound emotional connections of conflict in the marital pair with older sources of conflict in the families of origin.

To illustrate, in one such dream the patient finds herself in an automobile, a convertible, accompanied by her husband and another woman, his office secretary, who is the object of her paranoid sexual jealousy. The three of them drive to the home of the patient's former husband, where she finds other people. First she spots her father hiding in the bedroom, as if he were up to some mischief.

Although he offers a plausible excuse for his presence, she knows that this is a complete lie. Then she becomes aware of the presence of other people—children, her husband's parents, his office secretary's parents, etc.

In this dream we see three generations of family relationships: the husband's family, the wife's family, and the family of the office secretary. We see the patient in the roles of both child and wife. At the very least, this dream reflects the complexity of the origins of marital jealousy in a way that embraces an extensive network of conflicted family relationships stretching across three generations. Marital disorders, therefore, are anything but simple. They are an aspect, a focal one to be sure, but nonetheless one aspect of an ongoing family phenomenon.

In our studies at the Family Mental Health Clinic, we have been mainly oriented to these problems in the wider context of evaluating and treating the family as a whole. We have preferred, at least in the first phase, to interview distressed marital partners together with their children and sometimes with their own parents. The procedure is first to conduct a series of exploratory interviews with the whole family and then with appropriate timing to shift gear to specialize on the marital part of the broader family problem.

We learn to diagnose marital disorders by treating them. The marital relationship neither exists nor evolves in isolation. It has family in back of it; it has family ahead of it. Where there is marital conflict, it often involves a prior conflict of the respective partners with their families of origin. Marital conflict is often displaced and reprojected, in modified form, into the relations of each partner with the offspring. Thus the original problems of each partner with the family of origin become projected across time into the husband-wife relations and parent-child relations. The marital relationship does not and cannot stand still. It moves forward or backward. It grows or it withers. It must be nourished, it must make way for change, it must respond to new experience; otherwise it dies. As the marital balance shifts across time from one stage of the family cycle to the next, the diagnostic judgment must change accordingly. The diagnosis of marital disorders is complicated. It is influenced by the way in which the disorder is viewed from different places, by different people, with different interests and purposes: (1) by the marital partners themselves, (2) by other parts of the nuclear and extended families and community, (3) by the professional worker. The range and diversity of marital disorders in our culture is enormous. Our interest is not only in how the relationship works, but also to what ends. Diagnosis can be approached at three levels: descriptive, dynamic, and genetic.

At the descriptive level, one can classify disorders of the marital partnership in terms of symptom clusters reflecting deviant patterns of interaction; for example, in sexual failure; economic or social failure; in persistent quarreling, misunderstanding, alienation; in disturbances of communication, sharing, and identification.

At the dynamic level, diagnosis means the definition of the core conflicts, the ways of coping, the patterns of complementarity and failure of complementarity, the distortion and imbalance of the multiple functions of the marital interaction, and finally, the realism, maturity, stability, and growth potential of the relationship. From an estimate of these characteristics, one can delineate what is inappropriate and warped alongside of what is preserved and healthy in the quality of the marital adaptation.

At the genetic level, one traces the dynamic evolution of the relationship through the phases of courtship, early marriage, the arrival of the first child, and finally the expansion of the family with more children.

Diagnosis of marital interaction may be divided into subitems: (1) current performance, (2) level of achievement, (3) origin and development, (4) deviation measured against an ideal of a healthy marital relationship.

1. Current performance.
   a. Capacity for love.
   b. Mutual adaptation, adaptation to external change, and adaptation for growth.
   c. Levels of benign conflict, destructive conflict; the patterns of coping; the interplay of shared defense of the continuity of the marriage relationship, and individual defense against conflict and anxiety; finally, the characteristic patterns of complementarity. In clinical terms, two features of defense are of special importance: first, the use of the relationship and adaptation to the marital roles to compensate anxiety in one or the other partner, i.e., to offer support against emotional breakdown; and second, the use of external relationships to mitigate failure in the marital relationship and to provide compensatory satisfactions of individual need.
   d. The quality of integration of each of the partners into the marital role, and the fit of marital with other family roles.
2. Level of achievement.
   a. The strivings, expectations, values, and needs of the relationship and of each partner.
   b. The maturity, realism, stablity of the relationship.
   c. The trends toward fixation, regression, disintegration, etc.

3. Origin and development of the relationship; the relationship from courtship to the time of referral.

   a. Influence of the evolving patterns of motivation, the ideals and images of future marriage and family on the development of the marital partnership.

   b. Influence of the same on the development of the parental partnership; influence of the children on the parental partnership.

   c. Areas of satisfaction, dissatisfaction, harmony and conflict, healthy and unhealthy functioning.

   d. Past achievement in relation to values, expectations, and strivings.

4. Discrepancy between the actual performance and an ideal model of healthy marital functioning.

Disorders of the marital relationship are clinically expressed in two ways, conflict over difference and failure of complementarity.

Conflict over difference becomes organized in a special way. Neither of the marital partners fights the battle alone. Each tends to form a protective alliance with other family members, children, grandparents, collateral relatives. In this way the family splits up into opposing factions. One partner engages in prejudicial scapegoating of the other. Each warring partner puts on blinders and attaches a menacing meaning to the felt difference. The inevitable result is a war of prejudice revolving around subjectively distorted representations of difference, rather than actual ones. This is a war that rests on the false belief that the striving for one way of life automatically excludes another. Each faction then tries to impose its preferred set of aims and values on the relationship. The manifestations of this conflict are then seen as disturbances of empathy, union, and identification; in chronic, destructive quarreling, often about wrong or trivial matters; in defects of communication; in the failure of the devices of restoration of balance following an upset; finally, in progressive alienation of the partners.

The outcome of such conflict depends less on the nature of the conflict and rather more on the way of coping with it. Coping with marital conflict is a shared function. It is carried on both at the interpersonal and the intrapersonal levels. In this connection, it is of the essence to trace the interplay between specific patterns of group defense of the continuity of the marriage relationship and individual defense against the destructive effects of conflict and anxiety. At the relationship level, one may specify the following patterns of defense:

1. An enhancement of the bond of love, sharing, cooperation, and identification.

2. A shift in the complementarity of marital role adaptation brought about by:

    a. A shared quest for the solution of conflict

    b. Improved mutual need satisfaction

    c. Mutual support of self-esteem

    d. Support for the needed defenses against anxiety

    e. Support of the growth of the relationship and of each partner as an individual

3. Rigidification of the marital roles, or loosening of the marital roles.

4. Reduction of the intensity of conflict by means of manipulation, coercion, bribery, compromise, compensation, denial, or escape.

5. A shift of alignments and splits within the family, and prejudicial scapegoating of one part of the family by another.

6. Repeopling of the group, i.e., the elimination of one member or the addition of another, or a significant change of environment.

Failure in these patterns of coping produces, in turn, progressive failure of the quality of complementarity. The manifestations of such failure can then be identified as particular units of interaction which become rigidified, automatized, inappropriate, and no longer useful for the shared tasks of marital living.

The marital partnership may be oriented mainly to different goals, as indicated in the following:

1. Each partner egocentrically preserves his premarital individuality, largely untouched by the requirements of the marital bond.

2. The individualities of each partner are mainly subordinated to the requirements of the marital role.

3. The individualities of each partner are mainly subordinated to the requirements of the parental role.

4. The individualities of each partner are mainly subordinated to the requirements of successful conformity to the surrounding community.

From the genetic or developmental viewpoint:

1. The accidental or unintended marriage, one that is forced by external circumstance, as, for example, a marriage brought about by pregnancy or other accidental circumstance.

2. The abortive or temporary marriage. This is a type of marriage entered into on a tentative basis as a kind of adventure, a trial

marriage, a conversion of a sexual affair, not intended basically to endure or to evolve into a family group.

3. The marriage of flight. This is a marriage mainly by way of escape from conflict and rebellion in the family of origin, or one brought about as a rebound from a prior disappointment in love.

4. The arranged marriage. This is a pact of security, expediency, or one which has a purpose of joining two larger families.

From the functional point of view:

1. The immature or protective marriage. This is a marriage motivated mainly by the need of one partner, in the role of child, to relate to the other, in the role of parent.

2. The competitive marriage. This type of union is based on concealed motives of envy, jealousy, and competitive admiration.

3. The marriage of neurotic complementarity. This is a marriage in which the special neurotic needs of one partner are complemented by those of the other; one partner serves as the healer of the conflicts and anxieties of the other. The stronger partner in this arrangement is intended to serve as a provider of immunity against emotional breakdown in the more vulnerable partner.

4. The marriage of complementary acting-out. This is a marriage in which the two partners join in a shared pattern of acting out conflicted urges. There is unconscious complicity in the acting-out pattern.

5. The marriage of mutual emotional detachment. This is a marriage in which a tolerable balance is struck between the partners on the condition of maintaining a required degree of emotional distance and isolation.

6. The master-slave marriage. This is a role partnership in which one partner seeks omnipotent control of the other. Neither partner is a complete being. The master needs the slave; the slave needs the master. The one is aggrandized as the other is demeaned. The natural goal of love—sharing and identification—is perverted to the goal of power to dominate, degrade, and ultimately destroy the partner. In essence, this is a symbiotic bond, in which one partner expands at the expense of the other. A pathological balance of this type can be maintained only by means of coercion and intimidation.

7. The regressive marriage. This is a type of marriage dominated by a negative orientation to life. There is a shared fear of and prejudice against life and growth. There is a shared expectation of imminent catastrophe. Implicit in the emotional content of such a partnership is the theme of total sacrifice. One of the partners must surrender the right to live and breathe, in order to assure the con-

tinued life of the other. In emotional orientation, the persons involved move backward in life, rather than forward. This is the type of marital couple which is most apt to produce psychotic offspring.

8. The healthy marriage. In this theoretical model, or "pure" type, the partners have a good "fit" in the marital role. They are able to share realistic goals and compatible values. When conflict arises, there may be a transitory upset; yet, in the main, they are able to cooperate in the search for a solution or appropriate compromise. A temporary disturbance does not involve an excess or persistence of accusation, guilt feelings, or scapegoating. Each partner has a genuine respect for and acceptance of the other as a person with not only a tolerance of differences, but more than that, a use of them for creative growth of the relationship.

To a large extent, diagnosis rests on one's special interest—what one is trying to do about the marital condition. In this context, diagnosis is no mere label; it is an integral aspect of a plan of action, a strategy for inducing change. Through the implementation of the previously described principles and criteria, we seek a more precise definition of the functional pattern of the marital partnership, not only how it works, but to what ends. We want to know what it stands for, its goals and aspirations, what keeps the couple together, what pulls the partners apart. In essence, what is separate and what is joined in the relationship.

Now, the challenge of treatment. In keeping with the concepts we have outlined, the psychotherapy of marital disorders is viewed as the focused treatment of a component part of a family disorder. In other words, it is a phase of family therapy, adapted to and specialized for the specific features of a marital problem. Since family begins with marriage, the disorder of marital interaction holds a place of focal importance in family dynamics and development.

Since I have elsewhere discussed my view of the method of family psychotherapy, I shall here merely highlight those special considerations that pertain to the focused dealings with problems of marital interaction.

Professional contact begins with exploration of the salient problems, a function of any therapeutically oriented interview. In fact, we initiate the process of treating the couple before we know what it is all about. Only as we become engaged in the on-going adventure of therapy do we achieve, step by step, a systematic diagnosis.

How is the marital trouble viewed? How do the partners see the problem; how do the family and the community see it? What is the same and what is different in these several views? What alternatives loom up? What have the partners tried? What have they not tried?

Or, perhaps, what have they tried in the wrong way? Do they now feel discouraged, beaten down; have they surrendered hope and given way to feelings of despair? Do they console themselves with mutual punishment? In any case, what do the partners now want? What does the family want of them; what does the community expect; what does each partner need of the other, of family and community; in turn, what is each partner willing to do for the other, for family, and for community? Finally, what is the orientation of the therapist? What does he, in turn, propose to do?

These are the pertinent questions that confront the therapist at the outset. To make effective progress in clarifying the issues and exploring the alternatives, the therapist must cultivate an optimal quality of contact, rapport, and communication between the marital partners, and between them and himself. He uses this rapport to catalyze the main kinds of conflict and coping. He clarifies the real content of conflict by dissolving barriers, defensive disguises, confusions, and misunderstandings. By stages, he moves toward a more mutual and accurate understanding with the marital partners as to what is wrong. By stirring a desired quality of empathy and communication, he seeks to arouse and enhance a live, honest, and meaningful emotional interchange. Figuratively speaking, he strives to lend to the contact the quality of a touching experience, a spontaneous and deeply genuine kind of communion. As the members feel in touch with the therapist, they come into better touch with one another. Through the quality of the therapist's use of self, his open, earnest sharing of his own emotions, he sets an example for the desired quality of interaction between the marital partners.

In the therapy of marital disorders, the therapist must know what he stands for, what he is trying to do; he must also know what he can and cannot do. He must have explicit awareness of his own ideology regarding marriage and family life. He must clearly define in his own mind whatever discrepancy prevails between his personal family values and those of the marital couple.

So often, a central feature of marital conflict is the competitive one. Both partners are dedicated to the game of one-upmanship. They engage in ploys with the intent to be one up on the partner. Each seeks to get the best of the other. It is as if the business ethic of profit and loss invades the inner life of the married couple. Neither can be convinced of a gain unless he or she imposes upon the partner a loss, a semblance of sacrifice. The game of one-upmanship is the pursuit of a delusion. It is misleading; it can only end in a sense of futility. The essence of the delusion is that the well-being of the one partner comes only with a measure of sacrifice and surrender in the other. In the marital relation, it cannot be true that what is good for the one is bad for the other. In the long view, what is good or bad for the one must likewise be good or bad for the other. The very survival, continuity, and growth of marriage and family hinges on the acceptance of the principle of love, sharing, and cooperation. Without this, marriage and family have no meaning.

The goals of therapy of marital disorders are to alleviate emotional distress and disablement, and to promote the level of well-being, both of the relationship and of each partner as an individual. In a general way, a therapist moves toward these goals by: (1) strengthening the shared resources for problem-solving; (2) encouraging the substitution of more adequate controls and defenses for pathogenic ones; (3) enhancing immunity against the disintegrative effects of emotional upset; (4) enhancing the complementarity of the relationship; (5) promoting the growth of the realtionship and also of each partner as an individual.

The therapist is a participant-observer. To achieve the goals of marital therapy, the clinician must integrate his trained knowledge and his use of self in the therapeutic role in a unique way. He must be active, open, flexible, forthright, at times even blunt. He must make the most free, undefensive use of himself. Alternately, he moves in and out of the pool of marital conflict. He moves in to energize and influence the interactional process; he moves out to distance himself, to survey and assess significant events, to objectify his experience; and then he moves in again. The marital partners engage in a selective process of joining and separating from specific elements of the therapist's identity. The marital partners absorb, interact with, and use the therapist's influence in a variety of ways. The partial emotional joinings and separations reflect elements of transference and realism. The therapist must be adroit, ever ready and alert to move his influence from one aspect of the marital relationship to another, following the shift of the core of most destructive conflict. He engages the partners in a progressive process of working through these conflicts. In so doing, he fulfills multiple functions. He is catalyst, supporter, regulator, interpreter, and resynthesizer. These functions cannot be conceived of in isolation, but rather as a harmony of influences expressed through the unity of the therapist's use of self.

He undercuts the tendency of the marital partners to console themselves by engaging in a process of mutual blame and punishment. He stirs hope of something new and better in the relationship. He pierces the misunderstandings, confusions, and distortions, so as to reach a consensus with the partners as to what is really wrong. In working through the conflicts over difference, the frustrations, defeats, and the failure of complementarity, he shakes up the old and deviant patterns of alignment and makes way for new avenues of interaction. He weighs and balances the healthy and sick emotional forces in the relationship. He supports the health-maintaining tendencies and counteracts the sickness-inducing ones by shifting his function in accordance with need at changing stages of the treatment.

To sum up in more specific terms, once having established the needed quality of rapport, empathy, and communication, and having reached a consensus as to what is wrong, he moves ahead by implementing the following special techniques:

1. The counteraction of inappropriate denials, displacements, and rationalizations of conflict.

2. The transformation of dormant, concealed interpersonal conflict into open interactional expression.

3. The lifting of hidden intrapersonal conflict to the level of interpersonal interaction.

4. The neutralization of patterns of prejudicial scapegoating that fortify the position of one marital partner while victimizing the other.

5. The penetration of resistances; the reduction of shared currents of conflict, guilt, and fear. This is done with the use of confrontation and interpretation.

6. The use of the therapist's self in the role of a real parent as a controller of interpersonal danger, as a source of emotional support and satisfaction, as a provider of emotional elements which the marital couple needs but lacks. The latter function is a kind of substitutive therapy in which the therapist feeds into the emotional life of the parties certain more appropriate attitudes, emotions, and images of marital and family relationships which the couple has not previously had. By these means, the therapist improves the level of complementarity of the relationship.

7. The therapist's use of self as the instrument of reality testing.

8. The therapist's use of self as educator, also as the personifier of useful models of health in marital interaction.

Using these various techniques, he proceeds, together with the marital couple, to test a series of alternative solutions to the marital distress.

JAY HALEY

Marriage Therapy

Jay Haley brings to the problem of the study of the process of psychotherapy his background as a communications expert. This rather unorthodox preparation enables him to order the data in new and delightful ways.

The article on marriage therapy which follows is not only a highly provocative account of the technique of marriage therapy but is also a splendid introduction to his entire conception of therapy. It is interesting to note that the approach he describes, while arrived at completely independently, has many elements in common with the work of Marie Coleman Nelson, Spotnitz, Frankl, and Greenwald.

It is also interesting to note that Haley's rationale for suggesting to the patient that he continue to do what he is doing differs from the rationale of the other practitioners who use similar methods. Those who approach this from a psychoanalytic background usually describe it as "joining the resistance" and still view it from the framework of leading to increased self-understanding. Haley and his associates tend to be closer to the model of those learning theorists who do not believe that self-

From *The Archives of General Psychiatry*, Vol. 8, March 1963, pp. 213-34. Copyright 1963, by American Medical Association.

This paper was written while the author was a member of the Project for the Study of Schizophrenic Communication, directed by Gregory Bateson. The staff consisted of Jay Haley and John Weakland, Research Associates; Dr. Don D. Jackson and Dr. William F. Fry, Consultants. The research was financed by Grant OM-324 from the National Institute of Mental Health and administered by the Palo Alto Medical Research Foundation. The project was part of the research program of the Veterans Administration Hospital, Palo Alto.

understanding is necessary for change. Others who approach it from a psychoanalytic background may agree that self-understanding is not a necessary prerequisite for change, but believe that such understanding increases the possibility of generalization and leads to more permanent change. The paper by Peterson and London on the neobehaviorist approach also stresses the value of cognition as an additive force for behavior modification.

INTRODUCTION

ALTHOUGH IT IS BECOMING more common for psychotherapists to interview married partners together, there are no orthodox procedures for the treatment of a marriage. In fact there is no formal description of pathological marriages and therefore no theory of what changes must be brought about. The psychodynamic approach, or role theory emphasis, leads to discussions of the individual problems of husband and wife and not to descriptions of the marital relationship.

The emphasis here will be upon types of relationship in marriage, but no attempt will be made to present a full exposition of the complexities of marriage; the focus will be upon marital distress and symptom formation. After a description of certain types of relationship, there will be a discussion of the kinds of conflicts which arise, and finally a description of ways a marriage therapist intervenes to produce shifts in relationship.

When Marriage Therapy Is Indicated

Marriage therapy differs from individual therapy because the focus is upon the marital relationship rather than the intrapsychic forces within the individual. It also differs from family therapy where the emphasis is upon the total family unit with a child typically chosen to be the problem. Technically the term should be confined to that type of treatment where the therapist interviews the couple together. However, the variations are many: some therapists will see both marital partners separately, others will see one partner while occasionally seeing the spouse for an interview, and others will see one partner while referring the other elsewhere, with collaboration between the two therapists. Actually the psychotherapist who does only individual psychotherapy and refuses to see the spouse of a married patient is involved in indirect marriage therapy. Not only is much of the time of individual treatment devoted to discussions of marital affairs, but if the individual changes, the marital relationship will change—or terminate.

There are certain situations where marriage therapy is specifically indicated:

1. When methods of individual psychotherapy have failed, marriage therapy is appropriate. Often in such cases the patient is involved in a marital relationship which is inhibiting his improvement and perpetuating his distress to the point where individual psychotherapy is too small a lever to make a large change. For example, a woman with constantly recurring anxiety attacks and insomnia failed to improve in individual psychotherapy despite considerable exploration of her childhood. When her husband was brought into the treatment it was discovered that he was continually behaving in an irresponsible and unpredictable way. He was not only failing in business without taking any steps to prevent this failure, but he was surreptitiously writing bad checks time after time, despite his protests to his wife that he would never do so again. The onset of her anxiety attacks occurred with his first failure in business and his cavalier dismissal of this event. The continual conflict between husband and wife over his refusal to take responsibility in his business or in his family was handled by the wife with recurrent attacks of helpless anxiety, and her problem was more marital than individual.

2. Marriage therapy is indicated when methods of individual psychotherapy cannot be used. Since most individual psychotherapy consists of countering what a patient offers, the therapist is incapacitated if the patient offers nothing. Marriage therapy then becomes one of the few possible procedures. For example, a woman developed a fear of heart failure as part of a series of anxiety attacks which forced her to quit her job and remain at home, unable to go out anywhere alone. She sought psychotherapy, and the therapist asked her to say whatever came to her mind. She said nothing. She would answer specific questions as briefly as possible, but she would not volunteer statements about her feelings or her life in general. After two sessions in which the woman said nothing and the therapist said nothing, the woman discontinued treatment and sought another therapist. Clearly the woman would not permit the therapist to wait her out in the hope that the cost of treatment would ultimately force her to say what was on her mind. When she began marriage therapy with her husband present in the interviews, the wife became more loquacious, since she found it necessary to correct her husband when he was asked about her problems. She could not let her husband's portrait of her difficulties stand. To revise his version she had to provide her own and demonstrate her feelings about him, providing the leverage to start a change.

3. Marriage therapy would seem indicated when a patient has a sudden onset of symptoms which coincides with a marital conflict. Although most patients with symptoms tend to minimize their marital difficulties—in fact, the symptom is apparently used to deny marital problems—there are times when symptoms erupt in obvious relation to a spouse. For example, a husband developed an anxiety state which confined him to bed and cost him his job. His collapse occurred when his wife went to work over his objections. In another case a woman developed a variety of hysterical symptoms while on vacation with her husband. They quarreled, and her husband gambled away the vacation money, knowing that her greatest fear in life was of gambling, because her father had continually gambled away all the family money. Although the onset of a symptom can always be seen as a product of a change in a family relationship, in some cases the connection is so obvious that treatment of the marriage is indicated.

4. Of course this type of therapy is indicated when it is requested by a couple who are in conflict and distress and unable to resolve it. (However, it is not unusual even in this circumstance for some therapists to advise them to seek individual treatment separately.) Typically one spouse, usually the wife, seeks marriage therapy, while the other comes in reluctantly. Even though one spouse may need a special request, both partners will usually come in, because if one partner in a marriage is miserable the other is too.

5. Finally, marriage therapy is indicated when it appears that improvement in a patient will result in a divorce or in the eruption of symptoms in the spouse. Therapists have a responsibility to the relatives of a patient if they bring about a change. If a patient with severe symptoms says his marriage is perfect, and if his spouse also indicates this idea, then it is likely that improvement in the patient will lead to divorce or symptoms in the spouse.

THE FORMAL THEMES OF MARRIAGE

A marriage is an extraordinarily complex and continually changing affair. To select a few aspects of the marital relationship and emphasize them is to do some violence to the incredible entanglement of two people who have lived together many years. A few formal themes, those most relevant to marital strife and symptom formation, will be mentioned here.

When a man and woman decide their association should be solemnized and legalized with a marriage ceremony, they pose themselves a problem which will continue through the marriage: now that they are married are they staying together because they wish to or because they must? The inevitable conflicts which arise in a marriage occur within a framework of a more or less voluntary relationship. A marriage seems to function best when there is some balance between the voluntary and compulsory aspects of the relationship. In a successful marriage, the couple define their association as one of choice, and yet they have sufficient compulsion in law and custom to stay together through the conflicts which arise. If divorce is too easy, there is too little compulsion in the marriage to survive the problems. When divorce is too difficult, the couple can begin to suspect that they are together because they must be and not out of choice. At either extreme, a marriage can be in difficulty. It is not so much whether a marriage *is* a compulsory or a voluntary relationship, but how the couple choose to define it. For example, a woman may wish to stay with her husband but be unwilling to concede that her choice is voluntary, and therefore she says that they cannot separate for religious reasons. Another wife might insist that she could leave her husband at any time, defining the relationship as voluntary, although her history would indicate that she had a rather desperate need of him and could not leave him.

An example of a marriage which was so voluntary that the wife did not feel committed to her husband can be used for illustration. A woman in business for herself prior to her marriage agreed to sell the business at her husband's request because he wished to be the provider for the family. However, she took the money obtained in the sale and placed it in the bank in her own name "just in case the marriage did not work out." The marriage foundered on this act. The husband felt the wife was unwilling to commit herself to him: the wife behaved as if the marriage was a voluntary association which she could leave at any time, so she would make no concessions in her relationship with her husband.

At the other extreme is the type of relationship where the couple behave as if they are compelled to stay together. This type of relationship occurs where there are strict religious rules about marriage, when one of the spouses develops incapacitating symptoms, or when one of them puts up with "impossible" behavior from the other.

A compulsory marriage is like the relationship between cell mates in a prison. The two people get along because they must, but they are uncertain whether they would choose to be together if they had a free choice. A wife who suffers incapacitating symptoms will be indicating to her husband that she is unable to survive alone. A husband who turns to drink whenever his wife must go away for a day, or when she threatens to leave him, will persuade her that he cannot live without her. This is not necessarily taken as a compliment if a spouse indicates he cannot do without his mate; implicit in such an arrangement is the idea that they are only together because they must be and perhaps any other person in the house might do, but no one else would have them. When spouses begin to think of their relationship as compulsory, bad feeling is generated.

A marriage may begin as a compulsory relationship. For example, a man attempted to discuss breaking off his engagement with his fiancée, and the girl jumped out of his parked automobile into oncoming traffic and ran wildly down the street. Later she told him she would kill herself if he did not marry her. He married her. From that point on, he was in doubt whether she really wished to marry him or was only desperately trying to escape a dreadful home situation. The girl was in doubt whether he married her because he wanted to or because of fear she would kill herself.

When one spouse continues the marriage even though treated badly by the other, a compulsory type of relationship occurs. If a husband puts up with more than is reasonable from his wife, the wife may begin to assume that he must be staying with her because he has to, not because he wants to, and the marriage is in difficulty. Sometimes a spouse will appear to test whether he or she is really wanted by driving the other to the point of separation. It is as if they say, "If my mate will put up with anything from me, I am really wanted." However, if the spouse passes the test and puts up with impossible behavior, the tester is not reassured about being wanted but becomes convinced the spouse is doing so because of an inability to leave. Once this pattern has begun, it tends to be self-perpetuating. A wife who believes that her husband stays with her because of his inner desperation rather than because he wants her will dismiss his affectionate approaches as mere bribes to stay with her rather than indications of real affection. When she dismisses her husband's affection, he tries even harder to please her and so increases her belief that he stays with her out of desperation rather than choice. When the husband can no longer tolerate the situation, he may make a move to leave her. The moment he indicates he can do without her, the wife begins to feel she may be a voluntary choice and be attracted to him again. However, such a wife will then test her husband again by extreme behavior. When he responds permissively she again feels he is unable to leave her, and the cycle continues.

The extreme oscillation which can occur in a marriage is typical of those cases where a couple comes to a therapist for help in getting separated from each other. Some spouses will separate and go back together and separate again over the years, unable to get together and unable to get apart. The major problem in helping the separating couple is discovering in which direction they seem most to want to go. Sometimes a couple merely wants an excuse from an outsider to go back together so that neither will have to risk being the first to suggest living together again. In more complex separations there is usually a pattern of one spouse wanting to end the marriage until the other also wants it; then there is temporary reconciliation. For example, a young couple began to have trouble after a few years of marriage and the wife had an extramarital affair. The husband forgave her. She had another affair; they separated. After a while they tried living together again, but the affairs still rankled. The husband continued to blame her for her actions; the wife blamed him for depriving her in such a way that she turned to someone else. They separated but continued to associate. When they entered therapy the husband wanted them to go back together again but was uncertain about it. The wife, having taken up with another man, did not want to live with her husband, yet she wanted to associate with him and consider possible future reconciliation. At one moment the husband insisted on immediate divorce; at the next he asked for a reconciliation. Each time he spoke more firmly about his plans for a divorce, the wife began to discuss the great potential of their marriage and how fond she was of him. When the husband talked about going back together, the wife discussed how miserable their marriage had been. After several sessions attempting to clarify the situation, the issue was forced by a suggestion that if the couple continue treatment they do so in a trial period of living together. Faced with returning to her husband, the wife refused. The husband managed to arrange a divorce, although when he was no longer compulsively involved with her, the wife was finding him attractive again.

The Progress of a Marriage

Though their information about one another may be minimal, two people have already established ways of relating to each other at the time they marry. The act of marriage, typically an act of conceding they really want each other, requires a different sort of relationship and can provoke rather sudden shifts in behavior. A woman, for example, might be forgiving of all her fiancée's defects until the marriage ceremony, and then she might set about reforming him. A man might be quite tolerant of his fiancée's inability to show affection, but when they are married he might insist she undergo a major change. The man who was pleased to find such a submissive girl may discover after marriage that she is quite insistent about taking charge of him. Usually, however, the patterns which appear in a marriage existed in some form prior to the ceremony. People have a remarkable skill in choosing mates who will fit their needs, although they may insist later they married the unexpected. The girl who needs to be treated badly usually finds someone who will cooperate. If someone feels he deserves very little from life, he tends to find a wife who feels she deserves very little; both get what they seek.

The process of working out a satisfactory marital relationship can be seen as a process of working out shared agreements, largely undiscussed, between the two people. There are a multitude of areas in living together which a couple must agree about. For example, is a husband to decide what sort of work he will do, or will his wife's concern about prestige dictate his employment? Will the husband be allowed to freely criticize his wife's housekeeping, or is that her domain? Who is to handle the budget? Is the wife to comfort her husband when he is unhappy or become exasperated with him? How much are outsiders to intrude into the marriage, and are in-laws outsiders? Will the wife or the husband be the irresponsible one in the marriage?

Each situation that a newly married couple meets must be dealt with by establishing explicit or implicit rules to follow. When the situation is met again, the rule established is either reinforced or changed. These rules are of three sorts: (1) those rules the couple would announce, such as a rule that the husband can have a night out with his friends each week; (2) those rules the couple would not mention but would agree to if they were pointed out, such as the rule that the husband turns to his wife when faced with major decisions; and (3) those rules an observer would note but the couple would probably deny, such as the rule that the wife is continually to be on the defensive and the husband accusatory, and never the reverse. It is important to note that the couple cannot avoid establishing these rules: whenever they complete a transaction, a rule is being established. Even if they should set out to behave entirely spontaneously, they would be establishing the rule that they are to behave in that way.

The couple must not only set rules, but they must also reach agreement on which of them is to be the one to set the rules in each area of their marriage. The process of working out a particular rule always occurs within a context of resolving who is setting the rule. For example, a wife might not object if her husband has an evening out—unless he insists upon it; then she might object, but her objection would be at a different level. Similarly, a husband might not protest if his wife wishes to send her mother money, but if the wife implies that he has no say in the matter he might then announce objections. In the early days of a marriage each spouse might graciously let the other be labeled as the one in charge of the various areas of the relationship, but ultimately a struggle will set in over this problem.

As a part of the struggle to reach agreement on rules for living with each other, a couple is inevitably establishing another set of rules—those rules to be followed to resolve disagreements. The process of working out conflict over rules becomes a set of meta-rules, or rules for making rules. For example, two people might establish the rule that they will resolve a difference only after the husband has made an issue of the matter. When the wife has tested his concern by provoking him until he treats the matter as important, then they will resolve it. Or a couple might establish the meta-rule that they will never fully reach agreement on any rule, and so they maintain a state of indecision. Similarly, the act of avoiding certain areas of discussion is an establishing of meta-rules about how to deal with those areas.

If a marital relationship could be worked out by the application of agreement on rules, who is to make them, and how to make them, a marriage would be quite a rational affair. Obviously it is not. Couples find themselves struggling with great intensity of feeling over minor matters in a most irrational way. This intensity of feeling about who is to set rules in the marriage would seem to have several sources. A major cause is the fact that any marital partner was raised in a family and so given long and thorough training in implicit and explicit rules for how people should deal with each other. When a person gets married, he attempts to deal with a spouse who was given training in a different institution. The couple must reconcile long-term expectations which have all the emotional force of laws of life. The wife raised in a family where an open show of emotion was forbidden will become disturbed when her husband expresses his feelings strongly, even though she might have married him because she wished to move in that direction. The husband whose mother made an issue of being an excellent housekeeper may find it difficult to tolerate a wife who is not, and he may take her inability as a personal comment on him rather than mere inefficiency. It is sometimes difficult to realize how subtle are the patterns we learn in our families, where we are exposed to millions of messages over time. For example, the "proper" distance one should stand from another person while talking to him will vary from family to family. A person may feel uneasy because the other person is too close or too far away, without ever realizing that there is a disagreement in how far apart they should stand. The transition to a person's own family from a previous one requires considerable compromise with inevitable conflict.

Describing marriage in terms of working out rules for living together is another way of describing marriage as a process of defining relationships. Any rule established by a couple defines a certain type of relationship, and all relationships can be roughly classified into two types; complementary or symmetrical. A complementary relationship is one where the two people exchange *different* sorts of behavior, such as one giving and the other receiving. A symmetrical relationship is one where they exchange the *same* sorts of behavior, such as both giving. A rule that a husband is to comfort his wife when she is in distress defines a relationship as complementary. Similarly, an agreement that the wife is to have equal say about the budget is a mutual definition of a symmetrical relationship in that area. In a reasonably successful marriage a couple is capable of establishing both complementary and symmetrical relationships in various areas of their marriage. The husband can take care of his wife and she can accept this, the wife can take care of her husband and he can accept it, and they are able to exchange the same sort of behavior. When a couple is unable to form one of these types of relationship, the marriage is restricted. If a marital partner has had unfortunate experiences with certain types of relationship in the past, he or she might be unable to permit this type in a marriage. For example, if a wife has been disappointed in complementary relationships with her parents, she will respond to her husband's attempts to take care of her in a way that indicates she would prefer a symmetrical type of relationship. A wife might be unable to follow any directions given by her husband if following directions in her past cost her too much. Once when a wife was asked why she did not do what her husband told her, she said, "Why, I'd just disappear. I'd have no identity." Similarly, a husband might be unable to take direction from his wife or even let her take care of him when he is ill (and so he only retires to a sick bed when he has collapsed). He may indicate that he wants her to be an equal, but he does not want her to "mother" him. An inability to accept a range of types of relationship creates a marriage which is to some extent a depriving situation for both spouses.

Conflict in Marriage

Marital conflict centers in (1) disagreements about the rules for living together, (2) disagreements about who is to set those rules, and (3) attempts to enforce rules which are incompatible with each other.

For a honeymoon period after marriage each spouse is willing to overlook the disagreements which develop. When the husband is treated by his wife in a way he does not like, he avoids mentioning it for fear of hurting her feelings. When the wife discovers some aspect of her husband which irritates her, she does not bring the matter up because she wishes to avoid conflict. After a period of time the couple have a rousing fight in which they express their opinions. After such a quarrel, there are changes made, and each is willing to compromise. Often they overcompensate by going too far as they give in to each other, and this overcompensation provides the need for the next conflict.

If a couple is unable to have a fight and so bring up what is on their minds, they are dealing with each other by withdrawal techniques and avoiding any discussion of certain areas of their relationship. With each avoidance, the area that cannot be discussed grows larger until ultimately they may have nothing they can safely talk about. One of the functions of a marriage therapist might be to provoke a couple to fight and say what is on their minds so they do not continue to punish each other indirectly for crimes which have never been brought up as accusations. When a couple cannot fight, all issues which require defining an area of the relationship are avoided. The couple will then eat together and watch television side by side, but their life has little shared intimacy. At the other extreme a couple may stabilize into a relationship which requires constant fighting. They repeatedly share demonstrations of strong feeling for each other, but they cannot reach amiable agreement on who is to control what in the marriage.

The more easily resolved conflicts in a marriage are those involving which rules the couple will follow. The two people may disagree about an aspect of living together or about how they should deal with each other, but they can reach a compromise which resolves the matter. Sharing the work about the house, agreeing on friends or types of social life, and problems of consideration for each other in various areas of living can lead to disagreement which is reasonably easy to resolve.

Although disagreements tend to be about which rules to follow, emotional fights tend to be about *who* is to make the rules, and this problem is not so easily solved by compromise. For example, a wife may insist that her husband hang up his clothes so that she does not have to pick up after him like a servant. The husband might agree with his wife that she should not be his servant, and so agree to the definition of the relationship, but he still might not agree that *she* should be the one to give him orders on what to do about his clothes. What rule to follow is more easily discussable than who is to make the rules to follow. The process of defining who is to make the rules in the marriage will inevitably consist of a struggle between any couple. The tactics in this struggle are those of any conflict: threats, violent assault, withdrawal, sabotage, passive resistance, and helplessness or physical inability to do what the other wants. The power struggle is not necessarily pathological. However, it can become pathological if the conflict continues in a circular pattern or if one or the other spouse attempts to circumscribe the mate's behavior while indicating that he or she cannot help it. Labeling behavior as "involuntary" requires symptomatic behavior and leads to pathological relationships.

When the issue between two people centers on who is to make the rules, they will behave as if basic rights are being violated. Similarly, the internal burning which goes on within spouses who have withdrawn from each other and are not speaking will center in conflict over who is to define what sort of relationship they will have. Typically the two spouses will be silent but busy rehearsing conversation in their heads; this conversation will include lines such as "Who does he think he is?" and "If she thinks I'll put up with that she has another think coming." The question of rights involves a complicated labeling procedure in any discussion. The wife might not mind being advised by her husband, and so be cooperating in a complementary relationship, if he offers the advice in just the right way or if she has asked for it. However, she may stoutly oppose such a relationship if her husband has initiated it or insisted upon it. Similarly, a husband might be quite willing to treat his wife as an equal in a certain area, but if she demands that he do so he may lose his willingness. The physical violence which can occur over minor matters is generated by a struggle at this control level of marriage. Whether to go to one movie or another may lead to threats of divorce when the conflict centers on who is to tell who what to do in the marriage.

If marital partners communicated only a single-level message, conflicts would be more easily resolvable because cycles of conflict would not be generated. For example, if a husband only bids for a complementary relationship and the wife only responds with an acceptance or with a counteroffer for a symmetrical relationship, then the issue can be resolved between them. However, people do not communicate only on a single level, so they offer each other messages which define one type of relationship at one level of communication and an incompatible type of relationship at another level of communication. The conflict produced cannot easily be resolved and in fact usually provokes a response which perpetuates the conflict. For example, if a wife *orders* her husband to *dominate* her, the couple is caught in a network of incompatible definitions of the relationship. If the husband dominates her at her insistence, he is being dominated. To put this another way, if he accepts the secondary end of a complementary relationship by doing what she says, he is faced with a paradox if what she says is that he must tell her what to do. This is like the paradox involved in the statement "Disobey me." If the respondent disobeys, he is obeying and if he obeys he is disobeying. A similar situation occurs if a husband orders his wife to supervise or take care of him. Similarly, the paradox occurs if a wife insists that her husband assert himself in relation to his mother and not be a "mama's boy" by letting himself be dominated by a woman. The more he is forced by his wife to assert himself with mother, the more he is accepting being dominated. Two incompatible types of relationship are simultaneously being imposed. Sometimes a wife will quite explicitly say that she wants her husband to dominate her in the way she tells him to—without realizing the incompatibility of her requests.

The communication of bids for two incompatible types of relationship can occur whenever there is an incompatibility between (1) the behavior defining the relationship and (2) the type of relationship implicit at the level of *who* is defining the relationship. For example, if a wife tells her husband to pick up his clothes she is indicating that their relationship should be symmetrical; each person should pick up his own clothes. However, *when she tells him to do this* she is defining the relationship as complementary—she orders and he is to follow the orders. The husband is then faced with two different definitions of the relationship, so that whichever way he responds he cannot satisfy both requests. If he picks up his clothes, accepting the symmetrical definition, he is following her directions and so accepting a complementary definition. He cannot accept one definition without the other unless he comments on the situation in a way that redefines it. More likely he will erupt in indignation while uncertain what he is indignant about, and his wife will similarly be indignant because he erupts over this simple request.

A further area of conflict for a couple occurs if there is an incompatibility between (1) the meta-rules they establish for resolving disagreements about rules, and (2) the rules themselves. For example, a couple might reach an agreement that whenever they are in conflict about the rules for dealing with each other, the husband will make the final decision and set the rules. However, the final decision he might make could be that he and his wife are to be equals, or in a symmetrical relationship. If they are equals, he cannot be the rule-setter, yet that is the rule he sets. Similarly, a couple may establish the rule that they will resolve all disagreements in a mutually satisfactory way—by discussion and compromise. However, when the wife attempts to express her opinion on a particular issue, the husband may point out that getting emotional does not solve anything, and since she won't listen to him, he will withdraw from the field. His behavior defining the relationship as complementary on a particular issue is incompatible with their agreement to handle issues symmetrically, and the result is mutual dissatisfaction and indignation.

In summary, conflict between a married couple can arise in several areas: (1) conflict over what sort of rules to follow in dealing with each other and so what sort of relationship to have, (2) conflict over who is to set the rules with the types of relationship defined by the ways this conflict is worked out, and (3) a conflict over the incompatibility between these two levels; a relationship defined in one way on the first level conflicts with the relationship defined another way on the other level. Besides these conflicts, another may be generated by (4) an incompatibility between the process of working out conflicts and the conflicts themselves, so that what will be resolved at one level is incompatible with what can be resolved at another.

Almost any marital conflict which occurs can be described within this formal scheme, even though the description is confined to two levels instead of the multiple levels of communication which occur in human relations. Presumably, too, this scheme would apply to marriages in different cultures, since it is not a description of which rules a couple follows, which would be culture-bound, but a description at a more formal level. A couple in any culture must deal with what rules to follow, who is to enact them, and what rules to follow to resolve disagreements. In a changing culture there will inevitably be more conflict, as there will be in cross-cultural marriages. The shift in the status of women in America has produced a breakdown in many of the elaborate ways of defining relationships between men and women which were once taken for granted as courtesy procedures. As a result a man is often faced with a wife who insists that she be treated as an equal while simultaneously insisting that he take charge of her in a complementary relationship.

If one describes marital relationships in terms of conflicting levels of communication, the description is complex, but any less complex description is too oversimplified to be useful. For example, to describe a marriage as one where there is "a dominating wife and a dependent husband" does not include the idea that the husband might be provoking his wife to be dominating so that actually he is "dominating" what sort of relationship they have. Similarly, the "submissive" wife can actually be the one who, by helpless maneuvers, is managing whatever happens in the relationship.

When paradoxical communication occurs in a marriage, the conflicts are the most difficult type for a couple to resolve on their own. Such situations occur with any incompatible set of messages. For example, a double bind occurs when a husband indicates his wife should show an interest in sex and initiate the activity, but when she does he behaves unresponsively because she is being demanding and managing. If a husband receives his wife's advances as too demanding and her absence of advances as prudishness, the wife is wrong whatever she does. Similarly, a wife may encourage her husband to initiate sexual relations, but when he does she may indicate that he is imposing on her, and if he does not, that he is disinterested in her.

When these paradoxes occur in the sexual area they represent themes which appear throughout the marriage as incompatible definitions of the relationship. A husband is defining the relationship as symmetrical when he encourages his wife to initiate sexual relations, and if he also indicates she should not do so, he defines the relationship as complementary. The two incompatible definitions in this area place the wife in a double bind: whichever way she responds, agreeing to his definition of the relationship, will be opposed by him as a wrong definition. The wife might find a solution by posing incompatible definitions of the relationship in return. She might do this in "normal" ways or by devolping symptoms. As an example of a "normal" way to offer an incompatible definition of the relationship in response, the wife might talk about initiating sex, and so define the relationship as symmetrical, but leave all such initiating up to her husband, and so define the relationship as complementary. Or she might indicate an interest in sexual relations and then appear indifferent so that her husband must pursue her; she has then initiated sexual relations, but she also has not, since the major move resides with him.

Symptoms can be seen as a product of, or a way of handling,

a relationship in which there are incompatible definitions of the relationship. It is easy to assume that a wife's symptoms which interfere with sexual relations are only expressions of her guilts and fears about sex, but she might be demanding less of her husband in this involuntary way because he has indicated that she should (in such a way that she cannot accuse him of doing so). If a husband asks his wife to show an interest in sexual relations and opposes her when she does, the wife can become unable to because of symptomatic distress. Similarly, a wife who cannot tolerate "surrendering" to her husband in a complementary relationship but insists that he take charge in the relationship, may produce impotency in the husband as a convenience to them both. If one is asked to do something and not do it at the same time, a possible response is to be unable to do it—which means indicating that one's behavior is involuntary. The physiology of the human being seems to cooperate in this situation even to the point of producing somatic symptoms.

Resistance to Change

A married couple in difficulty cannot be rational about the matter. Both husband and wife might know perfectly well how they could treat each other to relieve their distress, despite an appearance of misunderstanding, but they continue to provoke discomfort in themselves and each other. When a therapist tries to bring about a change, he finds two central problems that inhibit a shift in the relationship.

One problem in the way of change is a couple's persistence in protecting each other. Although they could be making wild attacks upon each other, or be appearing to tear each other down constantly, a little probing usually reveals that they are protecting each other in a variety of ways, thus keeping the system stable. For example, a wife who was the manager in a marriage would insult her husband in the therapy session for his drinking, lack of consideration, bad behavior, and general boorishness. Alone with the therapist one day she said the real problem was the fact that her husband was just a big baby and she was tired of mothering him. When the therapist asked why she had not brought this up in a session with her husband present, the woman was shocked at the idea of hurting his feelings in that way. Yet she was consistently indicating that he was a baby in her eyes without ever making the accusation explicit so the husband could deal with it.

One of the functions of an angry quarrel in a marriage would seem to be to give the participants permission to stop protecting each other temporarily. Typically a wife and husband will let each other know what areas are too sensitive for discussion. When one of these areas is touched upon, they will respond in an anxious or angry way, so that further discussion will not occur. When a spouse finds one of these undiscussable areas to be a central problem in their relationship, he or she often will not discuss it because of the other person's sensitivity there. Yet often a change can occur only if there is discussion, not necessarily because understanding is brought about, but because a change is being made in the rules for who is to talk about what. That is, if a wife has established the implicit rule that something is not to be discussed and then the husband discusses it, his act of discussing it signifies a change in the relationship quite independent of whatever enlightenment may occur because of the discussion.

Although it might be considered a natural aspect of marriage that the couple protect each other, there are aspects of protectiveness which are not so amiable. If a wife does not discuss something because she feels her husband cannot tolerate it, she will be exhibiting a lack of respect for him which may be unjustified and which he will feel as patronizing. The problem in the marriage can center more in her lack of respect for her husband than it does in the content of the sensitive area. Similarly, if a wife restrains her own abilities and accomplishments so that she will not outshine her husband, she is not necessarily doing him a favor. For example, a wife decided not to continue in school and get a higher degree because she would then have had a higher academic status than her husband. When a wife decides to restrain herself for such a purpose, not only will she be patronizing her husband, but she may be using this protection as an excuse when there are a number of other reasons why she would not seek a higher degree. Usually if one mate is protective of another, there are unexpressed needs being served. For example, there may be a bargain involved. If a man protects his wife on a certain issue, it is often with the implicit agreement that she will therefore protect him on another issue. This may be all right unless the marriage is in distress. Such a state usually indicates that one or the other is getting the poorer part of the bargain. Should one cease such protection, the other does also, and changes can occur. A further aspect of protection is the confusion that occurs over who is protecting whom. Rather typically, if a spouse prefers not to discuss something to protect the other spouse, there is self-deceit involved. For example, a husband might indicate that his wife cannot tolerate a discussion of sex when, in fact, he is the one who becomes uncomfortable in such a discussion, but his wife will accept the label as the sensitive one.

One of the more severe forms of resistance to change in a marriage occurs with the development of symptoms in one or both of the partners. The symptom is then used by the couple, as a disturbed child is used in a family, to avoid defining their relationship and so avoid dealing with the marital distress. Typically the couple will say they would be perfectly happy if it were not for the husband's headaches or if it were not for the wife's anxiety attacks. However, as the symptom is alleviated, they do not evidence this happiness; in fact, their conflict may increase to the point where the disappearance of the symptom may mean separation or divorce. Psychotherapists who see only individuals are likely to miss discovering how a relationship with an intimate family member affects the patient's rate of improvement.

Typically, symptoms not only protect the individual as an intrapsychic defense, they also protect the marital partner and the marriage itself. A woman with a variety of hysterical symptoms was treated by joint interviews with her husband. The husband was reluctant to enter therapy because he insisted the problems resided in his wife, not in himself or the marriage. The wife, too, indicated that she could not see the relevance of her husband to the physical distress she was experiencing. As her symptoms improved, the couple began to fight more openly. The wife's dissatisfactions became more easily expressed. In the process of treatment, the woman revealed almost accidentally that for many years she had also suffered from claustrophobia. Since she could not ride in an elevator, the couple could not go for a drink at a popular bar on the top of a tall building. As the woman was encouraged in the interview toward planning a drink at the top of that building, both she and her husband became rather anxious. The woman said her symptom was not at all an inconvenience and she would prefer to retain it. Further inquiry revealed that the husband suffered from a fear of heights. However, no issue was ever made of this fear because of the "agreement" between the two of them that she had problems and he did not. Should this woman overcome her fear of enclosed places and ride an elevator, she would expose her husband's inability to go with her. Such an admission would require a revision of a basic premise that their marriage was a complementary relationship with the husband the strong one and the wife the one with symptoms and difficulties.

One finds, if he explores this kind of marriage, that characteristically one spouse carries symptoms which are a protective concealment for the symptoms of the other spouse. Improvement in the patient can be a severe threat to the marriage. For example, a wife may appear quite inadequate and helpless because of her emotional problems, but exploration reveals an even more helpless and inadequate husband who is constantly required by his wife's difficulties to maintain the fiction that he is taking care of *her*. Often in such cases, despite the wife's helpless incapacity, one finds that she handles the budget, organizes the family activities, deals with the outside world, and generally manages the home. The credit for strength in the family, however, is handed to the man by mutual agreement.

In this type of marriage the wife will develop her symptoms when the husband is so shaken by something in his life that he is threatened with a breakdown or the development of symptoms. At that moment the wife develops her problems, and the man must pull himself together to help her. Occasionally the wife may develop her symptoms at the time the husband takes a step forward and begins to assert himself with more self-confidence in the marriage. As he makes more demands upon her the wife may gain control of the relationship by becoming too "ill" to meet the demands. Sometimes these two circumstances may occur simultaneously; the husband experiences some success in his field of endeavor which causes him to assert himself more at home and at the same time shakes him because of his uneasiness about added responsibilities. As he oscillates between breaking down under the threat of greater success and becoming more self-assertive, he offers his wife incompatible definitions of the relationship and she cooperates by developing symptoms which stabilize the situation.

An example of this type of situation is the graduate student who receives his degree and begins his first job. Threatened with a change in his relationship to the world because he must go out and deal with people as an equal adult after years as a student, he, in this time of success, enters a crisis. In the case of a particular student, the wife, who had been supporting him through college, was the one who collapsed. She was suddenly faced with a shift in their relationship as he went to work and started supporting her. He became both more assertive at home and more shaken by his new responsibilities in life. At the moment he was expressing his uncertainty about leaving his new job and going back to school, the wife developed anxiety attacks. She was unable to continue work because of these anxiety attacks, or even to leave the house alone, and so he was required to continue in his new job and support her. When the wife moved in the direction of getting on her feet, the husband indicated he might collapse. Yet when the husband attempted to take more charge of the marriage, which the wife indicated she wished, she would become uncooperative but indicated she "could not help it." Whenever the couple began to deal with their conflicts with each other, the wife would indicate that she would respond to her husband differently if it were not for her anxiety. The husband would indicate that the problem was not between them but centered in her internal anxiety. As long as the couple maintained an emphasis upon the wife's symptoms when threatened with change, the marital relationship could not be worked out in a more satisfying way.

THERAPEUTIC INTERVENTION

The typical marriage therapist brings a couple together and tells them he wants them to talk and correct the misunderstandings which have arisen, to express their feelings, and to gain some insight into their difficulties. However, merely because this procedure for change is outlined to the married couple does not necessarily mean that therapeutic change is brought about by self-expression, correcting misunderstandings, or gaining insight into difficulties. The explanation to a patient of what will bring about this change need not be confused with what actually brings about a change.

The argument that insight and self-understanding are the primary factors in producing change cannot be sufficiently supported. Some couples will undergo a change from following directives without insight. Other couples will evidence considerable understanding, particularly of the effects of the past on their present behavior, and yet they will continue to behave in distressing ways. More important, understanding and self-expression cannot be separated from the effects of the therapeutic context in which they occur. Shifts in relationship with the therapist can effect a change which appears as a shift in understanding. For example, a wife may "discover" that she is unwilling to let her husband be the authority in the home because of the inadequacies of her father in the past. However, when she makes this discovery in the therapeutic context, she will be presenting the idea to the therapist and so accepting him as the authority on the point she is making. What change occurs may not be brought about by her self-understanding but by her acceptance of the therapist as an authority when she has never allowed anyone to be in that position with her.

The Effect of the Third Person

When a couple comes to a marriage therapist, changes can occur in their relationship because of the mere existence of the therapeutic triangle. The marital partners may have various motivations for entering therapy, including a determination to prove that the other is the villain in the marriage. The ways spouses attempt to use third parties are often what need to be changed about their relationship. Most couples have managed to use in-laws, intimate friends, or children against each other. A marriage therapist, by dealing fairly with each spouse, deals differently with them than others have. By not letting himself be provoked into condemning either marital partner, the therapist disarms a couple and prevents many of their usual maneuvers. (Actually, on the basis of his fee alone the therapist is involved with a couple in a different way from that of family members.)

The mere presence of the therapist, as a fair participant, requires the spouses to deal with each other differently. Each spouse must respond to both therapist and mate instead of merely to mate. For example, a husband who handles his wife by withdrawing into silence will find that he cannot easily continue with this maneuver in the therapy setting. Instead of being incapacitated by his silence, the wife can discuss it with the therapist and use it to prove her point. The husband must change his tactics to deal with both people. Many maneuvers a spouse habitually uses to provoke a response in his partner can lose their effectiveness when used against two people at once, particularly if the third party is not easily provoked.

Although it is not possible for a marriage therapist to be "objective" with a couple, since he rapidly becomes a participant in the interaction, it is possible for him to side first with one spouse and then with the other and so be fair. It is convenient for some therapists to argue that they do not take sides in a marital struggle but merely "reflect" back to the couple what they are expressing. Such an argument requires considerable naïveté. If a therapist listens to a wife's complaints and then turns to her husband and says, "How do you feel about that?" he cannot make this classic statement without his inquiry being in some sense directive. A therapist cannot make a neutral comment; his voice, his expression, the context, or the mere act of choosing a particular statement to inquire about introduces directiveness into the situation. When the therapist is being directive, coalition patterns are being defined and redefined, and a crucial aspect of this type of therapy is continually changing coalition patterns between therapist and each spouse. The wife who drags her husband into marriage therapy soon finds that the therapist does not join her in condemnation of the fellow, and the dragged-in husband discovers with some relief that the focus also shifts to how difficult his wife can be.

A further effect of the presence of the therapist is the change brought about by each spouse when he has the opportunity to observe the other dealing with the therapist. For example, a man who had paid little attention to his wife's protests must sit and observe an authority figure treat her in a symmetrical way by paying careful attention to what she says and encouraging her to say more. Not only do questions of coalition arise in such circumstances, but a model is being set for the spouse. Similarly, a therapist may prevent a wife or husband from dealing with him the way he or she has habitually provoked the marriage partner. For example, by commenting on how he is being handled the therapist may set a model for dealing with such provocations.

The difficulty a couple have in accepting a complementary relationship with each other is profoundly affected by the fact that they place themselves individually and collectively in a complementary relationship with a marriage therapist by asking for his services. When the therapist cooperates in such a relationship by taking charge, as most marriage therapists tend to do, he is accepting this type of relationship. Although such a therapist is not necessarily overtly authoritarian (in fact, that may not be wise or possible except in special circumstances) he is willing to listen and explore the problems. If a couple is to pay attention to him, he must be an authority figure, although not so omnipotent that it is necessary for the couple to topple him. Their acceptance of an authority figure, and therefore the acceptance of a complimentary relationship, becomes a part of the process of working out types of relationship with each other.

Defining the Rules

Besides intervening in a marriage merely by being present, a marriage therapist will actively intervene by relabeling, or redefining, the activity of the two people with each other. In the early stages of treatment his comments and directives tend to be permissive as he encourages the couple to express themselves in a context where each will have a fair hearing. Accusations and protests are nurtured so that as much as possible is made explicit. One way of encouraging a more free discussion is to define the consultation room as a special place, a "no man's land," where the rules are different from those of ordinary situations. In this special place it is appropriate to bring up matters which they have on their minds but have avoided discussing. Although this framing of the therapy situation appears a mild directive, couples will often accept the idea that they can protect each other less in that room. Sometimes a therapist may forbid the couple to discuss certain topics between sessions so that only in that special place are they discussed.

As a couple express themselves, the therapist comments upon what they say. His comments tend to be of two sorts: those comments which emphasize the positive side of their interaction together, and those comments which redefine the situation as different from, if not opposite to, the way they are defining it.

An emphasis upon the positive typically occurs when the therapist redefines the couple's motives or goals. For example, if a husband is protesting his wife's constant nagging, the therapist may comment that the wife seems to be trying to reach her husband and achieve more closeness with him. If the wife protests that her husband constantly withdraws from her, the husband may be defined as one who wants to avoid discord and seeks an amiable relationship. Particularly savage maneuvers will not be minimized but may be labeled as responses to disappointment (rather than the behavior of a cad). In general, whenever it can be done, the therapist defines the couple as attempting to bring about an amiable closeness but going about it wrongly, being misunderstood, or being driven by forces beyond their control. The way the couple characterize each other may also be redefined in a positive way. If a husband is objecting to his wife as an irresponsible and disorganized person, the therapist may define these characteristics as feminine. If the husband is passive and inactive, he may be defined as stable and enduring. When the therapist relabels a spouse in a positive way, he is not only providing support, but he is making it difficult for the couple to continue their usual classification. In addition, when the therapist redefines a spouse, he is labeling himself as the one who classifies the couple. By emphasizing the positive, he does his classifying in such a way that they cannot easily oppose him.

The other type of comments by the therapist emphasize the opposite of what the couple is emphasizing. If both husband and wife are protesting that they remain married only because they must, for religious reasons or for the children's sake, the therapist focuses upon the voluntary aspects of their relationship. Emphasizing how they chose each other and have remained together for many years, he minimizes the compulsion in the relationship. When husband and wife are protesting that their relationship is strictly voluntary and they can separate at any time, the therapist indicates that they have remained together so long despite their difficulties and they obviously have a deep unwillingness to end their association.

The therapist also relabels the type of relationship of a couple. If a wife protests that she is the responsible one in the family and must supervise her husband, the therapist not only commiserates with her for depriving herself by cooperating in this arrangement, he also points out the husband's supervision and responsible acts. In addition, he may suggest to the wife that the husband is arranging that she be the responsible one, thereby raising the question who is supervising whom. Similarly, if a husband labels his wife as the helpless one, the therapist points them in the direction of discovering who gets her own way. By focusing upon the opposite, or a different, aspect of a relationship, the therapist undermines the couple's typical ways of labeling the relationship, and they must define it in a different way and so undergo a change.

A further product of encouraging a couple to talk about each other is to make explicit many of the implicit or covert marital rules. When they are explicit, they are more difficult to follow. For example, if an implicit agreement between a couple is that they will visit his in-laws but not hers, the therapist may inquire whether they both prefer this arrangement. If they have not discussed the matter explicitly, an issue is then raised where a decision can be made. Similarly, there may be an implicit agreement that the wife never lets her husband speak. When the therapist points out that the wife seems to be interrupting her husband before he has a chance to say what is on his mind, the wife will be less able to do so, even though the therapist is not suggesting a change but "merely" commenting on what is happening. A comment can also make mutual protection less effective. By suggesting to a husband that his wife seems to be treating him like a sensitive plant, the therapist can provoke a more straightforward discussion. Conflicts about what rules to follow can be resolved by encouraging a couple to discuss their lives together and to work out compromises with a therapist emphasizing the positive. However, conflicts about who is to set the rules require more active direction from a therapist.

Resolving Problems of Who Is to Set the Rules

Although the major conflicts in a marriage center in the problem of who is to tell whom what to do under what circumstances, the therapist may never discuss this conflict explicitly with the couple. If a husband says that he gets angry because his wife always gets her own way and is constantly supervising him, the therapist will not emphasize the struggle for control but will emphasize the strong feeling in the situation. Explicitly talking about the control problem can solidify it. However, specific directives given by the therapist are most effective when they are designed to resolve the struggle over who is to set the rules for the relationship.

Any comment by a therapist has directive aspects, if only to indicate "pay attention to this," but the marriage therapist often specifically directs a marital couple to behave in certain ways. These directives can be classed for convenience into two types: the suggestion that the couple behave differently, and the suggestion that they continue to behave as they have been.

A marriage therapist will direct a spouse to behave differently only in those cases where the conflict is minor or where it is likely that the spouse will behave that way anyhow and is only looking for an excuse. That is, a husband who never takes his wife out may be advised to take her out to dinner, but usually only if the husband is moving in that direction. Such a suggestion permits a couple an evening out without either spouse having to admit they wish it. Mere advice to a couple to treat each other in more reasonable ways is rarely followed or goes badly if it is followed. A couple, like an individual patient, can only be diverted into more productive directions and cannot be forced to reverse themselves. To tell a husband and wife that they should treat each other more amiably does not provide them with new information or give them an opportunity to follow the directive. More important, if a therapist directs a couple to behave differently, he has often been led into this directive by the couple and so is responding to their directive. A couple in distress have provoked many people to advise them to behave more sensibly; such advice only proves to the couple that the other person does not understand them and they continue in their distress. In general, when a therapist is provoked into giving advice, the advice will be on the terms of the person doing the provoking and therefore will perpetuate the distress. For example, a wife might say to the therapist, "Don't you think my husband should stay home nights instead of going out every night of the week?" If the therapist agrees, he is being led down the garden path. If instead of agreeing and so offering such advice the therapist says, "I think it's important to understand what this is about," the therapist is not only encouraging understanding but making it clear that he offers advice only on his own terms, not when provoked into it.

However, this does not mean that the therapist should not offer advice or directives on his own terms. The psychoanalytic approach to couples is largely to listen, and such a procedure avoids being led into directives by the couple. Although there may be theoretical rationales for remaining silent, such as developing deeper layers of the intrapsychic conflicts, the main function of silence is to avoid behaving on the patient's terms. However, a therapist who remains silent also avoids taking those actions which would move a couple in the direction of a more satisfactory relationship. To be silent when provoked by the couple may be necessary; to remain silent when directives which would produce change could be given on the therapist's terms is wasting time.

A couple can be instructed to behave differently if the request is small enough so that the implications of it are not immediately apparent. For example, if a husband says he always gives in and lets his wife have her own way, he may be asked to say "no" to his wife on some issue once during the week. When this is said in the wife's presence, the groundwork is laid for the suggestion to be more easily followed. Further, the suggestion is more likely followed if a rationale is provided, such as saying that any wife should feel free to do what she pleases with confidence that her husband will say "no" to her if she goes too far. Given such a directive, the couple may at first treat the "no" lightly. However, if it is on a major issue, or if the instruction is followed for several weeks, there will be repercussions in their relationship. The more rigid the previous "agreement" that the wife will always have her own way, the greater the response in both of them if he says "no" and thereby defines the relationship differently. The fact that he is doing so under direction, and so still accepting a complementary relationship, will ease the situation. But since the message comes from him, the wife will react. Similarly, an overly responsible wife may be asked to do some small irresponsible act during the week, perhaps buy something she does not need that costs a dollar or two. If the previous agreement was that she was the responsible one and her husband the irresponsible one, a small request of this sort undermines this definition of the relationship. Even though the wife is being irresponsible under therapeutic direction, and so doing her duty by doing what the therapist says, she is still spending money for something she does not need and so behaving irresponsibly. However, in general, when a directive is given for a husband or wife to behave differently, and so break the marital rules they have established, the request must be so small that it appears trivial.

Actually it is extremely difficult to devise a directive which is a request for marital partners to behave differently from their usual ways when their usual ways of behaving are conflictual. That is, a wife who insists that she is the responsible one in the marriage is usually irresponsible at another level. For example, she may be so responsible about the budget that she is irresponsible because she is overemphasizing money at a cost to her husband and children. To ask her to do something irresponsible is not necessarily to ask something new of her. Similarly, a husband who never says "no" to his wife directly is usually a man who is constantly saying "no" by passive resistance. To tell him to say "no" is only partly asking for different behavior. Even if one should suggest that a husband who is treating his wife coldly be more considerate of his wife, this may not be a request for a change in behavior because treating her coldly may be considerate of this type of woman. In fact if her husband treated her more amiably she might feel great demands were being put upon her or become so overwhelmed with guilt that sudden amiable behavior on his part would actually be inconsiderate.

Often a directive may appear as a request for different behavior when actually it is not. For example, a husband had spent some years crusading to have his wife enjoy a sexual orgasm. He had made such an issue of the matter and become so angry and exasperated with her, that the issue had become a grim one between husband and wife. The wife was told, in the husband's presence, that one of these days she might enjoy some sexual pleasure and when she did she was to tell her husband that she did not enjoy it. If her husband insisted on her saying whether she had *really* not enjoyed it or was just following this directive, she should say that she had really not enjoyed it. This directive had various purposes, including the purpose of introducing uncertainty into the situation and freeing the man from his overconcern about his wife's pleasure (he suffered from *ejaculatio praecox*). However, from what had been said, there was some indication that the wife was enjoying sex while denying it and so the directive actually was an encouragement of her usual behavior.

Encouraging a couple to behave in their usual way is, paradoxically, one of the most rapid ways to bring about a change. Such a directive may be calculated or it may occur as a natural result of encouraging a couple to express themselves. A wife may say that her husband should stop being so ineffectual, and the therapist may respond that perhaps he needs to behave in that way at times and they should try to understand his reasons for it. When the therapist makes such a statement, he is permitting—if not encouraging—the husband to continue to be ineffectual. Most procedures which ostensibly emphasize bringing about understanding can be seen as subtle encouragement of usual behavior. Note that this procedure is quite different from the way the spouse typically handles the problem: a spouse usually tells the other to stop certain behavior, and the result is a continuation of it. When the therapist permits and encourages usual behavior, the person tends to discontinue it.

When a therapist "accepts" the way a couple is behaving he begins to gain some control of that behavior. He is placed immediately in the center of their problem: who is to lay down the rules for the relationship. Although a couple cannot easily oppose the sort of relationship the therapist is prescribing if they are already interacting that way, they can still respond to the idea of someone else defining their relationship for them, and this response will produce a shift. For example, if a wife is managing her husband by being self-sacrificing and labeling all her behavior as for the good of others, the husband cannot easily oppose her, even though he may not wish to be in a secondary position in a complementary relationship with her. Such a woman will tend to handle the therapist in a similar way. However, if the therapist encourages her to be self-sacrificing, the woman is placed in a difficult position. She cannot manage him by this method when it is at his request. If she continues to behave that way, she is conceding that she is managed by the therapist. If she does not, then she must shift to a different type of relationship. If the therapist goes further and encourages the wife to be self-sacrificing and the husband to attempt to oppose her and fail, then the couple must shift their relationship with each other to deal with being managed by the therapist.

As an example of a typical problem, a couple may be continually fighting, and if the therapist directs them to go home and keep the peace this will doubtfully happen. However, if he directs the couple to go home and have a fight, the fight will be a different sort when it happens. This difference may reside only in the fact that they are now fighting at the direction of someone else, or the therapist may have relabeled their fighting in such a way that it is a different sort. For example, a husband may say that they fight continually because his wife constantly nags. The wife may say they fight because the husband does not understand her and never does what she asks. The therapist may relabel, or redefine, their fighting in a variety of ways: he may suggest that they are not fighting effectively because they are not expressing what is really on their minds; he may suggest that their fighting is a way of gaining an emotional response from each other and they both need that response; he may say that when they begin to feel closer to each other they panic and have a fight; or he may suggest they fight because inside themselves is the feeling that they do not deserve a happy marriage. With a new label upon their fighting, and directed to go home and have a fight, the couple will find their conflict redefined in such a way that it is difficult for them to continue in their usual pattern. They are particularly tempted toward more peace at home if the therapist says they *must* fight and that they must for certain reasons which they do not like. The couple can only disprove him by fighting less.

As a marriage therapist encourages a couple to behave in their usual ways he gains some control of their behavior because what occurs is being defined as occurring under his direction. At this point he may shift his direction to bring about a change. The change he brings about may be an expansion of the limits of the type of relationship of a couple, or a shift to a different type of relationship.

An example of extending the limits of a type of relationship is a classic case reported by Milton Erickson. A woman came to him and said that she and her husband were finally going to purchase a home, as they had hoped to all their married life; however, her husband was a tyrant and would not permit her any part in the choice of home or in the choice of furnishings for it. Her husband insisted that everything connected with the new house would be entirely his choice and she would have no voice in the matter. The woman was quite unhappy because of this extreme version of a complementary relationship. Erickson told the woman that he wished to see her husband. When the old gentleman came in, Erickson emphasized the fact that a husband should be absolute boss in the home. The husband fully agreed with him. Both of them also enjoyed a full agreement that the man of the house should have complete say in the choice of a house to buy and the choice of furnishings for it. After a period of discussion, Erickson shifted to talking about the type of man who was *really* the boss in the house. When the old gentleman expressed a curiosity about what sort of man was really the boss, Erickson indicated that the real boss was the type of man who was so fully in charge that he could allow his underlings a say in minor matters. Such a boss kept full control of everything, but he could *permit* certain decisions to be made by those beneath him. Using this line of approach, Erickson persuaded the tyrannical old gentleman to lay out twenty plans of houses and twenty plans of house furnishings. Then the husband permitted his wife to choose among *his* plans. She chose a house she liked and the furnishings she liked. In this way the husband was still fully in charge of all aspects of the house purchase, but the wife could choose what she wanted. The limits of a complementary relationship were extended to satisfy both partners' needs.

Accepting what a couple offers, or encouraging them to behave in their usual ways and later suggesting a change, can also provoke a shift in the type of relationship. For example, a wife was protesting that her husband avoided her, that he would often leave the dinner table when the family was eating to sit in the living room alone and later make himself some dinner. Although the husband at first indicated he did not know why he behaved this way, he also indicated that his wife spent the time at the dinner table nagging the kids and nagging at him. At the first suggestion that she was behaving in this way at the table, the wife said that she had to correct the children at the table because he never did. The husband said that when he attempted to, she interrupted, and it was not worth a battle.

The wife was instructed to correct the children at the table during the coming week, and to observe the effect of this upon her husband. Her husband was instructed to observe the way his wife dealt with the children, and if he strongly disagreed with it he was to get up and leave the table. Actually the instruction was merely to continue to behave as they had been. However, when they were instructed to do so, the couple found it difficult to behave in their usual ways because the behavior both became deliberate and occurred under duress. After a week of this procedure, the couple was instructed to shift their behavior: for a week the wife was to be relieved of all responsibility for discipline at the table and could just enjoy her meal, and the husband was to take full charge at the dinner table. The wife was not even to point at one of the children to indicate that her husband should take some action. Since their behavior was defined as occurring at the instigation of the therapist, rather than originating within each other, the couple could tolerate this shift in their relationship at the table with a consequent carryover into other aspects of their lives together.

Similar encouragement of typical behavior occurs if the therapist instructs a distant couple to maintain a certain distance from each other and not risk becoming too close for a period of time, if he instructs a nonfighting couple to avoid a fight but to rehearse in their minds what they would like to say to each other, if he instructs a spouse who always gives in to give in for a period of time, and so on. This procedure not only gives the therapist some control of what the couple is doing and lays the groundwork for a later shift, but it also utilizes whatever rebellious forces are latent within the couple.

Often an instruction to one spouse in the presence of the other has its effects on them both. For example, a couple who are constantly fighting, with the wife flaunting her extramarital affairs before her husband, will see their struggle from a particular point of view. They will usually see what they do to each other in terms of revenge. If the therapist, from his vantage point of an expert, advises the wife that she is protecting her husband by her dalliances with other men because he is uneasy about sex, the wife is faced with a different point of view. To label her behavior as protective, when she sees it as vengeful, makes it more difficult for her to continue it, particularly if the therapist suggests that it may be necessary for her to continue to help her husband in this way. When such a comment is made in the husband's presence, he is almost obligated to prove that he does not need such protection by attempting a closer relationship with his wife. Naturally the couple will disagree with such a comment, but the idea will continue to work upon them. If there is sufficient disagreement, the therapist may suggest they should experiment; if they manage a closer relationship, they will find that they panic. To disprove this, they must manage a closer relationship. If they become upset as they become closer, they are accepting the therapist's conception of the situation and so accepting him as someone who can arrange a change. If they do not become upset, they have a closer relationship, which is the therapist's goal.

When a therapist provides a framework which is to bring about a change, and within that framework he encourages a couple to continue in their usual ways, the couple is faced with a situation which is difficult to deal with without undergoing change. If, in addition, the therapist makes it an ordeal for them to continue in their usual ways, the problem is compounded for the couple. Labeling in a different way what they do often makes it more of an ordeal for the couple to continue their usual patterns. This "different way" may be a relabeling of negative behavior as something positive; it may also be the reverse. The therapist may suggest that certain behavior by one of the spouses which they consider positive is really negative. For example, the therapist may define protectivness as really selfishness because the protecting person's needs are being satisfied. Another procedure is to raise the question with the marital partners of how they usually punish each other. Typically they say they do not, but when the punishment is defined as that behavior which the other spouse feels as punishing, they become more loquacious. Couples will then discuss such behavior as withdrawing, complaining, arguing, refusing to do what the other asks, and so on. Such a discussion makes explicit many of the maneuvers a couple use against each other, and also leads to a relabeling of those maneuvers. It is possible to lead up to the idea of symptomatic behavior as punishing. Since symptoms in one spouse are always hard on the other, one can suggest that a symptom is a way of punishing the other. A spouse with an obesity problem, headaches, hysterical symptoms, or compulsions usually prefers to define the symptom as something occurring independent of the spouse. To call such a symptom a way of punishing makes it more difficult to exist. At times a spouse may be asked to inquire of the other "Why are you punishing me?" when the other complains of a symptom. Such an inquiry provokes a denial but also provokes an inhibition of the symptomatic experience. This procedure is similar to other relabeling of symptoms so that they are characterized differently and thus a change is induced. For example, one may ask a spouse, in the presence of the other spouse, to choose a time when the symptom is better that week and announce that it is worse. Such an instruction increases the uncertainty of the severity of the symptom and lays the groundwork for change.

The idea of a therapist's encouraging a couple to behave in their usual ways can be varied by a therapist's directing a spouse to encourage the other spouse to exhibit symptomatic behavior. Typically the mate of a spouse with symptoms opposes the symptomatic behavior but also encourages it. If a marriage therapist directs a mate only to encourage symptomatic behavior in the spouse, there is often a rather drastic response. For example, a wife became anxious whenever she tried to leave the house alone. When she attempted to go out, she suffered anxiety feelings and a terrible pain in the eyes. She had suffered this problem for years, and her husband was constantly assuring her that she should go out alone and that it was perfectly safe. However, he was also fully cooperating in her staying at home by doing all the shopping, escorting her where she needed to go, and indicating some uneasiness whenever she started to go out alone. After several sessions of marriage therapy, the husband was asked, in the presence of the wife, to do something he might think was silly. He was asked to tell the wife each day as he left for work that she was to stay home that day and not go out alone. He could say this seriously, or as a joke, or however he pleased. The husband agreed to follow this procedure. On the third day that he told her to stay at home the wife went out to the store alone for the first time in eight years. However, the next interview was devoted to the husband's expressions of concern about what his wife might do if she went out alone, where she might go, whom she might meet, and would she even get a job and become so independent that she would leave him.

This directive to the husband to tell his wife to stay at home was actually a double encouragement of usual behavior: the husband was directed to encourage his wife to stay at home, as he had been covertly doing, and the wife was being encouraged by the husband to stay at home, as she had been doing. The product of such a directive is a shift in type of relationship. Although the wife had been behaving like the helpless one, *she was in charge* of being the helpless one by insisting on staying home. When her husband directed her to stay at home, the question of *who* was laying down the rules for their relationship was called in question. The wife responded by a symmetrical move, leaving the house, which was her only way of taking charge in this situation. Although it seems a mild directive when a therapist directs a spouse to encourage the other spouse to behave as usual, there is inevitably a marital upheaval because such a directive centers on the crucial problem of a marriage; who is to define what sort of relationship the two people will have.

Changing the Stability of a System: Summary

A marital couple in difficulty tend to perpetuate their distress by attempting to resolve conflict in such a way that it continues. The goal of a marriage therapist is not only to shift, or to expand, the types of relationship of a couple, but also to provoke a change in the ways the couple keep the marital system stable. Such a change requires influencing the corrective variables in the system so the system itself may undergo a change.

An appearance at the door of a marriage therapist is essentially an attempt by a couple to find a more satisfying means of perpetuating their relationship. The therapist provides an opportunity for change in a variety of ways: to resolve conflict he encourages discussion rather than pervious methods, such as withdrawal and silence; he provides a reasonably impartial advisor and judge; he encourages a couple to examine motivations of which they might have outside awareness; he makes many maneuvers explicit and therefore more difficult to follow; and he engenders habits of dealing with sensitive topics. Granting that discussion, encouragement of understanding, and new points of view are offered in the marriage therapy context, there is another source of change which has been emphasized in this paper—the paradoxical position in which a couple is placed if they continue distressing behavior when undergoing marriage therapy.

For the purposes of this paper a paradoxical position is defined as the position a person is in when he is faced with messages which conflict with one another at different levels. For example, when faced with a marriage therapist a couple is faced with someone offering benevolent help for their difficulties. Yet at the same time the benevolent helper is requiring the couple to go through an ordeal which they can feel as punishing. It is not easy for a couple to expose their problems and petty conflicts, and the situations which couples are most sensitive about are often those most explored, so that the therapy can be a process of exacerbating old and new wounds. In so far as the couple is faced with a benevolent therapist who is helping them to feel better by putting them through an ordeal, they are faced with a paradoxical situation. Still another dimension of paradox occurs when the therapist encourages them to continue in their distress while communicating to them at another level that he is helping them over that distress. Still another paradox is involved when the therapist assumes the posture of an expert who can help the couple and then declines to instruct or direct them as an expert would.

The question of why paradoxical situations are evident in therapy is related to the question of how change is brought about and how difficult it is for a couple to bring about a change in their relationship without assistance. It would seem reasonable that if a couple who are obviously compounding their difficulties by their behavior were advised to behave in more sensible ways they would do so and their conflicts would be resolved. However, such advice is not usually offered in marriage therapy, and, if offered it is not usually accepted. It is possible to postulate deeply rooted psychodynamic causes to explain why change in a marital relationship is so difficult, but it is also possible to approach the problem from a relationship rather than an individual point of view.

People in relationship to each other tend to govern each other's behavior so that their relationship remains stable, and it is in the nature of governors that they act so as to diminish change. Implicit in this way of looking at relationships is a premise which might be called the first law of human relations: *when one individual indicates a change in relation to another, the other will respond in such a way as to diminish that change.* Granting the operation of this law in relationships, it would follow that each attempt by a spouse to change the marital relationship would provoke a response to diminish that change. A distressing relationship would be perpetuated by the act of attempting to change it. As it is sometimes said, if a wife wishes her husband to remain unchanged, she should set out to reform him.

Assuming that people follow such a law in their relationships, family relations would tend to be stable and difficult to change, and it would follow that psychotherapy of any sort would be faced with the problem that each attempt to change a patient could provoke a response to diminish that change. This would not mean that psychotherapy was impossible, but it would mean that tactics of psychotherapy would have to take this law into account. Therefore therapists would not say to a patient, "I'm going to change you." Instead, they would avoid indicating that a change was to be brought about, by emphasizing other factors in the interchange, such as self-understanding. They would decline the position of one who is explicitly attempting to bring about change, by saying to a patient, "I'm only trying to help you understand yourself" or "The best therapist for you is you and I can only try to help you help yourself." The therapist would be assuming the posture of the expert who can help bring about change, but he could not merely offer advice because that would be an indication for change which the couple would need to diminish. The various tactics of a therapist to avoid indicating a change would make paradoxes evident in the therapeutic setting, since he must bring about change without asking for it to occur.

It would also follow, granted this law, that an obvious way to bring about change in a symptom would be to encourage a change toward an increase in symptomatic behavior; the couple could only diminish that change by a lessening of symptomatic behavior. Again, a paradox becomes resolved if one assumes that people act to diminish those changes which are indicated by others.

Although a marriage therapist typically emphasizes to a couple the need for self-understanding, there is little evidence that achieving understanding causes a change in a marital relationship. More apparently, marriage therapy offers a context where a couple can learn alternative ways of behaving while being forced to abandon those past procedures which induced distress. By advice, counsel, and example the therapist offers other ways of resolving conflict. By imposing paradoxical situations, the therapist both forces and frees the couple to develop new ways of relating to one another.

K. I. PLATONOV

Methods of Verbal Suggestion

Platonov's work is typical of a great deal of Soviet writing in the field of psychotherapy in its heavily Pavlovian emphasis. While the insistence on suggestion and consistent attempts to word all interventions in physiological terminology may seem somewhat strange to other psychotherapists, it is fascinating to note how many parallels may be found with Western psychotherapeutic ideas.

The description of the technique of persuasion is similar to Albert Ellis's rational-emotive psychotherapy. However, the emphasis on direct authoritative suggestion would seem to be directly opposed to the methods of Jay Haley as described in the preceding selection. Closer examination of Platonov's work indicates that, being a good clinician, he obviously modifies his therapeutic endeavor to meet the individual needs of his patients. Platonov not only stresses the need for understanding the patient but rejects "unjustified interference" in the personal life of the patient on the grounds that it "may defeat the purpose of the suggestion because it will inevitably meet with the patient's direct resistance." Obviously Platonov is aware of resistance and makes suggestions for dealing with this phenomenon.

Although Platonov is opposed to psychoanalysis, his clinical suggestions show certain striking resemblances to psychoanalytically oriented psychotherapy. He quotes with approval the old Roman saying, "Medicine is the art of being silent"; he insists on the importance of paying close attention to the patient in order to establish a working relationship; and his statement,

From *The World as a Physiological and Therapeutic Factor* (Moscow: Progress Publishers, 1959).

"The psychotherapist must not only understand but also feel the agony of his soul, put himself as it were in the patient's place but so that the patient may also feel it," could fit into a psychoanalytic text.

His emphasis on the therapist's attitude to his patient sounds similar to analysts' injunctions against pathological countertransference.

Of course, on the whole Platonov's work is quite different from that of psychoanalysts, but this difference must be examined from the viewpoint of the different cultural context within which it occurs.

The emphasis on the psychotherapeutic task of physicians other than psychiatrists seems sound, but it also indicates how much more authoritatively physicians' words are accepted by Soviet patients as contrasted with, say, the middle-class Americans who are the chief targets of psychotherapy in the United States.

Suggestibility is a phenomenon inherent in everybody. It is deeply rooted in the nature of man and is based on the direct influence of words and other psychic impulses on the course of associations, the actions and deeds and various functions of the organism. V. BEKHTEREV

GENERAL PRINCIPLES OF BUILDING THE FORMULAS OF SUGGESTION AND PERSUASION

IT SHOULD BE TAKEN into account that under favorable conditions the words of suggestion may exert an enormous influence on all processes occurring in the cerebral cortex. These words comprise the formula of suggestion.

The formula of persuasion is built on a system of logical arguments and consistent proof, for example, "teaching of parturition" in the system of psychoprophylaxis of labor pains, anti-alcoholic chats, etc. The physician explains to the patient the real state of affairs, the groundlessness of the inferences made by the patient as regards the facts that trouble him or the events that traumatize him, etc. Thus, the physician's words must give rise to a new system of relations in the cerebral cortex limiting the significance of the pathological dynamic structures which have developed in it and must form new vital principles correctly orientating the patient in the given sphere.

In other cases, therapeutic suggestions must imperatively inform the patient of what the suggestion has already done. For example: "The event you have experienced has already receded into the distant past and no longer troubles you; you think of it very calmly, your life now proceeds very normally, you feel good, your night sleep is deep and undisturbed." Or: "You have already forgotten all your distressing past experiences and when you happen to think of them casually they no longer worry you." Or in treating a dipsomaniac: "You no longer have any desire for alcoholic drinks; on the contrary, you feel an overwhelming aversion for them or regard them indifferently."

At the same time, the formula of suggestion must be expressed in a few simple and understandable words corresponding in their nature to the individual peculiarities of the patient, the level of his intellectual development, the form of his ailment, etc. It must not contain anything superfluous.

In more complicated cases the formula of suggestion must be extended, the text of the suggestion thought out and edited in advance. In this case, it may be prepared in written form beforehand. When making a suggestion, the physician must pronounce the words authoritatively and firmly, confidently and calmly, repeating the formula of suggestion several times (at certain intervals) in order that the conditioned-reflex bonds created by it may become sufficiently consolidated. It should be particularly emphasized that each word intended for suggestive influence during suggested sleep is for the patient's cerebral cortex a precisely differentiated stimulus, the meaning of which will have the necessary therapeutic force and significance only if the patient understands it.

The success of a verbal suggestion is in certain measure determined not only by the content of the formula of suggestion itself but also by the expressiveness of speech, i.e., the sound intensity, the intonation of the voice, particular accents corresponding to the meaning of the uttered words, etc. Besides, during hypnotic sleep the suggestions must not be made in a loud voice.

The content of the formula of therapeutic suggestion, its structure, its direct and clear pathogenetic purposefulness, are of enormous importance. Complete removal of the pathological syndrome not infrequently requires a number of repeated sessions of suggestion.

The words of suggestion must not reflect the attitudes of the physician himself, especially if they do not correspond to the patient's social principles or point of view, or affect his pride, his relations with his relatives, etc. It is but natural that such unjustified interference in the personal life of the patient may defeat the purpose of the suggestion because it will inevitably meet with the patient's direct resistance.

At the same time, the formula of suggestion must always be

very clear and definite. The suggestion must not be referred to some indefinite future; the physician must not say, for example: "Your nervous system will improve"; "Your attacks will cease"; "You will feel good"; etc. In this uncertain formula of suggestion the physician deals with some unknown future when all this will have to happen.

As stated before, in some cases suggestion during suggested sleep may have the nature either of a motivated explanation or persuasion, or an authoritative instruction or advice (motivated suggestion according to V. Bekhterev and G. Löwenfeld).

The formula of suggestion may envisage its immediate or deferred effectuation. The latter case must provide for a definite time or definite conditions for the effectuation of the suggestion.

There can be no doubt that the patient's emotional state while the therapeutic suggestion is made must be in the center of the physician's attention. The formula of suggestion he uses must fully reflect it. At the same time, the words of suggestion must also be emotionally colored.

Formation of a dynamic structure connected with an excessively strong emotion sets up the conditions for the emergence of a trigger point with more or less complex neurotic syndromes.

A suggestion: "The event you experienced is already a thing of the past and no longer troubles you" repeated several times on end produces inhibition at the focus of concentrated stimulation which, in turn, leads to a weakening of the surrounding zone of negative induction and by virtue of this, to the removal of the "trigger point" itself. The words: "Your experience is a thing of the past" are an inhibitory conditioned reflex (conditioned inhibition) aimed directly at removing the pathological state which the "trigger point" is.

Thus, the construction of the formula of therapeutic suggestion is the result of a detailed study by the physician of the conditions under which the neurosis developed. The psychotherapist must therefore prepare himself in a certain measure for every session of therapeutic suggestion as, say, a surgeon prepares himself for a surgical operation, by thinking out his tactics beforehand and foreseeing the possible circumstances and complications by virtue of which the suggested word may act contrary to the physician's intentions.

The formula of suggestion used by the physician really assumes very great importance because it is precisely this formula that contains the key to the success of psychotherapy. It is essential that the physician's suggestion act on the patient's cerebral cortex, which is in a state of reduced tone conditioned both by the suggested sleep and the neurotic ailment, and is connected with it by a negative asthenizing emotion. By virtue of this the words of the suggestive therapeutic influence exerted during suggested sleep may be fixed for a long time and firmly enter the cortical dynamic structures. Any possibility of their iatrogenizing influence must therefore be foreseen by the physician and fully removed. That is why the words of the therapeutic verbal suggestion must be chosen very carefully and must be sufficiently well thought out and weighed, and presented in the form which does not admit of any ambiguous interpretation. This is the crux of the matter, because the entire skill of a physician consists in the *pathogenetically correct administration of the suggestion.* The physician's mission thus becomes particularly clearly creative and at the same time extraordinarily responsible. The formula of the verbal suggestion must be not only very clear, but also properly aimed. It must produce the necessary stable and deep reorganization in the patient's cortical dynamics.

It should be emphasized that the generally accepted expression "to treat by hypnosis" is in this case not quite exact, because the very state of suggested sleep "treats" only to the extent to which it is a prolonged restorative sleep inhibition, and may be referred to as hypnotherapy. As for the direct therapeutic effect in the form of "forgetting" the events that traumatized the mind, it is produced, of course, only by the very content of the therapeutic suggestions, which may be referred to as hypnosuggestive therapy.

It should be added that upon the patient's awakening after the session of suggested sleep the physician must make sure the patient has entirely freed himself of sleep inhibition. In case of incomplete awakening, i.e., incomplete disinhibition of the cerebral cortex, phenomena of sleepiness may persist for a long time. To avoid this, a light drowse must be induced and the patient must be awakened from it with the words: "You are now completely awake and are as usually alert."

As V. Bekhterev observes, this repeated suggestion "removes all the undesirable phenomena resulting from hypnosis." "Hence, it should be clear," he emphasizes, "that only a physician should have the right to hypnotize and that sessions of hypnosis and suggestion by incompetent people, especially nonphysicians, are under no circumstances admissible."

Thus, we are arriving at the conclusion that it is not the hypnotic state itself, of which many people were formerly afraid, that can be harmful, but precisely the words of the physician or the unskillfully made suggestion which traumatize the mind.

We consider ungrounded the fears that frequent sessions of

verbal suggestions during suggested sleep may weaken the patient's volition or that he may develop high suggestibility. By virtue of the extensive functional mosaics of the cerebral cortex the physician can influence by verbal suggestion only certain cortical dynamic structures without affecting the enormous number of the other structures. This excludes the danger of a general increase in suggestibility or of any weakening of the patient's volitional traits. However, certain increase in suggestibility as regards the hypnotist can and must take place.

Phenomena of increased suggestibility may also develop in the waking state; this is observed, for example, in all cases of close association of people in which this increased suggestibility is determined by the growing confidence of one person in another.

A weakening of the volitional traits may occur only if a special verbal suggestion aimed precisely in this direction is made, which, of course, is opposed to the basic moral principles of a physician. This danger does not, therefore, exist at all. If enormous confidence has been displayed in the physician by placing a considerable assortment of various physical and chemical means at his disposal, though they may prove toxic, poisonous, or excessively active if incorrectly used, there are no reasons to deprive him of the right to induce with the same degree of responsibility a state of suggested sleep in the patient and to make the corresponding physiologically substantiated verbal suggestions to the patient in this state.

We must also note the circumstance, very well known in literature, which testifies that suggestions opposed to the direct personal interests of the subject or to his moral principles are, as a rule, never effectuated. We had ample opportunity of repeatedly convincing ourselves of this during the studies of people with a somnambulistic phase in hypnosis. Despite their seemingly uncommonly high suggestibility they far from effectuated all the suggestions made to them.

Taking all this into consideration, we emphasize the necessity of observing the rules of "asepsis" of the suggested word. The physician can and must use verbal suggestion during suggested sleep and do it with the confidence and calm with which a surgeon wields his knife.

Thus, the state of suggested sleep as such and the pathogenetically correct therapeutic verbal suggestion are harmless. There is, therefore, every opportunity for making use of the hypnosuggestive method for therapeutic, diagnostic, or research purposes connected, for example, with the study of a number of physiological processes and states observed in the human organism.

ADMINISTRATION OF INDIRECT SUGGESTION

Indirect suggestion is sometimes extremely valuable in psychotherapeutic practice when direct verbal suggestion proves ineffective. In this case, the formula of suggestion is enhanced by the very definite and concrete conditions under which the suggestion will have to be effectuated. These conditions may be either simple or more or less complex.

Thus, if the therapeutic objective is confined, say, to obtaining the effect of painlessness (for example, during parturition) the method of indirect suggestion is very simple. It comes down to about the following suggestion made to the patient on the conscious level: "You will now be given an injection (or a medicinal microenema, etc.) after which your pains will immediately disappear, you will fall asleep and will sleep well for two hours." To carry out this prescription of the physician, some neutral substance (physiological saline solution, a streptocide or vitamin pill, etc.) is usually administered, which under corresponding conditions may, nevertheless, very quickly result in the effectuation of the suggestion.

In a more complicated case, in which the objective is thus to treat a neurotic ailment, the physician acts as follows: After analyzing the ailment he prescribes for the patient some indifferent mixture (or physiotherapeutic procedure unrelated to this particular ailment) and accompanies this prescription by the following words of suggestion to the patient on the conscious level: "I have prescribed a mixture (or procedures) for you which should be taken so many times per day for a period of so many days. *Each time you take the mixture* (or carry out the procedure) your ailment will grow noticeably weaker, you will feel much better, and your appetite and night sleep will greatly improve. When you *finish taking this prescription* you will be entirely well: this mixture (or procedure) will cure you." This suggestion must be daily reinforced by the physician in the same form, say, during his morning rounds.

Thus we have in both cases a definite prescription of the physician, the action of which is concrete, purposeful, and reinforced by verbal suggestion. It should be emphasized that the effectuation of these suggestions is not very probable if this concrete form of the therapeutic prescription is not imparted to them. On the other hand, if this method is used the effect will in some measure manifest itself after the mixture (or procedure) is taken the first few times and will subsequently increase, finally reaching the highest value by the time *all* the physician's prescriptions are carried out.

As we see, the positive result of the therapeutic influence is obtained with the given method precisely by *suggestion reinforced through the first signal system* by the concrete therapeutic prescription.

What physiological mechanisms are involved in its effectuation?

The simultaneous, concerted and purposeful action of two factors on the patient's cortical regulatory function, i.e., the verbal suggestions of the physician and the very process of carrying out his prescription, which constitute a single complex of therapeutic influence, is apparently of decisive importance in this case. It aims not only at *mobilizing* the regulatory function of the patient's cerebral cortex by *imparting to it the necessary direction,* but also by *reinforcing* it with corresponding first signal conditioned reflex bonds.

Furthermore, since during a complex suggestion the carrying out of the therapeutic prescriptions is spread over several (five to six) days, its result becomes palpable to the patient himself, which enhances still more the degree of the suggestive influence of the entire complex. It will also be noted that for the suggested changes to occur in the state of the patient's organism requires time not only for their effectuation, but also for their consolidation.

The method of indirect therapeutic suggestion contains a conditioned-reflex factor concealed from the patient, this factor directly influencing his cortical regulatory activity. This method is of very great importance to therapeutic medicine. There are many observations emphasizing the considerable efficacy of psychotherapy administered by indirect suggestion. A few examples are:

1. Woman in childbirth named K., 33 years old, giving birth for the first time, reacts strongly to labor pains, is extremely excited and worried. After corresponding persuasions of the necessity of injecting an anodyne subcutaneously, 1 milliliter of an indifferent substance was injected into a buttock, following which the woman quickly calmed down and observed with satisfaction that she had no more pains and felt, as she said, only a sort of "numbness in the small of the back." Examination by mirrors showed that the cervix of the uterus opened by 1½ fingers. Labor pains continued, in view of which the same injections were repeated. The woman did not complain of pain any more and was calm until the very delivery of the baby. In her testimonial she wrote: "After the administration of the anodyne I felt absolutely no pain with the exception of a pressure in the small of the back throughout the

remaining period of the parturition." The uterine curettage and the sutures of the cervix were also painless. (Observation by K. Pronayeva.)

2. Woman in childbirth named S., 25 years old, giving birth to her first child. Complains of keen pain. During the reassuring interview she was given sodium bicarbonate with the suggestion: "This is a hypnotic. You will now fall asleep and will feel no pains." Several minutes later the woman fell asleep and slept well for an hour and 15 minutes. After awakening she complained of "tolerable pain." The same powder with the same assertion was given again; the patient fell asleep again and slept for an hour. After awakening she no longer complained of pain. Judging by her behavior and composure there were really no pains. Spasms occurred more frequently, but the woman was perfectly calm. A water micro-enema as "preventing pain" was administered in the beginning of the labor in order to maintain the obtained effect. There were no pains until the end of the period of expulsion and the woman had no pain when the baby's head was coming out. (Observation by I. Tsvetkov.)

I. Tsvetkov and K. Pronayeva anaesthetized the childbirth of 197 women by the method of indirect suggestion with the following results (according to the 5-grade system): grade 5 for 28.4 per cent, grade 4 for 29.4 per cent, grade 3 for 24.4 per cent, and grade 0 for 18.8 per cent. These figures ought to command serious attention.

Thus we see that indirect therapeutic suggestion is always connected with a concrete object, *is made through the second signal system, but is effectuated by a stimulus acting on the first signal system.* Besides, it must always be made in an unconditional imperative form.

During the administration of *any* drug or physiotherapeutic procedure, the role of suggestion cannot be excluded, which must be taken into consideration when evaluating the efficacy of the particular therapeutic means. It is not always possible, however, to determine how much of the effect is due to either the purely medicinal or the physiotherapeutic influence. At any rate, we believe that all therapeutic measures should necessarily *be accompanied* by corresponding pathogenetically purposeful verbal reinforcement.

The therapeutic suggestion *accompanying* and *reinforcing* the physician's prescription may be effected as follows. After ascertaining the conditions and peculiarities of the given ailment the physician prescribes the necessary treatments (medicinal, physiotherapeutic) and in addition addresses approximately the following words of suggestion to the patient in the waking state: "You have been given a prescription which you will receive for a period of so many days on end. Each dose of the mixture prescribed and the procedure will produce a very favorable effect on you. With each dose taken by you your ailment will weaken markedly, you will gain strength, and your appetite and night sleep will improve. As soon as you have taken all of the medicine you will be entirely well because the treatments prescribed for you will cure you." The same suggestion must be daily reinforced by the treating physician in a similar form as he makes his rounds.

In this case the action of the therapeutic prescriptions will be *augmented* and *reinforced* by verbal suggestion. This method very often greatly enhances the efficacy of the medicine.

USE OF AUTOSUGGESTION AND DREAMS IN PSYCHOTHERAPY

In observations on the necessity of elaborating the problem of the use of autosuggestion V. Bekhterev said: ". . . there can be no doubt that it is essentially important to make use of autosuggestion for therapeutic purposes and that special methods must be elaborated for it." According to his observations, the best time for autosuggestion is before going to sleep and after awakening when the cells of the cerebral cortex are in a phasic state.

Bekhterev believes that a definite formula of autosuggestion should be worked out for each individual patient and that this formula "should correspond to the given case and should be uttered by the patient in the first person in an affirmative form and in the present rather than in the future tense." Let us assume, says Bekhterev, that a person with a habit of drinking wine wants to cure himself of this ailment by autosuggestion. He must utter the autosuggestion in the following form: "I have pledged not only to stop drinking, but even not to think of wine; I have now fully freed myself of the pernicious temptation and no longer think about it." These words of autosuggestion must be uttered in a low voice "many times before going to sleep and in the morning, hardly awake and with full concentration." Bekhterev believes that many patients can benefit from such autosuggestion. It should also be borne in mind that effectuation of autosuggestion requires a certain positive emotional state.

Bekhterev proposed one more method of autosuggestion used during suggested drowsing. The patient repeats in a low voice the formula of suggestion uttered by the physician, but in the first person. For example: "Recollections of my insult no longer worry me," or: "I'm now absolutely indifferent to alcoholic drink," etc. The physician and then the patient repeat these suggestions two or three times. There can be no doubt that this method, based on the physiological mechanisms of conditioned-reflex bonds, elaborated and fixed in the sphere of second signal activity, particularly the activity of the speech-motor analyser, is also of practical value.

When the patients are taught the methods of autosuggestion it is good to demonstrate to them the ideomotor phenomenon described by I. Tarkhanov, which, as is commonly known, very well illustrates the proposition that the "idea of movement is already the beginning of the movement."

This purely didactic method consists of the following: a small weight—a metal ball, a teaspoon, etc.—is suspended from a string 30 to 35 centimeters long, the physician holding its free end between the thumb and index finger of his right hand; while sitting on a chair before the patients surrounding him he raises his right hand to the level of his head and slightly bending his arm at the elbow holds it motionless in this position. Waiting until the oscillations of the suspended weight stop, the physician tells the patents that he will now imagine (i.e., will begin to talk it in to himself) that the weight is starting to swing like a pendulum in a certain direction —for example, from him toward the patient sitting opposite him. All those present immediately begin to observe that though the arm of the physician is motionless the suspended weight begins to swing, gradually swinging higher and higher precisely in the direction indicated by the physician. By changing the direction of the intended motion it is possible similarly to force the load to swing in a different direction, or instead of swinging lke a pendulum to swing in a circle either clockwise or counterclockwise. Finally, by imagining that the weight is stopping and has stopped it is possible to stop it.

In this connection Pavlov observes that "as long as you think of a certain movement (i.e., you have a kinaesthetic idea) *you involuntarily perform it without noticing it*[1] (italics by the author). Thus, "each time we think of a movement we actually perform it abortively. Consequently, the innervational process may go on, though it really does not."[2]

Such an "experiment" usually impresses the patients very much,

1. I. Pavlov, *Twenty Years of Objective Study of the Higher Nervous Activity (Behavior) of Animals* (Medgiz Publishing House, 1951), p. 446.
2. *Ibid.*, p. 360.

convinces them that the phenomena of autosuggestion are real, and impels them to work in this direction.

The following is an example of autosuggestion successfully used by a patient in the treatment of dermatosis (eczema of the hands) developed against a background of a neurasthenic ailment.

Patient I., 43 years old, a physician, familiar with the methods of suggestion, complained of psychogenic eczema she had developed on both hands, of a general neurasthenic state, and considerable emaciation of several years' standing, caused by her itching eczema which sharply reduced her efficiency.

After useless customary treatments the patient applied to us for psychotherapy. The conditioned-reflex mechanism underlying the formation and development of her eczema was explained to her, after which she read A. Kartamyshev's monograph and saw a demonstration of Tarkhanov's ideomotor phenomenon; following this she began resolutely to combat her strong desire to scratch the skin where it itched, barely succeeding by means of distracting her own attention. This, nevertheless, somewhat relieved the itch. But the moment she looked at her hands the sensation of the itch recurred and a blister with a serious liquid appeared and soon began to fester before her very eyes *without any scratching*. Owing to this she developed an obsession, a tense expectation of these blisters to form. To fight this obsession she began to *suppress this fear and these expectations* by efforts of her will. She talked calm and indifference into herself and disregarded the itch. After a month of stubborn work she ceased *noticing the itch* and being afraid of it, but not by means of distracting her attention from it (which was very hard); on the contrary, she began to *think of the itch*, but think of it *calmly, without anxiety*.

This struggle lasted about two weeks and as a result no thought, idea, or mention of the eczema occurring without any excitement *provoked the itch or the eczema any more*.

Six years later, after a long-continued psychic trauma (it lasted about six months) she suddenly developed an itch on the right forearm. Scratching this place produced blisters with a serious liquid. By persuading herself that this was a relapse of the same eczema and by using the previously described methods she cured herself. It will be observed that the new psychic trauma produced an eczematous affection in a new place without provoking a relapse in the old.

In this case the patient managed by autosuggestion, which required enormous effort, to create in the cerebral cortex strong foci of concentrated excitation which negatively inducted the regions of pathological stimulation; in other words, she was able purposefully to influence her own cortical activity and through it the cutaneous trophics.

In such cases we sometimes use the suggestion of dreams as an auxiliary therapeutic method.

Thus, to a patient who was stubbornly afraid of standing and walking by herself (stasibasiphobia) we suggested during suggested sleep a dream in which she "saw herself walking freely and easily through shops." By becoming effectuated this dream impressed her so much that she grew confident of recovery and was now ready to persist in the exercises prescribed for her which consisted of walking through the apartment and then through the streets by herself. After this dream her condition radically improved and she was more confident of her recovery than she had ever been.

It is possible to "revive in the memory" of the patient who is in a state of suggested sleep the content of forgotten nocturnal dreams which were indirectly connected with the development of some particular neurotic symptoms. It will be well to remember this when analyzing the genesis of a neurotic state. We illustrate this by one of our observations (1925).

1. Applying to us in reference to her neurotic condition, patient B., 22 years old, told us that it developed after she had once awakened in a state of inexplicable anxiety. Since that day she had anxiously expected something terrible to happen, had been continuously worried and irritable, and had palpitations, cold extremities, and insomnia.

The sudden development of the neurotic condition after nocturnal sleep made us suspect the possibility of some dream which might in some way or other have been connected with the onset of the ailment. To make sure, we induced a state of suggested sleep in the patient and made her recall her forgotten dream by deepening the suggested sleep with a series of repeated awakenings and sleep inductions and corresponding suggestions. The patient told us she "had dreamed that burglars had broken into her apartment." Without bringing her out of the suggested sleep we gave her an explanatory suggestion and also suggested that she forget her dream, after which she was given a one-hour suggested rest. Upon awakening the patient was perfectly calm and cheerful, all the phenomena of the former neurotic condition having disappeared. After that she was under our observation for a period of several months, and felt fine.

Nocturnal dreams sometimes reflect the efficacy of the already administered psychotherapy.

2. Patient K., 32 years old, was shell-shocked at the front in 1921 and lost consciousness; since then and until 1923 he had suffered from fits of "commanding hysteria"; six months after the shell shock he developed epileptoid attacks (convulsions, loss of consciousness, and involuntary micturition). The following symptoms were observed from the very onset of the disease: profuse perspiration, irritability, facial tic, nightmares, and inability to endure loud sounds and music. Once, after attending the opera, he had to stay in bed for two weeks. Began stuttering in 1921. In 1931 he applied to a railway psychoneurological dispensary in reference to the aggravation of all these phenomena following a serious psychic trauma (sudden illness and death of his wife).

General improvement was observed at the third session of suggestions administered during suggested sleep. Besides, there was a change for the better in the nature of his constant nightmares. This expressed itself in the fact that instead of dreaming of *fleeing* from the attacking enemy the patient began to dream of *defending* himself and, after the fifth session of psychotherapy, of *attacking* his enemy. In addition, after the seventh session he saw, on the advice of the physician who was treating him, a sound motion picture through to the end, whereas before the treatment he could not endure even the sound of a metronome (when attempts were made to induce sleep with its aid). The treatment was discontinued after the tenth session. The patient grew much calmer, his behavior was adequate, there were no more crying spells, his spirits rose, and he stuttered much less. He could now calmly endure even strong sound stimuli, slept well, the hyperhidrosis diminished, and he put on some weight. Several months later he wrote to the dispensary expressing his gratitude for "the new lease on life"; he considered himself healthy. (Observation by M. Kholodenko.)

3. Three sessions of hypnosuggestive therapy with suggestions of reassurance and recovery were administered to a patient, an artist by occupation, in order to relieve a reactive neurotic condition. After the first session he felt considerably relieved and during the third session dreamed that the physician who was treating him was confidently cutting a "tumor" out of his chest with a sharp knife. The operation was painless and bloodless. Following the operation (in his dream) he had a feeling of relief in his chest and awakened with a sense of joy and elation. After this session all of the unpleasant sensations and pains in the chest, as well

as the anxiety and compulsive thoughts and ideas, disappeared completely and he regained normal sleep and efficiency. (Observation by M. Kashpur.)

Thus, in the given case, the experienced feeling of relief in the patient, apparently belonging to the artistic type of higher nervous activity, reflected itself in his first signal system in the form of a symbolic picture of a dream.

The foregoing examples show convincingly enough that the content of dreams may in a number of cases indirectly testify to the degree of efficacy of the administered psychotherapy.

METHODS OF SLEEP INDUCTION AND AWAKENING

In conclusion we shall consider the methods of inducing sleep and of awakening by suggestion.

Before putting the patient to sleep for the first time it is necessary to have a preparatory interview with him for the purpose of explaining the essence of this therapeutic method, why he needs is, how it may help restore the activity of his nervous system and remove the disorders.

If the patient is afraid of hypnosis this fear must be removed by explaining to him that there are no reasons for it, because hypnosis is a necessary and beneficial therapeutic method which puts the patient in a state of incomplete sleep. It may at this time be explained that to hypnotize means to put to sleep the way a mother puts her child to sleep and that it has been scientifically demonstrated that in the state of a suggested drowse or suggested sleep the brain reacts better to the words of suggestion made by the physician and that they are better fixed in the brain, by virtue of which they exert a long-continued influence.

Before sleep is induced the patient should be placed in a comfortable armchair or on a couch and told to assume the posture in which he usually falls asleep; the patient may lie either on the back or one side with his back to the light, facing the physician. It should be pleasantly warm in the room or else the patient should be well covered. The room should be isolated from noise, have somewhat dim lights, and contain nothing bright or gaily colored that might distract the patient's attention, because the fewer the outside stimuli the sooner will inhibition spread over the cerebral cortex.

When hypnotizing the patient it should be borne in mind that the success of psychotherapy does not require that the patient be fast asleep. In a number of cases it is sufficient to induce only a light drowse—i.e., the initial phase of the division of the cerebral cortex into sleeping and waking sections. The patient should be told about this beforehand, considering the fact that he may be bewildered and may doubt the success of the treatment if he is not fast asleep.

At the same time the patient should be warned that while being hypnotized he must not be tense and must not "force" himself to fall asleep because this may interfere with his falling asleep. He must only calmly and peacefully prepare himself for sleep. As for the physician himself, he must make ready to hypnotize the patient and devote all his attention to it, manifesting necessary firmness and persistence and at the same time retaining complete calm and self-confidence.

To induce sleep the physician must use corresponding words and if need be auxiliary physical methods. The latter may express themselves, for example, in the form of weak rhythmic stimulations of one of the analyzers or simultaneously several analyzers for the purpose of developing the inhibitory process in them. The physician may use rare beats of a metronome (one beat every 1 or 2 seconds), ticking of a clock or watch, monotonous stroking of the patient's hand, head, or forehead; sometimes the patient is asked to fix his eyes on some bright point, etc.

At the same time the physician should say approximately the following sleep-inducing words: "You are already calm enough to doze off and fall asleep. You are beginning to feel pleasantly languid, sleepy; your arms and legs are growing heavy, your eyelids are also growing heavy, they seem to be filling with lead and you can no longer resist sleep. You can hear my voice very well. I shall now count *slowly* to ten and with each count you will feel more and more sleepy: one . . . two . . . three . . . (and so on until ten). You are falling asleep, you are falling fast and pleasantly asleep."

These words should be uttered in a low voice, monotonously, slowly, and calmly but at the same time sufficiently clearly and confidently. Individual sentences should be repeated several times.

The patient should be firmly convinced that the sleep which is being suggested to him really *comes as it were of itself* and that he increasingly succumbs to this state.

The subsequent sleep-inducing words may be as follows: "You are now in a state of complete rest, you are breathing evenly, easily, and deeply. You have become completely oblivious of all your daily troubles, concerns, and impressions and you are paying no attention to your surroundings. You continue to perceive my words very clearly. Nothing seems to trouble you, you have no unpleasant sensations, you feel a pleasant weakness, your arms and legs have grown heavy, your eyelids have become heavy, you feel more and more drowsy, you have no desire to move or open your eyes, your eyelids are closed, you are falling asleep, you are falling fast asleep, you are asleep."

These sleep-inducing suggestions should be repeated from time to time, gradually assuming the nature of something that has *already happened*: "You no longer feel your body, your eyelids are firmly closed, you already feel pleasantly relaxed, you have already acquired a peace of mind, you have no more worries, you perceive my words still more clearly and increasingly yield to them."

If the patient still shows no signs of falling asleep, the physician should continue with the hypnotization and emphasize more insistently: "You can no longer move any member of your body and you want to lie perfectly quietly. The more you hear my voice, my words, the firmer do your eyelids close and the faster you fall asleep."

Some persons become sleepy two or three minutes after the beginning of sleep induction and soon fall fast asleep; in others sleepiness and sleep develop more slowly, only ten to twenty minutes after the beginning of the session; in still others it is impossible to induce even a light drowse during the first session and it appears only in the subsequent sessions. This circumstance undoubtedly prevents the physician from producing a sufficiently rapid effect in all cases. To expedite the onset of sleepiness and sleep it is therefore recommended that the physician tell the patient at the very first session that "with each session the patient will become sleepy faster and faster and will fall deeper and deeper asleep.

By these methods, which contribute to the formation and fixation of positive conditioned reflexes to the word "sleep" in the patient, it is possible very soon to reach a point where the patient in the subsequent sessions begins to feel drowsy and falls asleep at the very first words uttered by the physician. In addition, to put the patient to sleep it does well in some cases suddenly and imperatively to utter in a loud voice the command: "Sleep!" This method, as we know, puts in operation the physiological mechanism of transmarginal inhibition underlying the "ancient hypnosis" (hypnosis of animals) used by Charcot, Danilevsky, et al.

As stated already, to influence the patient by suggestion there is no necessity at all of inducing *deep* sleep. In most cases it is enough to elicit the lightest drowse or the lightest general torpor in order to effectuate the suggestion. In some cases, however, deep sleep is necessary—for example, when the therapeutic suggestion deals with the cause which traumatized the mind and which may provoke in the patient an undesirable negative emotional reaction.

At the same time excessively deep sleep inhibition is also undesirable because it may prevent the effectuation of the suggestion, especially if suggested sleep shows a tendency for transition to a state of complete sleep. It will be remembered that all these peculiarities of falling asleep and of sleep vary greatly with individuals and that for the successful effectuation of the suggestions the most favorable depth of suggested sleep is the one in which (retaining the rapport) there is a subsequent amnesia of the content of the suggestions made. This will apparently be the "somnambulistic phase" of sleep characterized by a deep dissociation of the cerebral cortex into sleeping and waking divisions produced by the verbal sleep induction. (F. Maiorov.)

Various attendant circumstances which aid sleep induction should also be taken into consideration. Some persons fall asleep more easily mainly under the influence of first stimulations (beats of a metronome, ticking of a watch, stroking the hand or head) and do not fall asleep in response to the word "sleep," while others, on the contrary, easily yield to verbal suggestions but cannot fall asleep when stimulated by first signal influences. In still others sleep is induced by the point action of the second and first signal stimuli. These peculiarities were ascertained by I. Strelchuk. The *customary conditions* under which a person falls asleep may be of great importance.

Thus, we were able to induce sleep in a certain patient only by stroking his back. It turned out that in his early childhood he had always been put to sleep by this method. After useless attempts to put another patient to sleep we were able to do so only by letting him have a book because, as he told us, he was in the habit of falling asleep with a book in his hands. In this case several words suggesting sleep were enough for the book to fall out of his hands and the patient to fall asleep.

When it is necessary to induce sleep rapidly in a person who yields with difficulty, we can recommend the so-called Oskar Vogt fractional method. For this purpose the attempts to induce sleep are repeated *many times* in one session. In addition, various methods of *disguised* (indirect) suggestion may be used—i.e., instead of hypnotics the patient may be given various placebo substances (for example a coated soda pill).

Lastly, an auxiliary dose of a hypnotic (for example, 0.75 to 1.0 chloral hydrate or 0.1 barbamil about ten to fifteen minutes before inducing sleep) is now widely used in daily practice.

In concluding our few remarks on the methods of sleep induction we deem it necessary to observe that in some extremely rare cases the hysterical patient, while being put to sleep, may have a reactive hysterical fit in the form of crying or convulsive jerks. A similar hysterical reaction may also develop in an anxiously nervous person who fears hypnosis.

Thus one of our patients became extremely excited once when he felt that, while he was falling asleep, his extremities began to grow numb, because this revived the traces of the sensations experienced by him in the past under chloroform anaesthesia.

All these conditions can be easily relieved by persistent reassuring countersuggestions: "Take it easy, the attack is over, everything is all right, and you may now calmly go to sleep." If necessary, the hypnotic session must be discontinued until the patient grows perfectly calm. In these cases it is sometimes possible to ascertain the reason for such reactions by means of corresponding questions made during suggested sleep or after awakening the patient from it.

It will be observed, furthermore, that sleep induction may sometimes be extraordinarily complicated if the patient's neurotic ailment has deranged the activity of one or several of his analyzers—especially if it has impaired his auditory analyzer.

As for awakening from suggested sleep, the following words are customarily used: "Wake up. Upon awakening you will feel well rested and cheerful. I shall count to three and, as I count, you will gradually awaken and will be completely awake at the count of 'three.' I am beginning to count: one . . . two . . . three. . . . Open your eyes; you are fully awake." It is not advisable to awaken the subject from suggested sleep rapidly; the physician must avoid a too rapid, sudden transition from sleep to wakefulness. In cases of incomplete awakening the continued drowsiness can be easily removed by corresponding verbal influences on the conscious level.

It sometimes happens that upon returning home from a session the patient continues to be sleepy, which may worry him and the people around him. The patients should be warned about this possible sleepiness and told that there is nothing unusual about it. Moreover, the patient may even be advised to have a little more sleep upon coming home, if necessary.

A difficulty of awakening after a session is sometimes observed. It usually occurs in people who have difficulty in awakening even from natural sleep. In these cases it is necessary repeatedly and more energetically to awaken the patient, which should in no way disconcert the physician.

Some people believe that awakening from deep suggested sleep is possible only within a few days. This, however, is not true. At any rate, neither our associates nor we have ever observed it.

> *If the patient does not feel better after an interview with a physician, the latter is no physician.*
> V. BEKHTEREV

PHYSICIANS' TACTICS

Even in early antiquity, when there was no scientific medicine, it was believed that a physician must display a maximum of attention and tact for the patient and be able to safeguard him against harmful influences and worries.

Thus, the Indian Brahman medical laws forbade the physicans to tell the patient about a possibly unfavorable outcome of the disease or about events connected with material damage to the patient and demanded that the physician "refrain from any manifestations of rage, hatred, cunningness or greed," etc.

Russian internists have long attached great importance to "psychic treatment." Thus, G. Zakharyin laid special stress on the fact that "with rare exceptions the seriously ill are by the very virtue of their morbid state in a depressed mood and regard the future gloomily and with little hope." For the success of the treatment the physician "must therefore encourage the patient and instill in him the hope of recovery or improvement in his health, as the case may be." Zakharyin says that "this encouragement sometimes immediately induces sleep which the patient has not had for some time. And this is not the only thing that raises the patient's spirits. If we recall the facts belonging to the sphere of what is known as *suggestion* we shall understand that here prognosis coincides with treatment," whereas telling the patient about all the apprehensions of the physician "is always a mistake on the part of the latter and sometimes as actual crime."

"Everybody knows," says Bekhterev, "what magic health-giving influence one reassuring word on the part of a physician is likely to exert and, contrariwise, how fatally, in the literal sense of the word, the severe cold verdict of the physician sometimes acts if the latter does not know or won't know the power of suggestion."

Psychotherapists of other countries (P. Dubois, I. Déjèrine, A.

Forel, et al.) were of the same opinion. "The first crossing of swords between the physician and the neuropath," writes Déjèrine, "determines the outcome of the battle. If no mutual sympathy is born from the very first interviews, it is useless to go on."

All authors attached great importance to the emotional sphere, i.e., to the necessary affective connection without which psychotherapy cannot be successful. It was not ascertained, however, what the essence of these important conditions was and why the state of the patient's emotional sphere was of such great importance. And only Pavlov succeeded by a strictly scientific objective method in getting the answer to the question why precisely the "affectiveness" and "emotions" of the patient played such an essential part and insured the success of psychotherapeutic influence.

In connection with this, let us recall Y. Popov's early investigations, which showed that the elaboration of a motor conditioned reflex on the basis of an electrocutaneous pain stimulation was directly connected with the emotional (respiratory) reaction in the subject: in people suffering from Parkinson's disease, in addition to the absence of a respiratory reaction, the conditioned reflexes as a rule either failed to develop or arose only with great difficulty and were extremely unstable. These and other facts denote the important role played by the condition of the subjects' emotional sphere or, in other words, of the state of the closest subcortical region.

V. Gakkebush also showed that the verbal suggestions of emotional states in persons affected with Parkinson's disease were not effectuated, which he could judge by the absence of reactive hyperglycemia. Similar data were obtained by Hoff and Wermer.

The data obtained by V. Osipova (Leningrad Institute of the Brain) are instructive in this respect: in children kept in the "conditioned reflex cabin," the sight of which was associated in them with a negative emotion—a feeling of fear—it was impossible to develop stable conditioned reflexes. But when this cabin was rebuilt into a beautiful little children's home, the conditioned reflexes began to be rapidly elaborated, this time against the background of a positive emotion. Osipova's data were but recently confirmed by M. Linetsky.

A simultaneous elaboration of four conditioned reflexes to various light stimuli was attempted in patient B., who suffered from stasiphobia. Each attempt failed, however, whereas in healthy persons and in other patients these reflexes were usually elaborated after one or two combinations. The patient's fear of the study was the reason for the failure. The patient explained her persistent fear by the fact that she was "afraid she could not cope with the complicated task of the study." To rid the patient of her fear the following suggestion was made during suggested sleep: "Do not be afraid; there is nothing hard about it." When the patient awoke all the conditioned reflexes were obtained very quickly.

All the foregoing testifies that the success of psychotherapy directly depends on the patient's emotional state and that the physician's behavior and all the surroundings must evoke in the patient a corresponding *positive* reaction.

Besides, a very important part is also played by the emotional state of the physician. During his association with the physician the patient develops an intricate complex of conditioned-reflex bonds which determine the nature of his relations with the physician. With reference to this Bekhterev says that the patient comes to the physician "with an emotion of expectation," his nervous system is "in a state of readiness," with a ready "tendency" (A. Ukhtomsky) to react to a very definite stimulus. It is precisely this circumstance that can aid in the easy formation of new stable conditioned-reflex bonds developed in the patient under the influence of the physician's authoritative words.

It will be noted that G. Sorokhtin ascertained that during the elaboration of a conditioned reflex by the speech method the emotional coloring of the verbal signal was of very great importance. Thus a verbal signal uttered inertly produces no conditioned reflex, whereas a "verbal order" given in a higher tone may rapidly produce a stable conditioned reflex. We ourselves have observed that the word "Hurts" spoken in a loud voice caused a stronger reaction on the part of the respiration of the subject who was in a state of suggested sleep. Similarly, the fatigue of the investigator or various distracting external or internal factors which may influence the tone of his verbal orders, etc., evoke in the subject conditioned-reflex reactions of varying strength.

There can be no doubt that the physician plays the same part as the investigator and that his positive tone supports and strengthens the readiness of the patient's nervous system for a lively reaction to everything that is connected with the physician. We must not overlook the important circumstance that, as M. Yanovsky says, "psychotherapeutic influences begin the moment the patient comes to the physician. The patient thus proves that he has faith in the physician and is ready to follow his advice, and succumb to his influence in the hope of recovery."

It should be noted that to influence the patient verbally means to create new dynamic structures in his cerebral cortex, coupling in it new chains of positive and negative temporary bonds. A positive emotional state connected with corresponding endocrine-vegetative changes ensures rapid formation and firm fixation of these dynamic structures. Positive emotions, by influencing the tone of the cerebral cortex, enhance the functions of the cortical cells—i.e., new conditions facilitating formation of new dynamic structures arise.

How is the patient's confidence won and the necessary "inner bonds" between the physician and the patient insured?

The patient must feel that the physician is attentive to his morbid state, which is necessary for complete frankness between the patient and the physician.

A frank anamnestic interview in addition to a detailed somatic examination therefore plays an essential role, not only in disclosing the psychic and somatic etiological factors, but also as regards the confidence and sympathy of the patient for the physician and consequently the success of the treatment. That is why the more attention that is paid to the anamnesis the first time the physician sees the patient (and when necessary during their subsequent meetings)—i.e., the more attention devoted to discovering the causes of the ailment—*the greater are the physician's chances to win the patient's confidence* and hence to achieve success.

The following case may serve as a good illustration:

A 23-year-old man came to the psychoneurological dispensary of the Ukrainian Psychoneurological Institute in 1930 complaining of a highly depressed state; apathy; loss of interest in life and work; loss of faith in himself, his abilities, and efficiency; self-consciousness, weakening memory, irritability, and fear of gong insane. Before this ailment he had been active and sociable.

The anamnestic interview revealed that he had taken sick two years previously after a serious conflict manifesting itself, as he put it, in an unfair insult to him and very much hurting his pride. The patient could not endure the "unfair attacks" against him and the unhealthy atmosphere that arose around him in connection with this. Constant anxiety, nervousness, and disturbed sleep, according to the patient, "undermined his nervous system." Despite the fact that seven months after the beginning of the conflict everything was decided in favor of the patient he continued to be distressed for the subsequent two years. He saw many physicians but all of them gave him the stereotyped answer: "All your organs are healthy." The patient's anxiety increased and he lost faith in recovery and in physicians and medicines. "None of the physicians ever asked me about my troubles, while I myself did not dare tell them about them," the patient said on coming to the dispensary of his own accord after deciding to resort to treatment by suggestion as "the last means."

After three anamnestic interviews, explanatory and reassuring psychotherapy was administered on the conscious level and several sessions of suggested rest were conducted. A calm attitude to the past experiences and a faith in his abilities and efficiency were suggested to the patient. He left us with a sense of great satisfaction and in leaving exclaimed bitterly: "Why didn't any of the other physicians look into my soul?"

Subsequent observation for eighteen months showed that he again became the active worker he had been before. He went to school and continued to work on his former job. (Observation by F. Tseikinskaya.)

In conclusion we shall cite a case described by M. Yanovsky which throws light on some important intimate aspects of the "psychic treatments" that imbued the medical tactics of S. Botkin, the outstanding Russian physician.

A man who suspected he had some pulmonary ailment once came to the dispensary and was received by Botkin. Before then he had made the rounds of all therapeutic clinics but had been told everywhere that he was only "ill with his own self-consciousness." These answers did not satisfy him, however. After examining and questioning the patient very carefully, Botkin said: "Yes, you really have something, but so little that it is hard to notice. At any rate this is direct proof that your ailment is insignificant. Take this medicine and in a few days you will be all right." When the patient left, Botkin turned to the students who were there and said: "He is quite well physically; but he does have something, and that is his self-consciousness based on subjective sensations. If I had treated him as the other physicians did he would continue to suffer, but now he has left under the impression he had finally found a physician who understands his ailment and, consequently, can cure him whatever medicine he prescribes."

The new temporary bonds created by the physician must be systematically reinforced by other identical stimuli acting in the same direction in order that the new sound cortical dynamic structures become still stronger. That is why the junior medical personnel must also learn the fundamentals of psychotherapy to know that the success of treating a patient (by any method) is largely determined by skillful influence on his mind and always to have a curative and anodyne factor—the *word*. However, a word is a double-edged weapon that must be properly used. The patient should be talked to so as not to be traumatized. A great deal depends even on the construction of the sentence. Thus, it is not at all immaterial whether you say to the patient: "You may rest assured that with your health you will live many more years," or "You will die thirty years from now." Besides, it is necessary not only to be able to watch your words but also to *be able to keep quiet*. It is not for nothing that the Romans called medicine the "art of keeping silent" (*ars muta*): the patient does not have to be told everything. Practical nurses should also have some knowledge of this, because a casual, thoughtless word may sometimes cause irreparable harm both to psychotherapy and to any other method of treatment.

A favorable friendly atmosphere of the entire medical personnel must therefore be set up in every hospital. The entire personnel must be wholly devoted to the interests of the work because in any medical institution not only the *words* of the medical personnel, but also their behavior with respect to the patients and the entire hospital regimen, with all of the stimuli connected with it, are of psychotherapeutic importance. This last circumstance should be borne in mind when the medical personnel who must help the physician in everything he does and maintain his prestige in the eyes of the patient, are chosen.

Thus we see that not only the physician's prestige and his attitude to the patient but also the impression he makes on the latter already in large measure determine the success of the treatments, since *the very personality of the physician* is essential. Thus, for example, Pavlov characterized Botkin as follows: "He actually charmed the patients: one word, one visit of the patient frequently sufficed to cure him. How often I heard his pupils, clinicists, admit sadly that the same prescriptions and apparently in similar cases proved ineffective, while in the hands of the teacher they worked wonders."[3]

Calmness, even temper, and patience with respect to the patient, a sincere and warm striving to help him, tactfulness and mildness of treatment are the essential qualities which every physician must have if he wants to help the patient. Nothing brings the patient and the physician so close to each other as the physician's maximal attention to the patient's troubles. The psychotherapist must penetrate into his patient's mind (especially if the patient is a neurotic), must not only understand but also *feel* the agony of his soul, put himself, as it were, in the patient's place, but so that the patient may also feel it. Unfortunately, it is not always that way. Some

3. I. Pavlov, *Physiology of Digestion* (Publishing House of the U.S.S.R. Academy of Medical Sciences, Russian ed., 1952), p. 419.

physicians pay too little attention to it and at times do not even take into consideration that the patient before them is one who needs urgent, and precisely psychotherapeutic, aid.

It will be taken into account that it may be the first time the patient suffering from a neurosis has decided to be quite frank about his intimate experiences, which he not infrequently hides even from his closest relatives. This frankness is not infrequently the health-giving factor for his mental condition without which it seemed for a long time incurable.

An individual and tactful approach by the physician to a gravely suffering patient is most valuable and efficacious. All his medical erudition may turn out absolutely unnecessary and even useless if he does not wholeheartedly put himself in the patient's place.

According to A. Ivanov-Smolensky's testimony, Pavlov's approach to patients "was always uncommonly mild, tactful, and cordial," and Pavlov himself never forgot that when treating a patient he always faced a living, and frequently keenly suffering, human being.

Thus, the nature of the reactions that arise in the system of the patient's higher nervous activity depends in large measure precisely on the physician himself. The personality of the physician, his manners with respect to the patients, the tone of his voice and his emotional state, which determine his behavior toward the patients, are all complexes of enormously strong and significant stimuli capable of provoking very powerful, particularly emotional, reactions in the patient's nervous system. In M. Yanovsky's colorful expression, the foundation on which "the prestige of the physician rests," as far as the patient is concerned, is his "respect for his profession, love for his science, humane feeling for the patient, and a calm and serious attitude to his work."

Even the Indian Brahman medical laws of antiquity previously mentioned, attached great importance to the personal qualities of the physician, who must live a sober life and have a "nobility and purity of heart." Even his appearance was not disregarded: he had to have "a fine and decent appearance," he had to be "well dressed and his clothes had to smell sweet." An Indian adage said: "One may fear his mother, brother, and friend, but never a physician."

Thus it was believed even in early antiquity that the very appearance of the physician may influence the condition of the patient, the course of his disease, and the success of the treatments.

There can be no doubt that in our day, too, the success of all types of therapy, including psychotherapy, whatever the form in which it is administered, largely depends on the *prestige of the physician* and the relations established between him and the patient. S. Korsakov, V. Bekhterev, Y. Kannabikh, and V. Gilyarovsky in Russia, and Déjèrine, Forel, and Dubois abroad, pointed out a long time ago that the success of any treatment, particularly psychotherapy, depended on the confidence of the patient in the physician, the relations established between the patient and the physician, on the "feeling" of the patient that the physician wanted to help him, on the "sympathy" of the patient for the physician, etc. It will be observed that as early as the eighteenth century when Danilo Samoilovich spoke about the plague he observed that "the confidence in the physician greatly helped the patients resist the fatal attacks of the disease." "We may affirm," he said, "that the toxin of the plague loses its force in proportion to the patient's faith in medical aid; hope raises the spirits of the patients, rendered weak by fear, and the internal symptoms cease to be serious and numerous from the very onset of the disease."

JOSEPH WOLPE

Reciprocal Inhibition as the Main Basis of Psychotherapeutic Effects

Strongly influenced by the work of Pavlov and the learning theorists, Wolpe has developed a comprehensive systematic treatment of symptoms that result from specific anxieties. His assumption appears to be that there is a close similarity between the neurotic behavior induced in experimental animals under laboratory conditions and the neurotic problems of human beings in society. However, it is obvious that he also, like most good clinicians, including Platonov, aims at establishing a therapeutic atmosphere based more on subtle human characteristics than on mere conditioning.

The extensive history taking, the instruction in relaxation technique, and the hypnosis induction all aid in establishing the kind of dependent relationship from which a psychoanalyst might explain his results as a "transference cure."

Per contra, the intensive discussion of anxiety-arousing situations that usually takes place within the noncensorious accepting atmosphere of the psychoanalytic session could well be regarded as a form of reciprocal inhibition.

THE AIM of this paper is to show that when fundamental psychotherapeutic effects are obtained in neuroses—no matter by what therapist—these effects are nearly always really a consequence of

From *Archives of Neurology and Psychiatry*, Vol. 72, No. 2, August 1954, pp. 205-226. Copyright 1954, by American Medical Association.

A more comprehensive statement of the central argument of this paper is given in Wolpe's *Psychotherapy by Reciprocal Inhibition* (Stanford University Press, 1958). Further details of therapeutic techniques and summaries of controlled outcome studies are to be found in *Behavior Therapy Techniques* by J. Wolpe and A. A. Lazarus (Pergamon Press, 1966). This volume also contains references to a large number of recent papers on this subject.

the occurrence of reciprocal inhibition of neurotic anxiety responses, i.e., the complete or partial suppression of the anxiety responses as a consequence of the simultaneous evocation of other responses physiologically antagonistic to anxiety. Several new psychotherapeutic techniques are described that have been derived directly from the reciprocal inhibition principle and have turned out to be of value.

In previous writings[39, 41, 42]* I presented evidence in support of the view that neurotic behavior is persistent unadaptive learned behavior in which anxiety is almost always prominent and which is acquired in anxiety-generating situations. By "anxiety" is meant the autonomic response pattern or patterns that are characteristically part of the given organism's response to noxious stimulation, and the term is applied irrespective of the duration of the autonomic responses or of what has led to them. An anxiety response is unadaptive when it is evoked in circumstances in which there is objectively no threat.

Successful therapy of experimental neuroses[5, 22, 39, 42] seems to depend on obtaining reciprocal inhibition of neurotic responses,[39, 42] for conditioned (learned) inhibition of these responses evidently develops on the basis of their repeated reciprocal inhibition. The mechanisms presumed to be concerned in this process have been discussed in some detail in another connection.[43] Taking a cue from the experimental findings, it was decided to investigate the effects on human neuroses of measures designed specifically to bring about reciprocal inhibition of neurotic responses. Favorable early experiences[41] encouraged the use and further development of these measures, and in 1952 a series of 70 cases was reported,[44] in 86 per cent of which the condition had been either apparently cured or much improved after an average of 25 interviews. A short account of the techniques employed was included in that report. In the present paper these techniques, and some new ones, are described in more detail, and the results of treatment of 52 additional cases are set forth.

EXPERIMENTAL BACKGROUND OF PSYCHOTHERAPY BASED ON THE PRINCIPLE OF RECIPROCAL INHIBITION

In the course of experiments during the years 1947-1948,[39, 42] I found that cats could be made neurotic merely by placing them in a small cage and then, immediately after presenting an auditory

* Superior numbers refer to the list of references at the end of this article.

stimulus, subjecting them to a small number of high-voltage, low-amperage shocks from an induction coil. (Previous workers[1, 22] had mistakenly thought that neurosis would ensue only if the reaction to the shock was in conflict with a previously conditioned food-approach response.) The animals all reacted violently to the shock, showing various combinations of rushing to and fro; clawing at the roof, floor, and sides of the experimental cage; crouching, trembling, howling and spitting, mydriasis, tachypnea, piloerection, and, in some cases, urination or defecation. After a variable number of shocks these reactions would become stabilized, and it would then be found that if the animal was replaced in the experimental cage on a later occasion it would manifest a reaction pattern similar to that observed at the time of the shock. Confinement in the cage for several hours did not diminish the reactions, nor did they show remission when the animals were put in the cage day after day without ever again being shocked. The disturbance was such that an animal starved for 24 to 72 hours would not eat meat dropped in front of him in the cage. Months of absence from the experimental cage did not weaken the reactions evocable there.

It was thus clear that the usual means by which ineffectual responses are eliminated—experimental extinction, which depends upon a process associated with fatigue of the response[11, 43]—was ineffective as far as the anxiety responses were concerned. It seemed for a time as though these responses would have to be regarded as permanent and irreversible, but in our considering possible methods by which they might be eliminated, it seemed reasonable to try causing some other response to occur in the experimental situation that might be expected to be incompatible with the anxiety responses. The obvious response to try was feeding. Neurotic animals were placed inside the experimental cage after having been starved for 48 or 72 hours, and pellets of meat were tossed in front of them. As usual, no eating occurred. Now, since in their living cages the animals were accustomed to having food conveyed to them by the human hand, it was presumed that the hand had become a conditioned food-approach stimulus, and it was hoped that, added to the food-approach tendencies aroused by the sight and smell of the meat, the presentation of the human hand might lead to the overcoming of the inhibition of the feeding response. Accordingly, meat pellets were offered to the animals on an ebony rod held in the hand. Some of the animals ate the food after various periods of hesitation and then took subsequent offerings with increasing readiness.

In those animals that were not induced to eat by the above technique a method was tried that proved to be very instructive. In addition to their reactions in the experimental cage, the animals also reacted with anxiety anywhere in the experimental laboratory and also in each of a series of rooms that had varying degrees of resemblance to the experimental laboratory. They were offered meat pellets in each of these places, starting with the rooms that more closely resembled the laboratory. In the case of each cat a place was eventually found where the evocation of anxiety responses was not great enough to inhibit the feeding response. The animal would be fed about 20 pellets in this place and on the next day would usually be found to accept food in the room next closest in resemblance to the laboratory—as it would not have done previously. From day to day further advances were made, until the animal would eat in the laboratory and eventually, through several stages, in the experimental cage itself. There it would be given numerous pellets of meat on successive days and at last would move about in the cage freely, without any signs of anxiety.

But at this stage the anxiety responses could again be evoked by presenting the auditory stimulus that had preceded the neurosis-producing shocks. The effects of this stimulus could be eliminated in a manner parallel to that applied to the visual stimuli—by feeding the animal first at a considerable distance from the continuously sounding stimulus and then gradually coming nearer day by day. Meanwhile, the auditory stimulus would incidentally have become linked to a food-seeking response; but extinction of this by repeated nonreward did not lead to a recurrence of anxiety in any animal.

These experiments seemed clearly to confirm the expectation of a reciprocal antagonism between the anxiety responses and the feeding responses. As long as, in a given situation, the anxiety was strong enough to inhibit feeding, anxiety would continue to be dominant, and would even increase or spread, as certain supplementary experiments[39, 41, 46] showed. But if conditions were so changed that the feeding tendency was relatively stronger and feeding could occur in the face of some measure of anxiety, the strength of the tendency to respond by anxiety to the stimuli concerned was gradually weakened.

RECIPROCAL INHIBITION IN PSYCHOTHERAPY

The above findings led to the framing of the general hypothesis that if a response incompatible with anxiety can be made to occur in the presence of anxiety-evoking stimuli it will weaken the bond between these stimuli, and that anxiety responses can be produced in human subjects in a number of different ways. It is not surprising that this should be so, for although Sherringtonian reciprocal inhibition associated with spinal reflex activity is apparently rather specific, at higher levels of organization reciprocal inhibition is clearly often diffuse within the functional "modality" concerned —for example, accompanying the articulation of any word there is ordinarily an automatic inhibition of all simultaneous tendencies to pronounce other words.

The first requirement in a planned attack on neurotic anxieties on the principle of reciprocal inhibition is to determine in what circumstances anxieties are aroused in the patient. Sometimes, usually when the patient has been available for only a small number of interviews, it has been possible to obtain satisfactory results with the therapist's knowing only the general character of the situations producing anxiety and without his precisely identifying the disturbing elements. But it is always desirable, and nearly always possible, to examine the situations carefully and to determine in detail to what stimuli the patient reacts with anxiety. To this end, it has been found helpful in some cases to make use of the psychogalvanic response (PGR). A careful history of the patient's life and background is, of course, an essential preliminary to the foregoing.

Under the headings that follow it is explained how various responses incompatible with anxiety have their therapeutic effects. Sections 1 to 4 discuss, in the main, techniques that have emerged directly from the reciprocal inhibition principle, and sections 5 to 8 show how the effects of a number of procedures widely used in the treatment of neuroses are understandable in terms of reciprocal inhibition.

1. Assertive Responses

These responses are mainly employed in situations that occur spontaneously in the normal course of the patient's life. Great prominence has been given to their use by Salter,[30] who, having been led to them by a different theory, seems to apply them almost universally. I have found them of use only for overcoming unadaptive anxieties aroused in the patient by other people during his direct dealings with them. In these circumstances assertive responses are extremely effective. To take a common example, a patient feels hurt when members of his family criticize him and responds by trying to defend himself, by sulking, or by an outburst of petulant rage. Such responses are expressive of anxiety and helplessness. But some measure of resentment is, understandably, almost invariably present at the same time. The patient is unable to express this resentment because, for example, through previous training, the idea of talking back to his elders produces anxiety.

Now, just because this anxiety inhibits the expression of the resentment, it might be expected that if the patient could be motivated to express the resentment, the latter would, in turn, be reciprocally inhibitory to the anxiety and would thus suppress it, to some extent at least. The therapist provides this motivation by pointing out the emptiness of the patient's fears, emphasizing how his fearful patterns of behavior have incapacitated him and placed him at the mercy of others, and informing him that, though expression of resentment may be difficult at first, it becomes progressively easier with practice. It usually does not take long for patients to begin to perform the required behavior, although some need much initial exhortation and repeated promptings. Gradually the patient becomes able to behave assertively in progressively more exacting circumstances and reports a growing feeling of ease in all relevant situations. A conditioned inhibition of the anxiety responses is clearly developing, presumably on the basis of their repeated reciprocal inhibition—a process in all respects parallel to that involved in the overcoming of animal neuroses, as described above. Cases 3, 4, and 5 illustrate this technique.

Obviously, in advising assertive behavior, the therapist must be discreet. He should advise it only when the anxiety evoked in the patient by the other person concerned is unadaptive—in other words, an anxiety that occurs even though no unpleasant repercussions can reasonably be expected to follow from making a stand. For nothing can be gained, and sensitivity may even be increased, if the patient's assertiveness should meet with a swift and sharp punishment. For example, however much a person may resent his boss's surly manner, it would in most cases be foolhardy to give frank expression to this resentment. But it is quite frequently possible to express aggression indirectly, through gaining control of an interpersonal relationship by means subtler than overt assertiveness.

Occasionally, when there is unusual difficulty in the expression of aggression in the life situation, it is helpful to initiate the patient by means of a kind of "psychodrama" in the consulting room in which the therapist takes the role of some person who in life evokes anxiety in the patient.

2. Sexual Responses

These responses, of course, are mainly of use when anxiety responses have been conditioned to various aspects of sexual situations. When very high degrees of anxiety conditioning have been accompanied by a complete inhibition of sexual responsiveness, other measures, described later, have to be employed. But very often the sexual inhibition is partial and varies according to variations in definable properties of the relevant situations. The patient is told that he must on no account perform sexually unless he has an unmistakable positive desire to do so, for otherwise he may very well consolidate, or even extend, his sexual inhibitions. He is instructed to wait for or to seek out situations in which pleasurable sexual feelings are aroused, and in these he must "let himself go" as freely as possible. If he is able to act according to plan, he experiences a gradual increase in sexual responsiveness to the kind of situation of which he has made use, with varying degrees of generalization to sexual situations of other kinds.

Such favorable consequences occur, it seems, because each time a positive sexual feeling occurs and is intensified by a sexual approach there is reciprocal inhibition of whatever anxieties are also being evoked by the situation, and the strength of the anxiety-evocation tendency is each time slightly weakened. There is no apparent basic difference at all between this process and that which occurred in our cats, in which anxieties were overcome through appropriate manipulations with feeding reactions.

3. Relaxation Responses

(a) Relaxation responses in life situations. Jacobson's work has shown[12] that intense muscle relaxation is accompanied by autonomic effects that are antagonistic to the characteristic effects of anxiety. I have repeatedly found clinical confirmation of this in the rapid drop of a pulse rate from 120 to 80 or in the equally rapid drying of profusely sweating palms in a patient who is practiced in relaxation.

Relaxation can be used with lasting effects in the great majority of cases of neurosis, in my experience. Jacobson himself obtained impressive results by training patients in "progressive relaxation" and then urging them to be as relaxed as possible all the time. It would appear that the improvement in a patient who follows this program may be explained as follows: Persistent relaxation implies some measure of reciprocal inhibition of the effects of any anxiety-producing stimuli that happen to appear, and the occurrence of repeated temporary inhibitions of this kind enables conditioned inhibition of the anxiety responses gradually to develop.

I have sometimes obtained highly gratifying results in patients placed on Jacobson's regimen (Case 6), but oftener than not its value its limited, seemingly because the patient is unable to relax at short notice sufficiently deeply to counter the high degree of anxiety produced by the relevant stimulus situations. In a few patients this difficulty has been overcome when the subject has learned how to anticipate such situations and to relax deeply in preparation for them. The following technique, in which the therapist has a good deal of detailed control, has proved to have far wider application.

(b) Systematic desensitization based on relaxation. This method of systematic desensitization to anxiety-producing stimuli is carried out in the consulting room.

The patient is given training in progressive relaxation in the course of several interviews. Preliminary experiments on his responses to hypnotic techniques are meanwhile conducted, and during the same interviews steps are taken toward the construction of what is called an "anxiety hierarchy." This is a list of stimuli to which the patient reacts with unadaptive anxiety. The most disturbing items are placed at the top and the least disturbing at the bottom. The arrangement is usually derived solely from the patient's answers to questioning; but occasionally, when he has difficulty in assessing the relative effects of different stimuli, it has been necessary to base the hierarchy, or parts of it, on the psychogalvanic response (PGR). Multiple hierarchies are very often obtained.

In the session after the preliminaries have been completed, the patient is hypnotized and given powerful relaxation suggestions. (A good relaxer can do almost as well without hypnosis, just by closing his eyes.) He is then asked to imagine a scene embodying the feeblest member of the anxiety hierarchy. Sometimes it is advisable to start even more mildly, causing the name of the feared object to be visualized. The patient is instructed to signal if at any time he feels more than the slightest disturbance. Usually, two to four items from the hierarchy are presented at each session, the speed of progression depending on how much disturbance is shown or afterward reported. (It is always preferable to advance too slowly rather than too fast. During early experiments with the method I produced serious setbacks in two patients by the premature presentation of stimuli with a high anxiety-evoking potential.) It usually takes between ten and thirty desensitization sessions before the highest items in the hierarchy can be accepted by the patient without disturbance.

It is natural to ask: does it follow that because a patient can imagine a scene calmly, he will also be calm when he comes upon a similar scene in reality? Experience shows the answer to be in the affirmative. A very striking example is afforded by Case 7. Sometimes there is a tendency for the real-life improvement to lag behind somewhat, but even then it eventually catches up. The one proviso for success, given the ability to relax, is that the imagined stimulus must at the outset be able to evoke anxiety. A small minority of patients experience no anxiety when they imagine situations that in actuality are anxiety-producing, and in them desensitization is not accomplished by the above procedure. It is interesting to note that recently a patient who repeatedly failed to respond emotionally to images aroused by verbal cues from the therapist has shown considerable disturbance on verbalizing the same situations himself.

The above procedure, originally confined to "simple" phobias, has in the past year been applied to a wide variety of disturbing situations (see Case 8), often of a social nature. Sometimes there are multiple distinct, though usually interrelated, hierarchies. These may exist in parallel, or they may be, so to speak, "layered." For example, in a dentist phobic reactions to a variety of work situations were found after a time to depend on fears of criticism, which were, in their turn, partly based on a claustrophobic system. A separate hierarchy was derived from each of these three areas.

4. Conditioned Avoidance Responses

(a) Conditioned inhibition of anxiety through a dominating motor response. In 1948 Mowrer and Viek[27] performed an interesting experiment in which they showed that when rats are repeatedly exposed to a continuous mild electric shock, those animals who are enabled to learn a definite motor response in relation to the termination of the shock develop very little anxiety when placed in the experimental situation minus the shock; and, in contrast to these, much greater anxiety is shown by animals who have no opportunity to learn such a motor response. I have elsewhere[45] given reasons for rejecting Mowrer and Vick's own interpretation of their experiment and have argued that the less anxiety of the first-mentioned group of animals could be attributed to a gradual weakening of the autonomic anxiety responses due to their repeated reciprocal inhibition by the musculoskeletal response that regular reinforcement makes dominant.

It was reasonable to suppose that this experiment might have a therapeutic application. It was postulated that if in the presence of a stimulus evoking neurotic anxiety a mild noxious stimulus were to be applied on repeated occasions, and if this noxious stimulus were at the same time conditioned to produce a well-defined motor response, the neurotic anxiety would gradually be weakened. So far I have found only one case which has lent itself to the use of this method, and in which at the same time the response to other measures was poor enough to warrant the great expenditure of effort and time demanded.

CASE 1. The patient was a 23-year-old university graduate. She had been unbelievably overprotected during her childhood and adolescence. Three years previously she had had two fairly violent falls in the street within a few weeks and thereafter had been apprehensive of walking outside unaccompanied lest she should fall. As is apt to happen in such cases, her range of activity had then gradually become more and more circumscribed. At one stage she would walk in the street only if her mother held her arm; later she entirely refused to leave the house, and by the time I first saw her, she was practically bedridden, apart from very tense wall-hugging journey between her bed and a couch in the drawing room. After a year of interviews at approximately weekly intervals, she was feeling more confident and had greatly improved her handling of other people, but was only slightly more freely mobile. Her central fear—of falling—was undiminished, the hypnotic desensitization technique described above having turned out to be inapplicable to her case.

Then the following procedure, based on Mowrer and Viek's experiment, was adopted. Silver electrodes were attached to the patient's left hand and forearm. She was instructed to close her eyes and imagine a relatively easy (though, to her, slightly disturbing) fall and to signal at the commencement of the imagined movement. At this signal a mild electric shock (secondary of inductorium at 8.0 centimeters with 6-volt dry cell in primary) was passed into her forearm, being stopped only upon the occurrence of a brisk flexion of the forearm, which the patient had been directed to make. This movement soon became the instant response to the shock. When the whole sequence had been repeated a number of times, the patient reported that imagining the fall was becoming less unpleasant and disturbing, and, after further repetitions, that she could imagine it with ease. Thereafter, she was able to attempt this particular fall in actuality, and after practicing it a good many times a day, she could do it easily after a few days. Then she was ready for a slightly more difficult fall. Standing at increasing distances from chairs and other supports was later accomplished in similar fashion. The procedure was repeated at intervals of approximately five days, and as she became capable of falling farther and harder and, later, of standing farther from a support, she was able to walk and move around with increasing freedom. (It is intended to publish separately a detailed account of this case.)

(*b*) Conditioning of "anxiety-relief" responses. The possibility that "anxiety-relief responses might be directly conditioned to convenient stimuli and subsequently used to counter anxiety was suggested by an observation in a recent experiment by Zbrozyna.[47] This observation was that if a stimulus is repeatedly presented to an eating animal just before withdrawing the food, that stimulus acquires the property of inhibiting feeding even when the animal is in the middle of a meal. By analogy with this, it seemed reasonable to expect that if an uncomfortable induction shock were administered to a human subject for several seconds and were then made to cease immediately after a signal, that signal would become connected to such bodily responses as would follow cessation of the shock, and, furthermore, that these responses would be the negative of the anxiety that had been produced by the shock. This, it was hoped, would imply the acquisition of an additional means of inhibiting anxiety due to other stimuli.

This idea has been put into practice in eight patients, with results according to expectation in all but two. With the inductorium set at about 7.5 centimeters (but varying according to the subject's reaction) and a primary inflow of 6 volts, a continuous shock is administered to the subject's left forearm. He is told to bear it until the desire to have it removed becomes very strong, then to say aloud the word "calm." As soon as he says the word, the current is switched off. This is repeated ten to twenty times in a session. Most subjects report a feeling of relief at the cessation of shock that seems profoundly out of proportion to the disturbing effect of the shock and find, after one to three sessions, that using the word in disturbing situations decreases the disturbed feeling. In one case the word "calm" did not become the effective conditioned stimulus to the relief reaction, but the subject reported that she found herself automatically picturing the inductorium against the background of the consulting room whenever she experienced anxiety rising within her. This would bring on "surges of relief," under which the anxiety would melt away. Gradually, according to prediction on the reciprocal-inhibition principle, with repeated occurrences of this experience the amount of anxiety produced by the relevant stimuli became less and less. (It should be noted that this technique has in no case been the sole method of treatment.)

(*c*) Avoidance conditioning of obsessions. In the production of reactions of avoidance to obsessional stimuli, we have an instance of the application of the reciprocal-inhibition principle to a response other than anxiety, for here it is an intense and excessive approach that is being overcome. The essence of the method is to subject the patient to a very unpleasant electric shock in the presence of the obsessional object. It seems that the first to report the use of such a method was Kantorovich,[16] who employed it in the treatment of alcoholics—with considerable success. The technique was first applied to an obsessional patient by Max[23] a good many years ago and was then apparently ignored. Max administered to his patient an unusually severe induction shock in the presence of a fetishistic object. By doing this repeatedly and then reinforcing at intervals when required, he produced a persistent avoidance to this object, which alone, it seems, very greatly ameliorated the patient's emotionally disturbed state.

CASE 2. I have used a modification of Max's method in the treatment of a food obsession of 16 years' standing, which previously had completely resisted almost every current mode of therapy, from ECT to psychoanalysis. The patient was a very intelligent woman of 36 who had long suffered from cardiac insufficiency and was on a restricted diet. Besides the obsession, she had other exceptionally severe and distressing neurotic reactions, which had improved considerably on the more usual reciprocal-inhibition techniques. But the obsession was still present almost always and was worse when the patient was reacting to any persistent anxiety-producing stimulus. She would have visions of various items of delectable food and would be tortured by a conflict as to whether to eat or not. If she did eat, she soon felt a rising guilt (anxiety about something done) which would lead back to the obsession. Thus, a vicious circle of eating and anxiety would be started, which, within a few days, would leave her in a desperately helpless and exhausted state.

Avoidance conditioning was carried out as follows: The electrodes having been attached to her left forearm, the patient was told to raise her right hand as soon as she had formed a clear imaginary picture of some desirable foodstuff. An almost unbearable current from the inductorium at 7.0 centimeters (6 volts) was then instantly delivered and continued until she lowered her right hand as a signal that the shock could no longer be borne, as she usually did after a second or two. About ten reinforcements were given at each session, and two to three days were allowed to elapse between sessions. After the first session the "nagging" of the obsession was already markedly reduced. It was further reduced in four more sessions, which implicated the whole range of items of "delectable food." The patient reported that on imagining any such food she immediately had a feeling of fear and revulsion, accompanied by an image of the shock situation. (At an earlier stage this feeling was occasionally preceded by a momentary feeling of pleasure.) Within a few seconds she was able to return her attention to whatever she had been doing before the food image came up—a tremendous gain as contrasted with the old misery of hours spent debating, "Should I eat; should I not?" After her fifth, and last, session she stated that her tendency to think of food was also diminishing. Unfortunately, but not unexpectedly, there was also some generalization of the avoidance to permitted foods, i.e., nonfattening sodium-free foods eaten only at mealtime. This was a very considerable difficulty, but the patient regarded it as trivial in comparison with her obsession. The over-all lightening of the burden made it much easier to return to the usual procedures for overcoming the anxiety reactions. Gratifying progress was made, only to be brought to an end by the patient's sudden death from ventricular fibrillation due to chronic rheumatic heart disease.

5. Feeding Responses

I have not employed feeding responses to obtain reciprocal inhibition of anxiety in human subjects, but Jones[14] has done so successfully in young children. There is no reason why feeding should not be effective in overcoming fears in adults under certain circumstances. What is required is that in the presence of the anxiety-evoking stimulus food must be given under so intense a hunger drive that in the act of eating there will be an inhibition of anxiety. Probably, it is precisely this that is the explanation of the beneficial effects on neuroses of subcoma doses of insulin;[21, 32] and it is worth noting that the effects of this method have been greatest when the patient has eaten substantially more than usual and has put on weight. Presumably, in eating voraciously because of heightened hunger drive, the patient obtains a reciprocal inhibition of any anxiety responses that happen to be occurring within him at that particular time. This explanation, with its close parallel in animal experiments, gains credence when one takes into account the haziness of the explanations that have been offered in terms of gross physiology. However, from the results of a controlled experiment by Teitelbaum and associates,[34] as reviewed by Sargant and Slater,[33] it is clear that only a small percentage of patients are favorably affected by subcoma insulin. This finding is not surprising, because any effects depend on the fortuitous occurrence of anxiety-producing stimuli at the time of the eating (this implies, of course, that the patients who should respond best are those that have a good deal of so-called free-floating anxiety, i.e., secondary conditionings of anxiety to commonplace stimuli, such as room walls or voices).

6. Respiratory Responses

In 1947 Meduna[24] reported the very interesting discovery that in many patients neurotic reactions can be ameliorated, and sometimes even overcome, by inhalations of high concentrations of carbon dioxide. His usual technique has been to make the patient breathe a mixture of 30 per cent carbon dioxide and 70 per cent oxygen until consciousness is lost. More recently, La Verne[19] has claimed equally good or better results from single full-capacity inhalations of 70 per cent carbon dioxide and 30 per cent oxygen, usually producing no more than stupor. Meduna and his followers have assumed that the effects of this kind of treatment are due to the depressing action of carbon dioxide on nerve structures. Gellhorn[7] has criticized Meduna's theory (p. 463) and has gone on to suggest another explanation of these effects, also in terms of gross physiology. But from a psychological point of view any such theory is untenable, because the treatment apparently affects only neurotic anxiety responses. If the effects of carbon dioxide were due to its action on some chemical factor in certain nerve cells, all cells containing this factor would be influenced; and since the relevant cells are those that in one way or another subserve anxiety responses, all anxieties, even those aroused in response to real threats, would be similarly diminished by the treatment. Neither Meduna's case histories nor my own personal experience reveal any indication of this happening. Anxiety responses, as such, are by no means removed from the repertoire of the patient, who continues to have and display normal anxieties. It is therefore to be concluded that a specific unlearning of the connection between certain stimuli and the anxiety responses has occurred.[43] It is reasonable to suspect that the unlearning occurs by a process of reciprocal inhibition in this instance, too. Neurotic anxiety-producing stimuli are brought forth during the dreamy or confused stage of the treatment, or are already present if there is "free-floating" anxiety. Processes antagonistic to anxiety can be found both in the excitation that goes with intense respiratory stimulation and in association with the complete muscle relaxation that high concentrations of carbon dioxide produce.[7] (p. 459).

I have occasionally treated patients with carbon dioxide, employing La Verne's method because, in contrast to Meduna's, it arouses little or no anxiety. Of five patients, one was completely unaffected, two felt sedated afterward for the rest of each treatment day, one showed slight but definite lasting improvement, and one obtained very marked benefit. The last-mentioned had a war neurosis of 10 years' standing. He displayed, almost continuously, a high degree of "free-floating" anxiety and had a special sensitivity to all situations involving explosions or low-pitched rumblings. Desensitization under hypnosis could not even be started because when asked to imagine a scene the patient could never visualize anything but irregular black and white blotches. He had three treatments, each consisting of two full inhalations of the mixture of 70 per cent carbon dioxide and 30 per cent oxygen. There was a week between treatments, and he felt persistently better after each. After the third treatment he said he felt perfectly well. Three months later he was still well and reported that thunderstorms had left him quite undisturbed, in contrast with the past.

7. Interview-Induced Emotional Responses

Cures of neuroses seem to be obtained by all kinds of therapists, even though, owing to their different theories, they devote the interview period to procedures that differ in a large variety of ways. Such studies as have compared the success of various kinds of interviews have shown no important differences either in the percentage of cures or in their quality.[18, 35] Wilder,[35] for example, found that the psychotherapeutic results achieved by hospitals, mental hygiene clinics, psychoanalytic institutes, private psychoanalysts, and private psychotherapists were much the same. This finding strongly suggests that the various special points of procedure that the different therapists regarded as crucial to success were not crucial at all, and that the effective factor must have been something that all the therapeutic situations generated in common.

The only feature common to all the therapies seems to be that there is a private interview in which the patient confidentially reveals and talks about his difficulties to a person he believes to have the knowledge, skill, and desire to help him. This kind of situation undoubtedly excites emotional responses in patients, and both the character and the strength of these responses vary as functions of many factors, of which the personality and attitude of the therapist and the individual reactive potentialities of the patient are presumably the most important. If, in a patient, the emotional response evoked by the interview situation is (1) antagonistic to anxiety and (2) of sufficient strength, it may be supposed that it will reciprocally inhibit the anxiety responses that are almost certain to be evoked by some of the subject matter of the interview.

This hypothesis requires systematic testing, but it is my clinical impression that those patients who display strong emotions other than anxiety during the early anamnestic interviews are the ones who are likely to show improvement before special methods for obtaining reciprocal inhibition of anxiety responses are applied.

8. Abreaction

Abreaction may be defined as the emotional re-evocation of a fearful past experience. It is a special case of the interview-induced emotional reactions considered under the previous heading. It may occur under thiopental (pentothal), hypnosis, or deep relaxation, or even in the course of an ordinary interview. The emotion is of considerable intensity, and beneficial effects seem, by and large, to be positively correlated with its intensity. But, as Grinker and Spiegel[9] have pointed out (p. 81), if unrelieved terror is the only emotional component of the abreaction, the patient makes no progress. It is only when the patient can feel the impact of the therapeutic situation—e. g., the therapist's sympathetic acceptance of him—that beneficial abreaction can occur. This is emphasized by the observation of Grinker and Spiegel that "abreactions that occur spontaneously under alcohol are nontherapeutic"[8] (p. 392). In the case of abreaction, too, then, benefit depends on the evocation of other emotional responses in association with the fearful situation, so that, presumably, reciprocal inhibition of anxiety occurs. The specially dramatic changes sometimes produced by abreaction are in line with the experimental finding that modifications of response are likely to be more marked when there is a higher level of drive to be reduced.[11, 40]

If the above interpretation is correct, it would follow that the uprooting of "repressed memories" is not essential to the therapeutic effects of abreaction, although the ventilation of forgotten material often provides the subject matter. Many of Grinker's and Spiegel's patients[9] were improved by abreactions in which the battle experiences concerned were well-remembered ones (pp. 83-84). The case that follows demonstrates how irrelevant to a patient's recovery the restoration of forgotten memories can be.

> CASE 3. A 37-year-old miner was seen in a state of intense anxiety. He had had a very marked tremor and total amnesia for the previous four days. He gave a story that his wife, on whom he was greatly dependent, had cunningly got him to agree to a "temporary divorce" six months before and was now going to marry a friend of his. No attempt was made at this juncture to recall the lost memories. The patient was made to realize how ineffectual his previous attitudes had been and how he had been deceived. As a result, he angrily "had it

out" with his wife (and a few others, incidentally); anxiety rapidly decreased, and he soon felt strongly motivated to organize his whole life differently. At his fifth interview (ten days after treatment began), he said that he felt "a hundred per cent," and looked it, and he was full of plans for the future. Yet, he had still recalled nothing whatever of the forgotten four days.

Since the possible effects of restoring the memories at this stage were obviously a matter of great interest, the patient was then deeply hypnotized and told to recount the story of the four days. He narrated in detail how he had traveled 300 miles to his rival, meaning to strangle him; how he had been fobbed off; and how, returning, and at last hearing from his wife's own lips that she was in love with the rival, he had staggered out of the house, made his way to his sister's house, and there collapsed. He told all this quietly, with little emotion, except where he described meeting his rival. Then he moved his hands as if about to throttle someone. He was given the posthypnotic suggestion that he would remember the whole story on waking. When he woke, he told it again briefly, expressing slight amusement at it and surprise at having remembered. There were no important consequences. A few months later he married another woman and was apparently very well adjusted generally. After four years there has been no evidence of relapse.

RESULTS

In 1952 the results were reported of the treatment of 70 patients by the reciprocal-inhibition techniques that were then available.[44] In the 52 additional cases now presented, these were the techniques that were again chiefly employed; but, in addition, the three induction-coil methods described above and La Verne's method of carbon-dioxide therapy were occasionally used.

Both series include only patients whose treatment has ceased after they have been afforded a reasonable opportunity for the application of the available methods; i.e., they have had as a minimum both a course of instruction on the changing of behavior in the life situation and a proper initiation of a course of relaxation-desensitization. This minimum takes up to about fifteen interviews, including the anamnestic interviews, and no patient who has had fifteen or more interviews has been omitted from the series. Almost invariably, when a patient has experienced some early improvement, he continues until improvement is very marked, and then, oftener than not, breaks off treatment; even though I am not quite ready to discharge him.

The degree of response to treatment has been estimated by reference to Knight's five criteria[17]—symptomatic improvement, increased productiveness, improved adjustment and pleasure in sex, improved interpersonal relationships, and ability to handle ordinary psychological conflicts and reasonable reality stresses. In addition, the patient's score on Willoughby's questionnaire[36, 37] is compared with his score at the beginning of treatment, and no patient is regarded as greatly benefited unless his score has dropped markedly, preferably to 20 or less. On the basis of these criteria, results are grouped under the headings used by Knight: (1) apparently cured; (2) much improved; (3) moderately to slightly improved and (4) unimproved.

In Table 1 the cases are grouped according to the "type" of

TABLE 1. CLASSIFICATION OF CASES

Category	Number 1952 Series	Present Series	Total
Anxiety states	39	33	72
Hysteria	6	3	9
Reactive depression	7	3	10
Obsessions and compulsions	5	6	11
Neurasthenia	3	0	3
Mixed and unclassifiable	10	7	17
Totals	70	52	122

neurosis. This grouping has little value from any clinical angle, for almost all neuroses are really "mixed," and the compartment into which a case falls is no guide to its tractability.

Table 2 shows the results of reciprocal inhibition-based psy-

TABLE 2. RESULTS OF RECIPROCAL-INHIBITION-BASED PSYCHOTHERAPY

Series	No. of Cases	Apparently Cured	Much Improved	Slightly to Moderately Improved	Unimproved
1952	70	34	26	7	3
Present	52	20	30	1	1
Totals	122	54	56	8	4
		(44%)	(46%)	(7%)	(3%)

chotherapy in our two series. It will be noticed that in the present series the percentage of good results has risen slightly, but a more rigorous standard has been applied for "cure." Systematic long-term follow-up studies have not been done, but information has been received from 14 patients of the 1952 series. Not one of these has relapsed, and all but one have reported continuing progress two to five years after the end of therapy.

Table 3 subdivides the present 52 cases according to the number

TABLE 3. DISTRIBUTION OF INTERVIEWS

No. of interviews	Up to 10	11-20	21-30	31-40	Over 40	Total
No. of patients	12	17	12	3	8	52

Mean number of interviews per patient 26.1

of interviews given. Four-fifths of the patients had 30 interviews or less. The mean is 26.1, as compared with a mean of 24.9 in the earlier series. It may be noted that in the two series there was a total of 13 patients who had previously been psychoanalyzed, and these had an average of 51.7 interviews. Part of the reason for this high average was that some of these patients were exceedingly verbose and found difficulty in participating in treatment by objective techniques. Nevertheless, 10 of the 13 patients were either apparently cured or much improved. It is interesting to note that two psychoanalyzed patients, while repeatedly expressing skepticism regarding the present methods during their early interviews, nevertheless agreed to follow out instructions, and both did very well—one being apparently cured after 14 interviews and the other much improved after 16. Another such skeptic, however, was the only patient in the present series who made no improvement at all.

Table 4 compares the total results of our two series with those

TABLE 4. COMPARATIVE RESULTS

Series	No. of Cases	Apparently Cured or Much Improved	Improvement Moderate, Slight, or Nil
Berlin Psychoanalytic Institute[17]	263-402	163 (62-40.5%)	100-239 (38-59.5%)
New York Hospital[10]	100	53 (53%)	47 (47%)
Combined reciprocal-inhibition series	122	110 (90%)	12 (10%)

of the New York Hospital series of Hamilton and Wall[10] and those of the laregst reported psychoanalytically treated series[17]—from the Berlin Psychoanalytic Institute. In the case of the last series, two figures are given for both the total number of cases and the percentages. The larger total includes those patients who had less than six months' psychoanalysis. But for the purposes of our comparison the smaller, and more favorable, total is taken. The χ^2 test for significance yields a value of 44 when our results are compared with those of the New York Hospital series, and a value of 31 when they are compared with those of the psychoanalytic series. Thus both comparisons indicate that the probability that the higher proportion of successes in the present series is due to chance is negligible.

The crucial point of the comparative figures in Table 4 is that in our two series 90 per cent of the patients were either apparently cured or much improved, and only about 60 per cent of the cases in the other two series. If the favorable results of the present series are, to the extent of 60 per cent, regarded as due to the nonspecific reciprocal inhibition that would occur in any kind of interview situation, the additional 30 per cent of good results appears to be attributable to the special measures for obtaining reciprocal inhibition described above. Furthermore, the small average number of interviews needed suggests that the use of these special measures early in treatment greatly accelerates the improvement of those patients who would have responded to the nonspecific factors alone.

COMMENTS ON OTHER THEORIES OF
THE PSYCHOTHERAPEUTIC PROCESS

In reciprocal inhibition we have a single principle that can explain (1) the effectiveness of measures used to overcome animal neuroses, (2) the similar success of various, often widely different, interview techniques, and (3) the effectiveness of certain special measures—subcoma insulin and carbon-dioxide therapy. At the same time, the principle has led directly to the development of effective new psychotherapeutic techniques, as described above.

It is necessary at this point to examine some other current theories to see whether any of them can, with equal ease, cover the same range of facts. The theories will not be considered in relation to all the facts. If any theory is found to contradict even one major fact, that finding is sufficient to challenge the validity of that theory. It will be seen in what follows that on this basis there is cause to reject each of the more or less influential theories considered.

Psychoanalytic Types of Theory

(a) Pure psychoanalytic theory. The essential features of this type of theory have been described in great detail by Fenichel.[6] Neurotic symptoms are regarded as due to "distorted discharges" that come from the damming up of the energies of repressed memories, and the essential aim of psychoanalytic psychotherapy is to remove the repressions and so let the memories be reintegrated into the patient's conscious life. In Fenichel's words (p. 570), "The therapeutic task, then, is to reunite with the conscious ego the contents (both unconscious anxieties of the ego and instinctual impulses of the id) which have been withheld from consciousness by counter-cathexis." Now, the accomplishment of this "therapeutic task" cannot really be the essence of psychotherapy, because other methods which do nothing to lift repressions produce individual cures as impressive as any that psychoanalysis can claim, as often and at least as rapidly (in the present series apparently oftener and certainly more rapidly). Fenichel (p. 555) is well aware that methods other than psychoanalysis have psychotherapeutic effects; but, on the basis of his theoretical presuppositions, and without empirical support, he discards these effects as being limited in comparison with those of psychoanalysis. Meanwhile, the findings of Landis[18] and Wilder,[35] mentioned above, are contrary to Fenichel's presumption, as are the results of the treatment recorded here, with its high proportion of cases fully satisfying all of Knight's criteria.

Unfortunately, there is little likelihood that psychoanalysts in general will take the above considerations into account, any more than they have in the past taken account of facts or arguments unfavorable to their theories. It is not easy even for a strict scientist to give up a favorite hypothesis when the evidence fails to support it; but psychoanalysts seem especially liable to acquire habits of thought that do not conform to the requirements of science, as Ellis's recent monograph clearly shows.[3] Perhaps it is this that explains why such serious criticisms of the psychoanalytic position as those of Wohlgemuth,[38] Johnson,[13] Salter,[31] and Eysenck[4] are glossed over or ignored.

(b) A behavioristic translation of a psychoanalytic theory of psychotherapy. In an interesting book,[2] Dollard and Miller have tried to interpret the psychotherapeutic process in terms of the Hullian theory of learning.[11, 26] They accept as fact the psychoanalytic account of what happens. For instance, they say,[2] "The patient is sick just because his mind is lamed by repression, and he cannot use it freely to solve his problems" (p. 301), and imply (p. 322) that in a severe neurosis a therapist who is not concerned to remove repressions is unlikely to achieve "a complete cure." We have seen above that in view of the failure of psychoanalysis to obtain superior results there is no justification for this opinion. It is interesting, also, to note that, although the book is largely built around an account of a successfully treated case, that of Mrs. A. there is no point at which Mrs. A can clearly be seen to be benefiting from the lifting of repressions in the sense defined by the authors.

However, leaving repression aside, Dollard and Miller have given a very detailed and absorbing account of many of the occurrences that may be observed during psychotherapy. But on the matter of interpretation one must again quarrel with them. They regard extinction, i.e., conditioned inhibition based on reactive inhibition,[11, 43] as the main mechanism subserving elimination of neurotic habits (pp. 230-32). Now, while it cannot be denied that fear can undergo extinction, this process is usually very long and difficult, as Dollard and Miller themselves remark (pp. 71-73). For example, Miller found[25] that a fear-motivated motor habit required hundreds of trials to be extinguished. Thus, when fear responses are eliminated rather rapidly, either experimentally or clinically, it must be presumed that some mechanism other than extinction is at work—and reasons are given above for believing that reciprocal inhibition is the basis of this mechanism. Dollard and Miller do actually give consideration to the therapeutic effects of responses incompatible with neurotic responses (pp. 74; 383-87) but apparently regard these effects as having only minor importance. Yet, in most of the therapeutically effective events they describe in the case of Mrs. A it is possible to see how the anxiety is inhibited by antagonistic emotions arising either directly from the therapeutic relationship or as a consequence of the therapist's intervention. The following is an example: At a certain stage (p. 316) the therapist points out to Mrs. A that now that she is an adult she will not be punished if she acts independently. Dollard and Miller state that this suggestion had two important effects—to inhibit fear of taking necessary actions and to create hope of a way out. But the mere realization that she would not be punished could not be expected to have much fear-inhibiting effect. Patients are very often fully aware that their fears are unreasonable and yet go on having them. What the therapist really seems to have done is to motivate Mrs. A to take action, and it is the taking of this action which is "anti-anxiety" in effect and of far more potency in diminishing anxieties than talking or "realizing" could ever be.

Conditioned-Reflex Theories

(a) Pavlovian theory. Pavlov's theory of psychotherapeutic effects follows directly from his theory of the basis of neurosis. According to Pavlov,[28] normal cortical function requires a balance between excitatory and inhibitory processes. If at a given locus of the cortex excitation and inhibition come into conflict with each other at high intensity, the neural elements concerned may be unable to bear the strain and so undergo a pathological change by which the balance is overthrown; and then the animal presents neurotic symptoms (pp. 292-93). In accordance with this hypothesis, the essence of therapy would be to restore the balance, as Pavlov essayed to do by administering bromides, with the idea of strengthening the inhibitory process, and in many cases he succeeded in curing the neurosis. He later[29] obtained better results from a combination of bromides and caffeine. (pp. 95-97; 181). It has been shown elsewhere[39] that the curative effect of bromides could be due to the fact that they have a selectively greater depressing action on anxiety responses, favoring their reciprocal inhibition by any antagonistic responses that happen to occur. Pavlov's theory, on the other hand, would be hard put to it to explain how *lesions* in the nervous system could be healed either by a drug that depresses nervous activity or by retraining procedures that involve nothing more than the formation or undoing of specific neural connections.

(b) Salter's excitation theory. Salter[30] has recently offered a theory of psychotherapy which is broadly based on Pavlovian psychology but which apparently derives its special form from the clinical experience that if neurotic patients are encouraged to express their habitually inhibited nonanxious feelings, they often gradually overcome their neuroses. He holds that a person with a neurosis suffers from an excess of inhibition, and it is therefore through the arousal of excitation that this expression of feelings overcomes a neurosis. For Salter, it is on the basis of excitation alone that a neurosis can be cured.

There are several reasons for rejecting this theory. It may be noted that Pavlov himself did not regard an animal as neurotic just because its temperament was a highly inhibitory one but found that both excitatory and inhibitory animals could develop neuroses. The following criticisms are more directly relevant: First, even though it is true that in association with the anxiety many other responses are inhibited, the anxiety responses themselves, especially clearly in acute anxiety states, are quite evidently excitatory. Second, relaxation techniques, involving a negation of excitation, are, as described above, very effective in the treatment of neuroses. Third, electroconvulsive therapy, whose effects on the nervous system are eminently excitatory[7] (pp. 438-42) is not of great value in treating neuroses, with the exception of some depressions.[15] Even the most favorable series[20] give no better results than would be obtained from nonspecific interview-induced psychotherapeutic effects, and such effects would doubtless occur even when shock therapy is what the therapist is using.

FURTHER CASES ILLUSTRATING PSYCHOTHERAPY BASED ON RECIPROCAL INHIBITION

CASE 4. A married woman of 24 was first seen on April 14, 1951, complaining of chronic anxiety and a feeling of inadequacy in most of her social relationships, of which the most distressing was that with her mother-in-law. She had special phobic reactions to certain men, which turned out to depend on the degree of their resemblance to her father, and she also reacted with fear to the ringing of the front doorbell or the sound of footsteps up the garden path. All these reactions were tied up with the early behavior of her father, who was extremely sadistic and had terrorized her in her childhood in a great variety of ways. When she was 14, he removed her from school to work in one of his shops without pay. He would frequently creep up silently and pounce on her for not working hard enough. At 17 she ran away to Johannesburg from her family in Cape Town, and at 21 married a motor mechanic, with whom she was generally happy.

The patient had 65 therapeutic interviews, unevenly distributed over 27 months. The greater part of the time was devoted to discussions of how to gain control of her interpersonal relationships and stand up for herself. She had considerable difficulty with this at first, even though it had early become emotionally important to her to please the therapist. But she gradually mastered the assertive behavior required of her, overcame her anxieties, and became exceedingly self-reliant in all interpersonal dealings, including those with her mother-in-law. Finally, she deliberately made a trip to Cape Town to pit herself against her father. She experienced initial nervousness at their first meeting but after that was in complete control, during a three weeks' stay.

At the conclusion of therapy, in June, 1953, she was adjudged a very well-adjusted and competent person and early in 1954 reported that she was still going from strength to strength.

CASE 5. An attractive woman of 28 came for treatment because she was in acute distress as a result of her lover's casual treatment of her. Every one of very numerous love affairs had followed a similar pattern—first she would attract the man, then she would offer herself on a platter, crawling and cringing and leaning on him heavily. He would soon treat her with contempt and after a time leave her.

In general she lacked assurance, was very dependent, and was practically never free from feelings of tension and anxiety. Her Willoughby score was 45, reflecting very considerable neuroticism. A year previously she had terminated a two-year course of psychoanalysis, which had benefited her somewhat. She came to me only because her analyst was not available, and during the first few interviews she repeatedly expressed doubt regarding the value of my nonanalytic treatment.

At her fifth interview the unadaptiveness of her anxieties and the rationale of the reciprocal-inhibition principle were explained to her, and she left feeling optimistic. At the next interview she was told how to behave with firmness and take independent courses of action with her lover. This involved a good deal of subtle tactics. She performed well according to prescription and was able to terminate her relationship with him with dignity and with relatively little disturbance, and, indeed, with a certain feeling of triumph. Meanwhile, she was shown how to counterattack her nagging mother and to deal with her boss and other people who easily upset her. Through action she gradually developed a feeling of mastery, both at home and at work.

Soon she found that she was beginning to hold the reins in a variety of minor sexual situations. After her thirteenth interview, she went on a holiday and returned six weeks later to say that she had made continued efforts to control interpersonal situations and was feeling much more stable emotionally. She was much better poised and had been a social success for the first time in her life. She no longer felt, as in the past, that it was important to go out a lot. About this time she met a man who attracted her, and now her feelings had an adult, independent character. After handling many difficulties admirably, she married him three months later. Her Willoughby score had dropped to 17. She had 14 interviews in all, and a year later was reported to be well and happy.

CASE 6. Early in 1951 a divorceé of 39 stated that from as far back as she could remember she had been nervous and hypersensitive and perpetually worried about the future. Many ordinary situations, such as overhearing others quarrel, constituted stresses for her, made her anxious and left her fatigued, and sometimes produced epigastric pain. For seven years she had persistently suffered from fibrositic backaches. Her symptoms had improved somewhat after her divorce, two years previously.

She was encouraged to be more assertive and less subservient to the wishes of her friends. But her severest tensions arose from situations in which no direct action was possible, e. g., having visitors for dinner. Thus, from her seventh interview onward she was given lessons in relaxation. Her response was excellent. She became able to relax and to calm herself in an increasing range of situations, the anxiety-evoking power of which waned and eventually disappeared. The patient had 13 interviews over four months, during which she entirely overcame her neurotic nervousness and was functioning well in all areas. Her fibrositis disappeared completely after the first month. In a three-year follow-up there has been no recurrence but, instead, continued strengthening.

CASE 7. A 23-year-old divorced tram driver entered the consulting room in a state of acute anxiety. Eight hours before a woman had walked into his slowly moving tram. She had been "knocked out and her head was bleeding." Although a doctor had told him that the woman's injury was not serious, he had become increasingly shaky and had developed severe epigastric pain. He had recovered from previous accidents in an hour or two, but in these no human injury had been involved.

The significance of the statement that no human injury was involved is that when the patient was 13 his father had died after an accident and since then he had had a fear of human blood. Even the tiny bead of blood that might appear on his face during shaving gave him an uncomfortable feeling. He was quite indifferent to animal blood—had seen oxen killed and had himself cut the throats of fowls. It was clear that his grossly excessive reaction to the present accident was due to his phobia for human blood, and to overcome this probia was the central aim of therapy.

The first five interviews, which occurred over six days, were confined to obtaining an understanding of the patient's personality and background and to overcoming his immediate disturbed state by intense, hypnotically induced relaxation. At the fifth interview he reported feeling very well. He was told to drive a tram again for a short distance, which he did later that day, without any ill effect

At the sixth interview various situations involving human blood were arranged in ascending order of their disturbing effect. From this time onward, at each interview, while the patient was in a state of hypnotic relaxation, he was made to visualize "blood situations." The feeblest was a slightly blood-tinged bandage lying in a basket. When this failed to disturb his relaxation, he was presented with a tiny drop of blood on his own face while shaving. In this way, with the presentation of two or three images at each session, it was possible gradually to work up to a stage at which the patient could visualize a casualty ward full of carnage and not be disturbed by it.

The significance of this method for real-life situations was revealed in this case in a most dramatic way. Two days before his last interview the patient saw a man knocked over by a motorcycle. The victim was seriously injured and was bleeding profusely. The patient was absolutely unaffected by the blood and. when the ambulance arrived, helped to load the victim on to it.

CASE 8. A married woman of 32 came for treatment on March 23, 1953. She had been nervous and timid as long as she could remember. Rheumatic fever before puberty had been followed by chorea, which had improved very slowly at first but not at all since the age of 16, and she had been left with persistently troublesome choreiform movements, which were worse during any emotional upset. In December 1952, she had been injured in a motor accident and had spent three weeks in the hospital. There, as the pain of her injuries lessened, she noticed that she was very tense, that her twitchings were much worse, and that she had great difficulty in concentrating. These symptoms had been unremittingly present ever since. After her discharge from the hospital she had been especially anxious when in a car. This had improved a little through repeatedly forcing herself to go into cars and be driven around. But she still reacted with panic to every minor "threat" of an accident, e.g., if a driver 100 yards ahead were to fail to obey a "stop" sign, or if her husband took a bend "in a swerving way."

Treatment consisted, in the first place, in teaching her progressive relaxation. Her control of personal relations was also given attention, in particular the handling of her small son, which soon improved markedly. After a month's treatment (11 interviews) she was much better and had only occasional choreiform movements. But she was still reacting badly to motorcar situations. Hypnotic desensitization was then begun, and after 12 sessions of this, by the end of June she reported being completely unperturbed by all normal driving experiences. Her choreiform movements had almost stopped, and she said that never at any time, even in childhood, had she felt so well. On being interviewed in February 1954, she stated that she had, if anything, continued to improve.

CASE 9. A 47-year-old married male nurse, employed in an industrial first-aid room, was sent for psychiatric treatment by the medical officer who had observed him during the previous four years. For 17 years he had never been free from an uncontrollable impulse to mimic any rhythmic movements he saw, e.g., waving of arms and dancing. He would also automatically obey any command, no matter from whom. A command, though, could not stop a rhythmic movement. The workmen frequently exploited his compulsion, to amuse themselves, often exhausting him and distressing him sometimes so much that he was left trembling.

No anxiety component could be observed in this compulsive behavior, but it was resolved to employ hypnosis to try to break the compulsion by attaching to the cues to its occurrence new and incompatible behavior. The patient was a good hypnotic subject, and six inductions were done in the course of 3 interviews. Two were done at the first interview. At the first induction he was made to recall the first occasions of compulsive mimicry and obedience and was then given the direct suggestion that he would stop imitating. At the second he was simply hypnotized and wakened, as a control experiment. No change followed either of these trances.

At the second interview the posthypnotic suggestion was made that after waking he would copy only alternate movements of the therapist's right arm; but on being wakened, he still copied every movement, as before. He was then hypnotized again and told that on waking he would find that he would move only his hand when the therapist moved his whole arm rhythmically. This posthypnotic suggestion was obeyed. A third trance was induced in that session and the posthypnotic suggestion given that he would decrease his movement as the therapist continued to wave his arm rhythmically, also a general suggestion that he would move only his right hand when impulses to mimic anybody arose. When he awoke, his impulses did lessen.

At his third interview, two days later, the patient reported that he had entirely stopped being affected by other people's movements or commands. He showed no reaction at all to the therapist's beating his fist on the desk. He said that he was sleeping much better and was no longer startled at being awakened, and his fear of the dark had vanished. He was hypnotized again and told he would continue to be unaffected by people's movements or commands. During this trance, at the therapist's instigation, he told how the onset had followed a violent wakening by a nurse early one morning when he was in hospital with pneumonia.

Eighteen months later the patient was perfectly well and had not relapsed in any respect.

SUMMARY

The case is presented that conditioned inhibition founded on reciprocal inhibition is the basis of most fundamental psychotherapeutic effects. This principle is shown to explain a large number of widely used therapeutic methods and has led to some methods, which are described. Of 122 patients treated by these methods, 110 were apparently cured or much improved. It is shown that certain other current theories are unable to account for the same range of facts as that subsumed by the reciprocal inhibition hypothesis.

REFERENCES

1. Dimmick, F. L., Ludlow, N., and Whiteman, A., Study of "Experimental Neurosis" in Cats, *Journal of Comparative Psychology*, 28:39, 1939.
2. Dollard, J., and Miller, N. E., *Personality and Psychotherapy* (New York: McGraw-Hill, 1950).

3. Ellis, A., *Introduction to the Principles of Scientific Psychoanalysis*, Genetic Psychology Monograph 41 (Provincetown, Mass.: The Journal Press, 1950) p. 147.

4. Eysenck, H. J., *Uses and Abuses of Psychology* (Baltimore: Penguin Books, 1953).

5. Farber, I. E., Response Fixation Under Anxiety and Non-Anxiety Conditions, *Journal of Experimental Psychology*, 38:111, 1948.

6. Fenichel, O., *Psychoanalytic Theory of Neurosis* (New York: Norton, 1945).

7. Gellhorn, E., *Physiological Foundations of Neurology and Psychiatry* (Minneapolis: University of Minnesota Press, 1953).

8. Grinker, R. R., and Spiegel, J. P., *Men Under Stress* (London: J. & A. Churchill, Ltd., 1945).

9. Grinker, R. R., and Spiegel, J. P., *War Neuroses* (Philadelphia: Blakiston, 1945).

10. Hamilton, D. M., and Wall, J. H., Hospital Treatment of Patients with Psychoneurotic Disorders, *American Journal of Psychiatry*, 98:551, 1941.

11. Hull, C. L., *Principles of Behavior* (New York: Appleton-Century, 1943).

12. Jacobson, E., *Progressive Relaxation* (Chicago: University of Chicago Press, 1938).

13. Johnson, H. K., Psychoanalysis: A Critique, *Psychiatric Quarterly*, 22:321, 1948.

14. Jones, M. C., Elimination of Children's Fears, *Journal of Experimental Psychology*, 7:382, 1924.

15. Kalinowsky, L. B., and Hoch, P. H., *Shock Treatments* (London: Heinemann, 1946).

16. Kantorovich, N. V., An Attempt at Curing Alcoholism by Associated Reflexes, *Novoye v Reflexologii i Nervnoy Sistemy*, 3:436, 1929: cited by G. H. S. Razran, in Conditional Withdrawal Responses with Shock as the Conditioning Stimulus in Adult Human Subjects, *Psychological Bulletin*, 31:111, 1934.

17. Knight, R. P., Evaluation of the Results of Psychoanalytic Therapy, *American Journal of Psychiatry*, 98:434, 1941.

18. Landis, C., A Statistical Evaluation of Psychotherapeutic Methods, in L. E. Hinsie, *Concepts and Problems of Psychotherapy* (New York: Columbia University Press, 1937).

19. La Verne, A. A., Rapid Coma Technique of Carbon Dioxide Inhalation Therapy, *Diseases of the Nervous System*, 14:141, 1953.

20. Martin, C. A., and Lemieux, L. H., Electro-choc et psychonévroses, *Laval méd.*, 14:579, 1949; *Psychological Abstracts*, 25:467, 1951.

21. Martin, G. L., Sedative Insulin Treatment of Anxiety in the Anxiety Neurosis, *Journal of Nervous and Mental Diseases*, 109:347, 1949.

22. Masserman, J. H., *Behavior and Neurosis* (Chicago: University of Chicago Press, 1943).

23. Max, L. W., Breaking Up a Homosexual Fixation by the Conditioned Reaction Technique: A Case Study, *Psychological Bulletin*, 32:734, 1935.

24. Meduna, L. J., *Carbon Dioxide Therapy* (Springfield, Ill.: Charles C Thomas, 1950).

25. Miller, N. E., Learnable Drives and Rewards, in S. Stevens, ed., *Handbook of Experimental Psychology* (New York: Wiley, 1950).

26. Miller, N. E., and Dollard, J., *Social Learning and Imitation* (London: Routledge, 1945).

27. Mowrer, O. H., and Viek, P., Experimental Analogue of Fear from a Sense of Helplessness, *Journal of Abnormal and Social Psychology*, 43:193, 1948.

28. Pavlov, I. P., *Conditioned Reflexes*, G. V. Anrep, trans. and ed. (London: Oxford University Press, 1927).

29. Pavlov, I. P., *Conditioned Reflexes and Psychiatry*, W. H. Gantt, trans. and ed. (New York: International Publishers, 1941).

30. Salter, A., *Conditioned Reflex Therapy* (New York: Creative Age Press, 1950).
31. Salter, A., *The Case Against Psychoanalysis* (New York: Holt, 1952).
32. Sargant, W., and Craske, N., Modified Insulin Therapy in War Neuroses, *Lancet*, 2:212, 1941.
33. Sargant, W., and Slater, E., Treatment by Insulin in Sub-Shock Doses, *Journal of Nervous and Mental Diseases*, 105:493, 1947.
34. Teitelbaum, H. A., Hoekstra, C. S., Goldstein, D. N., Harris, I. D., Woods, R. M., and Cohen, D., Treatment of Psychiatric Disorders Due to Combat by Means of a Group Therapy Program and Insulin in Sub-Shock Doses, *Journal of Nervous and Mental Diseases*, 104:123, 1946.
35. Wilder, J., Facts and Figures on Psychotherapy, *Journal of Clinical Psychopathology*, 7:311, 1945.
36. Willoughby, R. R., Some Properties of the Thurstone Personality Schedule and a Suggested Revision, *Journal of Social Psychology*, 3:401, 1932.
37. Willoughby, R. R., Norms for the Clark-Thurstone Inventory, *Journal of Social Psychology*, 5:91, 1934.
38. Wohlgemuth, A., *Critical Examination of Psychoanalysis* (London: Allen & Unwin, 1923).
39. Wolpe, J., An Approach to the Problem of Neurosis Based on the Conditioned Response, Dissertation, University of the Witwatersrand, 1948.
40. Wolpe, J., Need-Reduction, Drive-Reduction and Reinforcement: A Neurophysiological View, *Psychological Review*, 57:19, 1950.
41. Wolpe, J., Genesis of Neurosis: An Objective Account, *South African Medical Journal*, 24:613, 1950.
42. Wolpe, J., Experimental Neuroses as Learned Behavior, *British Journal of Psychology*, Gen. Sect. 43:243, 1952.
43. Wolpe, J., Formation of Negative Habits: A Neurophysiological View, *Psychological Review*, 59:290, 1952.
44. Wolpe, J., Objective Psychotherapy of the Neuroses, *South African Medical Journal*, 26:825, 1952.
45. Wolpe, J., Learning Theory and "Abnormal Fixations," *Psychological Review*, 60:111, 1953.
46. Wolpe, J., Further Notes on Experimental Neuroses (to be published).
47. Zbrozyna, A. W., Phenomenon of Non-Identification of a Stimulus Operating Against Different Physiological Backgrounds in Dogs, *Lodzkie Towarzystwo Naukowe*, 3, 26, 1953 (in Polish with English summary).

ROBERT A. HOGAN

Implosive Therapy in the Short-Term Treatment of Psychotics

Implosive therapy bears certain resemblances to Wolpe's reciprocal inhibition.

As Hogan points out, both are based essentially on learning-theory techniques. The major difference seems to be that the implosive therapist stresses maximum anxiety experience without giving the client any instructions to relax.

The statistical pilot research study included in this paper is an interesting attempt to validate the effectiveness of the technique.

THEORETICAL BACKGROUND AND METHODOLOGY

IN MAY 1961, Stampfl[7]* presented a paper at the University of Illinois outlining a new form of treatment, implosive therapy, which is based on principles of learning theory. London[3] reviewed implosive therapy in his publication *Modes and Morals of Psychotherapy*. In brief, Stampfl viewed the emotional symptoms of the neurotic as avoidance responses which are learned and perpetuated on the basis of anxiety reduction. He indicated that anxiety (learned fear) drives the neurotic's symptoms; if anxiety could be extinguished, the symptoms would be eliminated. He hypothesized that extinction of the anxiety would take place when the conditioned

From *Psychotherapy: Theory, Research and Practice*, Vol. 3, No. 1, February 1966.

* Superior numbers refer to the list of references at the end of this article.

stimuli which elicit anxiety were present in the absence of primary reinforcement. According to his formulations, this would occur if the therapist could reproduce the conditioned stimulus (CS) cues associated with significant conflicts in the patient's life, and have the patient re-experience the emotions and anxiety related to these conflicts in the absence of primary reinforcement. These conditioned cues are reproduced by the therapist, for the patient, through the medium of imagery. The therapist directs the client·to play-act various scenes using imagery which is directly related to dynamically significant areas of disturbance. By this means the clinician symbolically reproduces or restates the original CS cues which elicit the symptoms. Since there is an absence of primary reinforcement (real occurrence of the feared event), extinction occurs. High levels of anxiety are obtained throughout this process and are considered by Stampfl essential for extinction.

Implosive treatment procedures developed jointly by Stampfl, Golias, and Hogan have been used with adults and children. In the typical implosive session, the client is instructed to shut his eyes and to picture, as clearly as possible, scenes directed by the therapist. The imagery and words of the therapist (conditioned cues) are related to significant dynamic areas of conflict in the person's life. It has been our experience that these conflicts are usually associated with fears of bodily injury, with the expression of overt and subtle aggression, with sexual conflicts, with feelings related to fears of rejection, and with guilt resulting from inappropriate prior behavior. The client is instructed to imagine these key scenes and is encouraged to experience as much anxiety, tension, and emotionality as possible during the session. He is requested to cooperate further in this experience by avoiding the impulse to open his eyes, to think of other scenes, to ask questions, or to make unnecessary movements, since these actions tend to help the patient avoid intense reactions.

By observing the overt behavior and reactions of the individual, the therapist is aided in the selection of appropriate cues. He can then place special emphasis on those pictures which seem to elicit the most anxiety. Typical responses by the client include sobs, crying, clenching of hands, muscle twitches, and anguished facial grimaces. These observed reactions act as feedback and usually indicate that the therapist is obtaining the desired reaction.

Dynamic areas are interrelated. Working through the conflicts in one area allows the therapist to move with greater ease through other areas of disturbance. For this reason, the implosive therapist will usually begin with themes related to fears, move on to expressions of aggression, and only later deal with conflicts related to past rejections, sexuality, and guilt. Since there appears to be a hierarchy of learned patterns of behavior, eliminating minor symptoms and dealing with less important areas of conflict first facilitate proceeding to the more significant areas of disturbance. Just as Little Albert's fear of a rat generalized to all furry animals and objects,[8] extinction of anxiety and conflict in one dynamic area tends to generalize to all similar situations. Extinction then is to a class of cues, to a stimulus compound, rather than to a single individual cue.

The therapist arrives so quickly at central areas of fear and conflict in implosion because of the following four points: (1) The information obtained in the intake interview points to the unique aspects of the patient's conflicts. (2) The therapist is guided by past experience and tends to employ implosive scenes that have been successful in the past. (Those scenes most often associated with the areas of conflict are described throughout this article.) (3) Observation of the bodily reactions of the client indicate the effectiveness of the probe. (4) The concept of generalization: the precise trauma does not have to be relived, but something similar to it aids in implosion. For example, a child who has been beaten many times by a parent could benefit from a series of cues wherein a monster attacks him. The closer one comes to an actual experience the more effective the procedure. But the principle that extinction is to a class of cues and not to an individual cue still prevails.

IMPLOSION OF PHOBIAS

In phobias the core of the conflict is specific and often associated with a clear real-life experience. Phobic reactions have been eliminated in a therapy session of one hour with implosive techniques. The typical session might be as follows:

A person afraid of a snake would be requested to view himself picking up and handling a snake. Attempts would be made to have him become aware of his reactions to the animal. He would be instructed to feel how slimy the snake was. Next, he would be asked to experience the snake crawling over his body and biting and ripping his flesh. Scenes of snakes crushing or swallowing him, or perhaps his falling into a pit of snakes, would be appropriate implosions.

Similarly, an acrophobic would be requested to imagine himself falling off a high building or cliff, or perhaps be instructed to picture himself falling through space and in complete darkness. Ideally, the person should be made aware of his feelings and sensations while falling. Then he should feel the impact of his body with the ground and view his crushed, broken body. It is important that the therapist emphasize how the person looks and feels throughout the scenes. If the client should recall an actual traumatic experience, the clinician should center succeeding imagery around that experience.

IMPLOSION AND AGGRESSION

In dealing with the dynamics of aggression, the implosive therapist employs images in which the client is encouraged to express hostility toward hated and despised persons in his life, such as parents, siblings, relatives, employers, or teachers. Little by little the person is encouraged to picture a violent scene in which he may beat up one of these significant people in his life. Such scenes might include whipping, cutting up the hated person with a knife or ax, destroying the hated person's personal possessions, or expressing any other appropriate imagery in which the client can relive sadistic feelings. The experience is intensified by having the patient verbalize his real or imagined grievances against the object of his hostility.

Humans learn not only the mode of expressing aggression, but they also learn to fear the aggressive expression of others. Fears of castration and of bodily injury are among the most common dynamics observed by the clinical psychologist. The implosive therapist attempts to work through and eliminate these learned fears through scenes in which the patient is symbolically beaten, whipped, castrated, mutilated, or killed. The vividness and detail of the session should not be limited in any way, since the most meaningful, clinically successful sessions are achieved in those periods when the client experiences maximum anxiety.

IMPLOSION AND REJECTION

Having the patient experience a series of imageries related to rejection is often crucial. Scenes in which the person imagines that no one loves him, or ever loved him, or in which he pictures a situation wherein everyone refuses to communicate with him are very effective. Imagining being abandoned, or being an uncared for, unloved, cold, hungry baby in a crib, for example, would produce an intense reaction.

IMPLOSION AND GUILT

In dealing with the dynamics of guilt, the implosive therapist, in the later stages of treatment, will have the individual symbolically and in imagery repeat the violations of his personal code, which result in high levels of anxiety. In the latter part of such imagery, there will be scenes where the individual is caught (more anxiety) and then punished. Combined implosive scenes such as violation of a value system and punishment may also include rejection by significant people in the person's life. A typical set of imagery might include the patient's masturbating, his being discovered by his parents, and finally his being punished and rejected by the family. Although an implosive therapist may have a client imagine that he is confessing a transgression of his personal code, such as infidelity, to an important person in his life, the implosive therapist would not advocate an actual confession, as suggested by Mowrer,[5] to important persons in the client's life. Such an admission in real life might result in primary reinforcement for the client. This type of reinforcement would occur if a client's parent, wife, or husband rejected or punished the client following a confession.

While we are considering scenes of guilt, confession, and punishment, we should mention that variation of imagery is desirable. A situation where the patient is not punished for inappropriate behavior sometimes produces more anxiety than a scene in which the person is punished for his transgressions. This is understandable, since in life, punishment often ends an uncomfortable period of time for a person who has committed a misdeed. This factor seems to be one of the dynamics behind some patients' unconscious drive for punishment.

CLINICAL IMPLOSIVE CASES

The following description of an unsuccessful case jointly treated by Golias and Hogan in 1961 on an experimental basis is illustrative of some of the techniques and difficulties in the short-term treatment of psychotics.

> Mr. D., a 29-year-old chronic schizophrenic, was exposed to over fifty sessions with one or both of the therapists. He had been hospitalized for over ten years with a history of hallucinations, delusions,

withdrawal, aggressiveness, heterosexual and homosexual contacts, chronic masturbation, and attempted suicide. Mr. D. was a typical chronic, back ward patient at the time of initial contact. His mother, a prostitute who had conceived the patient in a common-law marriage, died when Mr. D. was five. Subsequently, he had been rejected by relatives, and raised in an unending series of foster homes. He had been beaten, exploited, and had been the subject of homosexual assault on at least two known occasions. When in his most regressed phases, he would assume catatonic posturings and hallucinate. At other periods, he would attempt to preach religion to other patients, bother the chaplain, and verbalize paranoid thoughts that others were attempting to read his mind or seduce him.

Early in treatment, the therapists concentrated on the subject's fears of bodily injury and castration and on his hostility toward others. We had him express aggression toward his former foster parents. We tried to get him to relive assault traumas. We had him imagine that the therapists would beat him or sexually violate him, since these were the initial fears he verbalized. We sought to remove his avoidance responses of us. Throughout this period of treatment, the patient would dissociate affect connected with scenes. This defensive procedure was observable by his habit of rolling his eyes back into his head and partially hallucinating. Each time we would force him to stop and would reapply the imagery. After ten or fifteen sessions we began to move into other areas of conflict, such as his feelings toward parents, his rejection, and personal responsibility to others. When the patient began to miss appointments, we went up to his ward and continued verbal cues even though he refused to imagine scenes. During this period the patient completely withdrew from others, refused to talk, used catatonic mannerisms to avoid others, and seemed completely regressed. The therapists interpreted his behavior as an avoidance of the treatment sessions, and especially as an avoidance of cues associated with rejection by his mother, whom he hated. Under the assumption that Mr. D. knew and understood everything in his environment, we continued to bombard him with verbal cues. For example, we told him to imagine himself in his mother's womb, receiving her blood and nurturance upon which he was dependent. We had him nursing from her breasts. We gave verbal cues associated with his rejection of her, and associated with his known fantasy of wanting to drop hand grenades on her grave. We continued similar sessions for about six weeks, while the patient ignored us, and refused to speak. We frequently told him we knew he understood us, and that no matter what he did we were going to continue the visits. In spite of his defenses, we knew that the cues were partially effective because of occasional involuntary muscle spasms, eye movements, and other overt body signs. One day, with no warning, the patient came down to the therapists' office and said he was prepared to resume treatment. He stated that he could no longer fight us. From this point in treatment, we re-emphasized themes related to his fear of castration and assault, had him relive rejection by both parents, and allowed him to express, in imagery, his frustration and aggression toward those he hated. While expressing his true feelings toward his mother, the patient abandoned religious interests and began to avoid the hospital chaplain. Finally, he expressed and worked through feeling associated with religious conflict. He had equated religion with mother, and he hated both. We had him explore some of his narcissistic fantasies, such as his desire to rule and dominate the world. We explored his sexual conflicts by having him imagine being both aggressor and victim in homosexual and heterosexual conflicts. Finally, we explored his dependence on both the hospital and an elderly woman patient with whom he associated and whom he dominated as a mother substitute to wait on him and absorb his displaced aggression.

After approximately fifty sessions, the patient seemed to take on sociopathic behaviors which he never seemed to unlearn. He left the hospital during the day to attempt a job as a bus boy in a local restaurant. He lost the job because of his lack of responsibility and attempted manipulations of others. He was then hospitalized for a hernia operation. Prior to surgery the therapists imploded his fears of castration and bodily mutilation again. After surgery, Mr. D. secured a job in a factory, found an apartment, and obtained a release from the hospital. He would report back once a month for therapy sessions and seemed to enjoy the visits with his old patient friends. In his dealing with employers, he continued to manipulate and take advantage of their kindness. Existence outside of work was lonely and unrewarding as the patient had no friends. He remained at work for one and a half years before he was hospitalized.

The case illustrated the difficulty in getting psychotics to cooperate in treatment even though the therapist may be aware of the key dynamics. The psychotic's ability to dissociate or withdraw completely from his environment can be overcome, however, by forcing the person to experience emotion, if all fails. In dealing with neurotics and those suffering from acute, less chronic psychotic episodes, the defenses are not as ingrained and the person typically cooperates with the therapist after he is given a rationale for the procedures.

The case poses other issues concerning the chronically psychotic individual who must fit into society after a long period of absence with few skills or friends to help him. Our analysis of Mr. D. and his failure to make a final adjustment would stress his inability to learn the rewards of mature living, his return to habits of masturbation, partly to fill in periods of loneliness; his guilt over renewed violations of his personal code; and the fact that he was returning to friends and the protection of the hospital. Prolonged hospitalization offered many primary reinforcements that continued his dependence and made this life more attractive than the outside world.

In a second case treated by the author in private practice, Mrs. F. had a typical psychotic MMPI with the following "T" scores: L 43; F 70; K 38; Hs 68; D 78; Hy 77; Pd 81; Mf 68; Pa 85; Pt 83; Sc 101; Ma 65 on pretesting. She had been treated in a private sanitarium with an acute psychotic diagnosis. At first interview she was depressed; had fears of people, snakes, spiders, dogs, high places, and water; had sexual conflicts and, in our judgment, was very near rehospitalization. Mrs. F. was seen for five months or about twenty individual implosive sessions. Her husband, a rather passive person, was treated in five individual implosive sessions, and the couple had a few joint interviews. Following the treatment phase a post MMPI (L 43; F 60; K 44; Hs 58; D 65; Hy 63; Pd 86; Mf 45; Pa 73; Pt 65; Sc 67; Ma 68) was administered. Objectively, at least, great change had been made, and clinically the patient seemed to be lucid, controlled, and no longer afraid of going insane. Neither did she exhibit any of the previous fears. She had resolved many difficulties in her marriage relationship and seemed to have resolved her guilt associated with an extramarital affair.

However, in many ways her behavior was similar to Mr. D.'s as he approached his first job. She did not want to contact people outside of the family, including in-laws. She was afraid to face old friends who had known of her troubles, and she refused to take part in social and community activities as we had requested. Implosive techniques had resolved many of her avoidance responses and had allowed her to face repressed conflicts, but she had yet to try and find success in new learnings. For about one year, I lost contact with Mrs. F., but then we had a chance to interview her on a return visit to her home city. During that year, the patient had the opportunity to attempt new learning; she had taken part in community activities, had found time to invite relatives and friends to the home for visits, and had begun to express concern for others One manifestation of her maturity was her new-found sense of personal responsibility. She even reminded the therapist of his responsibility to others when I responded to her questions that I was not currently taking on private cases. None of the previously mentioned pathology had reappeared.

The key differences in the two cases appear to be the long-time effects of continued hospitalization on the chronic patient, the opportunity to learn new behaviors, the degree of original disturbance, and the fact that Mrs. F. had the support of her family.

COMPARISON OF IMPLOSION WITH OTHER THERAPISTS

In analyzing differences between implosive therapy and other systems of treatment, it appears that the implosive therapist is not limited by the manipulations (avoidance responses) so typically observed in nondirective and other verbal therapies. The implosive therapist determines on the basis of projective testing and the initial interview the key areas of conflict for each person. Then he begins to have the person imagine significant scenes almost immediately.

The experience of anxiety associated with significant conflicts and nonreinforcement of specific imagery is considered the primary key to the therapeutic success. It is not the relationship to the therapist. For example, clients have been told to go home and imagine specific scenes without the aid of a therapist. Relief from symptoms has followed such a procedure. The clinical relationship is necessary in enlisting the cooperation of the client, and, in the case of psychotics, in forcing him to experience certain feelings, but the nature of the experience and the type of cues the client eventually deals with determine the success of the treatment.

There is no attempt to have the client develop insight into his behavior, although typically patients do develop understanding of their behavior. This position agrees with some of the observations of Hobbs[1] on insight.

As a person relives traumatic events in verbal therapy, catharsis or an emotional release occurs. Often the emotional experiences or angry outbursts of clients are limited by verbal therapists; whereas, one who is implosively oriented would always attempt to extend and magnify any emotional experience.

Some clients seem to benefit from the emotional expression of role playing, and others seem to improve following catharsis in verbal therapy. However, the degree and scope of emotional expression, as well as the area of conflict emphasized, are usually limited by the client, both deliberately and through unconscious avoidance of anxiety. In implosive sessions the control of the experience rests primarily with the therapist, who develops the series of implosions based on his professional experience, the specific problems of the client, and the feedback from minute-to-minute interaction in treatment.

In those current attempts to modify psychotic behavior through the presentation of candy or other reinforcement, the psychologist seems to be dealing with the approach aspect of learning. Since much of the psychotic's behavior appears to be based on avoidance responses, the aforementioned implosive techniques have been directed at modification of these avoidance responses by extinguishing the anxiety which drives this behavior.

The treatment technique outlined by Wolpe[9] possesses certain similarities to implosive therapy. Both are based on learning-theory techniques. Wolpe employs imagery under hypnosis in an attempt to get the client to approach a hierarchy of anxiety cues. Some of the differences between the techniques are that the implosive therapist stresses maximum anxiety experience without giving the client any instructions to relax. The depth of cues evoked almost immediately in implosive sessions, the range of conflicts considered, and the requirement that the client consciously cooperate in therapy sessions constitute other distinctions between the two methods.

PILOT RESEARCH STUDY

To test the effectiveness of implosive therapy with psychotics, I hypothesized that patients treated by implosion would show significant improvement over traditionally treated controls. In this investigation, we evaluated 50 patients from the intensive treatment ward of Hawthorden State Hospital, Cleveland, Ohio. These patients were assigned to implosive and nonimplosive therapists by the ward physician. The assignment was made on the basis of time available in each therapist's schedule and without knowledge that the study was in progress. As a result, 26 patients were assigned to implosive therapy and 24 to nonimplosive treatment.

The hospital records were consulted to ascertain the similarity of the two groups on a series of variables which included sex, age, education, intellectual ability, prior hospitalization, and length of treatment.

Intellectual ability was established by assigning the patients to one of five ability levels: borderline, dull normal, average, bright normal, or superior, on the basis of the Wechsler Adult Intelligence Scale or the Kent Emergency Scale in addition to the test examiner's professional judgment of the level of intellectual functioning. These levels were subsequently averaged for statistical comparison. The median test described by Siegel,[6] was employed to test the significance of differences for each of these variables. There were no differences for each of the aforementioned variables.

When a patient was first accepted on the ward, he was administered the Minnesota Multiphasic Personality Inventory Short

Form corrected by K as a measure of his initial disturbance. The pretherapy MMPI scores were used to establish the similarity of the implosive and nonimplosive groups with regard to the character of the patient's initial disturbance. Analysis of variance procedures revealed that there were no significant differences between the experimental and control groups. The rounded means of the control group's MMPI's were L 55, F 69, K 50, Hs 55, D 69, Hy 60, Pd 70, Pa 68, Pt 64, Sc 72, and Ma 61. The approximate means of the experimental group were L 51, F 67, K 51, Hs 60, D 70, Hy 64, Pd 67, Pa 65, Pt 66, Sc 75, and Ma 63.

Each patient on the unit lived within a semicontrolled environment since he came into daily contact with the same fellow patients and the same members of the hospital staff. Every patient on the unit participated in group therapy and occupational therapy, in addition to recreation, work and educational programs. Full ground privileges were given.

The post MMPI's were administered at the time a patient was released from the hospital or transferred from the ward. This option was ultimately based on the decision of the physician, after consultation with the members of the intensive treatment staff. The interim between pre and post MMPI's established the period of time in treatment. Individual therapists, all psychologists, had similar academic and therapy experience prior to the investigation, and all therapists were aware that the study was in progress.

RESULTS

Comparison of the pre and post MMPI's of the experimental and control groups, using a simple analysis of variance technique, revealed no significant changes in the control groups from pre to post testing. The implosive group shifted significantly away from pathology on five MMPI scales: F, Hs, D, Hy Sc. These findings are summarized in the table on page 292.

The approximate post experimental group means are L 52, F 58, K 52, Hs 51, D 59, Hy 57, Pd 61, Pa 59, Pt 58, Sc 65, and Ma 59. The rounded-off post test means of the control group were L 51, F 70, K 52, Hs 52, D 62, Hy 58, Pd 70, Pa 66, Pt 65, Sc 73, and Ma 64.

Since clinical psychologists have traditionally considered MMPI T scores of 70 and above as a sign of pathology, we analyzed shifts in these extreme scores by means of chi square. All scores 70 and above, (pre- and post-experimental group, and pre- and post-control group), were placed in a fourfold table and evaluated. The results

ANALYSIS OF VARIANCE COMPARISON OF SELECT PRE
AND POST MMPI's OF THE EXPERIMENTAL GROUP

Scale	Implosive Pre-Mean	Implosive Post-Mean	Source of Variance	SS	df	MS	F
F	67.961	58.923	Within	6732.8	50	134.656	7.886**
			Between	1062.0	1	1062.030	
Hs	60.115	51.846	Within	6202.0	50	124.040	7.166*
			Between	888.9	1	888.940	
D	70.576	59.884	Within	8885.0	50	177.70	8.363**
			Between	1486.2	1	1486.23	
Hy	64.576	57.0	Within	5668.3	50	1113.367	6.583*
			Between	746.3	1	746.320	
Sc	75.346	65.153	Within	13929.2	50	278.585	4.847*
			Between	1350.4	1	1350.480	

* significant at .05.   ** significant at .01.

reveal a significant shift for the implosive group (at the .01 level of confidence) away from pathology. The chi square was 9.406. Similar results were obtained when all scores of 80 and above were considered. This evaluation resulted in a chi square of 9.3265, significant at the .01 level of confidence. The experimental group shifted an average of − 11.47 in the 70 and above analysis, and − 8.12 when scores 80 and above were considered. The nonimplosive group showed a mean shift of − .59 when scores 70 and above were evaluated and an average shift of + .88 for scores 80 and above.

The status of each patient was followed for one year after treatment. At the end of this time, cases released or discharged from the hospital were considered successful; whereas patients who were transferred to other units, and/or rehospitalized at Hawthornden or other institutions were classified as failures. Chi squares analysis of this data resulted in findings significant at the .02 level of confidence with a *chi* square of 6.445. Of the 26 implosive patients 18 were classified as successful, as opposed to 8 out of 24 controls in this category.

DISCUSSION

The results support the value of the implosive techniques over more traditional forms of treatment and suggest that short-term treatment of psychotics is possible. The evidence from the MMPI and the follow-up status of each subject were the major criteria for improvement; however, it should be understood that an evaluation of each patient's behavior was made by the psychiatrist in charge of the unit and members of the intensive treatment staff (representing all disciplines) before an individual was considered significantly improved and eligible for release.

Certain facts, however, may have influenced the results. All patients included in this study were on medication at one time or another during their hospitalization. There was no control over the amounts or types of medication administered. It was the policy on the intensive-treatment ward to keep the patients at low levels of tranquilization. Mendelsohn, Penman, and Schiele[4] studied the effects of medication on the MMPI and concluded that this instrument is relatively free from undesirable influence from medication. In general, the influence of medication on treatment is not clear from a review of the current literature.

Even though patients in both groups participated in group therapy (implosive cases with implosive therapists, and nonimplosive cases with traditional therapists) and other types of hospital programs during the experiment, these parallel activities do introduce uncontrolled variables that limit the value of the study.

In this investigation there was no set period of time in treatment for each patient. The implosive group averaged 4.88 months in treatment and the controls averaged 8.21 months. Each subject was given as much time as possible on the intensive-treatment ward and in all cases was permitted to remain if there appeared to be any chance of improvement. Typically, a patient was given one individual and one group session each week; however, when patients were upset or in a critical phase of treatment, it was not uncommon for the members of either group to be seen more frequently by their therapist. Statistically, the period of time in treatment as a variable between groups was not significantly different.

Variables associated with the therapist are difficult to evaluate. All therapists had at least master's level training in clinical psychology and from three to four years' clinical experience. Each therapist was under supervision of the chief psychologist, who treated one of the control cases. It is impossible to measure the effects of such variables as therapist enthusiasm for a new method, or the possible awareness on the part of patients that the experimental methods were something new or unusual. These variables, of course, could account for the observed changes.

SUMMARY

Implosive therapy, its theoretical foundation, and clinical techniques, supplemented by illustrative case histories, are presented in conjunction with the results of empirical research. The subjects, 26 experimental and 24 control, treated by implosive and traditional methods of psychotherapy respectively, and equated for degree of initial disturbance on the MMPI were evaluated after short-term treatment and upon a one-year follow-up. The experimental subjects (implosively treated) showed significant shifts away from pathology, improved on five MMPI scales, and were significantly successful (.02) in terms of release from a state hospital setting.

REFERENCES

1. Hobbs, N., Sources of Gain in Psychotherapy, *American Psychologist,* 17: 741-45, 1962.
2. Hogan, R. A., The Implosive Technique: A Process of Re-education Through the Application of Principles of Learning for Emotionally Disturbed Individuals. Unpublished Ph.D. dissertation, Western Reserve University, September 1963.
3. London, P., *Modes and Morals of Psychotherapy* (New York: Holt, Rinehart & Winston, 1964).
4. Mendelsohn, R. M., Penman, A. A., and Schiele, B. C., Massive Chlorpamazine Therapy: The Nature of Behavioral Changes, *Psychiatric Quarterly,* 33:55-75, 1959.
5. Mowrer, O. H., *The Crisis in Religion and Psychiatry* (Princeton, N.J.: Van Nostrand, 1961).
6. Siegel, S., *Nonparametric Statistics for the Behavior Sciences* (New York: McGraw-Hill, 1956).
7. Stampfl, T., Implosive Therapy: A Learning Theory Derived Psychodynamic Therapeutic Technique. In *Critical Issues in Clinical Psychology,* R. C. LaBarba and O. B. Dent, eds. (New York: Academic Press, 1967).
8. Watson, J. B., and Rayner, R., Conditioned Emotional Reactions, *Journal of Experimental Psychology,* 3: 1-14, 1920.
9. Wolpe, J., *Psychotherapy by Reciprocal Inhibition* (London: Oxford University Press, 1953).

E. LAKIN PHILLIPS
SALAH EL-BATRAWI

Learning Theory and Psychotherapy Revisited: *With Notes on Illustrative Cases*

This paper by Phillips and Batrawi is an unusually clear statement of the newer applications of learning theory to psychotherapy. They argue for emphasizing the response (R) rather than the stimulus (S) or cognitive (O) factors in psychotherapy. While they present cogent evidence for the necessity of changing the response it is unfortunate that they apparently do not realize that despite their theoretical differences many of the more traditional forms of psychotherapy may do the same thing. For example, many of the psychoanalysts' interpretations or labelings actually have the effect of extinguishing certain responses by making them ego-alien. When a patient is told repeatedly that his homosexuality is "infantile," the effect is to make the homosexual response unpleasant and aversive. If many of the non-learning-theory therapies in this volume are examined in this manner it will become clearer how this technique operates. When a psychotherapist, by keeping silent, does not supply the customary reward to neurotic statements, he is often helping to extinguish such attitudes. This is of course not all of psychoanalysis, but it may be an interesting way of looking at the material.

CLINICIANS INTERESTED in the experimental and conceptual bases for clinical theory and practice have often noted the importance of learning theory for psychotherapy (Eysenck,[6]* Bandura,[2]

From *Psychotherapy*, Vol. 1, No. 4, Fall 1964.

*Superior numbers refer to the list of references at the end of this article.

Phillips,[15] Wolpe,[22] Shaw[18]). A still wider influence of the applications of learning theory to psychotherapy has been seen in the contributions of Dollard and Miller,[4] Mowrer,[13] and Shoben.[19]

An earlier body of literature, stemming from the studies of Watson and Rayner,[20] Mary C. Jones,[9, 10] Lehner,[12] Burnham,[3] Holt,[8] and Willoughby, also illustrates attempts to relate experimental approaches to clinical problems. In many ways the earlier work of Watson and Jones (as Eysenck's volume[6] indicates) is more suggestive of heuristic leads than many later studies and theoretical developments. In essence, the theoretical and experimental work of Dollard and Miller, and of Shoben—as well as the stimulating volume by Pascal[14]—emphasize in relating psychotherapy to behavior theory *one* of several choices of learning theory variables—the stimulus variables.

The purpose in revisiting learning theory in relation to psychotherapy and behavior change is to suggest that the emphasis on stimulus variables may not be as promising as an emphasis on response variables.

The presumptive value of stimulus-centered learning theory to psychotherapy and behavior change will be reviewed first.

Alexander and French[1] stress the importance of the original stimulus and state the basis for the effectiveness of psychotherapy to be the re-exposure of the patient to the past emotional stress that gave rise to the problems. In most psychoanalytic writings there is a strong emphasis on the re-exposure to, and redintegration of, the original stimulus situation giving rise to the pathology, so that from the (therapeutic) redintegration new solutions to old problems will presumably arise.

Shoben[19] illustrates the same point in his discussion of catharsis: ". . . catharsis will be effective when it involves (a) the symbolic reinstatement of the repressed cues for anxiety, (b) within the context of a warm, permissive, nonjudgmental relationship" (p. 72).

Further discussion by Shoben adds that under the conditions described, counterconditioning can effectively take place. Thus the prerequisite for counterconditioning appears to be catharsis.

An even more explicit statement of the importance of the stimulus in overcoming psychopathology is contained in Pascal's writings:[14] "Failure to identify the pertinent stimulus situation results in a 'hit-or-miss' approach to behavior change" (p. 88).

And, "Failure to define the stimulus situation related to the deviant behavior not only results in variability in efforts to change behavior but also makes it impossible to gauge the effects of laboratory procedures calculated to change behavior" (p. 88).

And finally: ". . . the stimulus is all we can manipulate" (p. 89).

Coupled with these descriptive emphases on the original stimulus situation is a reliance on what Shoben[19] calls the "underlying anxiety" and its modification as the chief aim of the psychotherapeutic process (p. 54). As if to wrap up the whole therapeutic and behavior change enterprise in terms of the stimulus variables, Shoben says:

"Thus, the conversational content of counseling consists chiefly in the discussion of the patient's anxieties and the conditions which either currently evoke them or seem to be casually linked in some historical sense to them" (p. 59).

In constructing theory and practice in relation to psychotherapy and behavior change, we have in a sense three options. We can emphasize the original stimulus situations held to be related to the observable pathology. This is what we call an "S" type theory, and the quotations above amply illustrate this type.

We might also develop theory and practice based on "O" variables (phenomenological, "inner events," cognitive or central processes). The Rogerian position is the one most familiar to us employing O-centered variables, although a careful reading of much psychoanalytic literature shows that O-centered variables are often employed (principally in the ways in which the alleged original stimuli "flow" through the psychic economy in the form of "unconscious motivation"). Some types of eclectic therapy borrow now and again from cognitive variables, but Rogers has more exclusively dealt with O-centered variables than has any other therapist.

Our third choice, the one most neglected, but the one needing the strongest emphasis according to the present position, is a theory based on "R" variables. It is surprising that more R-centered theories have not been promulgated. There is only one volume in the annals of psychotherapy which gives much credence to R-centered theories of therapy, with good coverage of reciprocal inhibition therapy, symptom treatment, various negative practice and reconditioning theories, and some excursion into the uses of feedback to control the responses of the patient (Eysenck.)[6]

R-theories have been considered somewhat unworthy of serious attention. Psychoanalytic and cognitive therapists have contended that injury to the organism could occur if therapeutic efforts centered on removal of symptoms, reconditioning, or generally on what we here call response-centered methods. Response manipulation has been eschewed by all but a few. An example of strong dismissal of R-centered therapy is seen in the writings of English and Pearson,[5] in their discussion of enuresis in a male child:

"Treatment, therefore, will be directed toward the amelioration of his fear of his own sexual self in relation to persons of the opposite sex. It will not be directed toward the stopping of the enuresis, which after all is only an incidental part of the problem" (p. 272).

And the same authors state further:

"What is called for is intensive psychological treatment that will rid him of his fear of the opposite sex, and in our opinion this is best accomplished through a psychoanalysis, which will take a long time and will certainly have to be continued long after the bed-wetting itself has ceased" (pp. 272-73).

It has been held that attention given to S-centered or O-centered variables will, in the long run, produce changes in R. This is a much accepted but very moot point. The situation here is similar to that observed by Yates regarding "symptom substitution" under conditions of symptom treatment—it is more of a clinical conjecture than anything else.

Another facet of the rapproachement of learning theory and psychotherapy is how various drives or motivations give rise to behavior (or to tendencies to react in given ways) . Skinner, however, has been without a "drive" concept for some time, and other learning theorists have departed more in this respect from Hull than in almost any other respect (Harlow,[7] White[21]). It is now more heuristic and economical to exclude specific drive theory from the study of psychotherapy. (It is at once apparent that an emphasis on S-centered variables is contained in most drive theories, and it is just this choice of variables we wish to avoid.)

In simplest terms, R-centered therapies or theories of therapy allow for as much response manipulation as the ingenuity of the therapists or experimenter can name. The therapeutic problem from the R-theory viewpoint is to produce new responses, or to apply new discriminations to familiar circumstances. We are really much more in control over what the organism *does,* than we are in trying to learn *why* it behaves as it does in a genetic sense.

In an R-centered theory, we simply take the inadequate responses into the matrix of possibilities and ask what alternatives might exist. Thus, in the case of bedwetting, the obvious R-variable is that of "being dry" under a given set of circumstances. It takes very little doing to name the desired criterion or outcome in the case of enuresis or most habit disorders. When we come upon more complex situations, such as those associated with inadequate scholastic achievement under given ability conditions, we may consider the alternative responses to include better study habits, a schedule of studying, a different curriculum, and so forth. The more broad-based and complex the response capability called for, the more resourceful the subject has to become, and (perhaps) the more resourceful the therapeutic enterprise.

One may defend S-centered theories by pointing out that one never does away with the stimulus. One may also point to the logical sequence between S and R, as is commonly done. There is something fundamental in the S-R connection and something *a priori* about the stimulus, one may contend.

True as these arguments may be, they do not carry us far enough. It is more heuristic to distinguish between R-centered variables on the one hand, and S- or O-centered variables on the other hand, in terms of how instrumental they are in producing therapeutic gain, and in terms of their conceptual role in a behavior change theory. For example, in regard to therapeutic technique, we think it is not possible in most complex molar situations to redintegrate the stimulus. We do not think it is clinically feasible, even if it were theoretically desirable, to attempt, with Pascal, Shoben, French and Alexander, to reconstruct the stimulus situation allegedly responsible for the observed psychopathology. Also, "depth" psychology holds that the real core of a problem is hidden by anxiety and repression, and that repression has to be lifted before reliable change can occur. Again, we complicate the picture when, following Shoben,[19] our therapeutic movement is based on an S-centered approach: "A necessary concept in a theory of anxiety is that of repression" (p. 57).

If we pursue the original stimulus, we must deal with the anxiety surrogates or defenders, which, in turn, are bolstered by the phenomenon of repression! How any very cogent clinical practice can actually arise in reference to, or deliberately follow from, such a theory of behavior change is difficult to comprehend.

Aside from the unlikelihood of redintegration of the stimulus, the response itself becomes a cue to further responding. In terms of a feedback loop, we find it possible to leave behind the stimulus in its pristine originality and deal with continuous chains of responding in which each successive juncture is a stimulus to further reactions. We are given the opportunity, as our cybernetic fellows remind us, of continually *steering* the organism's behavior toward some selected behavioral objectives. We are, then, continually dealing with new behavioral discriminations or opportunities, and the behaving organism is, in a real sense, always up to date in its responding. All that is relevant from the past is present in the cogent sense of slanting or tipping the behavior in one or another direction.

What we have available to us as "therapeutic engineers" is a contribution to *immediately present* and *future* selections and discriminations, and not the alternative of doping out all the facets of some original stimulus that allegedly got the ball rolling.

We also object to the stimulus-centered theory in psychotherapy insofar as it states that each new behavioral juncture or choice situation is already determined by the factors involved in each previous juncture. We find it theoretically more useful to consider each juncture determined by the probabilities at hand. These "new choice" situations change to some extent the parameters and introduce different probabilities of responding one way or another (affected by reinforcement or feedback). If in some way changing the probabilities of responding in one direction can be brought about, this changes the response capability of the organism and leaves the importance of the original stimulus further behind.

The newer psychotherapies have at least one important element in common: *teaching the organism new ways of responding.* Such efforts are seen in connection with operant conditioning aversive methods, reciprocally inhibiting methods, structuring and interfering methods, and so forth (Eysenck,[6] Krasner[11]). Any method of behavior change which can increase the range of responding (or focus it, if this is required) can be therapeutic; and methods can be judged by the extent to which they accomplish a response change that is efficient and reliable. We have found it feasible to include in our psychotherapeutic armamentarium such additional resources as programmed instruction, study habits instruction, rigorous scheduling of time and effort, writing therapy, as well as some recourse to talking psychotherapy. We are beginning to prefer, in the university clinic setting at least, intervention that is not classified in the usual psychotherapeutic way at all, but which circumvents references to emotions, to diagnoses, to the history of the difficulty, and so on, and focuses immediately and clearly on the responses needed to overcome the stated problems.

A case in point is that of a 9-year-old girl referred for encopresis:

This child was the oldest of four siblings, having a 7-year-old brother and two sisters, 4 and 2. The child was able in school and had earned scores in the 115-120 I.Q. range.

Her encopresis had been evident for two years, off and on, despite help sought by parents from pediatricians and child guidance clinic personnel. Thorough physical examinations revealed no structural or anatomical reasons for the behavior, and the use of suppositories did not remedy the bad habit.

The mother's reactions had ranged from indulgence through

cajolery to utter exasperation—all without success. At first, the mother had the girl sit on the toilet after breakfast, but did not continue this plan after a week or two when it did not remedy the problem.

By and large, other problems with the child were minor and commonplace. The child attended well to her school work and had good peer relations; there were no other habit disorders, nor had other problems been reported previously at home or at school.

The most likely method of securing relief from the problem appeared to be one of reorganizing the child's schedule. We call this the "Change Plan." The mother had once tried having the girl sit on the toilet—a good beginning—but had not continued this practice long enough to secure results. Some reform of the child's behavior vis-à-vis the annoying symptom was called for. The Plan, therefore, included the following:

1. Seat the child on the toilet for 10 minutes after breakfast; if she defecated, praise her; if not, mention nothing but let her leave to play.

2. After one hour of play, call the child in from her activities and have her sit again on toilet for 10 minutes. (Child was told this plan would be followed.)

3. Continue on hourly scheduling of trips to toilet unless or until child defecated on that day. Repeat daily. Continue this schedule until it was apparent that it was working or its weaknesses were exposed. Report back to therapist within one month.

The parents reported happily that the new program trained the child within about two weeks. A follow-up three months later revealed no setbacks, and another follow-up after an additional four months revealed only one setback.

On the theoretical side of this treatment, we find no interest whatsoever in the possible stimulus origins of the bad habit, no interest in the expected relationship between the child's symptom and the birth of the youngest sibling about two years prior to the onset of the treatment, and so on.

This case was presented to a graduate seminar of clinical psychology students, most of whom had done clerkship tours in clinics, and some of whom had accumulated substantial clinical experience. Twenty-nine categories of spontaneous questions (and implicit theoretical notions) were offered, every one framed from an S-centered or O-centered standpoint.

This is an example of how rigidly clinical intervention is constricted by a strong theoretical bias. We are reminded in this connection of Eysenck's finding[6] that, in so far as he could determine, no child guidance clinics in England used symptom treatment measures for enuresis, despite experimental evidence as to the efficacy of such treatment. The armamentarium in clinical practice is determined largely by precedent (and perhaps to no small extent by folklore)!

Another similar case may illustrate further the reliance on R-centered variables. A boy, age 8½, developed periods of nausea and vomiting, particularly following recess and physical-education periods at school (although this confluence had to be ferreted out in discussions with parents and teachers). The problem had been in evidence off and on for about a year when consultation led to some restructuring of his schoolday experiences and routine. While no previous instance of vomiting had occurred at home, the weeks immediately prior to the beginning of treatment saw sporadic instances of nausea and vomiting at home on days apparently related to strenuous activities or demands at school.

The lad was the oldest of three siblings, one a boy of 6, the other a baby girl of 10 months. The patient had been very successful at school, and was in the 130-140 I.Q. range. He was reported to be willful, stubborn, and given to temper outbursts when thwarted.

This family had consulted a number of medical specialists, believing that the nausea and vomiting had some chemical or neurological basis.

In discussion with the parents it was noted that they yielded to the boy more frequently than they held to their requirements. They overlooked the possibility that the child might be suffering from some "exhaustion symptoms" and that his activity in some respects should be curtailed, particularly at school. They had erred, we feel, in allowing him freedom based on the assumption that their (faulty) attempts at control had caused the "nervous symptoms."

The regimen was extremely simple: disallowing his participation in physical education and recess periods for a tentatively agreed upon period of two weeks. During this period there were no overt instances of vomiting or nausea reported by the child (formerly associated with his requests to go to the nursing quarters of the school owing to his "not feeling well").

At the end of the two-week period, the child was readmitted to physical education (this was preferred to the recess period since more control over his activities could be exercised when the athletic instructor was present, allowing for a gradual reintroduction to games and strenuous activities). Followed by two weeks of symptom-free physical-education-class experience, the boy was admitted to recess periods, by prior plan, only 15 minutes per day (with the proper caution instilled in the observing teacher to report any instances of a return of the symptoms).

The child was able to continue his entire school program free from these symptoms. A follow-up check two years after the activation of treatment indicated no return of the original problems at school or at home.

Preventing the boy from going to the physical education class is not a case of manipulating the stimulus situation to extinguish the undesirable response; it is, rather, a case of temporarily removing the child from a situation in which the development of the new responses would be difficult if not impossible. We wanted to teach the child new ways of responding to a given situation; the stimulus situation itself—the physical education class—is simply a methodological necessity for the therapeutic change plan, not a source of reintegrative materials or an element in an extinction process. In our view, it would be uneconomical and very risky to attempt to extinguish directly or vicariously (through talk or play therapy) the undesirable nausea or vomiting; it was much more productive to teach new responses via a controlled change plan. The controlled change plan involved first removing the child from the prepotent influences (precluding his "practicing" the unwanted behavior), then reintroducing him to these influences on a guarded and tentative basis. The old pathological responses were supplanted by new discriminations, much the same as a new skill is taught with no intention to extinguish previous behavior (Phillips and Mattoon).[17]

While no formal reporting is intended at this time, an additional number of children with enuresis have been successfully treated in this general way: by altering some aspect of the response system of the child (Phillips).[16] One commonly used technique employs an electric clock (more economical than the expensive electrical buzzer systems) to arouse the child from his sleep. After learning the child's probable hour of wetting, the clock is set a comfortable period prior to the predicted wetting time. The child is given daytime training in getting out of bed, going some distance to the table on which the clock rests, pressing off the buzzer control switch, then going to the bathroom. Parental monitoring—which may be a desirable adjunct—can be economically maintained. The system works well and has been used by many with enuretic children without the usual complications of a "personality study," often associated with treatment of enuresis.

None of the strictures usually associated with psychotherapy, as per Shoben,[19] were employed in these instances of behavior change—rapport with the child (the child with encopresis was actually never seen—all change effort was carried out by the "change agent," the parent) ; purposeful reduction of underlying anxiety; the employment of a warm, accepting, nonjudgmental relationship. There was no vicarious re-exposure to the original stimulus situation held accountable for the pathology, as advocated by psychoanalytic formulations. None of the methods of Rogers and his students—understanding, reflecting, therapeutic relationship—was used.

Putting the problem of changing behavior in "imput-output" terms, in an R-centered theory we develop new output to replace the old (pathological) output. This is accomplished not by matching in some vicarious way the pristine original imput, but by commanding new imput which takes its cue from the *available alternatives* to the old output.

In these respects the present report is strikingly like some found in the Eysenck volume,[6] in Bandura's article,[2] in Krasner's paper,[11] and in scattered references to reconditioning, operant conditioning, interfering and restructuring methods (Phillips and Mattoon[17]). The scope of the recent literature on psychotherapy and behavior change —reminiscent as it is of work going back several decades—reveals inconsistencies in what students are traditionally taught about the relationships between learning theory and behavior change, and does not justify the way they are schooled to carry out psychotherapy.

REFERENCES

1. Alexander, F., and French, T., *Psychoanalytic Therapy* (New York: Ronald Press, 1946).
2. Bandura, A., Psychotherapy as a Learning Process, *Psychology Bulletin,* 58: 143-49, 1961.
3. Burnham, W. H., *The Normal Mind* (New York: Appleton, 1924).
4. Dollard, J., and Miller, N. E., *Personality and Psychotherapy* (New York: McGraw-Hill, 1951).
5. English, O. S., and Pearson, G. H. J., *Emotional Problems of Living* (New York: Norton, 1963).
6. Eysenck, H. J., ed., *Behavior Therapy and the Neuroses* (New York: Pergamon Press, 1960).
7. Harlow, H. F., Mice, Monkeys, Men and Motives, *Psychological Review,* 60:32, 1953.
8. Holt, E. B., *Animal Drive and the Learning Process* (New York: Holt, 1931).
9. Jones, Mary C., Conditioned Fear in Children, *Journal of Experimental Psychology,* 7:383-90, 1924.
10. Jones, Mary C., The Elimination of Children's Fears, *Pedagogical Sem.,* 31:308-15, 1924.

11. Krasner, L., The Therapist as a Social Reinforcement Machine, in H. H. Strupp and L. Luborsky, eds., *Research in Psychotherapy* (Washington, D.C.: American Psychological Association, 1962).
12. Lehner, G. F. J., Negative Practice as a Psychotherapeutic Technique, *Journal of General Psychology*, 51:69-82, 1954.
13. Mowrer, O. H., A Stimulus-Response Analysis of Anxiety and Its Role as a Reinforcing Agent, *Psychological Review*, 46:553-65, 1939.
14. Pascal, G. R., *Behavior Change in the Clinic—A Systematic Approach* (New York: Grune & Stratton, 1959).
15. Phillips, E. L., *Psychotherapy: A Modern Theory and Practice* (Englewood Cliffs, N.J.: Prentice-Hall, 1956).
16. Phillips, E., Logical Analysis of Childhood Behavior Problems and Their Treatment, *Psychological Reports*, 9: 705-12, 1961.
17. Phillips, E., and Mattoon, C. U., Interference vs. Extinction as Learning Models for Psychotherapy, *Journal of Psychology*, 51: 399-403, 1961.
18. Shaw, F. J., Behavioristic Approaches to Counseling and Psychotherapy, *University of Alabama Studies*, No. 13, 1961.
19. Shoben, E. J., Jr., Psychotherapy as a Problem in Learning Theory, in H. J. Eysenck, ed., *Behavior Therapy and the Neuroses* (New York: Pergamon Press, 1960).
20. Watson, J. B., and Rayner, Rosalie, Conditioned Emotional Reaction, *Journal of Experimental Psychology*, 3:1-14, 1920.
21. White, R. W., Motivation Reconsidered: The Concept of Competence, *Psychological Review*, 66:297-333, 1959.
22. Wolpe, J., *Psychotherapy by Reciprocal Inhibition* (Stanford, Calif.: Stanford University Press, 1958).

DONALD R. PETERSON
PERRY LONDON

Neobehavioristic Psychotherapy:
Quasi-hypnotic Suggestion and Multiple Reinforcement in the Treatment of a Case of Postinfantile Dyscopresis

In this paper, in addition to describing a simple method of dealing with a specific problem, Peterson and London make an effort to synthesize insight therapy with behavior therapy.

This paper is significant because it provides some experimental evidence for the value of cognition in therapy, which many other experimentalists tend to deprecate.

The importance of Peterson and London's work is that it leaves open the possibility of a synthesis of the developments in behavioral therapy with the "dynamic" therapies which depend on comprehension, awareness, cognition, hindsight, foresight, and insight. Work such as that described in this paper makes it more possible to use a variety of modalities in the psychotherapeutic endeavor.

MODERN BEHAVIOR therapy (Wolpe,[14]* Eysenck,[4, 5]) is currently enjoying a surge of popularity unequaled by any treatment innovation since Elisha Perkins applied tractors to hysterics. The principal reason for enthusiasm, apparently, is the combination of theoretical elegance and practical effectiveness which characterizes the approach. Behavior therapy is efficient and dependable. It is also objective, rigorous, and based on sound scientific principles, conceived and tested in formal laboratory research. Traditional insight ther-

From *The Psychological Record*, Vol. 14, 1964, pp. 469-74.

* Superior numbers refer to the list of references at the end of this article.

apy, by contrast, is subjective, mystical, inefficient, undependable, and unscientific.

Since global insight therapies are so hopelessly objectionable, insight is itself generally rejected by behaviorists as a legitimate goal or even as a tool of the therapeutic enterprise. The omission is most conspicuous in systems evolving from the work of Skinner and his disciples, but it also holds, in lesser extent, for most other versions of behavior therapy. For the most part, behavior therapists condition, extinguish, sensitize, desensitize, shape, and reshape their patient subjects in exclusive reference to behavioral functions. The problems are behavioral, the procedures are behavioral, and the changes sought are all behavioral. Insight, consciousness, awareness, cognition, understanding—the whole complex of responses which comprise verbal knowledge—have little or nothing to do with anything which transpires in the course of treatment.

The derogation of insight, however, is gradually becoming passé for enlightened behavior theory, and the neglect of awareness in therapy may turn out to be a gross error in the light of some of the most rigorous and elegant research produced by learning laboratories in recent years. The studies of Dulany,[1, 2] Kirman,[7] Levin,[8] Matarazzo et al.,[12] Spielberger et al.,[13] Eriksen,[3] and Farber[6] and his students, among still others, have demonstrated in myriad learning experiments, beyond any shadow of doubt, that if a subject knows what he is supposed to do in a learning situation, wants to do it, and can, then he might. An immediate demonstration of this principle comes from two identical but independently designed verbal learning experiments which London[9] and Bandura* never conducted. They indicated that the rate at which Ss used first person plural pronouns in an experimental interview increased dramatically among those who were instructed to use "we" as often as possible. Far less substantial increases were shown by control Ss who were not given such instructions, but received systematic verbal reinforcement for the emission of plural nouns. This result obtained, moreover, whether the correct response was reinforced in the latter group by "un-hunnh," "mmm," or "good," and despite the fact that no reinforcement was ever administered to Ss in the instructed group.

The point of the foregoing is not so much that comprehension is *essential* to learning—paramecia can be conditioned; pigeons can be trained; planaria who ingest their educated forebears can evidently crawl through mazes better than those on other diets—it is rather that comprehension, awareness, cognition, hindsight, fore-

* Interpersonal Communication, Stanford University, September 1962.

sight, and insight can be *useful* in learning. Human beings, more-over, appear to have unusual capacities for all of these. Without these capacities, indeed, they might not get into as many psychological difficulties as they do. But once possessing them, perhaps they might be enabled, by skillful use of them, to solve their psychological problems even more readily than pigeons do. Insight, in short, is neither necessary nor sufficient to the generation of behavior change, but it can be very helpful. Perhaps awareness of this fact will itself be as helpful to therapists, theoreticians, and researchers as the therapeutic insights which the architects of behavior therapy have recently made so clear.

These propositions are illustrated in the following case.

The child's name is Roger, and at the time of treatment he was three years and four months old. He was the third of four children born to upper-middle-class parents in a small urban community. His father is a university professor and his mother holds a Master's degree in Child Development in addition to two baccalaureate degrees. She has worked occasionally in her professional specialty but was not employed at the time the problem arose nor was she working when treatment was conducted. To all appearances, the members of the family are reasonably successful, content, and adapted to their lot. There has been some conflict between the parents over discipline, with the father tending toward leniency and the mother toward greater strictness, but this had never reached the point of open argument before the children, and had had no visible effect on Roger's emotional or social adjustment.

For his part, Roger had displayed no serious difficulties prior to his referral, aside from a certain accident proneness which seemed more a product of his exuberant energy than of any latent wish for self-destruction. As far as anyone could tell, he was loved by his parents, liked by his siblings, and enjoyed by most others with whom he came in contact.

Presenting Problem. The presenting problem, in brief, appeared circumscribed and limited to the fact that Roger did not defecate with either the frequency or aplomb that seemed meet in an other-wise normal and happy three-year-old. The interlude between elimi-nations was generally about five days, enough to concern the family pediatrician, and when they did occur, bowel movements were so painful that the child was reluctant to complete them. Eventually he would defecate, under increasing physical pressure, but he would hide under a bed (if indoors) or a bush (if outdoors) to perform the act. At the time of referral, he had not had a normal bowel movement in the usually appropriate location for more than three months.

Origin of the Problem. Toilet training had commenced, as with the older siblings, when Roger was about two years old. He had been placed on the toilet whenever he indicated by word or gesture that he "had to go," and effective performances were moderately praised. It seems the eliminative difficulty developed when Roger became so preoccupied in play, at times when the physical urge was present, that he did not ask to be taken to the toilet. His mother, in the adaptation which sometimes occurs with later children, had relaxed a good deal of her earlier watchfulness and did not notice the change in routine until Roger had failed to defecate for three days. By that time, elimination was quite painful. Roger cried throughout the act and remained slightly upset for the rest of the day. When he was taken to the toilet the next day, he became very upset. He cried, struggled to get down and refused to defecate. His mother did not insist, but she took Roger back to the bathroom two or three more times that same day and offered him additional opportunities over the days which followed. The patient did not eliminate again for six days, and the experience at that time was even more painful than before.

The mother called her pediatrician, who prescribed laxatives, but these had no effect, and after three months of increasing urgency and distress on the part of parents and child alike, Roger was referred, with the concurrence of the pediatrician, to the agency in which the writers were employed.

Strategy of Treatment. Although the origin of the symptom was partly obscure, it seemed plain enough that there were two separate components involved in its retention (so to speak): (1) Whenever the urge to defecate occurred, Roger experienced a primary negative reinforcement for responding to it, i.e., the initiation of a downward peristalsis toward the anal sphincter was immediately followed by pain, and (2) whatever primary drive may have initiated the sequence in the first place was of insufficient strength to sustain it against the combined presence of pain and absence of any secondary reinforced positive motivation. The only secondary motive of any consequence was the concern and displeasure which his parents manifested in connection with his symptom, and though Roger was uncomfortable with the parental pressure he experienced, the alternative of succumbing to fecal pressure seemed even less desirable.

The therapeutic strategy which was planned on the basis of the foregoing analysis consisted of (1) generation of insight (cognitive stimulation) to facilitate the initiation of the eliminative sequence, and (2) reinforcement of the adaptive, i.e., "target" behavior, upon its occurrence.

1. Generation of insight consisted in part of communicating to the child verbally that the issue of therapy was his eliminative reticence and that it would be "good" for him, and would feel good, to move his bowels. It was assumed that recognition of positive value in the behavior would interact with need for social approval and primary drive in a way that would make Roger desire, at least at a cognitive level, to undertake the behavior.

Hypnotic suggestion was elected as the means of changing expectancies regarding pain of sphincter pressure and the act of elimination itself. Hypnosis has been used successfully for the relief of pain in a variety of clinical settings, and in the present instance, where skeletal and other muscle tension contributed much of the painful sensation, the generally relaxing character of hypnosis might be even more than usually effective. In this case, the technique consisted largely in the delivery of a posthypnotic kind of suggestion to the general effect that well-timed defecation would not hurt. As it turned out, Roger did not satisfy *any* standard criteria for hypnotic behavior, though the therapist conducted himself as if the child were hypnotized.

2. The importance of selecting effective and immediate positive reinforcements is apparent when one considers the immediacy and potency of the negative reinforcement which generally applied in this case. Both verbal and nonverbal reinforcements were used here; the former consisted of parental praise (P_1), and the latter of the administration of popsicles (P_2). The efficacy of verbal reinforcement has, of course, been widely studied, though often with ambiguous or contradictory results (London & Rosenhan[11]). It is, at all events, only a secondary reinforcement. Popsicles, on the other hand, have both primary and secondary reinforcing characteristics. Though little laboratory research has reported their use as reinforcers, indications of their popularity, particularly with children high in hypnotic susceptibility, have been reported by London.

Course of Treatment. Roger was seen for three therapy sessions; the first (7/30/62) lasted for about twenty minutes, the second (8/1/62) for ten minutes, and the third (8/6/62) for about fifteen minutes. The entire course of treatment transpired over an 8-day period.

The first session began in a play therapy room. After about five minutes, in which Roger played quite happily with the therapist, he was escorted to the therapist's office. Seated there, he was first asked to draw a picture, which he willingly did. He was then presented with a Chevreul pendulum, and a formal hypnotic induction was attempted by means of the procedures of the Children's Hypnotic Susceptibility Scale (London[10]). This was totally unsuccessful because Roger became quickly bored. The therapist (T) then insisted that he lie down on the couch and, abandoning more formal procedure, began stroking his forehead, at the same time softly and monotonously talking to him about how T knew that Roger did not like to "go potty," that Mommy and Daddy wanted him to, etc. This gradually evolved into a soft hypnoidal chant, as follows:

"Mommy and Daddy want Roger to go potty all the time, but he doesn't like to, Roger doesn't like to. Everybody wants Roger to go potty, Roger to go potty, Roger's going potty. Everybody likes Roger to go potty, 'cause then he'll feel real good."

After about ten minutes of this, Roger quietly said, "Can I wake up now?" T agreed to this, and Roger said he wanted to go home. They returned to the waiting room, where his mother was waiting. His only comment on the session was that he had played. Another appointment was scheduled for two days later.

When he arrived home with his mother, Roger immediately went to the bathroom and defecated. Mother lavished praise on him (P_1) and gave him a popsicle (P_2). This did not recur the next day.

The second session occurred as scheduled. Roger did not wish to lie down this time, however, or to go into the therapist's office. He did go to the playroom, and while playing there, listened quietly to the therapist's hypnotic-like suggestions that it would not hurt when he went to the potty, that it would feel very good, and that Mommy and Daddy would be very happy. After ten minutes, he was returned to Mother, who took him home immediately. As before, there was no discussion of the session or other symptom-relevant material, but on arrival at home, Roger again went to the bathroom and moved his bowels, again followed immediately by P_1P_2. There was no further discussion of the matter, but for each of the next four days, Roger moved his bowels once daily with P_1P_2. (No inquiry was ever conducted to ascertain the extent to which he was aware of the reinforcement contingencies, since this was not important to the therapeutic procedure. Both parents and therapist, however, are of the opinion that there was some cognizance of them, with respect to both P_1 and P_2.)

The final therapy session came five days later. After a few minutes in the playroom, Roger again agreed to go to T's office. He was congratulated on his recent successes, asked if it felt good when he "went," and when he responded affirmatively, asked if he intended "to go" regularly and would never have any trouble again. He affirmed all these suggestive queries, which were then repeated at length by the therapist in a hypnotic fashion, accompanied by glowing descriptions of the joy in Roger's household at his good behavior and the plethora of praise and popsicles which would subsequently result. Roger was visibly pleased by this imagined scene, and after about five minutes of its repetition, the session was terminated and he was remanded to his mother. As in the previous session, no formal hypnotic induction was employed. Therapy was discontinued at this point by mutual agreement, for, though formal hypnosis plainly had not worked, the treatment apparently had.

Follow-up. At this writing, exactly one year after termination of treatment, Roger's remission is still complete. For some 75 days after treatment, P_1P_2 was administered directly in response to completion of bowel movements, which occurred approximately once each day. One day, at the end of that period, a movement occurred under circumstances where P_2 was not available. Roger did not seem to notice its absence, however, and continued the behavior pattern established during the previous three months. Approximately 290 trials have been successfully completed since that time with no visible signs of extinction. It may be safely concluded at this point that the desired behavior is habituated and the child cured.

REFERENCES

1. Dulany, D. E., Hypotheses and Habits in Verbal "Operant Conditioning," *Journal of Abnormal and Social Psychology*, 63:251-63, 1961.
2. Dulany, D. E., The Place of Hypotheses and Intentions: An Analysis of Verbal Control in Verbal Conditioning, *Journal of Personality*, Symposium on Behavior and Awareness, 30:102-29, 1962.
3. Eriksen, C. W., ed., *Behavior and Awareness: A Symposium of Research and Interpretation* (Durham, N.C.: Duke University Press, 1962).
4. Eysenck, H. J., *Behavior Therapy and the Neuroses* (New York: Pergamon Press, 1960).
5. Eysenck, H. J., The Effects of Psychotherapy, in H. J. Eysenck, ed., *Handbook of Abnormal Psychology* (New York: Basic Books, 1961).
6. Farber, I. E., The Things People Say to Themselves. *American Psychologist*, 18:185-97, 1963.
7. Kirman, W. J., The Relationship of Learning, with and without Awareness, to Personality Needs, *Dissertation Abstracts*, 19:362, 1958.
8. Levin, S., The Effects of Awareness on Verbal Conditioning, *Dissertation Abstracts*, 20:3835, 1959.
9. London, P., Hypnosis in Children: An Experimental Approach, *International Journal of Clinical & Experimental Hypnosis*, 18: 79-91, 1962.
10. London, P., *The Children's Hypnotic Susceptibility Scale* (Palo Alto, Calif.: Consulting Psychologists Press, 1963).

11. London, P., and Rosenhan, D. L., Personality Dynamics, in *Annual Review of Psychology*, Ch. 15, 447-92, 1964.
12. Matarazzo, J. D., Saslow, G., and Pareis, E. N., Verbal Conditioning of Two Response Classes: Some Methodological Considerations, *Journal of Abnormal & Social Psychology*, 61:190-206, 1960.
13. Spielberger, C. D., Levin, S. M., and Shepard, Mary, The Effects of Awareness and Attitude Toward the Reinforcement on the Operant Conditioning of Verbal Behavior, *Journal of Personality*, 30:106-21, 1962.
14. Wolpe, J., *Psychotherapy by Reciprocal Inhibition* (Stanford. Calif.: Stanford University Press, 1958).

MILTON H. ERICKSON

The Use of Symptoms as an Integral Part of Hypnotherapy

While Erickson is best known for his brilliant innovations in hypnotherapeutic technique, his approach has implications far beyond hypnosis. After reading many of his papers it was difficult to select only one. The paper which follows was chosen because it seemed to contain more than the others about the rationale for his approach.

In this paper Erickson makes clear a fundamental error which he believes interferes with the work of many therapists. The error flows out of the mistaken notion that patients are rational and are ready to be dealt with rationally. Erickson, on the other hand, is keenly aware that before any therapy can take place the patient has to be receptive. Often this receptivity can be accomplished only by fully accepting and making use of the patient's irrational beliefs and behaviors. It is in this area that Erickson is a master.

Emerging from a completely different background, his therapy shows considerable similarity to the work of Greenwald, Nelson, and Spotnitz, as contained in this volume. Of course Haley, who worked with Erickson, makes his influence quite clear, and Frankl's paradoxical intention also employs a technique with considerable similarity to Erickson's.

One of the innovations which Erickson uses with virtuosity in this paper is illustrated in the case of the patient who used "word salad" to avoid meaningful communication.

In Erickson's work the question of manipulation comes to

From *American Journal of Clinical Hypnosis*, Vol. VIII, No. 1, July 1965.

the fore. Is it manipulative of him to use the patient's own neurotic behavior for his cure?

Erickson states that his aim is to permit "the patient to use his own thinking, his own understandings, his own emotions in the way that best fits him in his scheme of life." Thus Erickson the consummate strategist and manipulator may have more respect for the patient's unique individuality than have many of the therapists who insist that the patient be sincere only in the fashion that the therapist finds compatible to his own standards.

IN DEALING with any type of patient clinically, there is a most important consideration that should be kept constantly in mind. This is that the patient's needs as a human personality should be an ever-present question for the therapist to insure recognition at each manifestation. Merely to make a correct diagnosis of the illness and to know the correct method of treatment is not enough. Fully as important is that the patient be receptive of the therapy and cooperative in regard to it. Without the patient's full cooperativeness, therapeutic results are delayed, distorted, limited or even prevented. Too often the therapist regards the patient as necessarily logical, understanding, in full possession of his faculties—in brief, a reasonable and informed human being. Yet it is a matter of common knowledge often overlooked, disregarded, or rejected that a patient can be silly, forgetful, absurd, unreasonable, illogical, incapable of acting with common sense, and very often governed and directed in his behavior by emotions and by unknown, unrecognizable, and perhaps undiscoverable unconscious needs and forces which are far from reasonable, logical, or sensible. To attempt therapy upon a patient only apparently sensible, reasonable and intelligent when that patient may actually be governed by unconscious forces and emotions neither overtly shown nor even known, to overlook the unconscious mind for possible significant information, can lead easily to failure or to unsatisfactory results. Nor should seemingly intelligent, rational, and cooperative behavior ever be allowed to mislead the therapist into an oversight of the fact that his patient is still human and hence easily the victim of fears and foibles, of all those unknown experiential learnings that have been relegated to his unconscious mind and that he may never become aware of or ever show just what the self may be like under the outward placid surface. Nor should the therapist have so little regard for his patient that he fails to make allowance for human weaknesses and irrationality. Too often it is not the strengths of the person that are vital in the therapeutic situation. Rather, the dominant forces that control the entire situation may derive from weaknesses, illogical behavior, unreasonableness, and obviously false and misleading attitudes of various sorts.

The therapist wishing to help his patient should never scorn, condemn, or reject any part of a patient's conduct simply because it is obstructive, unreasonable, or even irrational. The patient's behavior is a part of the problem brought into the office; it constitutes the personal environment within which the therapy must take effect; it may constitute the dominant force in the total patient-doctor relationship. Since whatever the patient brings into the office is in some way both a part of him and a part of his problem, the patient should be viewed with a sympathetic eye appraising the totality which confronts the therapist. In so doing the therapist should not limit himself to an appraisal of what is good and reasonable as offering possible foundations for therapeutic procedures. Sometimes—in fact, many more times than is realized—therapy can be firmly established on a sound basis only by the utilization of silly, absurd, irrational, and contradictory manifestations. One's professional dignity is not involved but one's professional competence is.

To illustrate from clinical experience, case history material will be cited, some from a nonhypnotic therapeutic situation, some from situations involving the use of hypnosis.

CASE REPORT 1

George had been a patient in a mental hospital for five years. His identity had never been established. He was simply a stranger around the age of 25 who had been picked up by the police for irrational behavior and committed to the state mental hospital. During those five years he had said, "My name is George," "Good morning," and "Good night," but these were his only rational utterances. He uttered otherwise a continuous word salad completely meaningless as far as could be determined. It was made up of sounds, syllables, words, and incomplete phrases. For the ..t three years he sat on a bench at the front door of the ward and eagerly leaped up and poured forth his word salad most urgently to everyone who entered the ward. Otherwise, he merely sat quietly mumbling his word salad to himself. Innumerable patient efforts had been made by psychiatrists, psychologists, nurses, social service workers, other personnel, and even fellow patients to secure intelligible remarks from him, all in vain. George talked only one way, the word salad way. After approximately three years he continued to greet persons who entered the ward with an outburst of meaningless words, but in between times he sat silently on the bench, appearing mildly depressed but somewhat angrily uttering a few minutes of word salad when approached and questioned.

The author joined the hospital staff in the sixth year of George's stay. The available information about his ward behavior was secured. It was learned also that patients or ward personnel could sit on the bench beside him without eliciting his word salad so long as they did not speak to him. With this total of information a therapeutic plan was devised. A secretary recorded in shorthand the word salads with which he so urgently greeted those who entered the ward. These transcribed recordings were studied but no meaning could be discovered. These word salads were carefully paraphrased, using words that were least likely to be found in George's productions, and an extensive study was made of these until the author could improvise a word salad similar in pattern to George's, but utilizing a different vocabulary.

All entrances to the ward were changed to a side door some distance down the corridor from George. The author then began the practice of sitting silently on the bench beside George daily for increasing lengths of time until the span of an hour was reached. At the next sitting, the author, addressing the empty air, identified himself verbally. George made no response.

The next day the identification was addressed directly to George. He spat out an angry stretch of word salad to which the author replied, in tones of courtesy and responsiveness, with an equal amount of his own carefully contrived word salad. George appeared puzzled and, when the author finished, George uttered another contribution with an inquiring intonation. As if replying, the author verbalized still further word salad.

After a half-dozen interchanges, George lapsed into silence and the author promptly went about other matters.

The next morning appropriate greetings were exchanged, employing proper names by both. Then George launched into a long word salad speech to which the author courteously replied in kind. There followed brief interchanges of long and short utterances of word salad until George fell silent and the author went to other duties.

This continued for some time. Then George, after returning the morning greeting, made meaningless utterances without pause for four hours. It taxed the author greatly to miss lunch and to make a full reply in kind. George listened attentively and made a two-hour reply to which a weary two-hour response was made. (George was noted to watch the clock throughout the day.)

The next morning George returned the usual greeting properly but added about two sentences of nonsense to which the author replied with a similar length of nonsense. George replied, "Talk sense, Doctor." "Certainly, I'll be glad to. What is your last name?" "O'Donovan, and it's about time somebody who knows how to talk asked. Over five years in this lousy joint". . . to which was added a sentence or two of word salad. The author replied, "I'm glad to get your name, George. Five years is too long a time" . . . and about two sentences of word salad were added.

The rest of the account is as might be expected. A complete history sprinkled with bits of word salad was obtained by inquiries judiciously salted with word salad. His clinical course, never completely free of word salad, which was eventually reduced to occasional unintelligible mumbles, was excellent. Within a year he had left the hospital, was gainfully employed, and at increasingly longer intervals returned to the hospital to report his continued and improving adjustment. Nevertheless, he invariably initiated his report or terminated it with a bit of word salad, always expecting the same from the author. Yet he could, as he frequently did on these visits, comment wryly, "Nothing like a little nonsense in life, is there, Doctor?" to which he obviously expected and received a sensible expression of agreement to which was added a brief utterance of nonsense. After he had been out of the hospital continuously for three years of fully satisfactory adjustment, contact was lost with him except for a cheerful postcard from another city. This bore a brief but satisfactory summary of his adjustments in a distant city. It was signed properly but following his name was a jumble of syllables. There was no return address. He was ending the relationship on his terms of adequate understanding.

During the course of his psychotherapy he was found hypnotizable, developing a medium to deep trance in about fifteen minutes. However, his trance behavior was entirely comparable to his waking behavior and it offered no therapeutic advantages, although repeated tests were made. Every therapeutic interview was characterized by the judicious use of an appropriate amount of word salad.

The above case represents a rather extreme example of meeting a patient at the level of his decidedly serious problem. The author was at first rather censoriously criticized by others but when it became apparent that inexplicable imperative needs of the patient were being met, there was no further adverse comment.

The next report is decidedly different. Although no psychosis was involved, there existed such an irrational rigidity of emotional conviction that the patient appeared to be inaccessible.

CASE REPORT 2

A man in his early forties approached a dentist friend of the author, explaining his situation at great length, perspiring freely as he did so and manifesting much fear and trepidation. His account was that he had recently read a news story about the use of hypnosis in dentistry. This reminded him of his college days when he had many times acted as a hypnotic subject for experimental purposes in the psychology laboratory. In these experiences he easily and invariably achieved the somnambulistic state, with profound amnesias still persisting for his trance experiences as such, but with a still-present fair memory of the experimental accounts subsequently shown to him.

For some reason not recalled by him but referred to as "some horribly painful experience connected with dentistry in some way" he had not visited a dentist for over twenty years, despite the fact that he was well aware that he was seriously in need of dental care. His direct explanation was, "I just can't bring myself to see a dentist. Dentistry is a painful thing. It has to be painful. There are no ifs, ands, or buts about it. Dentistry has to be connected with pain. Even with an anesthetic, there is pain after it wears off. No matter what you do in dentistry, there is some place that becomes terribly sensitive." There was more of this almost irrational obsessional thinking, but the foregoing is an adequate example.

The news story about hypnodontia made him hopeful that in some way his terror of dentistry could be overcome. Hence he made telephone calls about hypnodontia until he located the author's friend.

That dentist agreed to see him and in a preliminary session gave the patient a careful explanation of hypnoanesthesia. The man developed an excellent somnambulistic trance and easily developed glove anesthesia and then a profound anesthesia of the fingers as tested by overflexing forcibly the terminal phalanx. The dentist then attempted to produce mandibular anesthesia. This failed completely, arousing the dentist's intense interest in the problem apparently confronting him. An entire evening was spent the next day by the dentist endeavoring by one technique or another to produce dental anesthesia. The patient could develop surgical anesthesia anywhere except in relation to his mouth. Instead of anesthesia a seeming hyperesthesia developed.

Another dentist well experienced in hypnosis was called in to work with the patient hypnotically. The two dentists spent an intensive afternoon and evening with a profoundly somnambulistic hypnotic subject who was surgically anesthetic and able to withstand any painful stimulus they were willing to administer to his body. The patient had his eyes open throughout the trance and he was most interested in his hypnoanesthesia.

However, a touch on the patient's lip, chin, or the angle of his jaw would result in a flood of perspiration, a flushing of the skin, and complaints that the slightest touch seemed to be extremely painful, and the patient would break down hypnotically, establishing neck and body rigidity in order to wince and to withdraw from such touches.

Other dentists were questioned for suggestions and advice to no avail and the patient was finally sent to the author, together with a typed account of the findings of the two dentists and with a typed example of the patient's verbalizations about dental pain.

The interview with the patient and the induction of a deep trance permitted an easy confirmation of the report by the dentists.

Scrutiny of the typed account of his obsessive-like utterances about pain and dentistry, and close listening when he verbalized afresh his convictions about dentistry and pain, suggested a possible likely course of action. Since the dentists had expressed their interest in any experimental work the author might do, the patient was dismissed with an instruction to make an appointment with the first dentist. When the appointment was made the dentist telephoned his dentist friend and the author.

At the proper time the patient appeared and at the author's request took a seat in the dental chair, with his face flushed and perspiring and in a general state of utter fear. In spite of that he developed a deep somnambulistic trance in rapport with the two dentists as well as the author.

The intended approach to dental anesthesia and its rationale had been previously discussed with the dentists and the entire procedure, it was agreed, should be done with no preliminary preparation of the patient.

When all was in readiness, the patient, still in a deep somnambulistic trance, tremulous, and with his face flushed and perspiring, was asked to listen closely to a reading of a typed account of his statements about dentistry and pain, which included the statements quoted above. He listened with utter intensity and as the last statement was read, he was told seriously and impressively: "You are entirely right, absolutely right, and you summarize it most adequately in one of your statements. Let me read it again. 'No matter what you do in dentistry there is always some place that becomes terribly sensitive.' You are completely correct. As you sit there in the dental chair, the dentist will be to your right. Hence, you may now, at once, safely extend your left hand and arm, there to let it stay suspended as if frozen rigidly in place. And you may turn your face and see it there and as you do so you will note that your left hand, so completely out of reach of everything, safe from any touch, from the slightest breath of air, is becoming so terribly, so awfully, so horribly hypersensitive, so unbelievably hypersensitive, that in another minute all of the sensitivity of your entire body will drain into that hand. And since the dentist in working with you will not touch your hand where all the hypersensitivity is, he can easily do all the dental work you need. Now make an unforgettable mental note of just where that hypersensitive left hand is, and turn your head and let the dentist go to work."

The patient turned his head, fearfully voiced a plea that the dentist be careful of his left hand, and, comforted by the dentist's reassurance, opened his mouth in complete readiness.

The facial flush and the perspiration had vanished. It was noted that his left hand was flushed and perspiring. The dentist then took charge completely and, by means of posthypnotic suggestions, convinced the patient that each time he sat in the dental chair, he would develop left-hand hyperesthesia so that his dental work could be done. At no time was any oral anesthesia ever suggested.

The rationale of this approach is rather clear and simple. The patient was rigidly fixated on the idea that a painful hypersensitivity must inevitably accompany dentistry. Attempts at oral anesthesia fixated his attention on oral sensations. Acceptance of his neurotic belief and employing it to create hypnotically an area of extreme hypersensitivity met his need to be able to experience pain without having to do so. Thus all pain expectation was centered in his hand, resulting in an anesthesia of the rest of his body, including his mouth.

On the occasion of the termination of the last dental visit, the dentist tested the patient for pain sensitivity elsewhere in his body and found that a general surgical anesthesia existed.

This second case represents the hypnotic utilization, with an augmentation of it, of the actual barrier to the patient's capacity to develop the needful manifestation that he wished. It is true that the logic of the entire procedure is decidedly specious but it must be borne in mind that the patient's total attitudinal set was equally specious. Cold hard logic, presentation of scientific facts, any sensible reasonable approach would have been useless. Utilizing the patient's own neurotic irrationality to affirm and confirm a simple extension of his neurotic fixation relieved him of all unrecognized unconscious needs to defend his neurotism against all assaults. A systematic analysis of exactly what kind of thinking the patient brought into the office led readily to the solution of his problem. This same sort of situation existed in the third case, which follows.

CASE REPORT 3

A thrice-divorced young woman sought psychiatric help: "For just one problem, that's all, and I will tell you the problem right away but I don't want any treatment for anything else. That you must promise me."

The gist of her story was she had impulsively married at age 18 a handsome and, as she discovered later, dissolute man of 25, very much against parental wishes. The wedding night she discovered that he was a secret alcoholic and the attempted consummation of the marriage in his state of intoxication was a hideous travesty to her. He blamed her entirely, berated her unmercifully, described her rudely as "having a refrigerated derrière," left her alone, and spent the night with a prostitute. Nevertheless, she continued to live with him hopefully, despite his continued use of the description that he had bestowed on her the first night. After some months of wretched effort to prove to him that she was a woman of normal sexuality, she secured a divorce, secretly fearing that her former husband was correct in his appraisal of her lack of sexuality.

A year later, in an overcompensatory effort to avoid the kind of trouble she had encountered in her first marriage, she married a highly effeminate man whose latent homosexuality disclosed itself on their wedding night by his horrified aversion to her body. His reason for marrying her, since she did have some wealth in her own name, was to secure "proper social standing in the community." He was completely outraged and incensed by her "indecent haste" to consummate the marriage and administered a rather rigidly prim reprimand. He spent the night, as she learned later, with a male friend who helped him bemoan his unfortunate plight. Her reaction was one of complete self-blame, no understanding of her husband's actual sexuality, and she succeeded in convincing herself that he had applied the same derogatory description of her as had her first husband. The marriage continued for nearly a year, chiefly by virtue of the fact that he spent most of his nights at his mother's apartment. An actual attempt at consummation after about four months proved to be only a revolting experience for him and a conviction, because of her entire lack of response to him, that she was absolutely lacking in sexual feelings.

After they finally got a divorce, she secured employment and gave up any hope of a normal life. After about two years, while living a very sheltered, retiring life, she met by chance a man five years her senior who was successfully engaged in an exciting, but to soberer minds, a somewhat questionable, promotional activity in real estate. His charm, his easily likable personality, his knowledge of the world, his attentiveness and courtesy led her to make a third venture into matrimony.

They were married in the morning, and then went to an expensive suite in a hotel in a nearby town where he spent the day with her presenting innumerable plausible reasons in an effort to persuade her to turn over to him all of her property for him "to develop," thus to secure larger returns.

As he presented his arguments with increasing persuasiveness but with no display of emotional interest in her, a recollection of the beginnings of her first marriage raised sickening doubts in her mind. Her husband, becoming impatient with her slowness to accept his arguments, suddenly noted the horrified doubting expression on her face. Infuriated, he threw her on the bed and had violent intercourse with her while he denounced her for her lack of response, ridiculed her, told her how he had spent the previous night with a responsive prostitute and he finally walked out on her "to find someone who didn't have what my first husband said I had." A divorce was promptly secured by her.

Now she was interested in a young man who met the approval of her lawyer, her banker, her parents, her minister, and her friends. She desperately wanted to marry him, yet was equally desperate in her desire not to cause him any unhappiness. Her purpose in seeking psychiatric aid was to have her "deficiency corrected." With extreme embarrassment, in plain simple Anglo-Saxon words so that there could be no possibility of any misunderstanding by the author, she made matters painfully clear. She wanted, no more, no less, the chill she felt continuously, no matter what she wore, no matter how warm the seat she sat on, to be removed from her buttocks. This wretchedly cold feeling had been present, painfully present, since the first evening of her third marriage. The prompt dissolution of that marriage had not lessened the feeling of a subjectively recognizable coldness that had developed following the third husband's devastating criticism of her. This had plagued her continuously and she found herself to be too embarrassed to seek medical aid. Recently, in night school courses she was taking, she had read about hypnosis, hypnotic phenomena, and hypnotherapy. Seeing the author's name given as a reference, she had come to Arizona for immediate, direct, and specific therapy.

Her desire for therapy was almost irrational in its intensity. She was convinced of the circumscribed character of her problem and could not even listen to any attempted exposition of the general character of her difficulties. She was rigidly certain that once the "coldness" was removed, all would be well. She asserted an absolute willingness to cooperate in any way to achieve her goal of a slightly elevated temperature in place of the gluteal coldness. In the desperateness of her desire for help it was not possible for her to see the humorous effect of her use of vulgar language to insure the author's exact understanding of her problem in terms of the exact words that had been used to describe it to her originally.

After a laborious three-hour effort to secure her interest in the author's views, it became apparent that therapy would have to be accomplished, if possible at all, in full accord with her persistent demands.

Much speculative thought was given to the content of her limited understandings to devise some kind of therapeutic approach. Since she wanted hypnosis desperately she became an easy somnambulistic subject, as is sometimes the case with this type of patient. Indeed, she was one of the most receptive and amenable subjects the author has encountered, and she agreed readily to accept and act upon any hypnotic suggestion given her. The specious explanation given her was that, since she wanted her problem corrected by hypnosis, it was requisite that she be thoroughly trained in all hypnotic phenomena so that every possible necessary hypnotic element requisite for her cure would be experientially known to her. Actually, the real purpose was to develop in her a receptiveness, a responsiveness, a feeling of complete acceptance, and a willingness to execute adequately any suggestion offered her.

The next step was to ask her to make a systematic study by filling her bathtub with water of increasingly higher temperature until the water was hot enough to produce goose bumps on her legs, which were the only part of her to be immersed in the bathtub. After much labor she succeeded in achieving this. She was then presented with a laboriously detailed explanation of how an overloading of the thermal receptors by excessive warmth would overflow into the cold receptors of the skin, thereby resulting in goose flesh. The success of this venture, in the author's opinion, played a large part in the successful therapy. It supplied her with indisputable visual proof that heat can produce the concomitants of coldness and that this could be done in a definitely limited area of the body. From that point on there existed for her no doubts or fears of the author's understandings or competence.

Therapy was then continued by inducing a deep trance and by carefully worded suggestions, making her feel privately, a feeling just to be enjoyed within herself, an exaggerated, utterly intense, and inordinate pride in having the secret knowledge shared only with me that at least a part of her body could experience heat by a subjective cold response. Thus, by repetitious suggestion it was emphatically impressed upon her that this must always and forever be regarded as her own private pleasurable joy. The reason for this secrecy was to intensify her feeling and to preclude any disparagement by anyone in whom she might confide.

Then, bit by bit, suggestions were cautiously given her that, just as her calves had developed cold receptor responses to heat, so could the cold receptors of her thighs, of her buttocks, and her abdomen, Her acceptance of these ideas was insured by a sudden shift to a discussion of the "thrills and tingles of complete happiness and ecstatic joy that race so delightfully up and down the spine of the little girl who receives the new dolly so desperately wanted and never really expected."

This complex idea was impressed upon her with much repetition and with careful changes in the key words of "thrills" and "tingles" by making the phrase "thrills and chills and tingles" and then in a random fashion omitting one and then another of the three words. Also, since she came from a northern state and had a reasonably happy childhood, the "tingling delights of sledding down hill on a tinglingly cold day," "the rapturous joys of a cold, cold dish of ice cream on a hot summer's day," and similar plays on words associated with pleasures safely remote in her history, were woven into a whole series of suggestions.

This was repeated for a number of sessions, always impressing upon her the need for an unconscious retention of the ideas, the need to incorporate them, and everything else she had been taught in therapy, into the warp and woof of her very existence, and yet to keep the knowledge of all this safely secret forever from her conscious mind, just knowing in some vague and satisfying way that she possessed within her a knowledge and an understanding of a personal value, beauty, and happiness.

Very rapidly there occurred a marked change in her general behavior. The tension, the urgency, the over-all anxiety disappeared, she went for long scenic drives, and she began speaking of visiting Phoenix again.

Then one day she entered the office hesitantly, diffidently, blushing deeply and keeping her eyes downcast. After about fifteen minutes, almost in the voice of a small child, she asked, "Can I tell you a secret, a very important secret that's all mine, my special secret that belongs all to me?" The reply given her was, "I think that if you think it over very carefully you will find that you probably can tell your psychiatrist because he will understand."

After another seven minutes she said softly, "I've got to tell it in a special way that I know you will understand. It's what I said when I first came to you, only it's all different now." Then, in completely vulgar terms, with many blushes, she stated in essence, "I like being a frozen-posteriored creature."

To the author, that signified that she needed no further therapy and the years that have passed, her successful fourth marriage, her completion of college during the first years of this marriage and her subsequent entrance happily into the pleasures of motherhood have all confirmed the success of therapy.

And what was her problem? An impulsive marriage in the best of good faith but a wretchedly mistaken marriage as she immediately discovered; a second mistaken marriage to correct the trauma of the first, promptly discovered to be another mistake that was slowly corrected only so far as the marital state was concerned, but with only an intensification of her traumas; a third desperate marriage entered in good faith to correct, if possible, the injuries of the past, with only resulting further injury. Then came the acute realization of her therapeutic needs when a genuinely good marriage presented itself.

And what was her therapy? An unhappy succession of events had progressively emphasized the trauma centering about a vital need in her life, her fulfillment as a woman. These events had degraded her in her own eyes and had led her unconsciously to summarize her total unhappiness in a circumscribed way. Then she sought circumscribed therapy, only circumscribed therapy. This was presented to her in such a fashion that, even as she had circumscribed everything, she was in a position to enlarge properly her whole problem. Her thinking about her problem had been repressed emotionally largely at an unconscious level. Her therapy permitted her to do the same type of thinking but to include in it not only the events leading to her problem but the emotional values dating all the way back to her childhood. Then when once she had achieved her goals, at the level of unconscious motivation she felt compelled to verbalize her original presenting complaint, but with a totally different meaning and perspective. By doing this she freed herself from any dependency upon the therapist and then could go her way, finding her own proper goals in life.

CONCLUDING COMMENT

These three different case histories are presented to illustrate the importance in therapy of doing what appears to be most important to the patient, that which constitutes an expression of the distorted thoughts and emotions of the patient. The therapist's task should not be a proselytizing of the patient with his own beliefs and understandings. No patient can really understand the understandings of his therapist nor does he need them. What is needed is the development of a therapeutic situation permitting the patient to use his own thinking, his own understandings, his own emotions in the way that best fits him in his scheme of life.

Each of the patients reported on has no real understanding of what their therapist thinks, knows, believes, likes, or dislikes. They know primarily that in some peculiar way they began to unsnarl their lives in a fashion as inexplicable as was the fashion in which they had once snarled their thinking and their emotions.

ALBERT ELLIS

The Treatment of Frigidity and Impotence

Albert Ellis is one of the most prolific writers in the field; he has published more than 250 papers and about 25 books and monographs. His therapy is based on his theory that so-called emotional reactions and upsets can be traced to the concrete, simple, exclamatory sentences which people say to themselves to create their "emotional" states. He believes that almost any disturbed person can be taught to perceive the specific irrational internalized sentences that he employs to upset himself, and that he can learn to reorganize his own conflicting and self-defeating values, so that he can overcome his neurotic trends.

In observing Ellis in action one is impressed by his intense involvement in the act of arguing his patient out of his illogical beliefs. Many adherents of other points of view are occasionally either annoyed or amused by Ellis's frequent attacks on theories and techniques other than his own. Some therapists feel that rational-emotive psychotherapy is a useful partial technique which may profitably be incorporated into their treatment methods, but that it is not a sufficient form of treatment for all patients.

THERE ARE MANY reasons why women become frigid and men become impotent in our society, not the least of which is an over-

This chapter is expanded from "Guilt, Shame and Frigidity," *Quarterly Review of Surgery, Obstetrics, & Gynecology*, 16:259-61, 1959, and Chapter II, pp. 232-36 of *The Art and Science of Love* (New York: Lyle Stuart, 1960). It is found in this form in Albert Ellis, *Reason and Emotion in Psychotherapy* (New York: Lyle Stuart, 1963).

powering sense of guilt on the part of the sexually incapacitated female or male (Ellis,[2,][*][5] Hirsch,[7] Hitschmann and Bergler,[8] Kinsey, Pomeroy, Martin, and Gebhard.[9]) Thus, I have presented elsewhere considerable evidence to the effect that people in our Western world are usually overwhelmed with antisexual attitudes, with which we indoctrinate them almost literally from birth; and that consequently they are inordinately guilty about letting themselves go and fully enjoying themselves sexually. Varying degrees of frigidity and impotence naturally result (Ellis[3,][6]).

Be that as it may, another phenomenon has come to exist in contemporary society that is different from and in many ways more pernicious than the sexual guilt which was so prevalent in previous days, and upon the basis of which Freud constructed a considerable part of his psychoanalytic theory. This phenomenon is that of intense shame—which overlaps with guilt in some significant respects, but which is also somewhat different. Whereas when he feels guilty, an individual believes that he has acted wrongly or wickedly in the eyes of some God, fate, or social value system, when he feels ashamed or inadequate, he is more likely to believe that he has acted ineptly or weakly in his own eyes and in those of the people with whom he has immediate contact.

As Piers and Singer[12] and several other psychological and sociological thinkers have recently pointed out, shame and its concomitant feelings of inadequacy (as distinguished from guilt and its concomitant feelings of sinfulness) are likely to be particularly enhanced in a society such as our own, which stresses success rather than goodness, achievement rather than sainthood.

As a result of our having so many millions of shame-inculcated individuals in this country, I have been seeing, in my private practice of psychotherapy and marriage counseling, one person after another who, in spite of having had adequate sex education, is frigid or impotent. These sexually inadequate people are often highly sophisticated people who do not consider sex wicked and who have little or no guilt about engaging in premarital or marital relations. Indeed, most of them want very much to experience full sex satisfaction and will do anything in their power to experience it.

This goes for women, these days, as much as for men. Whereas, in previous years, it was frequently husbands who came to see me to complain that their wives weren't too interested in sex relations, today it is just as likely to be the wives who complain that *they*

* Superior numbers refer to the list of references at the end of this article.

want bigger and better orgasms and are not, alas, achieving them. The husbands come to complain—but largely about their own impotence rather than their wives' sexual inadequacies.

One of the major reasons, ironically, why both men and women in our society are not achieving full sex satisfaction is because they are often overdetermined to achieve it. Because of their upbringing, they are so ashamed if they do not reach the greatest heights of expressive sexuality that they tragically sabotage their own desires. That is to say, instead of focusing clearly on the real problem at hand—which baldly stated, is "How can I think of something sexually exciting enough and how can I concentrate on movements that are sufficiently stimulating to bring me to fulfillment?"—these people are focusing on quite a different problem —namely, "Oh, what an idiot and an incompetent person I am for not being able to copulate without any difficulty." Stated differently, sexually inadequate people are usually obsessed with the notion of *how* rather than *what* they are doing when they are having sex relations (Eichenlaub,[1] Ellis[6]).

The physiological and endocrinological aspects of impotence and frigidity are not to be ignored (Ellis,[4] Kleegman,[10] Kupperman,[11] Walker and Strauss[10]). It would nonetheless appear that most men and women who come for help because they are sexually inadequate are physiologically and endocrinologically normal and that there is little that can be done for them by prescribing sex hormones. Sex desire and fulfillment are largely mediated through the central nervous system and the cerebral cortex; and in order for arousal and satisfaction to be maximal, there must be a concerted focusing on specific sexual ideation.

If, instead of concentrating on sexually arousing stimuli, a person keeps telling himself that it would be terrible if he were sexually incompetent; that this would prove that he was worthless and inferior; that he simply must be able to get as many and as powerful orgasms as other people get; that when he comes to climax, bells should ring and lights should flash—if this is the kind of nonsense that a person keeps repeating to himself, it can only be expected that he will rarely achieve a high degree of excitement and fruition.

Another form that sex shame currently takes in our society is equally inhibiting—that is, as an inhibitor of varied coital and extracoital technique. Today, fewer college-educated and middle-class individuals are desisting from trying various coital positions or types of noncoital sex play which once were erroneously called "perversions." Having little sex guilt, in the old-fashioned sense, they do not deem these aspects of sex wicked.

At the same time, however, literally millions of Americans are employing extravaginal methods only as "preliminary" or "love play" techniques and are not using them, when necessary, up to and including the achievement of orgasm. Their reasons for so restricting themselves are again bound up with shame: that is, they feel that they "should" be able to achieve full satisfaction through "natural" coital means, and should not require digital manipulations of the genitals, oral-genital relations, or other techniques of coming to climax.

If people do require noncoital methods of achieving orgasm— as many of them quite normally do—they feel that there is something "wrong" with them, that they are sexually "inferior" or "incompetent." This feeling, of course, is perfectly illogical and is almost entirely a consequence of their arbitrary notions of what is "shameful." To compound the problem here, where many wives feel that they are abnormal because they cannot come to orgasm in the course of penile-vaginal copulation, many of their husbands also believe that they are inferior when they cannot give their wives orgasms except through noncoital methods. Both partners thereby shamefully—and most mistakenly—interfere with their own sex satisfactions.

As a case in point, I saw a 25-year-old wife who had never achieved an orgasm with her husband and was ready to divorce him because of her shame about her own and his sexual ineptness. Without even attempting at first to uncover any of her "deep" unconscious feelings of guilt, anxiety, or hostility, I merely forcefully explained to this woman how she was forestalling her own orgasms.

"From what you tell me," I said, "it seems clear that you are almost constantly telling yourself: 'Oh, how horrible I am because I never get an orgasm during intercourse!' and 'How can an incompetent person like me ever get a full climax?' and 'If I can't make it with this husband, who treats me so well, how will I possibly be able to be successfully married to anyone else?' and so forth."

"I'm sure you're right. That's just what I do keep telling myself."

"But how can you *possibly* focus on your sex pleasure when you are agitatedly focusing on this kind of self-blaming? In order to feel sexually aroused, you must *think* of sexually arousing things. And you are thinking of the most *un*arousing thing imaginable— that is, of your own unworthiness as a woman."

"But how can I consider myself to be a worthy woman if I am bad sexually?"

"How can you *not?* In the first place, as you told me before, your husband is not complaining at all, since *he* is being well satisfied by your mutual sex activity. And in the second place, even if he were complaining, it would merely mean that *he* has certain arbitrary prejudices—that he, for example, *insists* on your having an orgasm during intercourse, instead of telling himself that it would be nice if you did have one—and that he is just as disturbed, for having these prejudices, as you are for having yours. At the worst, in any event, you would prove to be a relatively poor sex partner to your husband. But that would hardly make you a worthless *woman*."

"You mean I might then be good for some other man—or good for myself, even though my husband would find me no good in bed?"

"Exactly. But you really seem to think that *you're* no good if you aren't a perfectly lovely sex partner to your husband. And that's only your *definition* of yourself, and has no relation to external facts."

I insisted, in session after session, that this patient was a worthwhile human being in her own right, no matter how poor she might be as a sex partner. I also kept pointing out that if she focused on sexually exciting stimuli, instead of on how worthless she was for not having orgasms, she could almost certainly bring herself to have fully satisfying climaxes.

She at first resisted my suggestions, but after eight sessions of fairly repetitive rational-emotive psychotherapy, I began to convince her. She tried, really for the first time, to let herself go in the course of her marital relations, and got so she could enjoy intercourse, even though she didn't have an orgasm while it was going on. She finally became sufficiently released to try mutual oral-genital relations with her husband and found that she was unusually aroused by this method, but that it was so exciting that she could not focus adequately on her own climax. When her husband was independently practicing cunnilinctus, however, she was able to focus quite well and soon experienced explosive orgasm.

After some practice, this patient was able to focus properly on sexual enjoyment during the act of coitus itself. As she reported during one of the closing psychotherapy sessions.

"I had considerable difficulty at first, because I found myself thinking, 'Will it happen this time? Will it happen this time?' And, of course, just as you explained to me, it didn't happen when I kept thinking that. Then I finally said to myself, 'All right, if it doesn't happen this time, so what? If I *never* get an orgasm this way it won't be too bad, either. But let me try to get it.' And I could feel myself, as I thought that it wouldn't be too bad, really, if it never happened at all, getting much more relaxed about the whole thing than I ever was before.

"Then I was able, without too much difficulty really, to focus on my own pleasure. Not even on Jim's, for a change, but just on my own. And I found that it started coming, almost immediately, and I kept focusing on the pleasant feeling I was getting, the sex feeling that is, and how I wanted to keep that feeling going. And before I knew it, after only about five minutes of active intercourse, there it was, and it was thrilling as all hell. Other times, we had tried for a half hour or more and nothing had happened. But this time, wow!"

At the last session I had with this patient, when we were talking about other aspects of her life (since sex was no longer a problem), she smilingly informed me that her husband had been away on a business trip for a few days and when he came home they had spent almost the entire night having sex relations in many different positions and ways. "And would you believe it?" she said, "I'm sure that I had about a hundred orgasms during the night!"

As an example of how rational-emotive therapy was employed with a male with serious sex problems, we may take the case of a 25-year-old patient whom I saw because he kept either losing his erection as soon as he started to have intercourse with his wife or ejaculating within a few seconds after penetration. It was quickly apparent in his case that this patient did have a somewhat classical Oedipus complex—which I by no means see in most of my patients today, but which from time to time does turn up—and that he always had felt guilty in having sex relations with any female partner because his mother, who was still young and attractive, had literally taught him that sex was for procreative purposes and that "more worthwhile" people enjoyed themselves with "higher and better" pursuits.

Consequently, this patient had had only two or three abortive attempts at intercourse before marriage and had married a rather unattractive physician, a few years older than himself, who was a highly intellectual and (according to his mother's and his own standards) "more worthwhile" sort of person. He had been potent with his wife until she became pregnant with their first and so far only child; and since that time, though the child was now two years of age, he had never been completely sexually adequate.

It was easy to see why this patient was afraid to be potent—or, to risk a pun, was scared unstiff—and it was not difficult to get him to accept the interpretation that his impotency originally stemmed from his indoctrinations concerning incest and his conscious belief that sex for the sake of fun was improper. Unfortunately, however, his acceptance of these interpretations had no particular effect on his sexual competence.

The patient was then shown that, while his *primary* disturbance may well have been connected with his relations with his mother and his antisexual beliefs thus engendered, his *secondary* (and for the moment *more* important) disturbance was connected with his feelings of shame, of incompetence, of failure. That is to say, his society (and, in his particular case, his father more than his mother) had taught him to believe wholeheartedly that the worst possible thing in the world, and in many ways even worse than enjoying himself sexually, was being a weakling, a nincompoop, a failure.

Consequently, when he first started to become incapable of sustaining an adequate erection, instead of asking himself the simple questions "*Why* am I failing sexually?" and "What can I do *not* to keep failing?" he kept telling himself, over and over, "See what a failure I am! This proves what I've always suspected: that I'm weak and no good! Oh, my God, how awful it is for me to be so incompetent and unmanly!" By repeating this kind of catastrophizing sentences the patient (of course!) kept focusing and refocusing on sexual failure rather than success, and he could not possibly overcome his disability.

It must again be remembered, in this connection, that both male and female sexual arousal and incitation to orgasm are mainly mediated through impulses from the cerebral cortex of the brain and are basically cognitive in origin. And when we focus upon nonsexual notions—such as the idea that it is awful or catastrophic when we are not becoming sufficiently erect or are prematurely achieving a climax—it is literally impossible for us to focus, simultaneously, on sexually exciting ideas. The result, in the male, is often inability to obtain or maintain erection.

I have not found a single case, recently, of male inadequacy in which, no matter what the *original* cause of the problem, the afflicted individual was not *secondarily* telling himself how horrible it was to be impotent, convincing himself that he was a terrible failure and that, as such, he would doubtless continue to be inadequate. So with this patient. He kept, once his first symptoms arose, ceaselessly watching himself, expecting sexual weakness to occur, worrying about his weakness, and continually giving himself a difficult time. When he was shown exactly what he was doing and what nonsensical catastrophizing sentences he was telling himself to sustain his erectile and ejaculatory difficulties, and when he was induced to start *contradicting* the nonsense that he kept telling himself, he quickly began to improve.

Thus, this patient began to see that it was *not* terrible—but only expectable—for him to be sexually inadequate, considering his upbringing. He was led to admit to himself that he was *not* an incompetent or a failure just because he had a sex problem. And he was forced, generally, to question his entire concept of masculinity and failure and to see that *doing, trying, working at* things are more important than necessarily *succeeding at* or doing them *perfectly*. Once he began to surrender his philosophy of the necessity of achieving absolute success and perfection, he was able to watch his sexual behavior more objectively and to focus on sexually exciting stimuli.

At the same time (though this seemed less necessary with this patient since he had already, by himself, worked through some of his original mother-inculcated puritanism), I also tackled his basic beliefs that sex was wicked outside of procreation and that incestuous desires toward one's own mother were horrible to contemplate.

On two levels, then, by attacking (1) his original antisexual philosophy that first led to his sex problem, and (2) his secondary philosophy of success and perfectionism that encouraged him to retain, sustain, and aggravate his original symptoms, I directed this patient to more rational modes of thinking about himself and his sexuality.

Whereas, when I used to do psychoanalysis, I mainly would have concentrated on the first of these points, I now, with the use of rational-emotive therapy, mainly concentrate on the second point and find this kind of focusing to be much more efficient. Almost invariably, I find this technique to be effective in case of male and female psychosexual disability.

I also note, that, although I see many people every year who specifically come to me with severe sexual problems, I rarely see one who has what I would call a pure sexual disturbance. With few exceptions, my patients have *general* emotional difficulties, which stem from their poor, illogical, and self-defeating *general* philosophies of life. Their sex symptoms almost always are derivatives of these idiotic general creeds or assumptions; and when their basic beliefs, of which they are unconscious in the sense of not knowing how important they are to their lives, are forthrightly brought to their attention, ruthlessly revealed and analyzed to show how ridiculous these are, and consistently attacked, discouraged, and rooted out, their sex problems do not automatically vanish but are at least much more susceptible to specific re-educating instructions.

In regard to the treatment of frigidity and impotence, therefore, rational-emotive psychotherapy is (as usual) no palliative, superficial, or symptom-removing technique. Rather, it is an intensive, theory-rooted form of therapy that goes right to the main philosophic roots of the individual's presenting disorder and that aims at fundamental attitudinal changes rather than any cursory "cures."

REFERENCES

1. Eichenlaub, John E., *The Marriage Art* (New York: Lyle Stuart, 1962).
2. Ellis, Albert, Application of Clinical Psychology to Sexual Disorders, in Brower, Daniel, and Lawrence A. Abt, eds. *Progress in Clinical Psychology* (New York: Grune & Stratton, 1952).
3. Ellis, Albert, *Sex Without Guilt* (New York: Lyle Stuart and Grove Press, 1965).
4. Ellis, Albert, *The Art and Science of Love* (New York: Lyle Stuart and Dell Books, 1966).
5. Ellis, Albert, Frigidity, in Albert Ellis and Albert Abarbanel, eds., *The Encyclopedia of Sexual Behavior* (New York: Hawthorn Books, 1967).
6. Ellis, Albert, *The American Sexual Tragedy* (New York: Lyle Stuart, 1962).
7. Hirsch, Edwin W., *Modern Sex Life* (New York: New American Library, 1957).
8. Hitschmann, E., and Bergler, E., Frigidity in Women, *Psychoanalytic Review*, 36:45-53, 1949.
9. Kinsey, Alfred C., Pomeroy, Wardell B., Martin, Clyde E., and Gebhard, Paul H., *Sexual Behavior in the Human Female* (Philadelphia: Saunders, 1953).
10. Kleegman, Sophia J., Frigidity, *Quarterly Review of Surgery, Obstetrics, & Gynecology*, 16:243-48, 1959.
11. Kupperman, Herbert S., Frigidity: Endocrinological Aspects, *Quarterly Review of Surgery, Obstetrics, & Gynecology*, 16:254-57, 1959.
12. Piers, G., and Singer, M. G., *Shame and Guilt* (Springfield, Ill.: Charles C Thomas, 1953).
13. Walker, Kenneth, and Strauss, E. B., *Sexual Disorders in the Male* (Baltimore: Williams & Wilkins, 1952).

VIKTOR E. FRANKL

Paradoxical Intention:

A Logotherapeutic Technique

Viktor E. Frankl is usually considered an existential analyst because his therapy (logotherapy) is a phenomenological approach
to what he sees as man's basic striving "for finding and fulfilling
meaning and purpose in life." The technique of paradoxical
intention, which is described in the following paper, is similar
to tactics employed by Marie Coleman Nelson, Spotnitz, Krich,
Erickson, Haley, and Greenwald, although their rationale may
be quite different from Frankl's. In phobias and obsessions,
Frankl encourages the patient to do, or wish to happen, the very
things he fears. Frankl believes that in this manner a paradoxical
wish is substituted for the pathogenic fear.

IT HAS FREQUENTLY been questioned to what extent psychotherapy can be taught and learned, since the psychotherapeutic
process consists of a continuous chain of improvisations. In addition, one must bear in mind the infinite diversity of patients which
precludes the possibility of extrapolating from one patient to another. Thus the psychotherapist is faced with the seemingly impossible twofold task of always considering the uniqueness of each
person as well as the uniqueness of the life situation with which
this person has to cope. Nevertheless, it is precisely this *individuali-*

From *American Journal of Psychotherapy*, Vol. XIV, No. 3, July 1960, pp.
520-535.
  I wish to acknowledge the kind assistance of D. F. Tweedie, Jr., Ph.D.,
Chairman, Dept. of Psychology, Gordon College, Mass., in the editing of this
manuscript.

zation and *improvisation* which must be taught and must be learned.

The choice of an appropriate treatment method to be applied in any concrete case depends not only upon the *individuality* of the patient involved, but also upon the *personality* of the therapist. The difficulty of the problem lies in the fact that the last two factors must be considered as "unknowns," at least initially. To illustrate this point, I frequently tell my students that the choice of the therapeutic method to be used in a specific situation may be compared to the following algebraic equation: $\psi = x + y$, wherein ψ is the therapeutic method, x represents the individuality of the patient, while y stands for the physician involved.

This equation highlights the fact that the crucial agency in psychotherapy is not so much the method but rather the relationship between the patient and his doctor, or, to use a currently popular expression, the "encounter" between the therapist and his patient. This human relationship between two persons is what seems to be the most significant aspect of the psychotherapeutic process, a more important factor than any method or technique. However, we should not be disdainful of technique, for in therapy a certain degree of detachment on the part of the therapist is indispensable. In fact, the human element must on occasion be disregarded in order to expedite the treatment.[1]*

The therapeutic relationship develops in a polar field of tension in which the poles are represented by the extremes of *human closeness* on the one hand, and *scientific detachment* on the other. Therefore, the therapist must beware lest he be beguiled into falling prey to either extreme in which only one of these poles is considered. This means that the therapist must neither be guided by mere sympathy, by his desire to help his patient, nor, conversely, repress his human interest in the other human being by dealing with him merely in terms of technique.[2] The therapist must beware of interpreting his own role as that of a technician, of a *médicin technicien*. This would amount to reducing the patient (in the words of the famous French materialist LaMettrie) to an *"homme machine."*

The question has often been posed as to whether Logotherapy includes what might be justifiably spoken of as a therapeutic technique. In spite of the fact that this inquiry is frequently accompanied by a measure of doubt, Logotherapy does utilize a special psychotherapeutic procedure. This method was first set forth by

* Superior numbers refer to the list of references at the end of this article.

the author in *The Doctor and the Soul*,[3] originally published in 1946, and in a more detailed manner in 1956.[4]

In order to understand fully what takes place when this technique is utilized, we shall use as a starting point a phenomenon which is known to every clinically trained psychiatrist, namely anticipatory anxiety. It is commonly observed that such anxiety often produces precisely that situation of which the patient is afraid. The erythrophobic individual, for example, who is afraid of blushing when he enters a room and faces a group of people, will actually blush at precisely that moment.

In case histories which display anticipatory anxiety, the fear of some pathologic event (thus, ironically, precipitating it), one may frequently observe an analogous phenomenon. This is the compulsion to self-observation. For instance, in cases of insomnia, the patients often report in the anamnesis that they become especially aware of the problem of falling asleep when they go to bed. Of course this very attention inhibits the sleeping process.

In addition to the fact that excessive *attention* proves to be an intrinsically pathogenic factor with regard to the etiology of neuroses, we also observe in many neurotic patients that excessive *intention* may also be pathogenic. Many sexual neuroses, at least according to the findings and teachings of logotherapy, may be traced back to the forced intention of attaining the goal of sexual intercourse—be it the male seeking to demonstrate his potency, or the female her ability to experience orgasm. The author has discussed this subject at length in various papers,[5, 6, 7] pointing out that as a rule the patient seeks pleasure intentionally (one might say that he takes the "pleasure principle" literally). However, pleasure belongs to that category of events which cannot be brought about by direct intention, but, on the contrary, is a mere side effect or by-product. Therefore, the more one strives for pleasure, the less one is able to attain it. Thus we see an interesting parallel in which anticipatory anxiety brings about precisely what the patient had feared, while excessive intention, as well as excessive self-observation with regard to one's own functioning makes this functioning impossible.

It is this twofold fact upon which logotherapy bases the technique known as "paradoxical intention." For instance, when a phobic patient is afraid that something will happen to him, the logotherapist encourages him to intend or wish, even if only for a second, precisely what he fears.

The following clinical reports will indicate what I mean:

A young physician came to our clinic because of a severe hidrophobia. He had for a long time been troubled by disturbances of the autonomic nervous system. One day he happened to meet his chief on the street and, as the young man extended his hand in greeting, he noticed that he was perspiring more than usually. The next time he was in a similar situation he expected to perspire again and this anticipatory anxiety precipitated excessive sweating. It was a vicious circle; hyperhidrosis provoked hidrophobia and hidrophobia, in turn, produced hyperhidrosis. We advised our patient, in the event that his anticipatory anxiety should recur, to resolve deliberately to show the people whom he confronted at the time how much he could really sweat. A week later he returned to report that whenever he met anyone who triggered his anticipatory anxiety, he said to himself, "I only sweated out a liter before, but now I'm going to pour out at least ten liters!" What was the result of this paradoxical resolution? After suffering from his phobia for four years, he was quickly able, after only one session, to free himself of it for good by this new procedure.

The reader will note that this treatment consists not only in a reversal of the patient's attitude toward his phobia—inasmuch as the usual "avoidance" response is replaced by an intentional effort—but also, that it is carried out in as humorous a setting as possible. This brings about a change of attitude toward the symptom which enables the patient to place himself at a distance from the symptom, to detach himself from his neurosis. This procedure is based on the fact that, according to logotherapeutic teaching, the pathogenesis in phobias and obsessive-compulsive neuroses is partially due to the increase of anxieties and compulsions that is caused by the endeavor to avoid or fight them. A phobic person usually tries to avoid the situation in which his anxiety arises, while the obsessive-compulsive tries to suppress, and thus to fight, his threatening ideas. In either case the result is a strengthening of the symptom. Conversely, if we succeed in bringing the patient to the point where he ceases to flee from or to fight his symptoms, but on the contrary, even exaggerates them, then we may observe that the symptom diminishes and that the patient is no longer haunted by it.

Such a procedure must make use of the unique potentiality for self-detachment inherent in a sense of humor. Along with Heidegger's assertion that "sorrowful concern" (*Sorge*) is the essential feature permeating human existence, and Binswanger's subsequent substitution of "loving togetherness" (*liebendes Miteinandersein*) as the chief human characteristic, I would venture to say that humor

also deserves to be mentioned among the basic human capacities.*
No animal is able to laugh.

As a matter of fact, when paradoxical intention is used, the
purpose is to enable the patient to develop a sense of detachment
toward his neurosis by laughing at it, to put it simply. A statement
somewhat consistent with this is found in Gordon Allport's book,
The Individual and His Religion:[8] "The neurotic who learns to
laugh at himself may be on the way to self-management, perhaps to
cure" (p. 92). Paradoxical intention is the clinical application of
Allport's statement.

A few more case reports may serve to develop and clarify this
method further:

> I once received a letter from a young medical student who had in
> the past listened to my clinical lectures on logotherapy. She reminded
> me of a demonstration of paradoxical intention that she had attended,
> and continued: "I tried to apply the method which you had used in
> the classroom demonstration to myself. I, too, suffered continually
> from the fear that, while dissecting at the Institute of Anatomy, I
> would begin to tremble when the anatomy instructor entered the
> room. Soon this fear actually did cause a tremor. Then, remembering
> what you had told us in the lecture that dealt with this very situation,
> I said to myself whenever the instructor entered the dissecting room
> 'Oh, here is the instructor! Now I'll show him what a good trembler
> I am—I'll really show him how to tremble!' But whenever I delib-
> erately tried to tremble, I was unable to do so!" †

> Another case, which was treated by one of my assistants, Dr. Kurt
> Kocourek, concerned a woman, Mary B., who had been undergoing
> various treatment methods for eleven years, yet her complaints,
> rather than being alleviated, had increased. She suffered from attacks
> of palpitation accompanied by marked anxiety and anticipatory fears
> of a sudden collapse. After the first attack she began to fear that it
> would recur and, consequently, it did. The patient reported that
> whenever she had this fear it was followed by palpitations. Her chief
> concern was, however, that she might collapse in the street. Dr. Ko-
> courek advised her to tell herself at such a moment: "My heart shall

---

* In addition to being a constituent element in man's existence, humor may
well be regarded as an attribute to deity. See Psalms 2:4; 37:13; and 59:8.

† Once I encountered the most severe case of stuttering that I have seen
in my many years of practice: I met a man who had stuttered severely all his
life—except once. This happened when he was twelve years old, and had hooked
a ride on a street car. When he was caught by the conductor, he thought that
the only way of escape would be to evoke his sympathy, and so he tried to
demonstrate that he was just a "poor, stuttering boy." But when he tried to
stutter, he was utterly unable to do it!

beat still faster! I will collapse right here on the sidewalk!" Furthermore, the patient was advised to seek out deliberately places which
she had experienced as disagreeable, or even dangerous, instead of
avoiding them. Two weeks later, the patient reported: "I am quite
well now and feel scarcely any palpitations. The fear has completely
disappeared." Some weeks after her discharge, she reported: "Occasionally mild palpitations occur, but when they do, I say to myself,
'My heart should beat even faster,' and at that moment the palpitations cease."

Paradoxical intention may even be used therapeutically in cases
which have an underlying somatic basis:

The patient was suffering from a coronary infarct. Subsequently
he developed anxiety as a psychic response to his somatic illness, and
this anxiety became so intense that it became his main complaint.
He began to withdraw from his professional and social contacts and
finally could not bear to leave the hospital where he had been a patient for six months and where a heart specialist was at hand. Finally
the patient was transferred to our clinic and logotherapeutic treatment was begun by Dr. Gerda Becker. The following is a brief summary of tape-recorded comments of the patient:
"I felt very anxious and the pain in my heart region began to
trouble me again. Then I asked the nurse to call the doctor. She
stopped in for a moment and told me to try to make my heart beat
faster and to *increase* the pain and fear until she could return
a little later. I tried this and when she came back after about a quarter
of an hour, I had to confess to her that, to my great surprise, my
endeavors had been in vain—I could increase neither the pain nor
the palpitations but, as a matter of fact, both had disappeared! . . .
Encouraged by this turn of events, I left the clinic for an hour or
so and went for a walk through the streets—something that I had not
attempted for more than six months. Upon entering a store I felt a
slight palpitation but, as the doctor had suggested, I immediately
started saying to myself, 'Try to feel even more anxiety!' Again it
was in vain, I simply could not do it! I returned to the clinic happy
over my achievement of leaving the hospital and strolling around
alone." We invited the patient to visit us six months later and he
reported that he was free of any complaints and had, meanwhile, resumed his professional work.

Now let us turn to the following case:

Mrs. H. R. had been suffering for fourteen years when she came to the
clinic. She was severely handicapped by a counting compulsion as well
as the compulsion to check whether her dresser drawers were in order
and securely locked. She did this by continually checking the contents

of the drawers, closing them by a sharp rapping of her knuckles, and finally by attempting to turn the key in the lock several times. Eventually this condition became so chronic that her knuckles were often bruised and bleeding and the keys and locks on the bureau were ruined.

On the day of her admission, Dr. Eva Niebauer demonstrated to the patient how to practice paradoxical intention. She was shown how to throw things carelessly into her dresser and closet, to try to create as much disorder as possible. She was to say to herself, "These drawers should be as messy as possible!" The result was that two days after admission her counting compulsion disappeared and, after the fourth day, she felt no need to recheck her dresser. She even forgot to lock it—something that she had not failed to do for decades! Sixteen days after hospitalization she felt free of any complaints or symptoms, was very proud of her achievement, and was able to do her daily chores without compulsive repetition. She admitted that obsessive-compulsive ideas occasionally recurred but reported that she was able to ignore them, or, to make light of them. Thus she overcame her compulsion not by frantically fighting it (which only strengthens it) but, on the contrary, by "making a joke of it"; in other words, by applying paradoxical intention.

A remarkable fact about this case is that after her symptoms had cleared up, the patient spontaneously, during a psychotherapeutic interview, revived some significant memories. She remembered that when she was five years old, her brother had destroyed a favorite doll and thereafter she began locking her toys in her dresser drawer. When she was sixteen, she caught her sister in the act of putting on some of the patient's best party clothes without her permission. From that time on she always carefully locked up her clothes. Thus, even if we take it for granted that her compulsions were rooted in these traumatic experiences, it is, nevertheless, the radical *change of attitude* toward her symptoms which was therapeutically effective. The bringing to consciousness of such psychic traumata cannot, at any rate, *in itself* be the appropriate treatment, inasmuch as a method which does not include such a procedure proved to be so efficient. This brings to mind a statement made by Edith Weisskopf-Joelson,[9] which seems to me to be noteworthy: "Although traditional psychotherapy has insisted that therapeutic practices have to be based on findings on etiology, it is possible that certain factors might cause neuroses during early childhood and that entirely different factors might relieve neuroses during adulthood." Even psychoanalysts are more and more inclined to assume that traumata in themselves do not directly cause neuroses. The traumata merely provide the contents of the respective obsessions, compulsions, and phobias. In some cases, I would dare to say that even the opposite is true: The trauma does not cause the neurosis, but rather, the neurosis makes the trauma reappear. One illustration may serve to clarify this point. A reef which appears at low tide is not the cause of the low tide; rather, it is the low tide which causes the reef to appear. Be that as it may, the therapy that we use must be independent of the validity of the etiologic assumptions of any particular neurotic symptoms. Thus Weisskopf-Joelson's comment is pertinent. At any rate, it is interesting to note that more or less "free associations" leading back to the traumatic experiences which produced certain habits and symptoms may occur *after* therapy has brought relief.

Thus we see that paradoxical intention works even in cases in which either the actual *somatic* basis (the patient with the coronary infarct) or the presumed *psychic* cause (the case of H. R.) were not touched upon. Paradoxical intention is effective irrespective of the underlying etiologic basis; in other words, it is an intrinsically nonspecific method. According to the author's opinion, based upon clinical experience, in every severe case involving phobic symptoms, one has to reckon with an autonomic-endocrine or an anancastic substructure. This does not entail a fatalistic viewpoint, however, for a full-fledged neurosis is nothing but a superstructure built upon these constitutional elements; it may well be that it can be psychotherapeutically alleviated without necessarily removing, or even taking into account, the underlying basis. Such a therapy is palliative rather than causal. This is not to say that it is a symptomatic therapy, however, for the logotherapist, when applying paradoxical intention, is concerned not so much with the symptom in itself but, rather, the patient's *attitude* toward his neurosis and its symptomatic manifestations. It is the very act of changing this attitude that is involved whenever an improvement is obtained.

This nonspecificity helps to clarify why paradoxical intention is sometimes effective in severe cases. I wish to emphasize "sometimes"; for I do not wish to convey the impression that beneficial results were *always* obtained, or that paradoxical intention is a universal panacea or a miracle method. On the other hand, however, I feel obliged to present the range of its applicability and the degree of its effectiveness accurately. I should like to add parenthetically that the percentage of cures or cases improved to a degree that has made further treatment unnecessary, is somewhat higher (75.7 per cent) than the figures reported in the literature.[10]

Paradoxical intention is also applicable in cases more complex than those involving monosymptomatic neurosis. The following will demonstrate that even instances of severe obsessive-compulsive character neurosis (in German clinical terminology referred to as anancastic psychopathic character structure) may be appropriately and beneficially treated by means of paradoxical intention.

> The patient was a 65-year-old woman who had suffered for 60 years from a washing compulsion of such severity that she was admitted to our clinic for a period of observation in order that I might certify her for a leucotomy (which I expected to be the only available procedure for bringing relief in this severe case).* Her symptoms began when she was four years of age. When she was prevented from indulging her washing compulsion, she would even lick her hands. Later on she was continually afraid of being infected by people with skin diseases. She would never touch a doorknob. She also insisted that her husband stick to a very complicated prophylactic ritual. For a long time the patient had been unable to do any housework, and finally she remained in bed all day. Nevertheless, even there she persisted in scrubbing things with a cloth for hours, up to 300 times or more, and having her husband repeatedly rinse out the cloth. "Life was hell for me," she confessed.
>
> In the hope of avoiding brain surgery, my assistant, Dr. Eva Niebauer, started logotherapeutic treatment by means of paradoxical intention. The result was that nine days after admission the patient began to help in the ward by mending the stockings of her fellow patients, assisting the nurses by cleaning the instrument tables and washing syringes, and finally even emptying pails of bloody and putrid waste materials! Thirteen days after admission she went home for a few hours and upon her return to the clinic, she triumphantly reported having eaten a roll with soiled hands. Two months later she was able to lead a normal life.
>
> It would not be accurate to say that she is completely symptom-free, for frequently obsessive-compulsive ideas come to her mind. However, she has been able to get relief by ceasing to fight her symptoms (fighting only serves to reinforce them) and, instead, by being ironical about them; in short, by applying paradoxical intention. She is even able to joke about her pathologic thoughts. This patient still kept in contact with the outpatient clinic, for she continued to need supportive logotherapy. The improvement in her condition persisted, however, and thus the leucotomy, which previously had seemed unavoidable, had now become unnecessary.

The author has included a number of cases that were treated by his collaborators rather than by himself. This is not accidental. It

---

* In this connection I should like to stress my conviction that in some cases this operation is the only way to help. I have ventured to give such indications in a few cases and have in no instance regretted my decision.

serves to indicate that it is the method that works and not the personality of the creator of the method (though, as has been pointed out at the beginning, the personal factor must never be neglected).

The reader has undoubtedly noticed, with respect to the above-mentioned case reports, that paradoxical intention is particularly useful as short-term therapy, especially in phobic cases* with an underlying anticipatory anxiety mechanism. The following is a remarkable instance of such short-term therapy that was successful in spite of long-standing pathologic manifestations. It is taken from a tape-recorded report of the patient, Mrs. Rosa L.

"... Once I had forgotten to lock the door and when I returned home it was open. That frightened me very much. After that, whenever I left the house, I couldn't get rid of the feeling that the door was still open. I would go back again and again to check. This went on for twenty years. I knew that the obsession was silly, for every time I went back the door would be locked, but I couldn't seem to keep from obeying the impulse. Life became unbearable. Since my interview with Dr. Becker, however, things have changed completely. Whenever I have the compulsion to check whether or not the door is locked, I say to myself: 'What if the door is open! Let them steal everything in the whole apartment!' and at that moment I am able to ignore the impulse and go calmly on my way."

Three months later we invited her back to report on her condition. She said: "I feel wonderful; not the slightest obsession. I can't even imagine how I could have had all those thoughts in the past years. *For twenty long years* I was tormented by them, but now they're gone and I'm very happy."

One should be careful to avoid the impression, held in many psychotherapeutic circles, that short-term therapy necessarily brings short-lived results. The following excerpts from another tape recording will illustrate this point:

"... There was practically not one minute during the day when I was free of the thought that I might break a store window. But Dr. Frankl told me to go right up to the window with the intention of smashing it. When I did this, the fear disappeared completely and I knew that I wouldn't go through with it. It all seems like a dream now; the fears and impulses to do these things have all vanished."

* At least in some instances, paradoxical intention seems to be effective in cases of psychosis as well; for example, a patient at our clinic reported to one of the doctors at the first interview that she had read about paradoxical intention and had successfully applied it with reference to the "voices" she was hearing. She had taken her acoustic hallucinations for a neurosis!

The noteworthy thing about this report is that it was given twenty years after the treatment!

In connection with short-term therapy, I should like to quote Gutheil's statement[11] regarding "the more common illusions of Freudian orthodoxy, such as that the length of therapy is synonymous with the depth of therapy; that the depth of therapy depends on the frequency of interviews; that the results of therapy are proportionate to the length and depth of treatment; that the durability of results corresponds to the length of therapy." Such a warning may point up the fact that paradoxical intention is not as superficial as it may first appear to be. Something is certainly happening at a deeper level whenever it is applied. Just as a phobic symptom originates beneath the surface of consciousness, so paradoxical intention also appears to affect the deeper level. The humoristic formulations of its method are based on a restoration of basic trust in Being (*Urvertrauen zum Dasein*)[12] (p. 41). What transpires is essentially more than a change of behavior patterns; rather, it is an existential reorientation (*existentielle Umstellung*).

It is in this respect that paradoxical intention represents a truly "logo"-therapeutic procedure in the truest sense of the word.[13] Jorge Marcelo David, a logotherapist from Argentina, has pointed out that its use is based on what is called in logotherapeutic terms psychonoetic antagonism (or, sometimes, *Die Trotzmacht des Geistes*), by which is meant the specifically human capacity to detach oneself, not only from the world but also from oneself. Paradoxical intention mobilizes this basic human potentiality for the therapeutic purpose of combating neuroses.

Of course one is bound to find individual differences in the degree to which this ability can be applied. It cannot be used indiscriminately, and the therapist must be aware of its limitation with regard to certain patients and situations.[14] It would undoubtedly be desirable to establish criteria for evaluating the extent to which a specific patient is likely to mobilize his own psychonoetic antagonism.* At any rate, such testing procedures have yet to be devised. The author himself insists that this ability is present in every human being, since it is an essential feature of being human.

With paradoxical intention one enters into the noetic dimension as the characteristic and constitutive dimension of human existence. Viewed from the point of view of logotherapeutic teachings, this

* Whether it would also be possible is another question inasmuch as, according to a statement of D. F. Tweedie, who is conducting logotherapeutic research, such "antagonism" is atypical for the neurotic patient's past and present experience, upon which, presumably, the criteria would be based.

dimension, the realm of the spiritual, covers more than merely rational or intellectual processes, although these are certainly included. Because of this inclusion, one can appreciate the statement that Gutheil made in his last paper, "Problems of Therapy in Obsessive-Compulsive Neurosis,"[15] namely, that "new therapeutic means must be introduced. . . . Appeal to reason, fruitless though it may be in other cases, holds promise in cases of obsessive-compulsive neurosis, in which rationalization and intellectualization play so great a part."

This, in turn, leads to another question; namely, whether or not paradoxical intention belongs to the persuasive methods, such as that of Paul Dubois, for example. As a matter of fact, paradoxical intention is the exact opposite of persuasion, since it is not suggested that the patient simply suppress his fears (by the rational conviction that they are groundless), but rather, that he overcome them by exaggerating them! The essential dissimilarity of paradoxical intention and suggestive techniques has been brought to our attention by Polak.[16]

Paradoxical intention can also be applied to cases of sleep disturbance, as mentioned before. The fear of sleeplessness increases sleep disturbance because anticipatory anxiety completes and perpetuates the vicious circle. In addition, it results in a forced intention to sleep which incapacitates the patient to do so. Dubois, the famous French psychiatrist, once compared sleep with a dove which has landed near one's hand and stays there as long as one does not pay any attention to it; if one attempts to grab it, it quickly flies away. But how can one remove the anticipatory anxiety which is the pathologic basis of forced intention? In order to take the wind out of the sails of this specific fearful expectation, we advise the patient not to try to force sleep, since the necessary amount of sleep will be automatically secured by the organism. Therefore, he can safely try to do just the opposite, to stay awake as long as possible. In other words, the forced intention to fall asleep, arising from the anticipatory anxiety of not being able to fall asleep, should be replaced by the paradoxical intention of not falling asleep at all! (Which in turn will be followed very rapidly by sleep.)*

In recent years the use of paradoxical intention has been in-

---

* It is noteworthy that this procedure, in cases of insomnia, has subsequently been worked out independently by two other workers in the field. One advises his patients to keep their eyes open as long as possible, while the other recommends to doctors who work with hospitalized patients that they let the patients punch a timeclock every quarter-hour. He reports that after a very few fifteen-minute intervals they succumb to increasing fatigue and sleepiness.

creasingly reported in the literature. Authors from various countries, as well as those collaborating in the work of the Neurological Polyclinic of Vienna, have published the results of the clinical application of this technique. In addition to David (Buenos Aires), mention may be made of the assistants of Professors Kretschmer (Psychiatric University-Clinic of Tübingen), Langen and Volhard, and Prill (Gynecologic University-Clinic of Würzburg) and Rehder (Hamburg). Professor Bazzi (University of Rome) has even worked out special indicators to enable the psychiatrist to distinguish in which cases paradoxical intention should be applied and in which the autogenous training method of Schultz is indicated.[17] At the International Congress for Psychotherapy, held in Barcelona, 1958, Ledermann (London) declared: "The results (of Logotherapy) are not to be denied. I have found the method helpful in cases of obsessional neurosis." Frick (Bolzano, Italy) goes still further by stating that there are cases of severe obsessive-compulsive neurosis in which a logotherapeutic procedure is the "only therapeutic way," and refers to some of his cases in which electroshock treatment had been tried in vain, whereas logotherapy alone served in the sense of an *ultima ratio*. Professor Lopez-Ibor (University of Madrid) makes a similar statement.

In addition to my associates, Kocourek and Niebauer, who have published papers about paradoxical intention, there has been among my co-workers a psychoanalyst, whose training and orientation are strictly Freudian. For a year he treated nearly all the cases of sexual disturbance in the outpatient ward of our clinic, and, inasmuch as short-term therapy was indicated, used logotherapeutic procedures exclusively. His experience is summarized in a paper, worked out in collaboration with me, which he read at a German Congress of Sexology.

We have previously stated that a compulsion to self-observation accompanies anticipatory anxiety, and in the etiology of a neurosis one often finds an excess of attention as well as intention. This is especially true in insomnia in which the forced intention to sleep is accompanied by the forced attention to observe whether the intention is becoming effective or not. This attention thus joins in perpetuating the waking state.

In reference to this phenomenon, logotherapy includes a therapeutic device known as *de-reflection*. Just as paradoxical intention is designed to counteract anticipatory anxiety, de-reflection is intended to counteract the compulsive inclination to self-observation. In other words, what has to be achieved in such cases is more than trying to ridicule the trouble by using paradoxical intention and its humorous formulation; one should also be able to *ignore* the trouble to some degree. Such ignoring, or de-reflection, however, can only be attained to the degree in which the patient's awareness is directed toward positive aspects. De-reflection, in itself, contains both a negative and a positive aspect. The patient must be de-reflected *from* his anticipatory anxiety *to* something else. This conviction is supported by Allport,[8] who once said: "As the focus of striving shifts from the conflict to selfless goals the life as a whole becomes sounder even though the neurosis may never completely disappear" (p. 95). Such goals may be discovered by a certain kind of analytic procedure which we call *Existenzanalyse*.[18, 19, 20] In this way the patient may discover the concrete meaning of his personal existence.[21]

Let us, in conclusion, review the indications of paradoxical intention from the perspective of what logotherapy presents as the four characteristic patterns of response toward neurotic problems:

I. *Wrong Passivity.* By this is meant the behavioral pattern which may be observed in cases of anxiety neurosis or phobic conditions, or both. It is the withdrawal from those situations in which the patient, because of his anticipatory anxiety, expects his fears to recur. What we have to deal with in this case is the *"flight* from fear"—most commonly fear of collapsing on the street or having a heart attack.

II. *Wrong Activity.* This behavioral pattern is characteristic, in the first place, of obsessive-compulsive neurosis. (1) The individual, rather than trying to avoid conflict situations, *fights* against his obsessive ideas and neurotic compulsions and thus reinforces them. This struggle is motivated by two basic fears: (*a*) that the obsessive ideas indicate an imminent, or actual, psychotic condition, and (*b*) that the compulsions will some day result in a homicidal or suicidal attempt. (2) Another aspect of "wrong activity" may be observed in sexual neurosis, namely, a struggle *for* something, rather than *against* something: a striving for orgasm and potency. The underlying motivation is usually as follows: the patient feels that competent sexual performance is "demanded" of him either by the partner, by the situation, or by himself, in the event that he may have, so to speak, "scheduled" it for that moment. Due to this very "pursuit of happiness" the sexually neurotic individual founders, like the obsessive-compulsive neurotic, by responses that are inappropriate to the situation: pressure precipitates counterpressure.

In contrast to these negative, neurotic, "wrong" behavioral patterns, there are two positive, normal ones:

III. *Right Passivity.* This is the case when the patient, by means of paradoxical intention, ridicules his symptoms rather than trying either to run away from them (phobias) or to fight them (obsessive compulsions).

IV. *Right Activity.* Through de-reflection, the patient is enabled to ignore his neurosis by focusing his attention away from himself. He will be directed to *a life full of potential meanings and values with a specific appeal to his personal potentialities.*

In addition to this personal aspect, a social factor is involved as well. More and more we meet individuals who are suffering from what logotherapy calls man's "existential vacuum."[2, 22, 23] Such patients complain of a feeling of a *total and ultimate meaninglessness* in their lives. They display an inner void or emptiness in which neurotic symptoms may abound. Filling this vacuum may thus assist the patient in overcoming his neurosis by helping him become aware of the full spectrum of his concrete and personal meaning and value possibilities, or, in other words, by confronting him with *the "logos" of his existence.*

SUMMARY

In the frame of logotherapy or existential analysis (*Existenzanalyse*), a specific technique has been developed to handle obsessive, compulsive, and phobic conditions. This procedure, called paradoxical intention, is based on the fact that a certain amount of pathogenesis in phobias and obsessive-compulsive neuroses is due to the increase of anxieties and compulsions that is caused by the endeavor to avoid or fight them. Paradoxical intention consists in a reversal of the patient's attitude toward his symptom, and enables him to detach himself from his neurosis. This technique mobilizes what is called in logotherapeutic terms the psychonoetic antagonism, i.e., the specifically human capacity for self-detachment. Paradoxical intention lends itself particularly as a useful tool in short-term therapy, especially in cases with an underlying anticipatory anxiety mechanism.[24, 25, 26, 27, 28]

REFERENCES

1. Frankl, Viktor E., On Logotherapy and Existential Analysis, *American Journal of Psychoanalysis*, 18:28, 1958.
2. Frankl, Viktor E., *From Death Camp to Existentialism, A Psychiatrist's Path to a New Therapy*, Preface by Gordon W. Allport (Boston: Beacon Press, 1959).
3. Frankl, Viktor E., *The Doctor and the Soul, An Introduction to Logotherapy* (New York: Knopf, 1955-57).

4. Frankl, Viktor E., *Theorie und Therapie der Neurosen, Einführung in Logotherapie und Existenzanalyse* (Vienna: Urban & Schwarzenberg, 1956).
5. Frankl, Viktor E., The Spiritual Dimension in Existential Analysis and Logotherapy, *Journal of Individual Psychology*, 15:157, 1959.
6. Frankl, Viktor E., Beyond Self-Actualization and Self-Expression, *Journal of Existential Psychiatry*, 1:5, 1960.
7. Frankl, Viktor E., Logotherapy and the Challenge of Suffering, *Review of Existential Psychology and Psychiatry*, 1:3, 1961.
8. Allport, G. W., The Individual and His Religion (New York: Macmillan, 1956).
9. Weisskopf-Joelson, Edith, Some Comments on a Viennese School of Psychiatry, *Journal of Abnormal and Social Psychology*, 51:701, 1955.
10. Kocourek, K., Niebauer, E., and Polak, P., Ergebnisse der klinischen Anwendung der Logotherapie, in *Handbuch der Neurosenlehre und Psychotherapie*, V. E. Frankl, V. E. v. Gebsattel, and J. H. Schultz, eds. (Munich and Berlin: Urban & Schwarzenzerg, 1959). Vol. III.
11. Gutheil, E. A., *American Journal of Psychotherapy*, 10:134, 1956.
12. Frankl, Viktor E., *Das Menschenbild der Seelenheilkunde, Drei Vorlesungen zur Kritik des dynamischen Psychologismus* (Stuttgart: Hippokrates-Verlag, 1959).
13. Weisskopf-Joelson, Edith, Logotherapy and Existential Analysis, *Acta Psychotherapeutica*, 6:193, 1958.
14. Frankl, Viktor E., in *Critical Incidents in Psychotherapy*, S. W. Standal and R. J. Corsini, eds. (Englewood Cliffs, N.J.: Prentice-Hall, 1959).
15. Gutheil, E. A., Problems of Therapy in Obsessive-Compulsive Neurosis, *American Journal of Psychotherapy*, 13:793, 1959.
16. Polak, P., *Frankls Existenzanalyse in ihrer Bedeutung für Anthropologie und Psychotherapie* (Innsbruck: Tyrolia-Verlag, 1949).
17. Bazzi, T., Considérations sur les limitations et les contraindications de la Logotherapie. Paper read before the Fourth International Congress of Psychotherapy in Barcelona, Spain, in 1958.
18. Frankl, Viktor E., Zur Grundlegung einer Existenzanalyse, *Schweiz. med. Wchnschr.*, 69:707, 1939.
19. Dienelt, K., *Die Existenzanalyse V. E. Frankls und ihre Bedeutung für die Erziehung* (Vienna: Oesterreichischer Bundesverlag, 1955).
20. Polak, P., Frankl's Existential Analysis, *American Journal of Psychotherapy*, 3:617, 1949.
21. Frankl, Viktor E., Logos and Existence in Psychotherapy, *American Journal of Psychotherapy*, 7:8, 1953.
22. Frankl, Viktor E., Logotherapy and the Collective Neuroses, in *Progress in Psychotherapy*, Vol. IV, J. H. Masserman and J. L. Moreno, eds. (New York: Grune & Stratton, 1959).
23. Arnold, M. B., and Gasson, J. A., The Human Person (New York: Ronald Press, 1954), chapter 16, Logotherapy and Existential Analysis.
24. Gerz, Hans O., The Treatment of the Phobic and the Obsessive-Compulsive Patient Using Paradoxical Intention sec. Viktor E. Frankl, *Journal of Neuropsychiatry*, 3:375-87, 1962.
25. Gerz, Hans O., Experience with the Logotherapeutic Technique of Paradoxical Intention in the Treatment of Phobic and Obsessive-Compulsive Patients, *The American Journal of Psychiatry*, 123:548, 1966.
26. Frankl, Viktor E., *Psychotherapy and Existentialism* (New York: Washington Square Press, 1967).
27. Kaczanowski, Godfrey, Logotherapy—A New Psychotherapeutic Tool, *Psychosomatics*, 8:158, 1967.
28. Frankl, Viktor E., Logotherapy and Existential Analysis—A Review, *American Journal of Psychotherapy*, 20:252, 1966.

LEWIS R. WOLBERG

Methodology in Short-Term Therapy

Effective short-term therapy is one of the major needs in the entire area of psychotherapy. Most of the papers in this volume reflect ways in which different therapists have tried to fill this need. Wolberg approaches the problem primarily from the viewpoint of providing insight but does not limit himself to this one modality. His approach is broadly eclectic and he advocates utilizing a variety of techniques, including psychoanalytic psychotherapy, interviewing procedures, hypnosis, and group therapy. He also provides a planned step-by-step procedure for the employment of these various techniques, examples of all of which are supplied in this volume.

THE ADVANTAGES of short-term over long-term therapy may be debated on various grounds. Financial savings, more efficient employment of psychotherapeutic resources, opportunities to reduce waiting lists—these and other expediencies are often presented as justification for short-term programs. Admitting that there may be pragmatic reasons for abbreviating treatment, we may ask a crucial question: "How truly effective are short-term approaches in modifying disturbed neurotic patterns?"

In a study of the results of patients treated by a team of psychoanalytically trained therapists from the Tavistock Clinic and Cassel

From *The American Journal of Psychiatry*, Vol. 122, No. 2, August, 1965.

Hospital, Malan[1] concludes that long-lasting "depth" changes are possible even in severely ill patients treated on a short-term basis. The findings in this study are similar in some respects to those I have observed among a large group of patients with whom I have worked briefly over the past 25 years. Follow-up visits persuade that not only have symptoms been controlled, but in a considerable number of patients reconstructive personality changes have been brought about. The rationale for short-term therapy and a detailed delineation of techniques have been elaborated elsewhere.[2] In this paper some stratagems found helpful will be outlined that may possibly be adaptable to the style of other therapists.

The psychotherapeutic process in short-term treatment may descriptively be broken down into four phases: a supportive phase, an apperceptive phase, an action phase, and an integrative phase.

THE SUPPORTIVE PHASE OF THERAPY

Turning to another human being for help is an inevitable consequence of feelings of helplessness, bewilderment, and anxiety. It represents a final acknowledgment by the individual that he is unable to cope with his difficulty through his own resources. More or less every emotionally ill patient overtly or covertly regards the helping authority as a source of inspiration from whom infusions of wisdom must flow that will heal his wounds and lead him to health and self-fulfillment. Such credences are powered by the helplessness that inevitably accompanies a shattering of the sense of mastery. Because his habitual coping mechanisms have failed him, the patient believes himself incapable of independent judgments and he delivers himself body and soul to the powerful therapeutic agent whose education and experience promise to take over the direction of his life.

This design is obviously unwholesome if it is permitted to continue, for elements will be released that undermine the patient's independence, inspire infantility, and mobilize anachronistic hopes and demands that superimpose themselves on the patient's other troubles, further complicating his existence.

Knowing that the patient covets a scheme to enmesh himself in

1. D. H. Malan, *A Study of Brief Psychotherapy* (Springfield, Ill.: Charles C Thomas, 1965).

2. L. R. Wolberg, The Technic of Short-Term Psychotherapy, in L. R. Wolberg, ed., *Short-Term Psychotherapy* (New York: Grune & Stratton, 1965).

a passive role with an omniscient deity, beneficent protector, and idealized parent, the therapist may plan his strategy.

First, it is essential to establish as rapidly as possible a working relationship with the patient. This can often be done by a skilled therapist in the initial interview. It is difficult, however, to designate any unalterable rules for the establishing of contact with a patient. Variable factors apply in one case that are not applicable in a second. However, there are certain general principles that are useful to observe, within the bounds of which one may operate flexibly. For instance, the expression on meeting the patient of a sympathetic and friendly attitude is remarkably helpful in relaxing him sufficiently to tell his story. As obvious as this may seem, many therapists greet a new patient with a detached and passive attitude in the effort to be objective and nondirective. This can freeze the patient in a resistive bind from which he may not recover during the span of his contact with the therapist.

Second, it is important to treat the patient, no matter how upset he seems, as a worthwhile individual who has somehow blundered into a neurotic impasse from which he will be able to extricate himself. Neurotic difficulties influence feelings in the direction of being unloved and unlovable. The patient may harbor doubts that he can be accepted or understood. Irrespective of denial mechanisms, he will crave extraordinary reassurance that the therapist is interested in him and cares about what happens to him. This obviously cannot be communicated verbally, but it may be expressed through a manner of respect, considerateness, tact, solicitude, and compassion.

Third, the patient must be inspired to verbalize as much as possible, while the therapist attends to what he is saying, encouraging him by facial expressions, gestures, utterances, and comments that reflect an interest in the patient and an understanding of what he is trying to say. The patient is constantly drawn out to express his problems, pointed questions being phrased to facilitate the flow of ideas and feelings.

Fourth, it is vital to avoid arguing or quarreling with the patient no matter how provocative he may be. The available time for therapy is so limited that one cannot indulge in the challenges and confrontations possible in long-term therapy. The therapist may not agree with what the patient says, but he should convey a respect for the patient's right to express his irritations and misconceptions.

Fifth, empathy is the keynote in establishing contact. Understandably one may not be able to sympathize with some of the attitudes, feelings, and behavior of the patient. It may also be difficult to put oneself in his place. Yet the therapist may be able to detect an essential dignity in the patient, considering that his problems, destructive to him and to other people, have deviated him away from creative and humanistic aims. While it is inexpedient therapeutically to reassure too readily or to praise, it is essential in the early stages of treatment not to underestimate the patient's constructive qualities. In concentrating his attention on his bad points, the patient will tend to minimize his worthwhile characteristics which may lend themselves to a recounting by the therapist after he has gathered sufficient data.

Sixth, the therapist may by his verbal and nonverbal behavior signal confidence in his ability to help the patient without promising him a cure. This presupposes that the therapist has faith in what he is doing and a conviction that all people, given even a minimal chance, have the capacity to develop.

Seventh, even in the first interview the patient may be told that the rapidity of his recovery will depend on his willingness to cooperate in working on his problems. The therapist will show him how he can do this and will help him to help himself.

THE APPERCEPTIVE PHASE

If we are to proceed beyond the supportive phase toward an attempt at reconstruction of personality, we must strive to bring the individual to some recognition of what is behind his disorder. The power of "insight" has, of course, been greatly exaggerated, but irrespective of how valid or invalid an "insight" may be, it constitutes, when it is accepted, a significant means of alleviating tension and of restoring to the individual his habitual sense of mastery. The fact that we couch our "insights" in scientific terminology, being assured that they validate our theoretical preconceptions, does not make them accurate, even though the patient responds to them with relief, hope, and abatement of his complaints.

Yet the principle is a correct one. Some explanation for his trouble is essential and we must give our patient one that is as close to our current scientific understanding of human nature as possible, always mindful of the fact that as behavioral scientists we are balanced precariously on the pinnacle of profound ambiguities. What seems like the truth of today may be the exploded myth of tomorrow.

But myth though it be, we have no other more tenable explanation; so we make it, hopeful that it will find its mark. The most effective vehicle that we have for this is the unique relationship that is set up between the patient and therapist which acts as a corrective experience for the patient. The patient may project into the relationship the same kinds of irrational demands, hopes, and fears as have shadowed his attitudes toward early authorities and other significant people in his past. But instead of meeting indignation, rejection, ridicule or hostility—the usual and expected rebuttals—the therapist interprets the patient's reactions with sympathy and understanding. Bringing these, if they are apparent, to his attention in a noncondemning manner helps the patient to arrive at an understanding of the meaning and possible origin of his drives while actually re-experiencing them in the protective relationship with the therapist. Under these circumstances the patient may come to realize that his responses toward the therapist are the product, not of any realistic situation that exists, but rather of what he anticipates or imagines must be as a result of past relationships. He may then appreciate that what is happening with the therapist also happens under some circumstances with other people. Thus varied defensive reactions become apparent to the patient, not as theories, but as real experiences.

In short-term therapy, time prevents the employment of the conventional tools of free association, extensive dream interpretation, and the building up of a transference neurosis. However, an experienced therapist will be able, perhaps even in the first session to gain knowledge of the operative dynamics from the history given by the patient, particularly the quality of his relationship with his parents and siblings, from one or two dreams, from the nature of the symptomatology, and from the patient's behavior with the therapist during the interview. He may then present at a propitious moment a cautious but firm explanation to the patient of the impact on him and his personality of some of the experiences and deprivations in his childhood, of the defenses he has developed, of how environmental precipitating factors have operated to bring his conflicts to a head and how these are registered in his immediate symptoms and sufferings. Only a fragment of the existing conflicts may lend itself to such exploration and interpretation in short-term therapy, but this can be like a biopsy of the total psychodynamic picture. If the patient grasps the significance of an interpretation and sees the continuity between problems in his development, their crystallizations in his general personality structure, and their relation to the current complaint factor, a deep penetration will have been achieved. By concerted self-examination, the patient may thereafter progressively widen his own insights. In any equation the shifting of one factor will bring other elements into realignment.

Obviously, interpretations will have to be made that coordinate with the patient's capacities for understanding. The therapist will need to employ language comprehensible to the patient, encouraging the patient to restate what has been expressed to test his comprehension. It is surprising how patients, even those without an extensive education, can grasp the meaning of relatively complex psychological concepts if these are presented in terms of the patient's own experience. When a good relationship exists between the therapist and patient, even unconscious repudiated aspects may be explored without provoking too severe reactions of resistance. If the patient is unable to acknowledge the accuracy of an interpretation, the therapist may ask him to consider it nevertheless before discarding it entirely. The patient may also be encouraged to alert himself to factors that stir up his tensions, to work on connections between these provocative factors and what is being mobilized inside himself. Are his reactions habitual ones, and if so how far back do they go? Are they related to important experiences in his childhood? Some patients may be able to get considerable understanding through the discipline of searching within themselves. Some may even learn to interpret their dreams in line with such percipience.

Sometimes the patient will, due to resistance or the lack of time, fail to arrive at any basic realizations in the course of short-term therapy. This need not deter the therapist from encouraging the patient to work on himself toward self-understanding after the treatment period is over. It is quite rewarding to observe how many patients, some months and even years later, arrive at insights which strike them with a dramatic force and which they can utilize constructively. Examining these one may recognize them as patterned after some of the therapist's original interpretations, which could not be accepted during the short treatment phase, but which were subjected to spontaneous "working-through" following treatment.

THE ACTION PHASE

The acid test of therapy lies in the patient's capacity to put his acquired new comprehensions into definitive action. This means that he must challenge conceptions that have up to this time ruled his life. A symptom may rapidly be overcome in the supportive phase of therapy; but a personality pattern, one that disorganizes relationships with other human beings, will scarcely be altered except after a period of resistance.

In short-term therapy even the tiniest action opposing neurotic misconceptions can be scored as a gain. The therapist may actively invite the patient to challenge his fears and engage in actions that hold promise of rewards. Discussion of the consequences of his movements may then prove fruitful. I have found several tactics of importance here. First, I actively outline specific courses of action, hoping that the patient, prompted to act on my suggestion, will achieve a small success which will reinforce his determination to try again. Even after a signal success, patients will need further urging. Having escaped hurt by the skin of their teeth, they may feel that their luck will collapse the next time they engage in an experience that threatens to set off anxiety. Second, a tranquilizer or a barbiturate taken prior to a challenge may reduce anxiety sufficiently so that the patient may allow himself to enter into a fearsome situation and see it through. As soon as possible, a repetition of this action with reduced and finally no drug will be indicated. In borderline patients, a phenothiazine derivative like trifluoperazine appears to work better than the tranquilizing drugs. Third, I sometimes teach the patient self-hypnosis.[3] In the trance the patient is trained to visualize himself successfully mastering situations that upset him. The patient may fantasy an overcoming of progressively challenging difficulties, gradually working himself up to more fearsome ones. Suggestions made to himself in the trance that he will have the desire to tackle his problems may enable him to handle these with greater and greater ease.

THE INTEGRATIVE PHASE

Consolidating ·therapeutic gains will require practice for the remainder of the individual's life. The chinks in the patient's defensive armor must be widened by constant challenges and repetitive salutary actions. Complacency, riding on the notion that one feels better and hence can remain at a standstill, invites a recrudescence of symptoms once stress exceeds existent coping capacities. Constant alertness to what is happening within oneself and a resisting of subversive neurotic temptations are mandatory.

In short-term therapy one must depend on the post-therapeutic

3. L. R. Wolberg, Hypnosis in Short-Term Psychotherapy, in L. R. Wolberg, ed., *Short-Term Psychotherapy, op. cit.*

period to harden what has been molded during the active treatment phases, and to restructure into new patterns aspects that were only casually perceived before. Encouraging is the fact that once the old way of life has been unbalanced in one dimension, new zones of activity and more wholesome modes of being and feeling may present themselves.

Before therapy is terminated, the patient may realize that it is possible to control tension and anxiety once it starts by making connections between symptomatic upsets, precipitating factors in his environment, and his operative personality forces; and by recognizing that he is capable of developing a different philosophy that can lend to his life a salutary meaning.

In some cases I encourage the patient to employ the technique of self-hypnosis or self-relaxation periodically when he is upset, both to resolve his tensions and to explore reasons for the revival of his symptoms.[4] Patients can easily learn to apply this twofold tactic by giving themselves the assignment to figure out the aspects within their environment and within themselves that have precipitated their anxiety. This may result in direct understanding, or stimulated fantasies and dreams may yield some leads. A helpful course of action may then spontaneously be evolved. No more than a few sessions are usually required to restore equilibrium.

The patient may also be counseled temporarily to employ a mild tranquilizing drug if his tensions do not resolve after a while. He must be cautioned, however, that drugs, while provisionally useful, cannot constitute a way of life. The basic therapeutic factor at all times is greater self-understanding. Drugs cannot and must not replace such self-directed efforts.

Finally, the patient is exhorted to adopt a few basic philosophical principles. Superficial as they sound, they sometimes make a profound impact on him. In long-term therapy the patient is expected to develop new values through his own spontaneous efforts. In short-term therapy a different way of looking at things may be presented in an active educational effort. For example, the following principle may be proffered: "It is useful to remember at all times that while you are not responsible for what happened to you in your childhood, and the faulty ideas and fears you learned in your past, you are responsible for carrying them over into your adult life." This principle, if accepted, may block the patient from making a career out of blaming his parents and crediting to past unfortunate episodes all of his current problems, justifying his neurotic carryings-on by

4. *Ibid.*

the terrible things done to him as a child over which he had no control.

Another principle is: "No matter what troubles or terrible scrapes you have gotten yourself into in the past, you can rise above these in the future with the knowledge you now have. You need not indulge in patterns which you know you should be able to control, and really want to control." This precept, if incorporated, may help some patients control certain neurotic patterns, realizing that they have powers to inhibit them. The putting together of certain persuasive formulations in this way can be useful to patients who are unable to structure a philosophic formula by themselves. This may help consolidate the gains they have made in therapy.

Within this broad framework, then, the therapist may apply himself flexibly to the problems of his patients, utilizing techniques from various fields blended in an eclectic approach. Hopefully, out of the experiences of workers from the various fields of human relationships there will eventually emerge a more scientific methodology in short-term psychotherapy that will enable us to help the greatest numbers of patients in the shortest possible time.

SUMMARY

Short-term therapy has more than utilitarian value. There are indications that it will, as its methodology becomes elaborated, develop into the treatment of choice for a considerable number of patients. This conviction is supported by observations from a variety of sources to the effect that patients suffering from a wide spectrum of emotional problems, treated over a short period of time, may obtain not only sustained relief, but also, in some cases, personality changes of a reconstructive nature that would have been considered significant had long-term treatment been employed. Four stages in the course of short-term therapy seem apparent: (1) a supportive phase during which homeostasis is brought about through the healing influences of the relationship with the therapist, the placebo effect of the therapeutic process, and the decompressive impact of emotional catharsis; (2) an apperceptive phase, characterized by the ability to understand, even minimally, the meaning of the complaint factor in terms of some of the operative conflicts and basic personality needs and defenses; (3) an action phase distinguished by a challenging of certain habitual neurotic patterns, facing them from a somewhat different perspective; and (4) an integrative relearning and reconditioning phase which continues after termination on the basis of the chain reaction started during the brief treatment period.

The specific techniques that are outlined in the paper are contingent, first, on the acceptance of eclecticism, adopting procedures from every field of psychiatry, psychology, sociology, education, and even philosophy that may be of help in the total treatment effort; second, on the existence of flexibility in the therapist that enables him to adjust his stratagems to the immediate needs of the patient and the therapeutic situation; and third, on the studied employment of activity in the relationship. All modalities are employed in those combinations that may be of value, including psychoanalytic techniques, interviewing procedures, drugs, hypnosis, reconditioning, and group therapy.

Among the procedures that may expedite treatment are the following: (1) establishing a rapid working relationship (rapport); (2) circumscribing the problem area as a focus for exploration; (3) evolving with the patient a working hypothesis of the psychodynamics of his difficulty; (4) employing dream interpretation where the therapist is analytically trained; (5) alerting oneself to resistances and resolving these as rapidly as possible; (6) dealing with target symptoms such as excessive tension, anxiety, and depression, through the careful use of drugs; phobic phenomena by conditioning techniques; obsessive-compulsive manifestations by persuasive tactics, etc.; (7) teaching the patient how to employ insight as a corrective force; (8) outlining with the patient a definite plan of action by which he can use his understanding in the direction of change; (9) searching for transference elements and resolving these quickly before they build up to destroy the relationship; (10) encouraging the development of a proper life philosophy.

HAROLD GREENWALD

Treatment of the Psychopath

The treatment of the psychopath is a subject that has received all too little attention in the literature, considering the wide social damage inflicted by this disorder. In the following paper the editor of this volume describes his own clinical experiences in dealing with this ill-defined but troublesome entity.

Greenwald's approach combines relationship therapy with what he has elsewhere described as "play-therapy with children over twenty-one," and some other techniques, in an essentially eclectic approach.

In DEALING with the severe character disorder of the psychopath we are dealing with more than individual pathology; we are also dealing with a problem that has broad social implications. The psychopath's aberrant behavior frequently consists of acting destructively toward others around him and toward society in general.

One of the problems in talking about psychopaths is that the term is not a very fashionable one. As a matter of fact many efforts have been made to change it. Psychopathy has also been called constitutional inferiority, moral insanity, perverse personality, and more recently, sociopathy.[4]

Henderson[10] described three basic types of psychopath: the predominantly aggressive, the predominantly passive or inadequate, and the predominantly creative. Because the term psychopath is often used in a judgmental sense and many authorities have stated

From *Voices*, Spring 1967.

that psychopaths cannot be treated, a new term that is more respectable had to be invented. For example, "neurotic character disorder" is a term that Abrahamsen[1] uses. He includes the rapist, the murderer, the pathological liar and swindler, the marriage wrecker, the Don Juan, the imposter, the nymphomaniac, the drug addict, the homosexual, and the alcoholic.

Another reason why psychopathy is an important social problem is stated by Ackerman[2] when he defines psychopathy as a social disease that is contagious and virulent. My subjective impression is that psychopathy has increased greatly in the last fifteen years. For more than ten years, I have been working on a book describing the kind of world that psychopaths inhabit, and I cannot finish the book because this world appears to be growing larger all the time. For example, "hip" language, which used to be primarily the property of people in this kind of world, is today familiar to many of us, and certainly to the youth generation. The language they speak, as well as many other of the characteristic behaviors which used to be confined mainly to psychopathic groups, such as smoking marijuana and participating in group sex, are now increasingly widespread.[15]

The behavioral symptoms, as described by Ackerman, include impulsiveness, antisocial conduct, defective control and judgment, lack of foresight, shallow emotionality, egocentricity, magic omnipotent thinking, power striving, grandiosity, inability to empathize with others, failure to respect the rights of others, lack of genuine guilt, failure to learn from experience, and deviant sexual behavior. In fact, so extreme are these symptoms in many cases that it is my impression that psychopathy is often a defense against a more serious disorder. I know from my clinical experience in dealing with psychopaths that when a psychopath stops acting out he will often either sink into a deep depression or begin to show overtly psychotic symptoms. Harry Stack Sullivan once said, "For the life of me, I can't tell the difference between psychopathic personality and psychosis."[14]

Usually when we talk about the psychopath we are talking about the *unsuccessful* psychopath. The reason why we generally do not discuss the successful psychopath is because we would then have to discuss many of the rulers of our world. The sociologists Sorokin and Lundeen maintain that when measured by the same yardstick, the moral behavior of any ruling group tends to be more criminal than that of the ruled population in the same society. Many of the symptoms discussed, such as lack of morals and apparent lack of guilt, exist widely among people of power and influence.

It is amazing how little empathy is shown for psychopathy. Many authors writing about schizophrenia have tried to see it from the inside. In discussing neurotics, and even homosexuals, we are willing to admit that there is possibly some neurosis or homosexuality in ourselves. But in practically all the literature discussing the psychopath there is a complete lack of the kind of empathic understanding that psychotherapists are supposed to have. I think that this inability to see the disorder from the "inside" may be one of the factors leading to our attitude of therapeutic nihilism and our belief that psychopaths cannot be treated. Perhaps this is a disorder so virulent and so contagious that most of us do not dare look at it too closely for fear of being contaminated. We must learn how to deal with this problem first in ourselves before our entire world is destroyed. One can readily imagine what might happen if some psychopath, in a position of really effective power (without any restraints), were suddenly to obtain possession of some of the nuclear weapons now in existence.

In discussing the psychopath, I feel there are two broad categories. There is the sociopath—the individual who is conforming to the norms of the milieu in which he grew up. Personally, I prefer to limit the term sociopath to that type of psychopath—the kind of person, for example, who grows up in certain sections of large urban communities where antisocial behavior, including drug addiction, prostitution, and robbery, is so widespread that in order to be properly adjusted to society, he grows up to be a deviant. This is how he successfully adapts to his social group. This kind of person is different from the second category of psychopath, who grows up in a milieu that does not share such norms. While I think one of the growing problems today is that our entire milieu is becoming one in which psychopathy is the norm, it is still true that when one finds people with similar symptoms and with the same way of behaving who grew up in supposedly more normal surroundings (by which psychotherapists generally mean middle-class surroundings), then we have the problem of the individual psychopath or the character neurotic.

The inability to see a differentiation between the two has caused much confusion in this area.

Now, what does the psychopath really feel like? This is what puzzled me, and only when I reached an understanding of this inner feeling was I able to get some perception of the condition. Can you imagine yourself a Jew suddenly dropped into Nazi Germany and surrounded by SS men during the height of the Hitler terror against the Jews? What feelings of morality would you have? What kind of ability would you have to empathize with the people around you?

What immediate gratification would you want to postpone? What would there be that you would not be willing to do? This is how the psychopath/sociopath views the world around him. He believes himself surrounded by deadly enemies. His early life experience has usually been such that this estimate is correct. He has grown up in the kind of milieu, whether broadly social or limited to his family, where he felt surrounded by enemies, and therefore had no hopes beyond survival and enjoyment of immediate gratifications because everyone was against him anyway.

Though we describe psychopaths as lacking morality, this is not completely true. What we do often find is that their morality may not be the morality of the majority culture. They frequently have a special morality of their own. For example, say a psychopath witnessed an acquaintance committing a murder. We would think it his duty to report it *to* the police. But the psychopath, because of his particular upbringing, would feel his duty was to protect his friend *from* the police. This would be a moral position, though different from the moral position that most of us have. Sometimes it seems to me that we may be witnessing the birth of a new morality. When I think of my younger patients I realize that their sexual behavior would have appeared highly immoral thirty years ago. Yet to them, the present day widespread premarital sexual freedom on the part of both males and females does not appear particularly immoral.

The use of marijuana was at one time confined to a small group. A girl in Mississippi recently wrote asking me what to do about a boy friend who smokes "doped" cigarettes. I could sense the moral horror she experienced. Yet many take a far more tolerant attitude about marijuana now, and there is even a movement afoot for its legalization.

One of the descriptions one reads again and again, which I find dubious, is that psychopaths are usually free of anxiety.[7] To me, their anxiety is obvious. My experience is that psychopaths will not admit to anxiety. However, if a workable relationship is established in therapy, then the anxiety becomes quite clear, despite their many ways of acting out in dealing with its avoidance.

One important factor in treatment, however, is the problem of countertransference—our own feelings about the psychopath. At a conference in Pittsburgh a year ago a frank psychiatrist confided to me: "You know, if I were going to go crazy, and if I could choose the way I would go crazy, I would prefer to be a psychopath." Similarly, some professions—psychologists, psychiatrists, or social workers—whom I have seen for training analyses, have asked if I could help them become psychopaths. One such trainee recently said at a first interview, "What I would like is to be able to do whatever I choose and not feel bad about it. The hell with everybody else; just get mine, that's what I would like to do." I believe that some aspect of psychopathy is in all of us because this kind of behavior sounds quite attractive to most of us. However, the problem is that while at one level it sounds attractive, at another level it is very difficult for any of us to accept the fact that we may have psychopathic traits. To accept our own psychopathy and to admit that we find some of this behavior attractive is so difficult that it becomes almost impossible for us really to establish a therapeutic relationship with psychopaths. Another difficulty arises from their skill in evoking hostile, punitive reactions by their compulsive aggressive rebelliousness and their calm assumption that our zeal is a hypocritical mask for our own selfish goals.

When I first started to treat psychopaths, I found it very difficult to establish a cooperative relationship, a relationship of the kind that is workable, the kind one gets with other types of patients. I can tell you some of the problems I encountered and some of the things I tried to do, and I admit that I had difficulty doing them. We therapists always maintain that we are free of moralizing, but many psychopathic patients have told me of going from therapist to therapist, and sooner or later in the treatment each therapist said, "How could you behave that way? What would this world be like if everybody behaved the way you do?"[7] These patients are very skillful in eliciting this kind of response. It is therefore absolutely essential for the therapist to keep his morality to himself, at least in the beginning. This was one thing that I had to learn to do in dealing with the psychopath. One way to help establish a working relationship is to be ready to use one's own psychopathy.

Psychopaths are frequently involved in manipulations. The ones in therapy are usually inadequate manipulators. Since they are inadequate, and continually manipulating, the therapist's job is to show them how to manipulate properly. For example, a woman came to see me for her first interview dressed in a rather ragged cloth coat. She said she just happened to find my name in the phone book; actually she did not want me to know that she had heard me speak at an expensive resort. It was six months before she wore the first of her three mink coats to a session. She had dressed poorly at first in order to be charged a low fee. It turned out that her husband was a "poor banker" (I had never heard of such a thing but that's the way she described him) and she was involved in an intense "life and death" struggle to get the things she wanted

from him; a 15-carat diamond, a larger and more expensive apartment, additional servants, a larger car, etc. Her husband was determined to give her as little as possible. So I helped her. I showed
her how to deal with him to get all the things she wanted. I was
perfectly willing to help her. Eventually, we established such a good
relationship that I treated her daughter and her son-in-law; the
son-in-law's parents came to see me several times; and even the
husband came. One major difference between the wife and husband
was that he was a much more successful manipulator than she was.

Another case concerns a young woman who came to see me some
years ago. She was being kept by a very wealthy man (to the tune
of about $30,000 to $40,000 a year). At the same time, she was having
a number of other affairs. The man who was keeping her had sent
her to an attorney for legal advice. Everything she discussed with
the attorney, such as her extracurricular sexual activities, was reported by the attorney back to her boy friend. The boy friend
naturally was not pleased when he found out that he was paying
so much for what others were receiving free. She had gone through
two or three similar experiences before she came to see me. Obviously the first thing I had to do was to establish a trusting relationship. When the boy friend called me and suggested that we have
lunch at an expensive restaurant, I accepted and explained to my
patient what I was planning to do. I met the boy friend, and when
he commented about the terrible situation between them, asking,
"Is she still sleeping around?" I responded, "Sleeping around? You
mean she never told you? She has tremendous fear of sex. Why do
you think you have given her two hundred and fifty thousand dollars so far, during which time you have only laid her five times?
Why do you think it has been so rare? It's because she is so frightened of sex." Of course, she got the message back from her boy
friend, who then became very tender and wanted her to go more
often for therapy so that she would get over this horrible fear of sex.
Now, I was scheming. I was apparently being more manipulative
than anyone else involved in the situation, but on this basis I was
able to establish a much better relationship and a much better transference with this girl than I had before. (Incidentally, despite her
acting-out, she actually *did* have serious sexual fears, and what I
had said was the literal truth.)

A major problem with psychopaths in office treatment is that
of fees. One of the things that often happens when a doctor does
establish a good transference is that the patient stops paying. If he
likes you, why should he pay you? This liking is such a rare gift that
surely payment isn't necessary. Therefore, the next problem in the

treatment of a psychopath is what to do about the fee. He tries to make you feel like the most crass, commercial, exploitative person in the world for even asking for a fee. The patient has had so much trouble, and finally has found you, the one person in the world who can understand him. How can you ask for money under those circumstances? When this point in therapy is reached, it is the key test in many ways. From bitter experience, I know that if you do not collect the fee, you can continue to treat them for the next three or four years without fee, but nothing will happen except that they will stop the therapy because they believe that if they succeed in this ploy, they are really smarter than you are. If they are smarter, why should they listen to you or do anything that you suggest? The question of the fee becomes crucial in the treatment of the psychopath, and the only thing I have found to be effective is to spend every session discussing the fee. Not setting limits; that does not appear to work. If you tell them, "All right, I will give you two months and if you do not pay we will stop treatment," the psychopath will be convinced that it is your fault he failed again. He will tell you that he could have been cured if only you had had a little more faith in him. But you're just like everybody else. So it does no good to set limits if you are interested in treating these people. What you have to do is to discuss payment of fee continually. Rather than face the anxiety that this provokes, they will sometimes pay. You must work this through or you cannot touch them in therapy.

The next problem in treating psychopaths is that of seduction. I am discussing not only sexual seduction, for psychopathic personalities practice many types of seductive behavior in their attempts to manipulate. A patient of mine who was a theatrical producer once said to me, "I've had several plays offered to me but I'm not going to take any of them because I'm waiting for your next book. I'm sure I can make a helluva play out of your next book." This was an attempt at seduction, because if I had given him the book, we would have gotten involved in details, and of course therapy would be impossible under those circumstances.

Another patient offered to double my fee. He said he could well afford it. I thanked him and explained that I did not think this was a good idea because I could not see that his financial condition had improved sufficiently to warrant an increase. If it should change, I would be willing to take an increase in fee, but until that time I saw no reason to do so. It was only then that he told me one of the reasons he had left his last analyst. That therapist had started with a fee of $50 per session. The patient then said, "I'm raising you to a hundred dollars a session," and the psychiatrist was very happy. After two months, the patient said, "I'm sorry I can't afford the fee of a hundred; I'm reducing it to fifty again." The psychiatrist was unhappy, but what could he do? Two weeks later, the patient left treatment and sought me out. If I had agreed to his raising my fee, he might also have left me, for once he was able to raise and lower the fee at will he felt he had outsmarted the therapist. A third patient who is a successful psychopath, a self-made millionaire and a wielder of great power at a comparatively young age, once started a session by saying, "You know what you do, Harold? Tell you what you do. Have you got your passport in order? I don't know when, but I'll call you one day—we'll hop on a plane—we'll go to Rome, Venice, and Paris."

There have also been attempts at sexual seduction by several female and two male patients. They do it quite cleverly, unlike the ordinary neurotic, who might just say, "I like you, I want you, I need you." One patient recently said to me, with a tear in her voice as she lowered her eyes, "I now know what my problem is. I never had any acceptance. Nobody ever accepted me." When I agreed, she continued, "I'm not even sure that you can accept me." When I asked her why, she replied, "Well, you might accept me verbally, but not really fully and completely." Slowly I drew from her (or so she made it seem) that the only acceptance a person with her kind of problem would really appreciate would be sexual. When I explained that I did not think such acceptance would be helpful, she said, "Won't you feel like a fool when it is discovered some day that this is the best kind of therapy for a patient like me?" For a while she had me wondering if she might be right.

One woman challenged me: "I know all the books say you're not supposed to sleep with your patient, but how do you know? Has there ever been a controlled experiment done on the effects of sleeping with a patient?" I had to admit that I knew of no such experiment.

Another patient made it very clear that she had been homosexual for a number of years and her last analyst had seduced her. She said, "He was a son of a bitch. It was nasty; he shouldn't have done such a thing and besides he was a lousy lay. But I was heterosexual for eight years after that incident." When I saw her, she was still acting heterosexually. She had a seven-year-old daughter. She was involved with another woman and at this point she indicated that we should have an affair. She implied that if we did, it would prevent her from getting involved in a homosexual relationship. She faced me with a choice that was morally difficult, because by refus-

ing, in a sense I permitted her to drift in.
relationship. However, she had organized it th.
and was willing to go through with a homosexual
pay me off for not having accepted her. I could give
examples of seductive behavior on the part of psychopathic p.
some of whom revealed a remarkably keen understanding about .
own sexual fantasies which they were offering to gratify.

The basic treatment plan that I follow or try to follow with psychopaths is to try to indicate to each patient the fact that he and I are not so different; that there are similarities between us. Advice about manipulation is one way of doing this. Another way is to be frank about my selfish needs. One patient said, "Don't give me any bullshit that the treatment won't be good without the money." I replied, "No, the most important thing is that I like to get paid because I like money. While it also happens that the treatment will not be effective without it, the most important reason for wanting the money is that I like to get paid."

This they can respect much more than moralizing. So one of the first things to do in treatment is to indicate our similarities. I will give an even more dramatic example. A pimp came to see me and started to discuss his way of life. He said, "You know I'm ashamed to show myself and so on, but after all, it's a pretty good way to live and most guys would want to live that way, you know, to live as a pimp. It's not bad—you get girls out hustling for you—why shouldn't you do it? Why shouldn't anybody do it?" I said, "You're a jerk." He asked why. I replied, "Look, I live off the earnings of call girls. I wrote a book about them;[9] I got respect for it; I got famous from it; they made a movie out of it. I made much more money off call girls than you ever will, and you, you schmuck, you can get arrested any day and be sent to jail for ten years, whereas I get respect, honor, and admiration." This he could understand. He saw that somebody whom he considered similar to him had a superior way of accomplishing the same ends.

Another patient with whom I dealt in this way had previously been extremely inadequate, unable to finish school or hold a job. She said to me once, referring to the fact that she had been enormously promiscuous before, "You know, I know you were as low in the gutter as I am, just like me, but somehow, you son of a bitch, you learned how to get out of it, and I'm going to learn that from you!" This is the beginning of a constructive relationship. They see that the therapist has similar problems, similar drives, similar feelings—that all of us have them, but that some of us have learned how to deal with them in ways that are more successful.

Another thing that helps foster the proper relationship is that when they attack society's hypocrisy, I find no necessity to defend it. I happen to agree with most of them that there is a tremendous amount of hypocrisy in our society, and I think it is because I agree with them that I have been better able to work with them.

What usually happens is that they develop a curiosity about how I did manage, since I am so much like them, to get away with it and be successful. At the point where they develop this curiosity I can begin to show them the self-destructiveness of their behavior. When they realize that the problem with their behavior is not that it is immoral or bad for society, but that it is self-destructive, it is an effective way of reaching them. After that, they will usually ask, "What should I do?" And it is at this point that they are ready to listen to the hard lesson the therapist has to drive home, which is—*to learn control.* I do this in a variety of ways. For example, in sessions with this kind of patient I will insist on certain controls. I will ask them not to smoke; I will ask them to lie down on the couch—something I do not necessarily demand all the time. In group therapy, I will ask them not to touch one another. Until I did that, I had a number of fights in groups. Now I do not permit group members to touch one another in affection, and that prevents them from hitting another group member over the head with a painting, as one did, or throwing a water carafe at me, as another did.

Almost every psychopath (this is practically a diagnostic sign) will, at one time or another, want to borrow one of the books in my library and usually there is a desperate urgency about it. One man, who had not completed elementary school and could hardly read, wanted to borrow a textbook of psychiatry (Henderson and Gillespie) so he could, as he put it, show his girl friend that we're buddies." And this, too, cannot be allowed (though you might do it with other patients), because they have to learn control. After some of these controls are established I go on to more, because it is in our battle over control that early problems are relived. Their major problem is that they did not learn controls when they were young; one of the characteristics of psychopaths is that many of them were enuretic as children and did not develop proper controls. So among the things I have done to make this conscious is to prohibit them from using the bathroom before a session, which leads to a big fight. I am willing to fight this out with argument and discussion, and even though they will defy me for a long time, I continue to insist. In group, of course, I prohibit socializing, and I try to prohibit their socializing with other patients, which they wlll frequently do. Psychopathic patients will very frequently try to get involved in a relationship with other patients they meet in the waiting room.

In addition to making the problem of control the central problem in therapy (by demanding control within the session), I indicate that the reason why they do not control themselves, is that they do not really *believe* that they *can* control themselves. (This type of treatment is useful not only with psychopaths but with many other character disorders.) Underneath the inability to control is lack of confidence in their ability. For example, a promiscuous girl complained that she did not understand her promiscuity. She explained that often she could have stopped herself from casual relations but did not think she would be able to, so she finally said to herself, "Oh, the hell with it," and gave up. This is why getting them to control themselves within the session becomes so valuable—because you demonstrate that they *are* able to control themselves under those circumstances. They are able not to smoke; they are able to sit in one place; they are able to say hello when they come in, and good-by when they leave, even if they were angry. These are things I request from such people, who have poor impulse control, which establishes the whole pattern of control.

Within this context it is important to indicate that the ability to control oneself leads to greater freedom. This is hard for them to see—that actually, if you know you have control, you are much freer. If every one of us knew we had complete control of our emotions, we would be free to experience the huge rage that might be boiling up in us, or to experience the lust that we might have for somebody who should be outside the pale. The ability to control leads to greater internal and external freedom. As a young woman said to me, "Now, as I am getting greater confidence in my ability to control myself, I can go out with a lot of men that I did not dare to go out with before because I didn't think I could control myself and would have to go to bed with them."

Another thing that happens as these people start to practice control is that they find that it gives them pleasure; it becomes one of the most ego-building experiences they have ever known. One young lady was very concerned about going out with a married man because, while she liked him and was attracted to him, she was very fearful that she would not be able to control herself; that she would have to go to bed with him, and that this would upset her other boy friend, who was aware of the situation. When for once she did control herself and did not go to bed with the married man, she was so excited and so pleased that she called me and said ecstatically, "I did it—I controlled myself and it was great! I said no, and I'm so happy."

Similarly, another patient, who had been involved in a homo-sexual affair, having decided that she was "going straight," that she did not need women any more and was able to control herself, also described this with great joy and happiness. A male patient who was always being fired because, upon being criticized by his boss, he would have to tell the boss off in no uncertain terms, was able to stop reacting in that way and reported, "I experienced the anger. It made me feel so good that I didn't have to blurt out and lose this job because it's a good job."

With control established, the next step is to facilitate the verbal expression both of their hostility and, even more important, of what is hidden behind the hostility in practically all these patients—their enormous dependency needs.

With the establishment of self-control, most patients find less need to control others. Frequently the need to control and manipu-late others is based on the fear of losing control if something unex-pected were to happen. Therefore they control and manipulate in an effort to prevent any unforeseen circumstance which might threaten their precarious self-control system.

Because I am interested in this whole problem of how to treat psychopaths, I have tried hypnotherapy on occasion. Robert Lindner in his book *Rebel Without a Cause* and Lewis Wolberg in a per-sonal conversation, as well as others who have dealt with psycho-paths, have pointed out that hypnoanalysis is useful in treatment. *Rebel Without a Cause* is a study of the treatment of the psycho-path with hypnoanalysis. Hypnosis of the psychopath is often a short-cut to a workable relationship. One girl, after the first hyp-notic session, said, "Did you see what happened? Did you see how my shoulders went down? What a pleasure, not to have to keep them up against the whole world, to let yourself go and for once be dependent on somebody else." Their deeply buried dependency is enormous and a great deal of their anger and hostility is often caused by the fact that this dependency has been frustrated for so long.

With a few, though all too few, it has been possible to transform psychopathy to creativity. Of course, not everyone is creative, but in one case, for example, a man who was never able to finish anything in his life was able to write a novel: a novel which described his experiences in therapy in a fictional way. He was able to vent much of his hostility and dependency in his writing. The creative person, one who can transform his psychopathy to creativity and utilize his creative potential, need not abide by all of the norms of ordinary society. Creative people often do not have to work from nine to five, for example, as do those of us who are less fortunately endowed. Also, the grandiosity of the psychopath is useful for the creative person. Every really creative person has a kind of grandiose self-esteem. A creative person gets an idea—those of us who lack that creative grandiosity know that other people have had that idea but they do not care—they feel that they are going to do more with it than anybody ever did before, so that grandiosity is useful to them on the creative side. Another way in which this sometimes works, and the reason why I had some success with it, is that several of them, as they established identification with me, identified with what they considered my creative ability. The fact that I had written books made it possible for the man I mentioned to write books. The fact that I had some of my own paintings hanging on the walls of my office (and obviously I am not a skilled painter) made it possible for some of them to start painting and to think seriously of painting or sculpture or some other of the graphic arts.

One of the biggest problems I used to have in dealing with psychopaths was the psychosis which often lies underneath the defense. On one hand, if they continue to operate as psychopaths, they can get themselves into such serious trouble that they may be jailed for many years, or even executed. On the other hand, if the psychopathic defense is removed, they may break down into a schizophrenic, paranoiac, or manic-depressive psychosis requiring hospitalization. However, by emphasizing the problem of control, you deal with the underlying problems, because, as they learn to control themselves, they can also control the psychoticlike behavior which lies underneath the psychopathy and the self-destructiveness. This technique gives you an opportunity to study the problem, and when you motivate and help establish controls, these help control possible psychotic behavior.

One thing I discovered in working with people who have had psychotic breaks is that most of them described a particular moment when there was a choice of whether to stay in control or let go. A patient who became catatonic described the particular moment when, as she was sitting in an airport, she found out that her lover had a date with somebody else. At that point she knew that she could get up or she could let herself drift into a catatonic stupor. She chose to let herself drift in, but the choice point was there. You will find, again and again, if you speak to patients who have broken down, and if you search for it, that there is always a point at which they had a choice, and it is at that point that they still have the possibility of controlling themselves. If they have confidence in their ability to control themselves they can exercise it.

Similarly, in every kind of acting out there often seems to be a choice point. The psychopathic problem of acting out has been indicated. Often, the major problem of psychopaths is impulsive behavior, and here again is a choice point at which they can exercise control.

In working with psychopaths, I have found some contributing factors which often show up. Frequently their history shows early lack of control, such as incontinence and enuresis. Frequently also, they have a confusion of lateral dominance which, too, leads to problems of control.

Many of them learned early in life that the way to survive was to play off one parent against the other, or one sibling against the other. In therapy they attempt to repeat this tactic by trying to play off the present therapist against previous therapists or simultaneously to visit other therapists. One such patient went to the length of seeing another therapist and myself for three months before she made her choice, and only then did she inform me of this choice.

Closely tied in with the tendency to divide and conquer is their enormous ability to arouse hostility in others. This they demonstrate most dramatically in group therapy, and if left to their own devices they will attempt to create such dissension in a group as to lead to its dissolution. Here firmness on the part of the therapist in demanding that the psychopathic patient cease his destructive behavior while indicating to the other patients how they are being provoked into anger is required.

One type of psychopath I have encountered chooses a psychopathic way of life out of feelings of profound despair. One such woman explained to me, "I was thinking of committing suicide and then I decided to choose evil instead. Now that I search for evil, I do not feel like committing suicide."

The establishment of the ability to control leads to more than a controlled psychopath. It leads to the development of an individual capable of substituting the verbal expression of hostility or anger when appropriate, rather than a driven creature who compulsively *has to* behave destructively. In turn, this new-found ability and self-confidence leads to the wish for the development of the ability to form meaningful and satisfying relationships, rather than self-destructive or exploitative ones. If the controlled psychopath has difficulties in this area, he is usually motivated to continue therapy as a neurotic and can be treated as such.

The therapist who is interested in treating the psychopath must not only be willing to withhold moralizing but must also be certain enough of his own controls to be nondefensive and free to be in contact with his own antisocial, manipulative, and psychopathic trends.

The ability to deal with psychopathy is an example of the ability really to deal with the dark destructive forces that stand ever ready to destroy the individual and society.

REFERENCES

1. Abrahamsen, David, *The Psychology of Crime* (New York: Columbia University Press, 1960).
2. Ackerman, Nathan, *Psychodynamics of Family Life* (New York: Basic Books, 1958).
3. Aichhorn, August, *Wayward Youth* (New York: Viking, 1935).
4. Chrzanowski, Gerard, The Psychotherapeutic Management of Sociopathy, *American Journal of Psychotherapy*, 19:3, July 1965.
5. Cleckley, H., *The Mask of Sanity* (St. Louis: Mosby, 1950).
6. Eissler, K. R., ed., *Searchlights on Delinquency* (New York: International Universities Press, 1949).
7. Ellis, Albert, The Treatment of a Psychopath with Rational Emotive Psychotherapy, in *Reason and Emotion in Psychotherapy* (New York: Lyle Stuart, 1963).
8. Glover, Edward, *The Roots of Crime* (New York: International Universities Press, 1960).
9. Greenwald, Harold, *The Call Girl, A Social and Psychoanalytic Study* (New York: Ballantine Books, 1958).
10. Henderson, David, *Psychopathic States* (New York: Norton, 1939).
11. Henderson, David, *A Textbook of Psychiatry* (New York: Oxford University Press, 1952).
12. McCord, William and Joan, *The Psychopath* (Princeton, N.J.: Van Nostrand, 1964).
13. Roche, Philip Q., *The Criminal Mind* (New York: Farrar, Straus, 1958).
14. Sullivan, Harry Stack, *Clinical Studies in Psychiatry* (New York: Norton, 1956).
15. Winick, Charles, Marihuana Use by Young People, in *Drug Addiction in Youth*, Ernest Harms, ed., (New York and Oxford: Pergamon Press, 1965).

INDEX

* *Page numbers in italic indicate complete article.*